21st Century Jet

Karl Sabbagh is a writer and television producer who lives in London. His previous books include *Skyscraper*, *The Living Body* and (with Robert Buckman) *Magic or Medicine?*

KARL SABBAGH

21st Century Jet

The Making of the Boeing 777

PAN BOOKS

First published 1995 by Macmillan

This edition published 1996 by Pan Books
an imprint of Macmillan Publishers Ltd
25 Eccleston Place, London SW1W 9NF
and Basingstoke

Associated companies throughout the world

ISBN 0 330 32890 5

1 3 5 7 9 8 6 4 2

A CIP catalogue record for this book is available from
the British Library

Typeset by Parker Typesetting Service, Leicester
Printed and bound in Great Britain by
Mackays of Chatham plc, Chatham, Kent

Acknowledgements

It goes without saying that my most important acknowledgement goes to the Boeing Company for allowing me access to the 777 project over the three years or so that led up to the plane's first commercial flight. It was not an easy decision for them to take, and I know that there were moments during those years when team leader Alan Mulally, in particular, wondered if he had made the right decision. (I'm sure there were other colleagues of his who *knew* that he hadn't, but I hope their minds may be changed now that the plane is a success.) Mulally himself was a key figure in allowing the access and accepting my terms, which included the desire to sit in on meetings, discussions and events that no outsider had been admitted to before. He also gave me generously of his time and answered my questions on a regular basis as honestly as he could, even when he suspected that I was digging for information that companies don't usually divulge to journalists. It was Mulally's support for the project that set the tone for the response of other colleagues who found themselves being told to tell me what I wanted to know, in a major departure from Boeing's normal public-relations response.

The other Boeing individual whose support was essential – and generously given – was Phil Condit, 777 programme manager when my researches started and now Chief Executive of the Boeing Company. Both Condit and Mulally exemplified in their relationship with me the characteristics of the phrase that was to dominate the management of the 777 project – Working Together. For a book like this to work, all parties have to agree on the goal and to feel that the enterprise is worthwhile. With that shared vision, it is possible to avoid conflict and secrecy. I wanted to tell the story of how a major modern airliner is built, and so did they. Once we had agreed the goal, the individual steps towards it were not in doubt.

This does not mean – I hope – that the story I have to tell is a cosy one.

While Boeing's collaboration was based on a degree of confidence in the way they do things and a belief that what would occur would always be the best they could achieve in the circumstances, they knew that there would be problems, mistakes and surprises. And, as you will see, there were. But there was no sense of shame in this. Instead, there was only a determination to *use* the things that go wrong to take aircraft manufacture to an ever higher plane of expertise and competence.

There were many other people in Boeing who gave me unstinting help. First, the other members of the 777 senior management team – Ron Ostrowski, Dale Hougardy, Neil Standal and Fred Howard. At the busiest phases of the project they could clearly ill afford the time that I sought, but they nevertheless gave it.

Second, I would like to give heartfelt thanks to John Cashman, Boeing's chief test pilot, who helped to simplify the complicated and humanize the mechanical in all my dealings with him. Much of this story is about the precise mathematical and physical disciplines of engineering, particularly during the phases when there were no completed airplanes. But time after time, in a vivid and human way, Cashman brought home to me the reality, and sometimes the danger, of piloting airplanes and, like all other Boeing staff, answered the most awkward questions politely and honestly.

Then many thanks are due to Donna Mikov, whose 777 Communications Division bore the brunt of my requests for interviews, visits, data, videotapes, dates, trips on the plane and research information. Bearing in mind that the peak of my needs coincided with the convergence of the world's journalists on her office as people became aware of the existence of the 777, she coped superbly with the demand. Barbara Murphy, Maureen Herward, Stephanie Mudgett, Greg Hunter and Kirsti Dunn shared the load and tried very hard to suppress their normal public-relations instincts in opening up the 777 project to my probings. The tone was set for their superb services by the support of their bosses, Gerry Hendin and Harold Carr. Thanks, too, to Boeing graphics staff Randy Hiatt and Howard Carter, who helped retrieve the line illustrations for the book from Boeing's capacious computer bank of images of the 777.

I shouldn't neglect to thank the person who first used the phrase 'Boeing 777' in my presence and who was really the progenitor of the project – Dick Kenny, Boeing's European public-relations manager. He and his colleague Don Ciminelli helped me climb the foothills of the

Boeing corporate structure, an essential step on the path to conquering the summit.

The other company which, from the beginning, gave wholehearted support to my project was United Airlines, whose decision to buy the 777 set the whole programme in motion. Gordon McKinzie was unfailingly helpful as United's first airplanes took shape in the factory and shared with me the viewpoint of the customer, which is not always identical to that of the aircraft manufacturer, even when they are meant to be Working Together. Bob Ireland, who was involved in the crucial 1000-cycle tests, gave me my first ride on the plane.

This whole project would not have been possible without the initial decision of Channel 4. Michael Attwell commissioned the television series on which the book was based and handed it over to Sara Ramsden, who brought equal enthusiasm to the project. Both were supported by their senior colleagues John Willis and Peter Salmon, and by Andrew Brann. At KCTS, the US PBS station that co-produced the series, Peggy Case gave frequent and effective on-the-spot support in Seattle when things moved too fast to cover from London. She was given moral support by Elizabeth Brock and Dave Davies. In gathering and assessing a mountain of data, I have enjoyed the enthusiasm of the television crews with whom I have worked. In a fast-moving situation, four pairs of eyes and ears are always better than one, and the colleagues who helped record the events for later analysis made an important contribution to the book as well as the television series. They are Keith Wood, Allan Palmer, John Blackman, Roger Pagel and Geoff de Lissavoy.

In Skyscraper Productions I was given invaluable support by Dick Pull, Jenny Matheson, Gillian Faulkner, Katherine English, Richard Thompson, Ulla Streib and Gail Morrison. In Melbourne, Richard Keddie kept on top of the all-important story of the rudder.

In Boeing, it can be taken as read that I was grateful to everyone mentioned in this book, and some not mentioned, for the time and care they took to explain things to me. The following people deserve special thanks for making me feel welcome, even at times of stress (for them): At Boeing: Lyle Eveland, Jim Metcalfe, Joe Macdonald, Dennis Floyd, Dennis Mahan, the brothers Higgins (Ken and Charlie), Tom Gaffney, Jeff Peace, Granny Frazier, Rocky Thomas, Terry Thomas, Sharon Macdonald-Schramm, Dick Blakeley, John Roundhill, Garnet Hizzey, Chet Ekstrand, Lars Andersen, Grace Chan, Valarie Kusuda-Smick, Sam Nakagawa.

At Pratt & Whitney: Mark Sullivan, Tom Davenport, Jim Johnson, Pete Chenard.

At BA: Jim Sullivan, Barry Gosnold, Andy d'Agata.

At ASTA in Melbourne: Al Tyler, Bob Ravarty, Pat Bogart.

At the Purrington Foundation, Mattapoisett, Massachusetts: Kathleen Lusk Brooke and George Letwin generously provided the calm and relaxing atmosphere in which the final draft of this book was written.

Bill Rosen at Simon & Schuster made the book what it is by allowing it to be so, and Roland Philipps, Georgina Morley and Claire Evans at Macmillan UK said all the things that authors like to hear.

My family, Sue, Bella, Susanna and Jonny, put up with my many absences from home without complaint, and I couldn't have written the book without the knowledge of their support and encouragement.

Last, I have to thank my friend Peter Pagnamenta who, in the way that so often happens with my friends and colleagues, brought me something – a magazine article – that he thought 'might just make a programme'. In fact, it was an article about the 747, not the 777, but it lit the fuse that exploded into a project that has dominated my life for four enjoyable years.

Contents

Introduction

There are two things I know about airplanes that surprised me when I first learned them. The first is that, when a plane is speeding down the runway and feels as if it is straining to get off the ground, the opposite is actually happening – at take-off speed the plane can do nothing else *but* leave the ground. Any straining is the force of gravity pulling the weight of the plane towards the ground as it rises inexorably in response to the upward pressure from the flow of air around the wings. The second interesting thing is the fact that when, in a turbulent patch of flight, you look out of the window and see the wings flapping up and down, they are really doing nothing of the sort. What is actually happening is that the *fuselage* is flapping up and down, while the wings are supporting it on a firm base of air pressure upwards. It's rather like a bouncing child sitting on a board between two chairs – the chairs are the upward pressure of the flowing air on the underside of the wings, and the child is the fuselage.

The reason for mentioning these two random facts is to illustrate the misconceptions that abound in people's minds about airplanes. Many, perhaps most, people experience some level of fear while flying, and some of this fear may be due to the fairly low levels of technical knowledge we have about planes and flight. Of all the marvels in the modern world, a Jumbo jet is one of the most counter-intuitive and the least accessible to unaided reason. In the normal world, heavy things fall, and the only things that rise are light, and yet here we have one of the heaviest free-standing man-made objects rising effortlessly into the air and, seen from a distance, floating serenely across a blue sky. I find it a little reassuring to know that the shape of the aircraft and the thrust of the engines collaborate to make its ascent inevitable at a certain speed, and perhaps your future flights will be made more interesting and slightly less fear-provoking by some of the things you read in this book.

But the purpose of this book is not to reduce fear – it is to tell an interesting story. As I began to think about the story in December 1991, I was sitting in a Boeing 747-200 somewhere over the West Coast of the United States. Like many regular travellers I take the whole business for granted. I ignore the stewardesses as they go through their balletic safety routines; I yawn as the plane speeds down the runway, barely glance up from my book as the landing gear retracts, and give only a moment's thought as I look down at a small town on the frozen shores of Hudson Bay, whose inhabitants are entirely unaware of my existence. Part of this nonchalance is a sense of trust in the vehicle. Now that planes are the size of buildings, we give as little thought to their inner workings as we do to the air-conditioning chiller unit on the roofs of our offices or the ducts that carry cabling from one floor of a building to another. But there is no strong analogy here. The demands on a plane are far greater than those on a land-based construction like a building. Because of the need to contain everything the plane, its passengers and crew need in a self-contained volume, miles away from land, there are levels of self-sufficiency, redundancy and compression that apply in plane-making that have no counterpart in making buildings. The even temperature, heated food and smooth movement that I experience in my flight are just a few of the hard-won benefits of a complex design and construction procedure that is applied to every modern airliner.

The 777, the subject of this book, did not exist in 1991, except in the form of electronic impulses in the massive computer design system that was being used to design the aircraft. As my 747 flew through the sky six miles high it was an aircraft of the 1990s embodying the technology of the 1970s. The 777 started from scratch – what Boeing people call a 'clean-paper' airplane. Materials, electronics, navigation, even cabin design, involved totally fresh thinking. And yet the functions of the plane are the same as any large passenger aircraft – to move several hundred people cost-effectively and safely from one part of the world to another. So in telling the story of the 777 I am also telling the story of modern airliner manufacture in general. When the plane was put through its paces by the Federal Aviation Administration to ensure that it conforms to safety standards, those standards were those applied to any modern twin-engine aircraft; when a client carries out his calculations to see whether the 777 is right for his route, they are similar calculations to those he will carry out for any aircraft, with some changes in the parameters; and when a 777 pilot sits down to fly the plane for the first time he will find a pleasing sense of familiarity as he looks around the flight-deck.

Part of the interest of the story, for me, lies in the fact that it highlights the extraordinary progression that has taken place since 17 December 1903. In the lifetime of a ninety-two-year-old, powered flight has gone from wood, canvas and a single passenger flying a few yards to 400-plus people flying round the world. And the *acceleration* of that progress is also impressive, in terms of safety, speed, payload, almost any criterion you care to name. A couple of facts: the US government's fleet of planes to carry airmail, largely composed of the de Havilland DH-4, modified by Boeing in 1919 to make it 'safer', crashed so often in a six-year period from 1919 that over three-quarters of the pilots who were hired by the Post Office to fly them were killed, 31 of 40. And in 1927 the flight from Chicago to San Francisco took twenty-three hours, compared with under five hours today.

The story ends on the first fare-paying passenger flight of the 777, UA921 from London's Heathrow Airport to Washington DC on 7 June 1995. Most of the passengers on that flight were either VIPs or plane enthusiasts – there are apparently people who try to collect 'first flights' on new airplanes. But even on that first day there were three 777s in service, the others flying with less ballyhoo and publicity, carrying passengers who were more concerned with how soon they would be doing business in New York or Denver than with the pioneering nature of their flight. When they checked in, walked to the gate and strolled through the entry tunnel, they were lulled by these stereotyped behaviours into believing that they were heading for a trip in 'just another plane', as one of the 777 people described it in the early stages of my research. And, as they walked through the doors of the plane, they probably noticed little difference from their last jet trip. They might have noticed the seats were a little wider – half an inch – and that the passenger-entertainment system had a few more buttons and clearer pictures. They may have found the overhead storage bins more capacious and easier to stow than in other planes. They might even have been pleased that the lavatories seemed easier to reach and the toilet bowl had a seat that didn't bang if you dropped it.

But if they were aware only of the comfort and facilities and failed to appreciate the 'common-parts' policy of the eight passenger doors, the power margins of the two large engines (if, that is, they realized that there were two rather than four), the fact that the commands to move the horizontal elevator were carried electronically by wires rather than by forces along cables – if all of these features of the new plane passed them by – the plane-makers would have been only too pleased. In a way that other manufacturing companies might think of emulating, the motivation for every single design decision was, in the end, traceable to a desire to please the customer. Direct comfort, of course, was one aim, in the design of the passenger cabin. But if a design feature made the plane cheaper to build, cheaper to operate, easier to maintain or safer, then at some level – journey time, ticket price or comfort – Boeing were also achieving the goals they had set themselves.

It is easy to think of the plane being built by 'Boeing' as if Boeing is some giant automated machine for making planes. But what I hope makes the story more interesting than a description of an assembly line is the fact that the plane is of course designed and built by people. And people, in turn, are interesting not only because they make planes but because they make decisions. Much of this book deals with processes that occur in the human brain rather than in the factory. Many of the interactions are between one person and another rather than between a hydraulic actuator and the surface it moves. The intellectual steps in the argument that led to the removal of an expensive alloy from the plane at a late stage are even more interesting than the metallurgical facts about why that alloy turned out to be wrong for the job. The chemistry that led to individuals working together who in previous Boeing planes might have been in a more adversarial relationship was to me even more interesting than the fact that their joint efforts led to a better windshield wiper or outboard flap.

And for me the 777 is a greater achievement by virtue of

emerging from ten thousand brains than if it had been the end result of a giant 'Boeing machine'. To paraphrase Alan Mulally, discussing the 777's state-of-the-art computer design system, 'Planes are made by people not computers', and that, in the end, is what this story is all about.

ONE

Why a New Plane?

The airlines of the world told us they wanted an airplane that was bigger than the 767 and smaller than the 747. And we said, 'Why don't you buy 767s?' And they said, 'We want an airplane that's bigger than the 767 and smaller than the 747, because on some of the city pairs that we fly we cannot get enough people to fill up a 747 and we have too many for a 767.' It took us two years to figure out that they really wanted an airplane that was bigger than the 767 and smaller than the 747. So we decided to make a new airplane.

Alan Mulally to Boeing's 777 team

Boeing had been giving away 350-seaters to McDonnell and Airbus. There's nothing special about the 777 other than that.

Tour guide at Boeing's Everett plant

In late 1986 John Roundhill, a tall lugubrious engineer in charge of new airplane design at the Boeing Company, was doing the rounds of the world's airlines, trying to market a new airliner that Boeing was hoping to make and sell. The designs he and his colleagues were showing were variants of the Boeing 767, a twin-engine airliner that still flies very successfully across the Atlantic if you don't mind arriving an hour or two later in New York than you would do if you were in a 747. For two years, in a constant shuttle between Boeing and its customers, men with briefcases spread out drawings of the latest variant of the 767 in front of the airlines, and went away, tail between their legs, armed with reasons why this model solved one problem but introduced another. The size was right but the range was too low; then the size and range were right but the 767 wing wasn't big enough to generate the lift needed to get to a high enough altitude to cruise efficiently in the thinner air. So they redesigned the wing. Now they had a version of the 767 that would carry people almost 7,000 miles. Then the airlines said they'd like some more seats, so the designers stretched the design, making it forty-six feet longer. You have to admire the patience of these men, locked into an escalation of consultation of the sort that had accompanied no previous Boeing plane. How they must have longed to make planes the old way, and say, 'Here's what we've made – how many will you take?'

And the airlines could be really rude. Roundhill remembers one variant that led to a British insult that he could barely understand, cultural differences being what they are:

> Some Englishmen ungraciously called it the Chipolata Sausage – that's a very long, skinny sausage, I understand. It turned out that the length created a concern about airport compatibility. With an airplane the length of a 747 in an area where 767-200 and A300s and DC-10s normally park, that could be an issue. So the airline said, 'The number of passengers is about right, the range looks attractive because you have this new wing, but we really can't stand the length.' So we worked on that through all of '87 and well into 1988.

Like the thin man concealed in the body of a fat one, the 767 must still have been detectable somewhere in these new designs, although with new wings, more seats and greater length it was more and more difficult to see the connection.

At this point the designers threw caution to the wind and seem to have gone a little mad. 'Let's put even more seats in,' they said, 'and while we're at it, to provide the space without increasing the length, we'll make it a double-decker. And we'll put the upper deck at the back.' Thus was born the Humpback of Mukilteo, named after a small ferry port a mile or two from Boeing's main assembly plant in the north-west of the United States. Not surprisingly, those picky airlines had problems with this design as well. More passengers meant more bags. Where were they to go? And the infamous hump increased the airdrag on the plane by an unacceptable amount, making it more fuel-inefficient. In one admirable – and final – return to the 767 drawing-board the team produced what they called the Advanced Twin Stretch. Very long fuselage – never mind the Brits and their funny sausages – winglets on the wing to increase the wing span, and increased thrust in the 767 engines. And the reply they got from the airlines was disappointingly predictable: 'It really isn't quite right, guys. Sorry.'

The rest, as they say, is history. Roundhill describes what happened next:

> In October of 1988 we held a meeting with our corporate leaders, where we as the commercial airplane company went over and laid out all of these product options. We had at that time, I think, seven product scenarios, all focused on a 767 derivative. And at the end of that five-hour meeting the simple question was asked: 'Why haven't you looked at a new airplane?' And our answer was: 'We haven't got round to it yet'. 'So go and do the homework.' And the next question was: 'When can we look at some data?' And the answer was: 'The last day before Christmas break in 1988.' So we went back to our team, which at this time was about 200 people, and said, 'Let's start working on a new airplane.'

Freed from the constraints of staying attached to some aspect of the 767, and perhaps weary of humps and chipolatas, the designers set to work to design a brand-new plane – the 777.

A surprising number of people ask, Why a new plane? The implication is, What's wrong with the old ones? We are used to seeing, and sometimes travelling in, a whole range of aircraft, from tiny twin-propeller commuter airplanes that ply between small sleepy towns in middle America to the majestic 747, large as several houses and capable of spanning the world. What else could anyone want? What gap would be filled by a new plane?

But of course we forget how, as car-owners for example, many of us collude with the relentless pursuit of novelty, speed and fuel-efficiency that marks the automobile industry, where new models spring up every year with little to distinguish them from previous models of the same car or existing models of different brands. Few of us would see it as a sign of progress to buy a car designed twenty-five years ago, apart from the case of that rare phenomenon the VW Beetle. But we have no problems travelling in the 747, also designed twenty-five years ago, and, who knows, we might be perfectly happy to fly the Jumbo as passengers in another twenty-five years if it's still around.

Because airplanes are built with a much longer shelf-life than cars, they eventually become very out of date in all sorts of ways. New materials, more fuel-efficient engines, better computers for navigation and flight control, more sophisticated inflight entertainment systems – all of these are difficult and expensive to 'retro-fit.'[1] There eventually comes a time when airplane manufacturers feel that enough advances in technology and improved manufacturing techniques have accumulated over the years for it to be worth going back to the drawing-board and starting from scratch.

There is a second reason why new planes come into existence. The 747 is a good example of this. While the latest technology helped to make it an improvement on earlier planes, its biggest asset was the fact that it filled a new niche in the market-place. In the 1970s, air travellers were increasing and so were the lengths of the routes they wanted to travel. Going to America from Europe or vice versa was no longer something only the privileged few wanted to do. Servicing mass air travel meant two alternatives – either increasing numbers of 707s or DC-8s, taking off at more frequent intervals and adding to congestion, airport noise and air-traffic-control problems, or a plane that could hold as many passengers as two or three of the existing aircraft types and carry them just as far or even further.

Market forces, then, can shape a new plane as well as new technology. And the fashions and tastes of air travellers are reflected not just in changing numbers and distances. The price people are willing to pay changes over time, and so do the proportions of business travellers compared with ordinary folk. Actual destinations

[1]This is one of a number of words we'll be meeting in this book that are either neologisms or misuses of existing words, coined by engineers to describe processes they have invented. Retro-fit: to install more up-to-date equipment or components in something that was not designed to take it – e.g. air-conditioning in an old car.

become more fashionable or less, and the availability, size, climate and altitude of airports at those destinations can affect what sort of planes can travel to them.

There are also changing costs. In the 1980s, oil had cost thirty dollars or so a barrel, and so planes that were economical to run were much appreciated by the airlines. Then the price of oil halved, and the airlines shifted their attention to the cost of buying and maintaining planes. Then the dollar fell, making planes more expensive for foreign airlines to buy. Because it takes so long to plan, design and produce large airplanes, factors like these – called by one Boeing executive 'unk-unks', for 'unknown unknowns' – keep companies like Boeing on their toes.

Each type of Boeing commercial jetliner is distinguished by a middle numerical between two 7s. The 707 should really have been the 700, the first of a new type of Boeing product, following earlier commercial aircraft or military aircraft whose numbers began with 2, 3 or 4. (5 and 6 were used by missiles and pilotless aircraft.) The only explanation – a feeble one – for why it became the 707 rather than the 700 was that the public-relations department thought it would

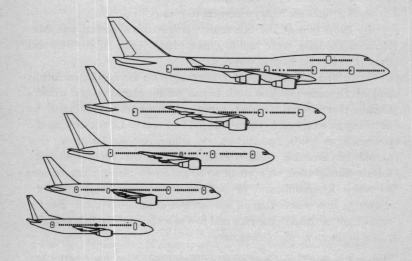

The Boeing family of '7s'

be a good idea.[2] The idea stuck, and, apart from the mysterious absence of the 717, Boeing planes have marched steadily up from 707, through 727, 737, 747, 757 and 767 to the newest 777.

In the airliner market there are really only three Western manufacturers: Boeing, McDonnell Douglas, and Airbus Industrie – two American companies and one European consortium. The competition between them is fierce, reflecting the need to sell a certain minimum number of new planes to justify the enormous cost of development. And without development a manufacturer stands in danger of being trumped by a new model from one of his competitors. Between deciding to build a new plane and the first fare-paying passengers flying in it, the lead time is so long that an airplane company can't afford to stand on the sidelines if it hears of a competitor's plan to build a new plane. The company can certainly decide not to compete – because it thinks the new plane won't sell or isn't really giving anything new to the market-place. But if there's half a chance that a rival could have a gleaming new, better-performing, more airline-friendly plane for sale in a few years' time, the company needs to put a lot of effort into making the right decision – to ignore or to imitate.

And airlines are hard customers to please.

In 1986 two of the big three plane-makers, Airbus and McDonnell Douglas, were building new planes – the A330/340 and the MD-11/12.[3] Boeing was not.

It seemed as if the company was caught on the hop when Airbus and McDonnell Douglas both began selling planes to the world's airlines that offered payload, range and economy unmatched by anything Boeing had to offer. The MD-11 was to be available to the airlines from 1990, and Airbus was selling two similar planes that would be available from 1993. Even on the most optimistic assumptions it takes six years or so to get a new plane in the air, and so when Roundhill and his colleagues were spinning out new drawings they knew that, if any of the designs took off, Boeing would still be third in the race and five years behind the first available plane in the new market position.

[2]Robert J. Serling, *Legend and Legacy* (St Martin's Press, New York, 1992), p.123
[3]The pairs of numbers indicate variations of capacity, range and number of engines in a model that is basically the same.

When it became apparent that, for a certain combination of passenger numbers and distance, the world's airlines would soon be able to choose from an Airbus plane or a McDonnell Douglas but not a Boeing, the company sat up and wondered whether this could be allowed to happen. Unusually, it turns out, the next step for Boeing was to investigate whether the airlines saw things the same way. It may seem unsurprising that a manufacturer would seek input from its customers before deciding on a new product, but for decades Boeing policy had been to dream up a new plane, design it, make it, and then sit around and hope that enough people would buy it. But the costs and uncertainties, helped by intense competition in the market, had necessitated a new approach – Boeing had to find out what the customers really wanted. Alan Mulally, the Boeing engineer who was to lead the 777 team through the most crucial phase of design and manufacture, explained in 1992:

The only way that we found to answer that question effectively is to spend lots of time with the airlines round the world. Not just listening to them and trying to understand where they think they're going, but walking in their shoes, asking ourselves, What is their world really like? We needed more than what the macro data say about the number of people travelling and the number of airports and the congestion and whether they need a small airplane or big airplane – we wanted to know what do they *really* need in range and in size and in capability. And not just now but in 1995 what do they need? And in 1998 what do they need? And then twenty years from now what do they need? What we found was that they think over a wide spectrum of capability, so it's not just one airplane they're thinking about, it's a family of airplanes so that they can match the airplane to the need.

But Boeing did more than send their executives to talk to airlines: they convened representatives of what became known as the 'Gang of Eight' – United, American, Delta, British Airways, Japan Air Lines, All-Nippon Airways, Qantas and Cathay Pacific. The group met with Boeing for about a year, and helped to design the plane that was to become the 777.

They spent a lot of time talking about apparently quite trivial matters like overhead bins for luggage, but this was just a reflection of the airlines' belief that the biggest impact on the customer, particularly the revenue-generating business traveller, is the comfort, convenience and attraction of the journey, rather than the fuel-burn, maintainability or manœuvrability at airports. They asked for a wider fuselage than the Airbus or McDonnell Douglas planes, to produce thirty or so more seats. And one airline, American, persuaded Boeing to offer a plane with folding wing tips so that it could use airport gates that had been built to accommodate American's fleet of DC-10s and 767s. In later years Boeing were to be surprisingly mild-mannered about the amount of work they put into acting on American's suggestion – many man-hours of design and prototype testing – in spite of the fact that, by mid-1995, American had not ordered the 777.

Once the decision had been taken to design a new plane, it seemed surprising that it hadn't been taken earlier, since the result fitted so neatly into Boeing's existing range of aircraft. Alan Mulally pointed out a picture on his office wall. It was just a PR graphic, showing all the Boeing '7' planes currently available, but he took as much pride in the picture as if it showed his wife and five children (who happen to be pictured on another wall). Of the planes, he said:

> This picture is a favourite because it shows the Boeing family. The broad market of the airlines around the world try to tailor the product they need to serve the travelling public, and they've been very pleased that they could tailor the size of the airplane to what they needed. With the 737, the 757 and the 767 and then the 747, that worked for them very well. When they were starting out a new city pair and establishing themselves on a segment like the East Coast of United States to Europe they could use the 767 to carry around 200 passengers and build up their loyalty and their market and their business plan, and then, when they got enough people, they could bring on a 747. But what they were finding was a pretty big gap between 200 passengers that the 767 could carry and 425 to 450 that the 747 could carry. And what they really wanted to do was to move up very carefully and very methodically and tailor the size of the airplane for the best economics and frequency to satisfy the travelling public. So all of a sudden there

seemed to be a hole or a gap in what they needed, and out of that need is where the 777 was born.

That birth had a gestation period of almost exactly 2,000 days, and its womb was in the Pacific north-west of the United States, in the state of Washington. The Puget Sound is the coastal area around the city of Seattle, and driving in a loop around Seattle and its suburbs you rarely see a clear patch of sky unoccupied by airplanes. Every few miles there is an airfield, from the twin major airports of Sea-Tac and Boeing Field, past other airfields at Renton, Everett, Auburn and Tacoma, and smaller airstrips for people who commute to the more rugged parts of the state in light propeller-driven aircraft.

There has been a Boeing presence in the area since 1915. A moving – and movable – reminder of Boeing history stands on the romantically named East Marginal Way, where in the early 1970s the red-painted wooden building that housed the original company set up by Bill Boeing was transported a couple of miles from a shipyard on the banks of the Duwamish River. In view of some of the main players in the story of the 777, it's interesting that one of the most significant steps the fledgling company took was to merge with an airline and an engine manufacturer in 1929 under a new multi-faceted holding company called United Air Transport Corporation. The engine manufacturer was Pratt & Whitney, and the airline – previously set up as Boeing Air Transport – was called United Airlines. The relationship that was set up between the separate companies ensured that United had to buy from Boeing and Boeing had to give United priority in deliveries. One ironic consequence of this arrangement was that when TWA wanted to buy Boeing's ten-passenger 247 in 1932 they were told that they'd have to wait a year, because an order from United had to have priority. Unwilling to wait, TWA went to a small California manufacturer and asked the owner, Donald Douglas, if he could make a better plane than the 247. And Douglas, thirty years later to team up with McDonnell, said 'Yes' and produced the forerunner of the best-selling, long-flying DC–3.

The marriage between Boeing and United was not to last for long. In 1934 the US Air Mail Act banned any connection between an airplane or engine manufacturer and an airline, as part of a squabble between the US government and the airlines over the carrying of mail. After the enforced divorce, Boeing ended up shorn of all its partners apart from Stearman Aircraft of Wichita, a company which was to become absorbed into the Boeing operations over the years and make significant contributions to the later successful manufacture of Boeing airliners. (Many years later, the lives of many of Boeing's commercial planes, including the 777, were to embody that severed relationship. United Airlines, now one of America's largest airlines, was the first to decide to order 777s, and that order was responsible for the board of Boeing giving the go-ahead for the plane. Once the order was confirmed, United had a choice of three engine manufacturers – Rolls-Royce, General Electric and, yes, Pratt & Whitney. They chose – on purely commercial grounds – the engine Pratt & Whitney were offering for the 777, the PW4084.)

It was during the Second World War that the company established its dominating presence. 'Boeing was like a gigantic baby dropped in Seattle's lap,' says one historian of the area.[4] In three years from 1939 the workforce went from 4,000 to 30,000, in response to a sudden hunger for B-17s for the Royal Air Force to respond to the German blitz of England. These days, the numbers of people working for the company fluctuate – unfortunately – between 70,000 and 140,000.

There is something about the company that makes grown men go gooey-eyed.

> Boeing . . .
> The very word, cold in print but rich in association, invokes images as vivid as man's memories and imagination can create.
> Images of mighty jetliners, leaving white contrails frozen against the blue sky as they streak across continents and oceans, shrinking a world that now measures distances in hours, not miles.
> Images of the great bombers defending the nation.
> Images of an American corporation whose name has become synonymous with technical excellence and integrity.[5]

---

[4]Roger Sale, *Seattle, Past to Present* (University of Washington Press, 1976), p.181
[5]Serling, *Legend and Legacy*, p.xiii

This kind of stuff, from a recent book about Boeing, reflects a widespread attitude among engineers, designers and managers who have imbibed company philosophy over years – often decades – of working for the company. Such sentiments would not be out of place in a brochure about an Albanian or Chinese company, but they come from free Americans, and are often expressed in similar vein in private as well as for public consumption.

The local TV stations run any news story about Boeing near the head of the bulletins, and the two main Seattle newspapers have aviation correspondents who are eager for any crumb of Boeing information that can be turned into a story. The number of people living in the area who are connected with the company and interested in its prosperity, including families and dependants, probably comes to three-quarters of a million or more in a state whose largest city, Seattle, has just over half a million inhabitants.

But to say – with slight exaggeration – that Seattle is a company town implies a greater concentration of the company's premises than really exists. The city is ringed with Boeing plants and offices in an arc from Everett, thirty miles to the north, right round to other plants far to the south of the city. You could just about visit all the plants in a day if you avoided the rush-hour snarl-ups on Interstates 90 and 405, but you'd have burned up a couple of hundred miles in the process. So the much vaunted quality of life that is bringing increasing numbers to the Pacific north-west can become a nightmare if a Boeing employee gets a job at Frederickson in the south, buys a nice ranch-style bungalow with an acre of land near the plant, sends his children to a school two miles away, and then after five years finds himself moved to Everett, and has to commute fifty miles each way.

Because of these vicissitudes of transportation, a car-pool culture pervades the company, encouraged by local government. Most of the freeways have car-pool lanes where cars with two or more people can glide past the stalled convoys of single-driver cars. In a well-meant but bathetic attempt to reinforce the segregation, notices exhort drivers who spot anyone using the car-pool lane illegally to report violators by dialling 764 HERO.

This symbiosis between company and city has advantages and disadvantages. For many years there was no local company which could compete in size with Boeing as an employer. When in the 1940s the company responded eagerly to the insatiable demand for military airplanes, its staff increased exponentially, and its subsequent success in diversifying from military aircraft to civilian air transport helped it keep up a similar level of employment for a decade or more after the Second World War. But the company's fortunes changed, and many Boeing managers still working for the company remember the effect on the city. Phil Condit, leader of the 777 team when the programme started, feels that he has scars from those years, as well as lessons learned:

> I was a young engineer here in 1969 when two-thirds of the Boeing population left and there was a big sign outside Seattle that said, 'Will the last person out please turn out the lights.' That clearly has affected the way I think about organizations and stability of organizations. 'Be more careful when you're going up, because on the other side of up is always down.' We went up way too fast. We weren't efficient in the process, and so when we got to the top we were way overmanned and the far side was very steep. I don't ever want to do that again. Watching people disappear literally – one day the people on either side of you are gone – is not something I want to do.

In spite of the fact that lay-offs still happen – Condit was reminiscing in 1992 in the midst of a programme of selective lay-offs on other Boeing planes whose orders had dropped – they no longer have such an effect on the city, which has attracted other large employers, notably the computer software giant Microsoft.

By the early 1990s, Seattle was acquiring a word-of-mouth reputation among people who had never been there as a desirable and attractive place to live. This reputation was partly a response to the tarnishing of other major American cities by reports of crime, sexual liberation, smog, bankruptcy and any other urban plague you care to name. People who flew into Seattle for a one-day business meeting sometimes returned for pleasure, and occasionally settled there. People who had never set boat shoe on decking spoke admiringly of the boating culture of the Puget Sound; those whose closest contact with nature had been the Central Park reservoir in

New York found themselves hugging the dark, evergreen trees that lined the hills of western Washington. And then there was the coffee.

Espresso and capuccino coffee-shops are more frequent than petrol stations in Seattle, and are used in the same way: to refuel during the course of a busy day. The main chain of coffee-shops, Starbucks, has made a fortune selling only coffee, but with a choice of beverages that runs to forty-two combinations not counting the different types of bean. You can have Espresso, Espresso Macchiato, Espresso con Panna, Capuccino, Caffè Mocha, Caffè Americano or Caffè Latte, and each of these comes in three sizes of cup – short, tall and grande. You can also have a single or a double shot of coffee with whichever choice of milk or cream you make.

Locals march up to the counter, rattle off 'Tall Macchiato, double shot', and are out of the shop before folks from other cities have managed to work out what the server means when she says, 'Would you like a hit on your capuccino?' Starbucks made a great splash in the US finance pages when it went public in 1992 and started franchising its operation outside Washington state. And Boeing cafeterias reflect this local preoccupation with coffee by installing in their cafeterias self-service espresso machines with technology that seems hardly less complicated to operate than a 747 flight-deck.

But there are drawbacks to offset the lifestyle. The weather, for example, is a shock to people who expect the entire West Coast to be like California. Seattlites (a word that looks odd however you spell it) resent the implication reinforced in films like *Sleepless in Seattle* that the place is permanently under a downpour, but many of the Boeing people are seduced to Seattle by the attractions of the job rather than the place, and they can be disappointed. Don Ciminelli, one of the sales force, said, 'People talked about the quality of life in the north-west – after the sixth week of rain I was suicidal. But it's helped by being away a third of the year.' In fact by standards other than Californian ones the weather is not particularly unusual – wetter than average, certainly, but with its fair share of breathtaking sparkling winter days and balmy summer ones, where the weather shows the dark green of the conifers and the deep blue of the bays and inlets at their best. And for those other aspects of lifestyle – food and drink, architecture and culture, leisure and home life – the people who live there feel quietly pleased that more people haven't discovered them.

Early this century, Bill Boeing was attracted to the Pacific north-west not so much by its charms as by the great distance it put between him and his stepfather in Detroit. In 1916 Boeing hired three engineers to work in his new airplane company. By 1939 two of them had risen to become Boeing's president and chairman of the board, setting a tradition that has endured until today, with a few exceptions. It's obviously easier for engineers to become managers than the other way round, but that doesn't quite explain why people who are trained to understand the behaviour of materials, the constraints of physical laws and the tools of mathematics end up being successful at organizing teams of unpredictable human beings into effectively managed plane-makers. Part of the success must lie in creating loyalty to Boeing and in the long service this leads to. As the world's largest plane-maker, Boeing could be seen as having a reasonably easy job inspiring loyalty in its employees – everyone likes to bask in the glory of being 'number one'. But, at the level of the individual, such a factor can count for only so much. People also have to feel appreciated and fairly rewarded, and to believe that they are making a worthwhile product to high professional standards. When times are tough, as they were to become during the most intensive periods of activity on the 777, particular employees would be singled out and suitably embarrassed by a display of corporate love that took the form of a speech by the team leader and the presentation of some token of gratitude in front of their colleagues. For the Boeing Company, making employees feel appreciated and rewarded was a small and intensive cottage industry within the main company, leading to the production of certificates, special jackets and T-shirts, badges and fake photographs with the awardee's face in some humorous montage.

The team that made the 777 was led by a group of men who were typical products of the Boeing ethos. There were five of them, each with twenty-five to thirty years of experience in the company. During the design phase they were led by Phil Condit, an engineer with experience on most Boeing aircraft built over the previous twenty-five years. As someone with a jovial openness among colleagues, clients and customers, he typified a Boeing paradox:

the coexistence of reticence, secrecy and coolness at a corporate level with personal qualities – essential for good management – that show warmth, humanity and humour. In fact, while this behaviour was not exactly a pose, Condit and his senior colleagues knew that it had to have limits. It could get you good copy with aviation journalists, and loyalty among workers, but there came times when hard decisions had to be made and commercial realities had to operate. With Boeing's policy of appointing from inside, Condit had had many years of corporate experience during which to imbibe, and increasingly create, the Boeing culture. He had no difficulty articulating what that culture is, and, like many Boeing senior executives, he spoke as if it permeated every fibre of his body:

> Buried in our culture is (1) you ought to respect your competitor and (2) you ought to go do everything you can to build a better product that does things that your competitor's doesn't do. You've got to listen harder. You've got to try to meet customers' needs better. You've got to try to anticipate their needs – where's the future? You ought to adapt your airplanes as the market changes. The 737 is a good example of how we do that. The 737 was the fourth airplane into that market segment: the Caravelle was first, the BAC1–11 was second, the DC-9 was third, and we were fourth. Twice during its lifetime the 737 programme was reviewed for cancellation. Orders were down; it wasn't going anywhere. Both times, what we chose to do was to make improvements to the airplane. One time we put a short-field package on, a gravel-runway capability, and we sold the airplane to people flying off gravel and grass strips and in and out of places like the Faroe Islands. It was a matter of, How do we make the product keep going? How do you make it better? Then we did the 737-300 with new engines. Now you look back and here we are just shy of 3,000 total orders. We've delivered number 2,300; the parts are out in the factory right now. It's the best selling jet airliner that ever was. That was not the first airplane. That was not the one we designed the first time. We had to keep working on it to get it there.

Alan Mulally, Condit's second-in-command on the team, although from a different social background – rural Kansas rather than urban San Francisco – has many of Condit's social skills, and the occasional hard edges. He sometimes gives the impression of being like a schoolboy in a candy factory:

> I'm just living a dream. There just couldn't be anything more rewarding than being part of a team doing something as spectacular as a new airplane . . . If you want to make airplanes and you want to work on big projects with lots of talented people it just doesn't get any better than this.

Although Mulally was younger than some of his senior management colleagues, he had had long experience in the company. He had worked on nearly every '7' airplane, from 727 up to 767, and had a fierce loyalty to Boeing that gave the impression the company could do no wrong. By personality as well as function, Mulally set the tone and style of the 777 team. It was as if his colleagues – even Phil Condit, the team leader when the project began – acknowledged his combination of charm and expertise and let him get on with the jokes, the folksy slogans and the hand-pressing that genuinely inspired many of his engineering colleagues and their subordinates, right down to people he bumped into on the factory floor.

The other members of the management team were Neil Standal, deputy general manager and vice-president in charge of production; Dale Hougardy, vice-president in charge of operations; and Fred Howard, the finance director of the team.

Standal had responsibility for all the people-related issues both among Boeing employees on the project and among the contractors who made many of the parts of the plane. 'I'm Mr Inside and Phil is Mr Outside,' he said, and he was the embodiment of calm, gentlemanly politeness – a skill that had particular value in Boeing's relationship with the Japanese manufacturers. In fact Standal's height – a good six feet – made it all the more essential that he did everything to counteract any impression of American dominance that might be conveyed inadvertently as he towered over the executives of Mitsubishi or Kawasaki at meetings. He had worked at

Boeing for over thirty-five years, having started at the company in a part-time role while at college. His role in the team was not as easy to define as engineering or finance, but over the years of the project he was to find himself dealing with a whole range of logistical and organizational challenges. His description of one particular Boeing initiative makes him sound more schoolmasterly than he really is. He was talking about something called 'The Five Ss' – a topic which makes other Boeing people rather embarrassed, particularly since most people can remember only four of them:

> The Five Ss are simple things of sorting, sweeping, standardizing, simplifying and self-discipline. And it's everything from what you have on your desk, how clean your office is, how clean your workstation is, and so on. When you go to other companies and see how things happen, you know when the automobile is going down the line, the mechanic is working, he can reach up and that tool that he needs is always in one location. You have simple things like a workstation where you put all tools that are required for that worker to do his job. And you hang them on a board in the same location every time and you can look up and see if it's there or not because there's an outline showing where it should be. Or in an office, there are certain things in your files: do you need everything? Should you go through there and screen out a lot of things? And we've had campaigns in the past where we put up large boxes and we have little campaigns where we go in an area and say, 'OK, clean out all the things you don't need.' And we get rid of tons of things. What we're now trying to do is to make that an ongoing thing, where people continually revisit the file and take things that are not needed out. It saves file space, we know where things are, we can find things, it's much simpler, and it's all-encompassing. It's a matter of 'Let's just discipline ourselves in everything we do.'

One of Standal's fellow 777 team members, Dale Hougardy, is a broad-faced amiable Westerner from Montana, given to wearing cowboy hats and jeans on special occasions. He also joined the company over thirty-five years ago, after he read an article about the 707 in the *Saturday Evening Post*. Hougardy was responsible for all the issues to do with manufacturing the plane – materials and machine tools; fasteners and finishes; flow diagrams and 'traffic-light' charts. With the 777 being touted as a forty-eight-month plane rather than having the usual sixty-month schedule, Hougardy would need to be on top of every aspect of this complex machine. And because the unique design method the team were planning would raise manufacturing issues very early in the design process, Hougardy and his managers played a key role right from the earliest days of the project.

To Fred Howard, in charge of finances for the project, fell the task of monitoring the unmonitorable. Everything has its price, although in the past it had sometimes been difficult to find out what it was. If a design team worked weekends on a particular component, they would be incurring overtime which made its own small contribution to the costs of the plane. But if a piece turned out to need redesigning *after* it reached the factory floor, that too incurred costs – potentially much greater. When Phil Condit or the sales staff discussed a price for the plane with a customer, that figure was a complex – and secret – mix of all sorts of elements, including an estimate of the actual costs of manufacture and a share of recovery of development costs, but also weighted one way or the other towards the desirability of getting that particular client hooked on to Boeing planes.

Each member of this top management team appeared to have a respect for the special skills of the others, and a willingness to accept judgements he might not wholeheartedly agree with. Perhaps the social and geographical differences had something to do with it: Condit might seem more patrician, Hougardy more down-to-earth and 'hands-on' through long experience of the manufacturing side, Howard clearly the fount of detailed financial expertise, and Standal comfortable with the logistics of choosing, moving, and influencing employees and contractors at every level. And darting among them all, by turns cajoling and conciliatory, innovative and humble, was the multi-talented Mulally, for whom *communication* dominated his daily life:

> One of my most favourite expressions is that the biggest problem with communication is the illusion that it has occurred. We think

when we express ourselves that, because *we* generally understand what we think, the person that we're expressing it to understands in the same way. Well, in my experience I've found that's very difficult. When you're creating something, you have to recognize that it's the *interaction* that will allow everybody to come to a fundamental understanding of what it's supposed to do, how it's going to be made. And I think we should always be striving to have an environment that allows those interactions to happen, and not have things be separate and sequential in the process.

The phrase that led to that homily was frequently heard at management meetings, along with other old favourites. Sometimes, watching Mulally at work, it was possible to believe that this was management by slogan. And his colleagues made the same observation. Ron Ostrowski, another engineering colleague:

We had a little party for Alan shortly after he got a new assignment. It was just a group of his engineering friends and his staff. We had it at a tavern, very informal, and one of the things that we did for Alan was to capture a list of his phrases, and Denny Wilson, who is our programme management director, put an entire speech together on the basis of it. It had nothing but Alan Mulally phrases in it, and it was a couple of pages long and lasted about twenty minutes.

Ostrowski himself on more than one occasion was subject to a familiar Mulally chant – 'Ron, Ron, he's our man. If he can't do it, no one can.'

Alan uses that prolifically, to recognize guys, to identify people. It's a way of focusing attention on that individual so that everybody recognizes what he is responsible for. Alan is also very good at cartooning. And he's also prolific at notes. We all give him a hard time. He'll go away on a road trip and there are many faxes coming from him as he goes back and forth across long distances. He also likes to doodle, and get his messages across with notations of that kind. So he has many methods of communicating. They're a bit unusual and yet very effective.

To the five vice-presidents and, as it turned out, Ron Ostrowski fell the task of leading Boeing's first important contribution to twenty-first-century air travel – the 777.

TWO

What Goes Fast Must Go Up

Pull joystick back – houses get smaller. Push joystick forwards – houses get bigger.

Pilots' joke about how to fly a plane

There is probably no other area of modern technology where the basic principles of function have changed so little as in flight. To put it another way, getting a plane to stay in the air means exploiting the same physical laws and principles with Concorde, the 777 or the Stealth Bomber that the Wright Brothers used at Kitty Hawk. Compare flying with, say, communicating at a distance, illuminating homes and workplaces, or even cooking, and the difference becomes clearer. There have been a whole range of technological advances over the last few hundred years that have transformed the process of information transmission from a man carrying a piece of parchment to electronic signals stimulating light transmission from a sheet of glass. The light that comes from the filament of a modern light-bulb or the heated gas in a fluorescent tube bear little relationship to a candle flame. And the heating of a join of meat in a microwave oven changes the state of its molecules in a fundamentally different way from suspending it on a spit over burning logs.

But, provided that it has wings, flying an airplane – however heavy or large it is – is still merely a matter of pushing it along the ground until it is going fast enough. What 'fast enough' means is dependent on the weight of the plane and the area and shape of the wings, but, as the speed increases, a vertical force is generated on the wings that should eventually overcome the weight and lift the plane off the ground.

Theoretically, pilots say, you could fly a barn door. Fix it at a shallow angle to the horizontal and accelerate it along a runway and some of the resulting air pressure will push upwards, eventually giving enough lift. But planes with wings like barn doors – just long, flat sheets of metal or wood – would need runways ten miles long to get off the ground, and they would have to land at a very high speed.[1] By giving the wing a subtler shape than a barn door – some variant of the familiar airfoil 'droplet' shape – aviation pioneers exploited a physical principle called the Bernoulli effect. One important characteristic of a successful wing is that when seen in cross-section the top surface is longer than the bottom. As this wing is pushed along, the front edge slices through the air, forcing the flow to split into two. The flow over the top of the wing meets up again with the flow underneath when they both arrive at the back of the wing. But the top flow has travelled further and faster than the bottom flow, and this greater speed generates negative pressure, or suction, over the top of the wing.

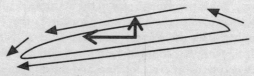

Two types of lift are generated when a wing moves at speed through the air

So, if you add the upward push that the wing gets at its bottom surface to the 'suction' acting at the top surface, the result is a combined force that when it acts on both wings equally lifts the whole aircraft symmetrically into the air. Both of these forces are proportional to speed, and when the plane reaches a speed where the upward forces are greater than the weight of the plane it begins to lift off the ground. To get the plane off the ground sooner, the pilot will tilt the nose up by pulling back on the control column. This puts the wings at a sharper angle to the ground and increases the lift contribution from the force on the lower surface. When the plane is at the required altitude, with no need for extra force upwards to keep the plane rising, the pilot will level the plane out by pushing the

[1] Richard L. Taylor, *Understanding Flying* (Delacorte Press, 1977), p.14

column forward and maintain a steady forward speed that generates just enough lift to balance the weight of the plane.

That's it, really, as far as *flying* is concerned. Once it is in motion, the shape of the plane forces it to rise. The rest is trimmings. The plane needs a source of force to propel it forwards to take advantage of the lift properties. It needs some system of steering so that it doesn't have to go in a straight line all the time. And it turns out that it needs ways to maintain its stability in the air, so that the inevitable vagaries of air pressure, speed and temperature don't send the plane pitching and rolling all over the sky.

Of course, all this may seem a gross oversimplification. Clearly there must be more to it than that. You only have to look at any modern airliner – and at its cost – to realize how complex and cumbersome an object it is. The Boeing people are fond of talking about the 777 as '4 million parts all moving in close formation' and, even if you don't allow them the poetic licence to call the fasteners – rivets, bolts, screws and suchlike – *parts*, there are many hundreds of

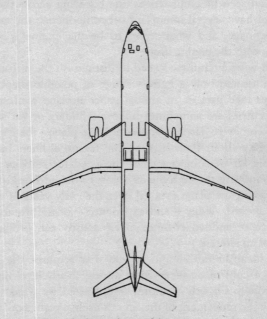

The basic shape of the 777

thousands of individually shaped pieces of metal, plastic, glass, and carbon-fibre composite in a modern plane. But most of these components are not so much to do with making the plane *fly* as with making it faster, lighter, more efficient or better controlled than any previous Boeing plane.

In the absence of any indication of scale, the 777 looks like 'just another plane' – with the proportions of wing, fuselage and engines not unlike the 767 or the 757.

The business part of the plane – in every sense of the word – is obviously the long tube in the middle: the fuselage. That's what generates the revenue for the owner. But, for reasons that are perhaps becoming obvious, the tube has to have add-ons in the form of projections of various sorts. Most of us can just about recognize and name wings, engines and tail on an airplane, and the 777 has its expected complement of those. But the terminology used by aircraft designers needs finer semantic divisions, and shows that what most of us call the principal parts of a plane are wrong. The 'wings' are really often seen by engineers as one big wing across the aircraft's width and have several important subcomponents; the tail is called the empennage; and what seems to be the engine is actually its covering, with the engine inside.

Fixed-wing aircraft (so-called to distinguish them from helicopters) can assume only a narrow range of possible shapes. Boeing employees take part in an annual paper-airplane contest, and the winning entries are sometimes hollow cylinders or flat sheets, but when it comes to large, people-carrying planes there's a boring predictability about their shapes. The reason airliners have such a predictable kit of components is the need for stability while the aircraft is moving through the air. Most of the add-ons to the wing and the aft of the plane evolved over the early years of aviation in response to knowledge – and experience – of the instabilities that turbulence or sudden changes in air density can produce in the motion of an aircraft.

The ideal aircraft design is one that requires the minimum amount of control or supervision during steady level flight. If air were a totally smooth medium, undisturbed by winds or ripples caused by the movement of the aircraft itself, a plane could probably make do with just a pair of wings. But, once it entered the world of real air, any odd gust of wind would tip the plane off balance – nose down, for example – and there would be nothing to stop the dive continuing. Each of the outcrops that makes up the familiar shape of the plane has a role in helping the plane resist such gusts and return to a more stable position. In effect, the laws of fluid dynamics predetermine or 'sculpt' the outside shape of airplanes.

Take, for example, the tail or empennage – a French word meaning the feathering of an arrow. The back end of the plane contains three main surfaces – the tail fin, fixed to the fuselage; the rudder, hinged to the fin; and the horizontal stabilizers, a linked pair of wing-shaped surfaces. The stabilizer works in the following way. If the aircraft tilts up, the angle of the stabilizer to the airflow increases and there is a vertical force on the underside of the stabilizer just like the force that helps to lift the plane. This vertical force, acting upwards on the back of the plane, swivels the plane around its centre of pressure – the point in the plane where all the forces cancel out – and pushes it back into level flight. This requires no intervention from the pilot: it's purely the geometry of the stabilizer that leads to the stabilizing force. And the sharper the angle of the plane,

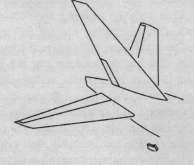

The empennage – or tail –
holds the rudder and the
horizontal stabilizers

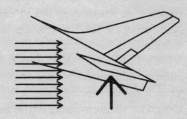

The horizontal stabilizers
automatically correct the plane's
attitude if it begins to tilt up

the stronger the force on the stabilizer tending to push it back in line.

Similarly if the nose pitches down, the stabilizer now presents its top surface to the airflow, and feels a pressure downwards to swivel the plane back to a level position. Again, this effect is purely a result of the position and shape of the fixed part of the stabilizers as it moves in the airflow. There are also movable surfaces, called elevators, but they have another purpose.

In a similar way to the stabilizer, the tail fin also keeps the plane on track. If the plane swivels in a horizontal plane so that it's no longer facing into the airflow, the side pressure on the fin tends to push it back into the flow. Of course there are times when the pilot doesn't want to go with the flow, and uses the movable control surfaces to change or maintain the position he wants.

So each of these surfaces owes its position and shape to the interplay of air currents and wind gusts on the solid three-dimensional shape of the aircraft. The greater the inherent stability given by the shape of the aircraft, the better the pilot (and the associated computers and controls) can cope with the task of sending the plane in the required direction at the desired speed.

That task is achieved by moving hinged surfaces that are attached to the wings, the tail fin or the stabilizers. The movable surfaces on the empennage are the rudder and the elevators; on the wings they are the ailerons and the flaps. Because of the need to travel in three dimensions, and to angle the plane in any of those same dimensions, any single manœuvre is achieved by moving a combination of surfaces. Essentially, however, they all do the same thing: like a rudder on a boat, they turn into the path of the flow whenever a force is needed at the point of attachment.

How these surfaces are moved, how the information about their positions is fed back to the pilot, how much of the task of dealing with the moment-by-moment changes that are required is auto-mated – these are design questions that are closely analysed by engineers whenever they design a new plane. And the factors that enter into making the right decision can be surprisingly philosophi-cal. Phil Condit summarized what he called 'three inviolate rules' for Boeing aircraft that had been laid down by previous Boeing engineers:

Rule number one was tameness – when a pilot loses an engine on any Boeing airplane, he must be able to control the aircraft with his feet on the floor, not with the rudder pedals – no rudder application should be necessary, and he can maintain stability with just the yoke [steering-column]. Rule number two involved stall recovery – no Boeing airplane should be put in a position in which elevator control is lost because the airflow to the tail is blocked out . . . Rule three – every Boeing airplane must be able to recover from a vertical or near-vertical dive.[2]

In addition to the wings, empennage and control surfaces, there's one other principal feature that fixes the familiar shape of a modern airliner – the engines. The 707 had four wing-mounted engines, as does the 747. The 737, 757 and 767 have worked very successfully with two, and that was the number decided for the 777.

No issue was to bedevil the acceptability of the 777 to the public

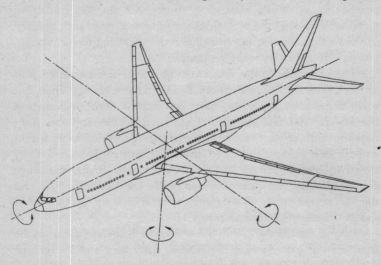

The three axes of movement produced by changing the angles of control surfaces on wings and tail

[2]Serling, *Legend and Legacy*, p.389

– or rather to the media – than the number of engines. In a way that never happened with the 767, attention was focused on the fact that the plane had 'only' two engines. It was to be the largest twin-engined plane so far, and therefore would require the largest engines, and the popular inference was that four engines, such as on the 747, were safer than two because if one engine went wrong you still had three-quarters of your power available, rather than being reduced to half.[3]

But there was a more complex reason for this close interest in the number of engines on the 777, triggered by a decision that Boeing made as part of an effort to make this plane the most reliable airliner they had ever sold. Boeing promised their customers that, on entry into service, the 777 would be reliable enough to fly routes that involved long flights across water, two or three hours away from the nearest airport. The significance of this was that with a twin-engine aircraft if one engine fails or has to be shut down the normal procedure is to fly as soon as possible on the other engine to the nearest airport. If you want to fly routes that can take you up to three hours' flying time away from any suitable airport, such as many of the world's shortest international routes between major capitals, you have to have very reliable engines.

The key phrase in this promise to the customers was 'entry into service'. With the 767, the process had been more gradual. In its first years of commercial service, safety certification authorities such as the Federal Aviation Administration in the USA and the Joint Aviation Authority in Europe required the 767 always to fly within an hour of a suitable airport to divert to if one engine failed. Only after two years of service had shown a very low engine-shutdown rate – as Boeing had claimed would be the case – did the FAA and the JAA authorize the 767 for routes that took it up to three hours away from a suitable diversion airport.

Boeing wanted the 777 to be certified to fly such routes from the time it went into service. To achieve that, they and the engine designers would have to carry out unprecedented levels of testing on the 777 before the plane ever took commercial passengers.

---

[3] John Cashman, the 777 chief test pilot, would point out that Lindbergh chose to fly the Atlantic on one engine because he thought it was safer than two.

But Boeing thought it was worth it. The advantage of a twin-engine plane to customers was large, in terms of purchase cost as well as running costs, fuel efficiency and maintenance. Boeing would not be making the engines – no plane manufacturers do – but they would specify very closely the thrust required, the size and position on the plane, and other key characteristics. Then the major engine manufacturers – Pratt & Whitney, General Electric and Rolls-Royce – would be likely each to offer engines for the 777. It would be up to them to offer variants of existing engines or, if they had nothing to do the job, they would have to weigh up the arguments in favour of designing and building a new engine type. Customers for the 777 would then choose which of the three engines to buy.

The choice of engine type is made for a mixture of reasons. Often, an airline will choose to go with an engine manufacturer who has already supplied engines for other planes in the fleet, so that the airline's maintenance engineers will have a familiar company and engine type to deal with. Sometimes, the decision will follow a fiercely competitive tendering process, as the airline tries to get the best price and payment conditions. And of course, the airlines will also pay some attention to the fuel economy and efficiency of the engines on offer.

But the amount of fuel used to fly a plane depends only partly on the efficiency of the engines. There are two key design factors that enter into the economics of a particular aircraft: weight and drag. The lower the empty weight of a plane for a given weight of passengers and cargo, the less useless weight the plane has to lift into the air on each take-off. And the smoother and more streamlined the surface of the plane, the less effort the engines have to make to push the plane through the air. These two factors were to preoccupy the designers as they went through the design phase of the project, trying continually to reduce the weight of every single component and to minimize unnecessary protuberances or roughness on the surface of the plane.

A tiny example of how much care is taken at the design phase occurred in discussions of the design of a handle for the passenger door. Each door required a handle that was accessible from the outside, so that it could be opened by ground staff. One suggested design involved a recess around the handle so that someone could get his hand in to open it. But this hollow in the surface of the door would create a roughness in the airflow during flight, as the air was diverted by the rim into the hole and out again, causing eddies and leading to a tiny source of drag. This roughness multiplied by eight – the number of doors on the 777 – would have the effect of causing the plane to burn slightly more fuel than it would if the doors were smoother. This type of drag is called 'excrescence drag', and the effect of each potential source, including even the raised heads of fasteners, is carefully monitored and attempts are made to minimize it. Since planes burn fuel to lift weight as well as to overcome drag, it has become customary to measure drag in terms of the amount of extra weight that would require the same amount of extra fuel to be burnt. Just that one recess in the doors, a few inches across, would create thirteen pounds of excrescence drag – causing the plane to burn the same amount of fuel as would be necessary to carry another thirteen pounds of passenger or luggage across the Atlantic. Too many sources of drag like that would reduce the number of passengers who could be carried for the same amount of fuel.

Of course there were much larger sources of drag, and the art of maximizing the efficiency of the plane lay in finding the best shape for each of them. Some of them were unavoidable, and indeed necessary. Some of the lift of the plane came from the angle the wing presented to the airflow, but that very design feature would generate drag at the same time as generating lift, and in proportion to it. A hand out of the car window will feel no lift and little drag if it's held horizontally. As it's tilted, it will feel a force upwards but will also be pushed backwards by the increased air pressure. The art of calculation had already come a long way since the earlier airliners, which were far heavier and far 'rougher' than they needed to be, but there was still room for improvement as the 777 team began to design the details of the aircraft.

Alan Mulally described some of the subtleties of the design process as they applied to the shape of the wing itself – the airfoil:

> The 777 airfoil is a significant advance in airfoil design over our past airplanes. And the way it looks to us to be significantly different is that it has more of a blunt nose and a different contour

and curve at the back end. We arrived at this shape by extensive analysis on the computer, plus validating these analyses in the wind tunnel. And we learned new things by testing the airfoil at more near-real flight conditions as far as temperature and pressures and air distributions are concerned. And so we've ended up with an airfoil that is a new standard at maximizing lift versus drag, where with the amount of lift that you can get it still minimizes the drag.

So the initial concept for the 777 was shaping up, in a way that would lead to none of the public perceptions of a brand-new aircraft that accompanied the first 747, but to an aircraft that nevertheless *was* brand-new – and in some respects pioneering.

One further invisible 777 characteristic, which was to generate a reaction of wary suspicion among some members of the public and the media, was the fly-by-wire control system – a means of passing the pilot's instructions to the control surfaces electronically, processing them through computers to obtain better handling characteristics and other advantages. Boeing were not the first to introduce this method to a large passenger airliner: the Anglo-French supersonic airplane, the Concorde, had used fly-by-wire very successfully from the beginning, and Airbus was already using fly-by-wire on its newer planes, although in a way that gave the pilot less freedom to override the computers than Boeing decided to incorporate in the 777 system.

There were other less visible innovations planned for the 777 as the Boeing team began to take seriously the task of building a new plane. Frank Shrontz, chief executive officer when the go-ahead was given for the 777, had already determined that Boeing's style of plane-making in the future would change in ways that identified Boeing people more closely with the common task of making the highest quality product possible. But the company also took the unprecedented step of involving potential customers – embodied in the Gang of Eight – in the design decisions about the new plane. Gordon McKinzie, a genial Harry Truman look-alike, was manager of new-technology engineering for United Airlines when Boeing first seriously started planning the 777, and he was surprised at the trouble Boeing took to consult the airlines:

Almost a year ahead of our decision date they were pulling airlines into Seattle and getting our opinions, but we didn't know if this was going to continue after a purchase. They made no reference to that, or didn't give us any clues, so I didn't know what was bubbling in the background in their minds, but they did want to get our inputs as to the best kind of airplane that they might design for the 1990–91 time period. They made a point inside the meetings of repeating back to us what we had told them, and then they followed up after each meeting with a little document that said, 'Here's what we thought we heard, and here's what you told us.' And if that didn't agree, we had a perfect opportunity to go back to them and say, 'That's not what we really said, and let's get on the record.' So, we were on the record. Everything was videotaped, and there were secretaries and clerks taking notes through those whole sessions, and I think we had three sessions – each one was about three days long – and there were a lot of airlines in attendance. It was great.

So far, good PR. But this turned out to be only the beginning. Once Boeing had digested the results of all this consultation and made the decision to commit, they then *continued* to talk to the airlines, about every aspect of the plane. And this is where another factor became important. Because every airline has different needs – some subtle, some major differences of range or number of passengers – Boeing decided to design a family of planes, not just one.

Jeff Peace was chief engineer for customer requirements. A cheery, outgoing man, with a passion for fishing, he was to present an unruffled exterior during the design phase of the plane, as the customers he and his colleagues had consulted and nurtured hummed and hawed about where they wanted their galleys, or changed their minds at the last minute about the height of a refuelling nozzle. He described the family concept as follows:

The Triple Seven family eventually will be at least five different airplanes. The first airplane – the A-market plane – is really designed for regional and domestic service. It's for medium-range routes over the North Atlantic, across the US, throughout Asia, that don't have the capacity for a 747, and where an airline would lose money on a 747. And yet the traffic is growing too large for the 767 to handle.

The B market is for the long, thin routes, ranging from the 5,550-nautical-miles up to 7,000-nautical-miles range – 'thin' meaning they don't carry the number of passengers where you can load up a 747 and make it profitable, but need to have a smaller airplane, so you can keep it at 65 to 70 per cent full, which is a profitable load factor.

The stretch airplane is designed primarily with Asia in mind – very high-volume routes, relatively short ranges. It's a people-mover, and it carries a tremendous number of people at a very low cost per seat. It is going to make the Asian carriers a bunch of money when they get it in instead of 747s.

Then eventually the airplane will be longer range at 300-passengers capacity, in the 8,500-nautical-mile range – that's like a sixteen- to seventeen-hour flight, to put it in context. It's going from Chicago to Hong Kong, for example – you're on the airplane for a *long time*.

And then we'd also use that capability in terms of range, and put it on the stretch airplane to make a twin-engine airplane about the same size as the early 747s that would now fly from South East Asia to Europe, across the northern Pacific.

The proposed 777 family could be summarized as follows:

Type	Range	Passengers (1, 2 or 3-class)
A	Medium distance	305 – 375 – 440
B	Longer distance	305 – 375 – 440
Stretch A	Medium distance	368 – 451 – 550
Stretch B	Very long distance	305 – 375 – 440

So the vision was of two planes, the A and the B, with the same number of passengers but with the B able to travel further because it could carry more fuel; then the stretch, with the same range as the A but carrying more passengers. And finally, not really even on the drawing-board, the longer-range higher payload stretch B. It was a grand vision – particularly since it was laid out before the company had sold a single plane, and before the first member of the family had even been designed. What's more, the Boeing vision, when it came down to the details, was not necessarily shared by the airlines, who, after they had come to Seattle and eaten Boeing's food and drunk its iced tea, actually told Boeing things they didn't particularly want to hear. For example, Gordon McKinzie, on behalf of United, ganged up with some of the other potential clients to make representations about the cockpit:

> We were very concerned that the cockpit not be another 767 cockpit, that we move up to the new technology of the 747-400, and that was not Boeing's original position, so we made quite a lot of noise in the airline meeting. We had great support from British Airways, who owned the 747-400, and Qantas also supported us. That was the great part of the airline meetings – you had people who knew the other airplanes and could put in the same kind of comments.

Another issue that had come up at those early meetings was the joystick. Since the 777 was to have a sophisticated electrical control system – fly-by-wire – there was no need for the normal control column coming out of the floor with the familiar half-steering-wheel on top. On previous planes this reflected the need for a column that could develop the leverage in three dimensions that operated the cables running to the control surfaces. British Airways engineering representatives wanted to have a small control lever with a button on the top, placed at the side of the pilot and similar to the joystick in an Airbus cockpit. But Boeing and United were concerned about this radical change in flight-deck philosophy and kept to the traditional control column. With its colourful glowing screens, the cockpit already looked like a giant video game – it would be adding insult to injury to equip it with a video-game joystick.

During this consultation phase of the 777 design process, Boeing had still not committed to make the plane. Millions of dollars had been spent on designers' and engineers' time and the support they required to make provisional drawings, calculations and models. Sooner or later, the main board of the Boeing Company would have to decide whether there was sufficient interest in the 777 to predict enough sales to justify the enormous costs of moving from drawing-board to factory. This decision could not be based merely on market forecasts – they had to have a commitment from someone to buy the plane, and in enough quantities to make the investment worthwhile.

The feedback from the airlines had been favourable. They had been impressed by the new, bright-eyed, 'Tell us what *you* think' approach, and the plane certainly seemed capable of filling several gaps in several different airlines' route patterns. But then there *were* other planes, some of them brand-new, that might fill the same gaps. The logical first purchaser for the plane was United Airlines, often in the past a loyal Boeing customer. But they were not *so* loyal that they didn't consider other options. Gordon McKinzie had returned to United's Chicago headquarters with a generally good impression of the 777 after the first consultation meetings, but he and his colleagues had to be fair to the other airplane manufacturers hammering on United's door.

> The 777 was part of a three-airplane competition – it was this airplane, it was the Airbus A330 and it was the MD-11: all about the same capacity, all about the same capability. My job then was to be the person that coordinated looking at all the new candidate aircraft for what we called the wide-body acquisition of 1990. There was a need to replace the ageing DC–10, which by the time this airplane delivers will be twenty-five years old – at the end of its life – and there was also a need to look forward to expansion aircraft for the whole aircraft growth problem. So we took an intensive look at what new aircraft were out there and what would best fit our needs.

United had thirty-three plane/engine combinations to consider, including the possibility of buying existing Boeing aircraft such as 747-400s and 767-300s. Airbus had the A330 and the A340, McDonnell Douglas had the MD-11 and MD-12, and each of these, like the 777, had two or three engine types it could use. The process of making the decision involved testing each of these combinations against a range of the routes that United would be flying in five years' time, and checking which combinations would perform most cost-effectively with the distances and passenger numbers involved.

> What we did was to isolate some city pairs that looked interesting to us. The first one, foremost for DC-10-type flying, was O'Hare [Chicago] to Honolulu, and then we looked at Denver to Honolulu. We also looked at the European operation, because May of 1990 is when we first started to Frankfurt in the 767s, so we were looking at Frankfurt westbound into Chicago and we were even looking beyond that at a Europe–West Coast route.

On the weekend of 15–16 October 1990, Phil Condit and his wife, Jan, had planned to visit one of their daughters at Colgate University, in upstate New York, and to take in a football game while they were there. Over the previous few weeks it had become clear that United were getting near to the final phase of their decision-making. The pieces were all in place as far as Boeing's 777 team was concerned – they had defined the preliminary design of the plane in some detail, and had also specified its range and payload. Now all they needed was a deal. United wanted the three airplane manufacturers to send teams to Chicago just at the time Condit had planned to be away. As leader of the team making the plane, Condit supposed that he would be required to go, but his senior colleagues from Boeing Commercial Aircraft Group said that they had done all the pre-planning, everyone agreed on what sort of plane they could offer, and the main decisions were to do with finance – outside Condit's remit. Condit seemed relieved but unconvinced:

> I said, 'OK, here's my phone number – I'm going to be at my younger daughter's Parents' Weekend, and I'm available by phone. I'll check in.' When I got there, we started into this process. I called and said, 'How are things going?' 'Well,' they said, 'we need a little of this and a little of that. And, besides that, Jim Guyette [executive vice-president of United] needs to talk to you – he's got some questions.' So I called and talked to Jim and answered some questions for him.

Condit paused and remembered the frustration of that long weekend:

The guys thought there was going to be an answer mid-afternoon on Saturday. And so, instead of going to the football game, I stayed in my daughter's dorm room and waited for the phone to ring. After a while I was reasonably certain that the phone was probably broken, because it didn't ring. I was just sitting there watching it while nothing happened. So I called Chicago. And they said, 'We're just sitting here. We expect something in the next couple of hours.' That then continued. The football game came and went. Finally I said, 'It doesn't look like it's going to happen tonight. It'll probably be tomorrow.' Next morning we started back into the same process all over again. A couple more conversations, I talked to some more people, went to breakfast with my wife and daughter. I went to the restaurant and then sat in the phone room while they had breakfast, and then I hurried back to my daughter's dorm room and we did this some more. So finally, at the end of the day, things were still about to happen and I said, 'I can't stand this any longer.' So I got an airplane and went to Chicago and joined the wait. And I sat and talked and worked on a crossword puzzle.

Gordon McKinzie played a key part in the decision-making. He and a colleague with a special knowledge of engines were the two United Airlines technical representatives. They were based in San Francisco, and had spent a lot of time putting together the technical recommendations on which United would base their decision about which plane/engine combination to buy. Then the call came to fly to Chicago, where they found a large group of people assembled.

There were six lawyers – one for each of the engine manufacturers and the airframe manufacturers – there were four financial-analysis types, and there were, of course, Jim Guyette and Jack Pope and Steven Wolf [United's top management]. When we went in there – I think it was a Thursday morning – we were told by the senior VP of finance that we weren't leaving that building until the deal was done, so we'd all checked into local hotels and we were there

watching the sun rise over our corporate headquarters, twice. We
went into seventy hours of non-stop negotiations, and it was very
emotional because we could tell by the faces on the people coming
out of the inquisition chamber that things had not gone well.
What was happening was that somebody would go in there from
one manufacturer and present a deal, and then he would be
dismissed and the next person would come in, and we'd try to
better the deal. So it was a ratcheting process through those
seventy hours, trying to get the best terms. Technically, we had
made our decision – we knew what we wanted to do – so we had
our technical recommendations already in place and the seventy
hours were really just financial negotiations – terms and conditions, a lot of contract talk. But it was emotional – huh!

At the end of the process, Condit's crossword-puzzling was
interrupted.

They finally came in and said they needed to see us in Jack Pope's
office. So we went down there and they said, 'You've got the deal.'
I was glad I was there – it was exciting to be there – but my
contribution probably can be measured in very small numbers at
that point. You know, it was just being there.

United had agreed to buy thirty-four 777s in the A-market
version and to take out an option on another thirty-four.
Mulally was fond of describing a piece of paper that played an
important role in clinching the deal:

It's a piece of paper that Jim Guyette wrote at 2.15 in the
morning. He woke up in a cold sweat, because he's going to walk
in and see Mr Wolf, who is the chairman of the board of United.
He had the chief financial officer that was voting for Airbus instead
of Boeing, and he had to walk in and make his vote. What airplane
should United Airlines go with for the next thirty years? And he
felt that Boeing would be the best choice. So he needed
something personal, something so that he could say, 'Boeing's
really committed to doing some things differently.' So he thought
about bringing in the attorneys. Well, you know what it's like to

deal with attorneys. So he said, 'No, I don't think that's it.' So he wrote a handwritten note with really sophisticated words like there's an agreement that he wanted Boeing to sign saying things like 'We agree to work together to deliver a service-ready airplane, an airplane that works.' And then he dragged Phil Condit and Dick Albrecht [a senior Boeing sales executive] into the room and he said, 'Will you sign this?' And he took that to Mr Wolf and he said, 'This is the new Boeing. The new Boeing is going to treat us at a new level of respect as a customer, and for the next five years they are going to work with us to deliver something Boeing's never delivered before on any other airplane.'

As the central contractual document for a multi-billion-dollar project, this must have been the least prepossessing document ever – a single sheet of paper, handwritten and consisting of a vaguely worded acknowledgement that Boeing and United, together with Pratt & Whitney, who had been awarded the engine contract, would work together to produce a really wonderful airplane. Of course there would be more official-looking documentation – several pounds of it, in the form of thick bound contracts – but in an apparently naïve but absolutely sincere way the single sheet represented what the Boeing people felt was the binding agreement between the parties.

The detailed contract document spelt out the terms of the deal that had emerged during the seventy hours of negotiations. Buying planes involves all sorts of financial considerations that are far more complex than the mere act of handing over a certain amount of money per plane and receiving your purchase in return. A bid package like that between United and Boeing has several elements. It might have as its starting-point a price per plane – of the order of $120 million for each 777. But this price would not necessarily be paid in full. There might be credit terms, by which Boeing lent United some money to buy the planes so that the initial amount was less. There would be elements in the deal that might specify favourable low interest rates for that credit, and a schedule of payments that helped the airline. There would be a lot of discussion of warranties. How long would Pratt guarantee the fan blades for? What promises would Boeing make about the durability of some of the materials they used, and when certain parts had to be replaced? There would also be a lot of hard bargaining about guarantees, by which Boeing assured the airline that the plane could fly on the routes that United wanted with the full number of passengers. Bearing in mind that these guarantees were given in 1990 – nearly five years before delivery, and when the detailed design was just getting into its stride – they can have been little more than hopeful promises. Rather than being guarantees, they were targets for the 777 team that they missed at their – and Boeing's – peril. If a plane doesn't meet some performance target – the guaranteed weight, for example – Boeing are obliged to pay the airline compensation. This payment can be a regular amount over the lifetime of the plane to cover loss of earnings. If a plane is heavier than guaranteed the airline can carry fewer passengers and will expect the lower revenue to be offset by money from Boeing or by reduced payments for the aircraft.

Other elements that United will have bargained for include a deal for the pricing of spare parts, and various clauses about resale value and the possibility of Boeing buying back the planes in the future if United should not need them.

There was also in the contract a combination of firm orders and options to purchase, so that United could monitor closely the market and react quickly with extra planes if things improved. An airline might pay about a tenth of the plane baseline price for an option to purchase, and that would entitle it to have a nominated plane in the assembly line until the date when it would either have to turn the option into a firm purchase or cancel it. In the latter case, if the market was good and Boeing wanted to be nice to the airline, they would sometimes give back the option price.

For the Boeing 777, the United order was a life-creating event. Boeing had not yet committed to make the plane, but the United deal now made that decision possible. For Condit and his colleagues, they *had* to have a reasonably big order to commit. They could not go ahead and make the plane and then take the chance that airlines would buy it when they saw it.

If United had gone for one of the others, we would have worked very hard to get American or Delta at that point to go with the airplane, or British Airways, JAL or ANA. We needed one of those big guys up front. Now, what would we have done if United, British Airways, ANA, JAL, Qantas, Cathay, Delta, American had all gone in another direction? Well, at that point I think you'd fold your tent up and decide you're going to work on something else. The good news is that that is not what happened. So I can smile and suspect what *might* have happened.

THREE

The Paperless Airplane

Alan Mulally's office during the early design phase of the project – between 1990 and 1992 – was on the corner of an engineering building at Renton, near the south end of Lake Washington. Intricately detailed computer printouts of part of the 777 lay unrolled on the floor, with a shaped piece of carbon-fibre composite acting as a paperweight. Low bookshelves around the office contained almost exclusively management textbooks, and there were usually half a dozen new arrivals piled on a chair or the floor waiting to be read. Like most long-term Boeing managers, Mulally had acquired over the years tributes from groups of colleagues – a signed basketball, a framed fake magazine cover, a group photo taken at some particular milestone. But the favourite art forms in these offices were, not surprisingly, variants of airplanes – framed illustrations and scale models of Boeing aircraft and of their competitors. In Mulally's office, one model airplane stood out. It resembled no Boeing aircraft, not indeed that of any other well-known plane-maker. It was a Fisher-Price plastic toy plane, and it had special significance for Mulally:

I know a lot about Fisher-Price toys because I've purchased a lot. First, they're very functional, they have lots of features. They're also very durable. That's a wonderful thing if you're a person that uses them or if you're a parent that has to replace them. The other thing is that they're very important on Christmas Eve. And the reason is if you have a relationship with your wife where you utilize her skills on getting the right toy and you utilize my skills on assembling them on Christmas Eve then it's real important that they're easy to assemble. You know what it's like on Christmas

Eve: you have to get everybody to bed, then you have a lot of pressure because Santa Claus will be coming in the morning so you only have a limited amount of time to assemble these toys. Fisher-Price do the best job of any toy company on making toys that are easy to fabricate and assemble.

So when we started this airplane programme, Dale [Hougardy] and I decided that one thing we could really do that would add value to our airline customers is to make the airplane easy to fabricate and assemble. Because if it's easier to fabricate and assemble it means it takes less flow time, and it takes less work, and you also have less rework because it's easier for people to do it correctly. And I kept thinking for a long time, How do we capture the imagination of a design and an operations community – having an assignment to design it so that it is easier to make it, fabricate it and assemble it? For example, if you have a right-hand thread, make it so it only goes on the right hand or on the right-hand part. If it's on the other side you should do something different with the design of the part so it can only be assembled from that side. Fisher-Price make a little notch in their wheels so that you can only put the right wheel on the right hub and you can only put the left wheel on the left hub. You also use simple tools. So I started saying what we're after on this programme is not just meeting cost targets, not just adding value to our airline customers, but we're going to do what Fisher-Price do on Christmas Eve. We're gonna make this easier to fabricate and assemble. So one time, as a present, the engineering guys gave me a whole bunch of Fisher-Price toys so I could pass them out and make the points to the other engineers. Isn't that funny?

The Boeing plant at Everett is littered with planes in every stage of manufacture. In early 1992 they were 747s, 757s and 767s. Wherever you looked there would be disembodied cockpits or unconnected cylinders of fuselage, waiting to be joined up as real functioning airplanes. But in one corner of one building there was a plane that would never fly, that *could* never fly. It was a reminder of how Boeing traditionally designed planes before the 777 came along. From the outside, it looked like a Boeing 747-400 freighter. And inside, too, in the stripped-down lower lobe, it had a full complement of wires, hydraulic tubing and control cables that you would expect to find in a 747. But this was a design mock-up, a plane built solely to check that the engineers who had produced the drawings that would be used to manufacture the parts of the plane had got it right, and had not made any silly mistakes such that one piece and another vied for the same space.

Traditionally, new planes had been designed in two dimensions: drawings on paper had been used as a basis for the manufacturing process. But to design a plane entirely this way, with over 100,000 different three-dimensional parts, and then to trust that the two-dimensional drawings had accounted for all the complexities of the three-dimensional airplane would have led to endless unpleasant discoveries at the assembly stage, as a piece designed by one designer arrived at the factory and turned out to be impossible to install because another designer had failed to leave the right amount of space. Furthermore, when it came down to the detail of the plane – the wiring and tubing that ran from one end to the other and required holes to be drilled or cut to allow free passage – the task of accounting for all that in two-dimensional drawings would have been impossible. So the drawings were backed up by what were called mock-ups – successively refined full-scale models of the plane.

Stage-1 mock-ups were usually made of plywood and foam and enabled all the large pieces to be visualized in three dimensions. The pieces would be cut on the basis of preliminary drawings, and then refinements would be carved in the foam or wood, and the changes would be fed back into the drawings.

Stage-2 mock-ups added some metal parts and began to address complicated issues of routing of wires and tubes as well as the accessibility of pieces that would have to be removed or inspected as part of regular maintenance. These mock-ups would also be pored over by manufacturing engineers, as they began to think about designing the machine tools that would make each of the larger components.

Finally, a stage-3 mock-up would be constructed, incorporating discoveries and changes made during the first two stages, with every component constructed by hand according to the engineering drawings. Although the materials were not always the same as in the real plane, and the accuracy was not to the fine tolerances of the finished engineering, this last mock-up provided an extremely good way to anticipate and avoid what are called errors, changes and reworks. But not good enough. With the inevitable imperfections and the overwhelming complexity of such a hand-crafted object, there were still unpleasant surprises on the shop floor as the first planes were assembled. The key word was 'interferences'. When two pieces overlap in space, they are said to interfere. This can happen with large pieces such as ribs or spars, or with tiny components such as a washer that is the wrong size, or a hole that is too small.

Henry Shomber is an engineer who has been with Boeing for nearly forty years. He was brought in very early on the 777 programme to help develop new ways of designing planes to avoid some of the problems of the old ways and to cut down the cost of mistakes:

> We needed to improve our ability to produce a product that is produced at lower cost and with less change, fewer errors and fewer requirements to make last-minute changes in order to produce it. We are the world leader, but often I think of it as largely because of our customer-support organization. If you own a Boeing airplane – it doesn't matter whether you are the first-tier owner or the third-tier owner – and that airplane is on the ground, we'll help you find a part or build a part for you and get it back in the air. And that's really what makes us the world's best today.

Shomber described graphically the Heath Robinson way in which all planes up to the 777 had their wiring bundles designed:

> We would literally thread the wire bundle through the mock-up and then take it out and flatten it on the board. We'd measure it, and that's the way we decided how long the wire needed to be. And then you would adjust as necessary, because the airplane which is not made of plywood and aluminium differs from the mock-up. So as you produce those first wire bundles then you make further adjustments to make them fit the real airplane. Hydraulics too were in a very similar situation.

Dick Johnson, Boeing's chief project engineer for digital product design, highlighted some of the problems that could occur:

> You have five thousand engineers designing the airplane. It's very difficult for those engineers to coordinate with two-dimensional pieces of paper, or for a designer who is designing an air-conditioning duct to walk over to somebody who is in structures and say, 'Now here's my duct. How does it match up with your structure?' Very difficult with two-dimensional pictures. So we ended up using the mock-up and – quite honestly – also using the final assembly line to finish up the integration. And it's very costly. You end up with an airplane that's very difficult to build. The first time that parts come together is on that assembly line. And they don't fit. So we have a tremendous cost on the first few airplanes of reworking to make sure all the parts fit together.

In the last quarter of the twentieth century, solving such problems was clearly a task for computers. In fact computer-aided design had been used for some time in the car industry and in architecture, essentially as a drawing tool. But Boeing were after something more ambitious than a draughtsman's visual aid, and that required number-crunching ability of a high order, as Alan Mulally explained:

> With digital computers before, we didn't have enough computational capacity to simulate an airplane. We've been able to use computers for parts of the task, and the best example is the flight-crew training simulators, where we simulated lots of the airplane's flying characteristics as well as the systems to teach pilots how to fly. It's much more effective than flying the real airplane, because you can do so many more different conditions and simulate so much more effectively the different systems and failures of the systems. But, as digital computers became larger and could handle more capacity, the next step was how we could make use of them as a design tool. And so in the past, where we had to make mock-up parts and try to figure out how to fit them together, now we can actually simulate the parts and assemblies and we can see ourselves whether all the parts are there and if they fit before we

release them to all of the makers around the world. So the essence of what really happened is that this tool allowed engineering to take responsibility for all their parts before they asked people to make them.

Now think about this. Before, you'd use a two-dimensional piece of paper and a yellow pencil and we would try to create a three-dimensional product. It was very difficult. It's very difficult for the mind, and it's a real skill just to think in two dimensions about all these parts that are really three. So for the first time the engineering creative process was enabled to think in terms of the way the world is, in terms of three dimensions, and to look at it and understand it and balance all the objectives of functionality and reliability. Now, computers don't design airplanes – we have not put the knowledge that's in the airplane designer's head into artificial intelligence that balances all these objectives. Some day we'll probably move to that end, but right now the *knowledge* to design airplanes is in the designer's head.

Nowadays the number of designers and drawings and the interconnectedness of the components of a plane as large as the 777 require systems of numbering, duplicating and releasing drawings such that the computer is about the only way to deal satisfactorily with the process. Gone are the days when more homely methods were sufficient. One retired Boeing engineer who worked during the Second World War on the design of the B-29 bombers reported that he had seen engineers make sketches on the cuffs of their shirtsleeves and then they'd give the shirt to someone else to copy. As planes got bigger and systems became more controlled, another Boeing engineer put a drawing number on his wrist and 'released' himself into circulation to see what happened to his own design drawings when they were sent off to the manufacturing engineers.

To see Boeing's computer design system in action is as pleasurable as watching a good animated cartoon. On 16 June 1992, John Mahoney, a designer with the Passenger Doors team, was working on a complex metal solid that would eventually hold the large handle that opened the door. The fineness of detail, the smoothness of rotation and the delicacy of colouring would have taken many hours to achieve if he had been working with a paper blueprint, but the workstation took all this in its stride, responding to the designer's instructions with the speed of light. Mahoney had called up the final three-dimensional contours for this piece, and was working out whether he could cut any more metal away and, if so, where. At this stage in the project, with 25 per cent or so of the drawings finalized, the various designers were paying a lot of attention to the weight requirements of the plane. Any unnecessary ounce or gram translates into extra metal to be carried on a long journey, and extra fuel to carry that metal, and then in an apparent infinite regress there's the extra fuel needed to carry the weight of the extra fuel needed to carry the extra weight of the part.

Mahoney rotated the component on his screen and drew a circle on one surface. He then told the computer to make a cylinder using that circle as one face. Then he made the cylinder become a hole in the component. A press of a couple of buttons produced an on-screen display of how much weight such a hole would lose (about a fifth of an ounce) compared with leaving it as solid metal. But, clearly, cutting holes in a piece to save weight can have a deleterious effect on other aspects of the component – particularly its load-bearing ability. Here another aspect of the system came into its own, as Mahoney gave instructions for the computer to display and then print out a view of the component under stress in a chosen direction, with coloured areas marking the different levels of force experienced throughout the metal. Like a colourful weather map, the piece showed one or two high-pressure areas that would be created if the hole was designed into the piece. But even in these high-pressure areas the pressure was well within the loads that the material could support, and Mahoney signed off the drawing. Now his design was accessible to any other designer, merely by calling it up on his own computer terminal. And if that designer had some problem with Mahoney's design – some interference, for example – he could take it right back to Mahoney there and then, rather than find out many months later. Says Mahoney:

> The old 'throw it over the wall' business of 'Here's what I insist being the case; now do what you can with it', that's gone away. But in order to really make it go away you still wind up throwing it

over the wall. You just have to accept it being thrown back – that's the difference.

Now that Mahoney had told the computer that the design was complete, the piece was then incorporated in the computer's memory. He could now look at the piece in its correct position in the door, highlighted to make it stand out from the mass of other coloured lines now surrounding it there. He could then zoom back to show the whole door on the screen, complete with the handle that fits into his component. He could move the handle and open the door. He could also zoom out further, seeing the door in its correct position in the fuselage as it opens and closes. He could view it from above, so that he was looking down on the top edge of the door, or from inside, so that he could see some of the other components that are in contact with the piece. He could check to see whether the new design led to any interferences that were not there before he made the change.

As he zoomed out further, he would see more of the whole plane, with other doors along the side of the fuselage, until the whole plane was visible, from tail to cockpit. Of course, as the plane got smaller, some of the detail was removed – otherwise the amount of redrawing as more and more components came into view would slow things down. But it was all there somewhere, stored in mainframe computers. And while Mahoney was looking at his door pieces, other designers would be using the same computers to draw or alter their own components, perhaps at the other end of the plane.

These miraculous events were made possible by two linked computer systems: CATIA – Computer-graphics Aided Three-dimensional Interactive Application – and EPIC – Electronic Preassembly in the CATIA – which allow the different components to be designed and integrated into one vast computer simulation of the whole plane.

Boeing started using a computer design system in 1978, for some parts of some aircraft. When they designed a wing strut of the 767 using this system, they found that it halved the number of changes they would have expected to make during manufacture. It was decided that the 777 would be the first plane to be fully built without mock-ups, entirely on the basis of 3-D computerized data. Boeing had introduced CATIA, using a Dassault/IBM system, in 1986. Then, when the 777 decision was made, Boeing computing staff devised the add-on program, EPIC, to allow the system to replace mock-ups entirely. The company distributed 2,200 computer terminals among the 777 design team, all of them connected to the world's largest grouping of IBM mainframe computers – eight of them – at Boeing's Bellevue offices. In addition, other key participants in the process, from airframe manufacturers in Japan to engine-makers in America and the UK, had immediate access to data and were made aware of updates and changes as soon as they were confirmed.

Dick Johnson identified one particular benefit of this system compared with the old system using mock-ups:

> With the mock-ups we had the three classes: class 1, class 2 and class 3. The engineer had three opportunities at three levels of detail to check his parts, and nothing in between. With CATIA he can do it day in and day out over the whole development of the airplane, and so it's a tremendous advantage.

Of course, this apparently limitless freedom to tinker with the design until the part is finalized could solve one problem by replacing it with another, as Johnson explained:

> As we go through the process of designing day in and day out, people continue to change their designs and they will interfere with other parts. But they have a tool to find it now, whereas in the past we had no idea until we tried to build an airplane. You may have checked against somebody else's part the day before, and when you check against it today he's changed his part and it goes right through your part. What we've done to try to help with the problem is to establish what we call a series of stages. There's six stages to the design process. In each stage the design is going to change daily. And designers just have to deal with the fact that parts are changing, and they have to coordinate with each other as best they can. But at the end of each of these six stages we go through what we call a freeze. I say, 'OK, no more designs. Now

go work out all the remaining fit problems.' So you get a few days where nobody is designing any more: all they're doing is comparing their designs with everybody else's design to make sure they have no more interferences. Interferences that exist they take action to go and fix. So it's a period in which people stop designing and do the fit check. Then they go back to designing at the end of the stage.

The negotiating that had to go on between designers whose parts interfered led to all sorts of interactions between people who wouldn't normally have any reason to meet, and sometimes found difficulty doing so, as Alan Mulally reported one day:

> I saw one of our senior structures people going up and down the 10-18 building the other day looking for a hydraulic guy. He wanted to put a bracket on his floor beam, and they had not come to an agreement on where the bracket was going to go on the floor beam, or how big it was going to be and whether it was going to create an interference. And he stopped me in the hall and he was so mad because he couldn't find the hydraulics engineer. And he said, 'What do they look like? Do they have tubes in their pockets? Do they have tubes coming out of their heads? What *do* those people look like?'

The main interferences were where one piece overlapped with another. But there are subtler and more complicated problems that can arise when a three-dimensional aircraft is designed on two-dimensional paper. For example, some components in the plane have to be removable for maintenance purposes. Steve Johnson was one of the designers responsible for parts of the wings. Inside each wing is a long cylindrical component called a torque tube:

> We've had a situation in the wing trailing edge where all the simple interferences were worked. We had a torque tube that fitted within the wing trailing edge and everything was OK. And then we found out through further analysis that we couldn't get the torque tube in, and we couldn't get it out. So we've had to go back and look at the swept volume – the space that this torque tube needs around it

so that it can be removed. It's really saved the company much money. Usually you don't find these things out until the first airplanes are built or till somebody tries to service them.

EPIC was intended to have a further benefit, by creating a more direct link between the design of the components and the engineering processes that were to manufacture them. In modern airplane production, design and manufacture are generally two entirely separate activities. In the Boeing Company in 1992 the separation of the two was embodied physically in the distances between the manufacturing and assembly areas and the offices of the designers and engineers. Communication was often by internal post as designers released their hitherto jealously guarded drawings to the people who were going to make the plane, who might be several miles away. Their task was then to look at the particular component and consider the materials involved, the intricacy of the design, the forces it had to support and the date it would be needed and to come up with a way of manufacturing it. When a solid mock-up was

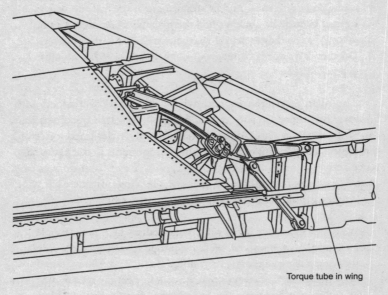

Torque tube in wing

The wing area containing the torque tube

involved, the part would often be hand-crafted in one of the Boeing machine shops and then the design would be tinkered with until it was right. Then, if it was a metal part of some complexity, the 3-D solid part would be used to design a production tool that would make it in quantity.

The 777 was to involve tools of some sophistication. In addition to the conventional drilling, riveting and milling machines that would be used to shape and connect the pieces of metal that made up the plane, there were more complex pieces of equipment, some of them costing hundreds of thousands of dollars, that simplified and streamlined the task of assembling multi-part components of the plane such as the wing.

Some of these machine tools filled half a factory. The wing spars, for example, which were to be the first pieces of the plane to be manufactured, would be assembled in a 200-foot-long device, called the ASAT tool, that consisted of a framework to hold the components and an automated carriage to move along and connect them in sequence and according to computerized specifications. There were two main types of components to be connected in this tool. There were the spars, each as long as a wing, to be made thirty miles from the design offices, in Auburn, and the ribs, to be made three thousand miles away, in Japan. These components would meet for the first time in the production tool, and would be expected to fit together, using three different types of fastener through thousands of holes drilled in the places the designers specified.

With the EPIC system, there could now be a direct link between the computer description of the design of a component and the instructions that a machine tool would need in order to make it. The tool has to know the size of the components, the breadth of the spar as it varies along the length, and the thickness of the pieces that are connected to the spars, which are also variable. For the first time in a Boeing plane, there was to be a direct – electronic – connection between the decisions made by the designers about the dimensions of a component and the data that the tool would need in order to put the pieces together.

But there was a further innovation which would be essential to ensure the success of this new tool. The link must not be solely electronic. Like the engineer Mulally saw in a corridor, each of the

many parties involved in the 777 must be made to meet other
species of engineer face to face to exchange ideas about matters of
mutual interest. The time was past when designers could 'throw stuff
over the wall' and wash their hands of it. This realization was what
led Boeing senior managers to develop two linked ideas, one called
Working Together and the other, which they had come across in
Japan, called design–build teams.

Working Together is a will-o'-the wisp idea which evaporates if
you think too hard about it, but it seemed to have a fierce power to
inspire men, and the few women, who worked on the 777. At one
extreme you have Alan Mulally at his most mystical describing what
are for him the roots of the Working Together philosophy:

> I think the human spirit is a fabulous thing, and I think there are
> beautiful butterflies in all of us, and I think that we come with no
> baggage and no burdens and no limitations in our own minds, and
> I think the environment we're trying to create is that we have a
> shared thought, a shared vision, a shared appreciation, a shared
> understanding of what it is we're really going to try to accomplish
> together. We would work out what each of us is going to do to use
> our unique talents to contribute. Then we'd know where we are.
> We'd know what needs special attention and we'll all bind
> together to help each other be a success.

At the other extreme you have Ron Ostrowski, also a very senior
engineer, as down-to-earth as Mulally is ebullient, suggesting how
he came to understand, to accept, and then wholeheartedly to
embrace the philosophy:

> It was a point of conflict to begin with. You know, an engineer
> with pride wants to find a solution to his problems. And it's not a
> natural thing to go out and explore publicly the particular
> problems you have. You'd like to be able to handle those yourself.
> So I'd say there was resistance at first. But it's interesting how
> attention can be given to a particular problem like that – a
> communication problem if you will – by just making it OK to do
> that sort of thing, to express your problems, get all the help you
> can. If you're working together, you're going to find that a great

assistance in finding the solution, because none of us singly can do nearly as well as we can as a group. And so I think over the years that resistance has gone away. We kind of shout it from the rooftops, in our programme reviews with large audiences, in our All Team Meeting. The same words have been used: 'It's OK.' It's almost like 'Celebrate our problems – get them out in the open so we can go work them.' So I think it's come a long way, and I don't think the resistance is there nearly so much any more, and it's overcome fairly easily. First of all you get a lot of folks that want to work that way, and the more people you get involved with that kind of an attitude the easier it is to break down the barriers of the few that don't. And so it just kind of feeds upon itself.

Working Together was to be the name of the first 777; it was to be painted on banners that went up around the factories, and on posters, baseball caps, badges and T-shirts. And it was to be repeated as a mantra in speeches and discussions between Boeing and its customers and contractors. But there was a lot riding on it. In 1992 Boeing believed in an almost theological way that this new way of working – whatever it was – could actually make a difference to the testable and costable quality of the plane they were making, an outcome that would not become demonstrable for another year if not two. But observing it in action in the new type of meetings that were happening every day in every 777 department revealed a very different atmosphere from that conveyed in a story from earlier Boeing days.

In the late 1950s there was a senior Boeing production manager called Bud Hurst:

Hurst had told one of his machinists the way he was drilling holes was unsafe. For several days Bud kept watching him and noticed he was still drilling the same way. Hurst went to the worker's foreman. 'Straighten that guy out,' he ordered.

That didn't accomplish anything either. Hurst brought the matter up at a production staff meeting and was told, 'The man's one of our best workers, he wouldn't hurt himself, and besides you can't tell him anything.'

The next day, Hurst approached the errant machinist.

'You gonna do that drilling the right way?' he asked.

The worker gave him the well-known freeway salute, and Hurst decked him with one punch.[1]

Now if only he'd told the machinist that he had a beautiful butterfly inside him.

[1]Serling, *Legend and Legacy*, p.169

FOUR

'No More Chainsaws'

'I wish that I could say that design–build teams were one of these wonderful ideas that leap forward and you say, "Aha!"' said Phil Condit one day, in his office in the executive building in Renton. It was March 1992, in the middle of the design phase, when the benefits of the new approach could still only be guessed at, but the tremendous amount of administrative work it engendered was only too apparent. The engineers were working in spaces that were not custom-designed, and the meetings of the design–build teams, or DBTs, were scattered through many different sites in Renton, requiring careful timetabling to avoid the situation where one engineer was meant to be in two different places at the same time – the human equivalent of interferences, you could call it. For some teams, such as the Propulsion DBTs, their life was complicated further by the fact that some of their members were three thousand miles away on the East Coast, and someone had to make sure that the video link had been booked and was operative to bring images of the Pratt & Whitney engineers in East Hartford into a conference room in Renton.

As Condit looked out of his panelled executive office on to a Japanese-style roof garden, he described how DBTs were, in some sense, a search for the past:

If you go back to the earlier planes that Boeing built, the factory was on the bottom floor and engineering was on the upper floor. Both manufacturing and engineering went back and forth. When there was a problem in the factory, the engineer went down and looked at it and said, 'Well you'd better do this.' The entire design department was within fifty feet of each other. As the scale goes up, that gets harder and harder and harder. And if you're not careful, organizations, just by the way they behave, want to form little enclaves, so Structures goes off over here and Air-Conditioning goes off over there; Manufacturing goes over here and Planning goes over there; and Finance goes somewhere else. And then one day you turn around and you've discovered there's an 'us and them' attitude. 'If only *they* would do this then *our* job would be easier.' And you look at that whole thing and you say, 'OK, what are the things that I can do to effect that outcome?'

I would love to have a building in which the entire organization was within fifty feet of each other. With ten thousand people that turns out to be really hard. So you start devising other tools to allow you to achieve that – the design–build team. You break the airplane down and bring manufacturing, tooling, planning, engineering, finance and materiel[1] all together in that little group. And they are effectively doing what those old design organizations did on their bit of the airplane.

Among all the secrets that Boeing guarded jealously during the design and manufacture of the 777, its management techniques were every bit as protected as any technical details of materials, wing shape, production rate or avionics. Superimposed on the design–build-team structure was a top-secret schedule of drawing freezes and design stages, each of which had been carefully planned to ensure smooth, error-free design, consultation and communication, and each of which generated its own flow charts, 'sign-off' documents, and progress reports. If 'the biggest problem with communication is the illusion that it has occurred', observing the DBTs at work left no doubt that communication was occurring, in detail and in triplicate.

In view of this range of Boeing secrets, identified by the label of 'Boeing Proprietary', it was surprising that the company nevertheless allowed into the heart of the 777 design and manufacturing process two groups of outsiders – representatives of the customer

---

[1] 'Materiel' – pronounced materi*ell* – refers to the department that deals with the purchase of airplane parts from other suppliers.

airlines, and engineers from foreign airplane manufacturers, notably the Japanese. Mulally explained why:

When we were getting ready to do the 777 we had these very clear customer–airline market imperatives. We were competing with three other airplanes. The customer had good choices, so it had to be a better airplane. Number-one criterion: so how can we make a better airplane? Well, engineering could try to do it by themselves, but then we realized, Well, do we know everything about manufacturing? Do we know everything about how the airplanes operate in the field? Do we know everything about what's happened in the past from an airline point of view? And the answer kept coming back, We can't make a better airplane unless we can figure how to get everybody's knowledge included in this design. So our first thought was: Let's send the engineers out around the world. We'll get them all an airplane ticket. They'll go out to the airlines and they'll watch how they operate. They'll watch how they refuel, they'll watch how they change the legs and how they do the galleys. And then they'll all know. And so we tried that and we learned a lot of things. And what we really learned was there's a lot of knowledge out there and there would be no way that we could train up a whole engineering workforce to bring all this knowledge inside. Then we'd do the same thing with manufacturing. We sent them all down to Auburn which is where we make all our detailed parts, and we showed them what big five-axis machine tools look like. And they were all very interested and they learned a lot, but there was no way that we could incorporate all of that manufacturing knowledge about what really happens when you make a part and how the dimensions change unless we brought that knowledge in.

So we thought, Why don't we get everybody together? Why don't we figure out an environment – a structure – that will allow this knowledge to flow into the designer? And that led to the design–build team concept, where airline customer services and manufacturers around the world would join with engineering and we'd sign a pact together that we would design a product that balanced all these objectives and we'd listen to each other and we'd include that knowledge. And then that, combined with

EPIC, would enable us to do three things. First, we would get it more right the first time, before people started to make it. Second, when we got it into test it would be closer to the final product. And third, it would allow us to test it more efficiently, so that the plane would be even more service-ready to deliver to the airlines.

Garnet Hizzey, an ornately named British engineer, helped devise Boeing's design–build teams. He was one of several British engineers who held senior positions on the 777 team and had travelled down the brain drain that has deprived British engineering of talent over the last thirty years. Like his compatriots, he had an unplaceable amalgam of a British regional accent spattered almost randomly with American vocabulary and pronunciation. He described his recruitment to Boeing:

I worked as an apprentice for the Rolls-Royce engine company in the British Isles, and after I'd finished my undergraduate studies I went to the Cranfield Institute of Technology for two years, and did a master's degree there. In those days Boeing used to make an annual trip to the United Kingdom and recruited from downtown London. So I went down one evening and had an interview, and I was very surprised that within three days I had a very attractive job offer and a telegram enquiring as to whether I had any counter-parts or peers who would like to join me. Unfortunately, I guess, from the college's point of view, many did, and so there was a mass exodus. This was 1966, when Boeing was in one of its boom eras, and there was a considerable drain on British talent. In fact I just joined a lot of British people and many other Europeans that were already here, so it was very painless. The immigration laws at that time very much favoured the Anglo-Saxons, and so within a six-week period Boeing had picked up all my goods and chattels and made everything so easy. My intentions were to come to Boeing for two or three years, and maybe then move on down to California, but in that short period of time I'd become what they call a tree-hugger. I'd come to enjoy the benefits of the north-west Seattle area, and that was twenty-seven years ago, and I'm still here.

In 1990 Hizzey and his colleagues looked at the tasks involved in designing a plane, and started to plan the best size and number of DBTs.

> At that time we anticipated maybe we would have 80 or 100 teams. I think if we'd known at the time we'd end up with 250 we would have probably dead-ended it right there. But it grew pretty much under its own momentum, and because of the success those early teams started to enjoy, it matured and blossomed. Obviously there are still improvements to be made to that process, but I think fundamentally it really set down the roots of Working Together, and it has established the relationships between engineering and operations that I think are now a distinct competitive advantage for us. From my association and travelling around the world I haven't seen anything that compares with the close alliance between design engineers and manufacturing people that exists on this programme. In fact it's even different within the Boeing Company, not just between Boeing and other companies.

Anyone who had shares in a company that made acetates for overhead projectors would have made a mint if they could have got their hands on the Boeing contract. Two hundred and fifty design–build teams met at least twice a week for a couple of hours, with reports from up to a dozen people, each slipping viewfoils on to the projector at a rate that was sometimes too fast for more than the first few lines to be read. Each team leader orchestrated the meeting like clockwork, with times allocated down to the minute, no rambling allowed, and very specific notes taken of what had been decided, who was to act on the decision, what reporting-back was required at the next meeting and what should be passed up the line to the next level of meetings. Meetings as a management tool had rarely been brought to such a pitch of organization.

The plane was divided up into large areas of responsibility such as wings, empennage, fuselage and so on, and then each of these units was broken down into subcomponents, each the responsibility of a DBT. The wing, for example, was divided into leading-edge and trailing-edge teams but, because they were dealing with such large and complex pieces, the role of these teams was more supervision than strict detailed design. Reporting to the trailing-edge team were ten DBTs, each responsible for a single piece of the trailing-edge.

Steve Johnson was in charge of the whole trailing edge, and had ten DBTs reporting to him, each responsible for one movable component of the trailing edge:

> The wing trailing edge has *spoilers*. We have five outboard spoilers and two inboard spoilers on each wing. Those are the relatively flat surfaces that lie on top of the trailing edge. They pop up when you touch down and land. They slow the airplane down when the airplane is landing, and the outboard spoilers are sometimes lifted up to change the roll or allow the airplane to roll while it's in flight. We have *ailerons*, which look just like a piece of the wing that is cut out and rotates about a single hinge. Those are used to make the airplane roll. We have an outboard aileron, which is only used at low speed, and then we have the inboard aileron/flaperon that is used at high speed. We have *flaps*, which are big airfoils that are extended on mechanisms to increase the chord of the wing at low speeds. These devices come back from the wing and also change their angle of attack to provide a lot more lift for the wing. This allows the wing to maintain its lift at low speed and allows the airplane to land at a reasonable speed.

The teams, each with between ten and twenty members, were named after a piece of the wing trailing edge. They were: Flap Supports, Inboard Flap, Outboard Flap, Outboard Fixed Wing, Flaperon, Aileron, Inboard Fixed Wing and Gear Support, Main Landing-Gear Doors, Spoilers, and Fairings. 'I kind of view each of the surfaces on the wing trailing edge as a little company,' said Johnson:

> And it's not the supplier's company and it's not the Boeing company. It's the Inboard Flap company, or the Outboard Flap company. They have all of the people necessary to design the structure, design the tools, develop the manufacturing plan, write the contracts – everything is in that little company. So we treat them like that.

One meeting on 26 March 1992 gave an idea of how these things worked. It was a meeting of the Outboard Flap design–build team. There were twenty people present, representing the following 'organizations' – some of them other departments in Boeing, others from outside companies: Customer Service, Weights, Alenia (the Italian company who would manufacture the flap), Design to Cost, Structures, Factory, Manufacturing Engineering, Tool Engineering, Materiel, Aerodynamics, and Quality Control. Even without precise definitions of these terms, it's possible to begin to see how the design of a part can have implications for many different aspects of the plane. Its weight, its cost, the tools that need to be made, the quality-control problems it might present during manufacture, the material it's made of (in this case the part is one of those that will be made of carbon-fibre composite) – information about all of these will fan out from this meeting to other meetings concerned with these more general issues. The current expected weight of the flap will be added into the total weight of the trailing edge, which in turn will be added to the data for the leading edge. Then, at a higher-level meeting, the total projected wing weight will be added to the weight projections for the fuselage, the empennage, the engines and so on.

The Outboard Flap DBT meeting took place in conference room 41C3 on one of the floors of Building 10-16 at Renton. Much of the floor was taken up with open-plan cubicles, and all the wing design engineers were in the same area, grouped in teams under signs hanging from the ceiling that indicated their own particular part. Most participants at the Outboard Flap meeting arrived punctually, until a few minutes after eight o'clock the room was full, with some people sitting round a long table and others on chairs around the edge of the room. An agenda was slapped on to the overhead projector, reminding participants who was to speak at what time. There was barely time to read it before the first speaker started on his report.

From the outside, the outboard flap looks like a long thin wing, tapered to a sharp edge along one side. Its outer envelope is comparatively simple, but under the skin are a framework and inner components that give it stiffness and enable it to rotate and maintain a position at an angle to the airflow, to help the plane slow down. The events at this DBT meeting were fairly typical. They included discussion of a change in the diameter of a metal pin from seven-eighths of an inch to three-quarters; a revised location for a washer that would be between two rotating surfaces; cancellation of a production order for eight parts of the flap, since there had recently been new calculations of the loads that the flap would experience and so the parts would have to be redesigned.

A section of the meeting was devoted to 'issue close-outs'. At each meeting some issues are identified that require the team to consider them and come to a decision. One issue was quite simple – what material to use for a particular tool that would be used to make the flap. Because it was such a long component, there could be expansion effects because of heat. If the tool expanded at a different rate from the material that the flap was made of, there could be nasty mismatches during the manufacturing process. There were two candidate materials for the tool, but one of them was far less durable than the other, and so the other was chosen. To indicate acceptance of this decision, every team member signed the 'issue close-out' form, which would be filed away as a record of who decided what, when and where. At that meeting, there were three more issue close-outs. The second was 'to study the costs and advantages of female spar tooling'. Whatever 'female spar tooling' was, it was clear from the team's discussions, and some tests that Alenia had done in Italy, that using a female tool showed 'thickness-control, bridging and wrinkling problems in the radius between the web and the flanges'. The decision was therefore made not to incorporate female spar tooling into the design. ('Male' and 'female' tools are honourable and traditional terms in engineering and merely refer, as you might expect, to items that poke into things and items that have things poked into them. So a jig that holds a component would be a female tool, and the drill or riveter that acts on the component would be male.)

In addition to 'close-outs' the team dealt with 'buy-offs' the final, detailed definition of what Boeing expected from a contractor. The purpose of these meetings at this stage in the design of the plane was to finalize as many drawings as possible so that they could be passed to the manufacturers – Alenia in this case – for tool design and factory planning to begin. Sometimes a plan would be complete apart from some final details of one small component, and the team would then fill in an 'exception record', saying effectively, 'You can start work on this piece, apart from the outboard seal interface with the fuel jettison panel support, for which we require clarification from another DBT.'

One impressive indication at this meeting of the power of CATIA/EPIC was a computer-calculated account of interferences that needed to be sorted out. A clash output report showed that the computer had been asked to check a three-dimensional assembly of twenty pieces of the flap and it had made 207,601 checks. This huge number came about because the computer was checking the relationship between pairs of the twenty pieces in turn to see whether they occupied the same coordinates in space. Today it found 251 interferences and printed out details of each one – which part numbers were interfering, by how much they overlapped, and so on, together with a drawing of each part with the area of interference outlined in red. On the basis of this document, the designers of the interfering components (assuming they weren't designed by the same person) would get together and decide who was to redesign one part to make room for the other, and to analyse what the implications would be, for strength in particular.

These interferences were within the DBT's own components, but of course many parts butted up or interacted with some other team's components, and there had to be ways of sorting out those interferences as well. Every few weeks during the main CATIA design phase a halt was called to all design activity – a design freeze – and everybody went into the system and looked for problems that had arisen because of the interfaces between one system or set of parts and another.

If representatives from any of the customer airlines wanted to attend these meetings they were welcome to do so. This would usually happen if there was a particular concern about some specific issue. In the early days it was with a degree of nervousness that the airline representatives took up the unusual invitation to become part of the design–build process. They expected a hostile reaction from the Boeing engineers. Gordon McKinzie began to attend a number of the DBTs as the United Airlines representative:

The die was cast at a high level at Boeing, saying that 'We're going to be having some airline folk sitting in on these design teams.' But the fact was these design–build teams were all new at Boeing, so, as all these people were sitting across the table from a production guy and a finance guy and a quality guy for the first time in their life, it really didn't make a whole lot of difference to see an airline guy there as well. We were all newcomers to this new culture that Phil Condit had brought on board. If they had already had this system over a period of years and then all of a sudden we showed up, I think it would have been a lot different. But the reception was great.

McKinzie cites examples from those early meetings where his presence avoided, or at least minimized, problems for United when the plane went into service:

The flap story is probably the biggest one and, and it's not a total win for United but it's a lot better than it could have been. The aft trailing-edge flap on this airplane is forty-three feet long. It's a beautiful flap, it's gap-free, and it's bump-free because it's made of composite material so it has no seams or anything in it. The problem is that our autoclave [an oven used to repair pieces made of carbon-fibre composite] is only twenty-five feet long, so our math quickly told us that if you put this thing in the autoclave at United to apply the heat and pressure you needed to fix it you wouldn't be able to close the door.

There may be occasions when a control surface like the trailing-edge flap is damaged while the plane is on the ground – by an airport truck running into it, for example. Since it is made of carbon-fibre composite rather than metal, any damage can't just be repaired with a riveted piece of metal over the surface: it needs a more substantial repair operation. United had tried to get Boeing to devise some kind of on-the-spot fix, but so far the only method they had come up with was to take the whole flap off.

Meanwhile Boeing was building a sixty-foot-long autoclave and they had no problem with it, so we said, 'You've either got to break this flap in half or at least make provision to have us saw it conveniently down the dotted line so we can get it in to the autoclave some day. And that's what they did. They actually beefed up the honeycomb inside the flap to permit us, if we ever had to, to saw through there, make a repair in our short autoclave, and then put it back together with a splice.

There were quite tough negotiations to deal with the flap issue, since there were costs for Boeing if they redesigned the flap and costs for United if they didn't. And, while United would really have liked a proper division halfway along the flap, Boeing came up with a compromise which United decided to accept. But that was what DBTs and Working Together were all about, as Ron Ostrowski explained:

It's a trade between weight, complexity of design and the functionality of the design when you're done. Now what we did on that particular issues was to come to a compromise where the internal structure is continuous and the external structure is not. In other words, the skins of the flap are separate. And we worked with United on that. And there are times when you'll debate these issues and you'll make the decision for the better of the airplane. And it's not like we drove a decision of that kind down their throats. We did not do that. They were a party to the decision-making process that led to the compromise that we produced for that particular situation. You just have to negotiate your way through those particular controversies.

There were many such examples of how allowing the airlines into the DBTs solved problems early:

Another one we just caught in time [says McKinzie] was the fuelling panel, and this is where the other airlines ganged up on Boeing because Boeing didn't think of the fact that our fuel stands only reach a certain height to fuel under the wing of the airplane. The 747 was about as high as our fuel stands could go to reach that fuelling panel, and this airplane was thirty-one inches higher than the 747 – it's a *big* airplane. We mentioned that to All-Nippon Airways and to British Airways, and they said their stands don't reach any higher either and unless we hire fuellers who are eight feet tall we're just not going to make it. That was pretty late in the game too, but Boeing agreed to move the panel down the wing, closer to the fuselage, and, because the wing is slanted up so much, by moving it inboard it also came closer to the ground, so now we're within six inches of reaching that panel and our safety folks have allowed us to put a stool on the top of the fuelling platform to get up there, so it's going to be fine. I don't know what would have happened if the airplane showed up at our stations and nobody could reach the fuel panel – that would have been very embarrassing.

The fuellers in our system were alerted to this and they got very upset. 'Have you ever fuelled an airplane in a high wind at O'Hare?' they said – 'it's really uncomfortable.' And to go any higher without additional stability they felt the safety guys would be on them. I think we'd have had a problem.

British Airways had a small team of people based in Seattle during the design of the 777. One of them, Andy d'Agata, was a very experienced maintenance engineer who had spent years helping to service Boeing planes at London Airport, and had 'tarmac cred' when it came to spotting assumptions made by Boeing designers who'd never had to prepare a plane for departure on a cold morning at Heathrow.

There's one DBT that was recently set up to study the power-up sequence of the aircraft. They had some rather different ideas of how the airlines powered their aircraft up on a cold morning from what really happens in real life. The designers considered that, because the aircraft is so complex and had so many new digital systems and so many new ways of doing things, it would be acceptable to wait for a significant period of warming-up, as it were. As an operational airline, we want the thing to come to life as soon as possible. We want to throw the switch and the airplane is live.

Although a lot of people involved in this project are highly experienced and qualified designers, they haven't been involved in the environment of operational aircraft. And it's relatively simple things which are overlooked – such as the location of units. If a box, for example, is placed in a path where somebody can stand on it, then somebody *will* stand on it. And the question I normally ask at that stage is, If you're going to put that box there, can we stand on it? Will it survive?

One of Alan Mulally's management slogans is 'No more chainsaws'. Ron Ostrowski describes how it came about:

That was an early one of Alan's phrases. One of our objectives was to design this airplane with customer input early in the process. Traditionally we found that, as we got more customers involved or if we didn't do a good communication job up front with the very initial customers, we would have to come in and change our design after we had put it in place. Maybe we'd even got hardware being built. Or maybe the airplane is sitting out there and it doesn't meet the customer's expectations in some specific way. The chainsaw approach was that you crank that chainsaw up and go into the plane and rip up structure, rip up systems, in a broad sense of the word, because you had to replace it with something that was closer to those expectations. It's very expensive. It disrupts the engineering process. And it's very difficult for manufacturing.

For an outside observer it's very difficult to appreciate the hideously complex interrelations between all the parts of the plane that leads to all sorts of problems at the design stage. In March 1993 Alan Mulally had a worried expression on his face as he headed for a meeting of engineers.

I'm feeling very anxious because I have a design meeting waiting. We're going to work one more time on the lower 41 section in the nose of the airplane[2] – trying to get all the wire bundles and the environmental-control system in and compatible with each other. And we want to get that done because in three weeks those wires need to be specified into the manufacturing shops who are going to make them.

---

[2]The 41 section is the front of the plane. It has an upper lobe, where the crew sit, and a lower lobe, housing different types of equipment.

It had been decided that the 777's section 41 would be the same as the 767's. The team felt that this was a good decision because it saved some design work, since the 767 data already existed. But this benefit carried with it a problem. Because the 777 is overall a larger plane, its systems were larger, and yet the electronic equipment under the cockpit floor had to be packaged to fit into the same space as in a 767 nose. Three months after that anxiogenic meeting, Mulally explained how things had turned out:

The packaging job was tough in the nose, under the floor and in the undercarriage, because we have the flight-control system, the environment-control system and the electrical system all vying for space. And we also improved the air-distribution system to the 777 pilots, because one of the things the airlines asked us to do was to create an environment that if one pilot were smoking, for example on the long-range flights, we could remove the smoke from one side and provide a cleaner environment on the other side. And so our design solution had more air inputs into the cockpit and more out, to manage this flow. So this meant that behind the overhead panels and the panels in the floor we had more things to integrate. We even made a special digital mock-up to look at all that together, and we got everybody in the room, from every discipline. It was really pretty exciting. And we just kept working on it. And we thought we'd have it done one day and then the air-conditioning guys would go back and find out that the way they had routed their air-conditioning ducts the velocities got to be too fast, so we wouldn't get the flow rates where it came out from the pilot at the right rate. And then they would come back to the next meeting and they would smooth out their environmental-control lines but that would run in to the hydraulics guy's lines. And we worked on just that solution for maybe six or seven weeks.

And we also had some other criteria that, as we worked on the detailed design, forced us to change our 'feel' system that gives the pilot the tactical feel for the aerodynamic loads and to be able to fly the airplane. We wanted to be able also to handle foreign-object damage that comes in through the nose of the airplane, because airplanes frequently run into tiny birds and they can go through the radome. We design so that bird penetration doesn't take out critical pieces of the systems such as the flight-control system, so we had to accommodate that requirement. There have been so many requirements and lots of design solutions, and the thing that made it come out in the end was everybody working together over and over and over again. And you had to keep your emotional resilience, because one day you had a solution and the next day you didn't because it didn't satisfy one person's requirements.

Day after day, an unquantifiable amount of data was digested and the important bits were passed on to the next level of synthesis, where the same process happened, with ever more information being boiled down to be passed even further up the line.

In 1992 the key regular management meeting was the Mega-Meeting, as it was called – a marathon gathering of all chief project engineers. This took place every Thursday afternoon on the seventh floor of Building 10-18 in Renton.

On Thursday 26 March 1992 the Mega-Meeting is scheduled to last five and three-quarter hours. This is Alan Mulally's meeting, although he plays a low-key role most of the time, sitting off to the left in the front row. There are two screens for the usual battery of overhead slides. The regular attenders at the meeting are all the chief engineers on the 777 project, sitting in sheepskin-covered chairs under signs bearing their names and responsibilities. They are responsible for broad categories of activity on the plane, such as Structures, Payloads, Systems or Propulsion, and each has hundreds of engineers working to him, spread across dozens of DBTs. The CEs make up the first three rows of the Mega-Meeting, and behind them are various other key individuals – sometimes subordinates or managers with non-engineering responsibilities at a senior level. The agenda at each Mega-Meeting is usually along the same lines. First, there are reports from three of the chief engineers in rotation, so that over the space of a month each will have given an indication of the status of his area's contribution to the plane. In March 1992 everyone is concerned about completing the design of 25 per cent of the plane. There is a design freeze on, which means that no one can get access to his design on the CATIA system in order to change it. At one point in the meeting, someone raises in a plaintive voice the fact that his team has been asked to carry out some task on CATIA by a certain date and can't do so because of the freeze. Another manager says that they can – it's just a matter of creating a separate file for them to play around in, making changes in a way that will not affect, or even be accessible to, anyone else.

The overwhelming impression is that this airplane depends on print or typescript to keep going. Chart after chart, histograms and flow diagrams, typed memos, all flow through the meeting in front of a group which is largely attentive. This is not a meeting like many senior management meetings in other companies where people resent the time they are spending away from the 'real work'. For Mulally and his colleagues this *is* the real work.

If anything brings home the complexity of running a project like this it is the Mega-Meeting. These people are not conventional managers, although most of their time is spent on traditional management tasks. They are all experienced and talented engineers, and yet today, for nearly six hours, they display only tenuous evidence of traditional engineering skills. What they do display is an astute understanding of the need for every person on the team to be aware of the significant aspects of every other person's progress.

If it is possible to summarize the drift of such a complex meeting it is that today, in March 1992, things are getting behind. As chief engineers rise one by one to speak, some of them show charts called traffic-light charts which incorporate easily visible indicators of status. These use the symbolism of traffic lights to indicate progress or lack of it, and such charts pepper many of the meetings at this stage, often in black and white, occasionally in colour. An open circle – or green – by a category indicates satisfactory progress, a half circle is a danger sign, and a black – or red – circle means things are unsatisfactory. There are more half-black or solid circles than anyone would like in many of these charts, and there is a steady build-up of worry during the meeting which goes largely unspoken until, near the end, one of the chief engineers says, 'Alan, I'm worried about us' – almost like a line from a soap opera where one partner sees a threat to the marriage. But the remark is not treated lightly, and the meeting spends several minutes on a mixture of self-analysis and reassurance.

Several aspects of this meeting throw a light on this group and the company its members work for. Almost everyone is wearing a tie, and that indicates, apart from a comfort in formality, that almost everyone is male. Only an occasional woman slips into the room – a secretary with a message for her boss, a woman delivering information about staff-purchasing possibilities for US bonds, a lone senior manager from Operations Division, a member of the Boeing public-relations team. The tone of the meeting is low-key but informal, in spite of the suits. There is little sense of hierarchy – even though Mulally is the undisputed leader of the team, people do no necessarily bow to his wisdom, and he doesn't expect them to. At one point a senior manager stands up at the back and presents a serious problem to the group, centring on relations between the 777 team and another Boeing division. It is a knotty problem, and it affects some CEs more than others. It can only be solved by some sort of meeting next week, but the Mega-Meeting has already heard of the need for a whole slew of meetings to be carried out in the next two weeks as part of the drawings review process. What is to be done? Can enough CEs spare the time for what it needs: a two-hour meeting some time in the next seven days? Mulally makes a point to the complainant: 'How about having a meeting with X?' With an expression of gentle contempt the man with the problem says, 'I've done that – I'm not from Kansas, but . . .' The implication of the uncompleted sentence is 'I'm not from Kansas, like you, but that doesn't mean I'm stupid.' The group erupts in laughter.

At certain points in the meeting, the name of Airbus is mentioned. Boeing's traditional stance on its competitors is to ignore them as a factor in the business of designing the best plane – whatever can be done to improve the design will be done in order to make the best possible plane, not to beat the competitors. But today Joe Ozimek, from Marketing, sums up the current status of orders and mentions an interesting piece of news about one of the foreign customers. An airline had to apply to its government for permission to buy six 777s. The government has given permission but told the airline to buy eight. This brings general delight in the meeting. 'Then', says Ozimek, 'the government also refused permission for the airline to buy Airbuses.' Mulally gives a whoop of happiness and leads a small round of applause, commenting, 'There's nothing like winning.'

The second piece of news in that area comes in a report by Brian Neal, an English engineer responsible for Propulsion. He has come back from a visit to Pratt & Whitney, who are making some of the engines for the 777. While there, he discovered that Pratt, who are also making engines for Airbus, have had a bad containment problem with an Airbus engine. 'Containment' refers to the need for an engine to contain any fragments that result from some kind of breakage or damage in the rapidly rotating turbine. Unfortunately – for Airbus – a recent engine test led to a turbine blade snapping and bursting out of the engine, unimpeded by the surrounding metal walls of the engine. This sounds like another piece of bad news for Airbus – and therefore good news for Boeing – but Neal goes on to say that, unfortunately, this is the same turbine that is to be in the P&W engines for the 777.

Halfway through the meeting Mulally peers over the heads of his colleagues towards the back of the room. 'Are the cookies here yet?' he says to no one in particular, for all the world like a little boy at a party. They are: a large cardboard tray of chocolate-chip cookies and another tray with lots of soft drinks – 'sodas' as Americans call Coke, Pepsi, 7-Up and so on. 'You'd better get there quick,' he says to a visitor to the meeting – 'the cookies are so good some people take three or four.'

It's at times like this that is it difficult to believe we are in a meeting at one of the largest corporations in the world, planning one of the most complex and innovative technological projects of the decade. It demonstrates the human side of a company that prides itself on looking after its people, and Mulally is in the vanguard of the managers who work away at that task. The management texts on his bookshelves demonstrate that, unlike some of his colleagues, he is entirely comfortable using some of the structured techniques that are designed to win friends and influence people.

When the main board of Boeing met to make a final commitment to the plane, all the people who were working on the 777 were gathered together in one of the Boeing hangars, to be addressed by the 'famous five' vice-presidents. It had been decided that, when Condit came in front of the crowd to make the announcement, the other VPs would change into football gear. Of all of them, Mulally looked most comfortable taking part in this pantomime. He had no fears of looking silly or of losing the dignity that befits a very senior manager in the company.

In a similar way, Mulally enters fully into the spirit of a typical Boeing ceremony at this Mega-Meeting. Just as one of the visiting managers called Elmer is about to deliver his report. Mulally stands up and says, 'Just a minute, everyone, it's time for one of those ceremonies we have from time to time. You know how it goes – look at this picture.' A slide appears on one screen – a picture of a baby. There is a mixture of laughs and groans as the assembled group prepare for one of them to be acutely embarrassed and secretly pleased.

'Anyone recognize this person?' says Mulally, looking around the room. 'Well, here he is again.' Another picture – of a toddler. In fact these are pictures of Elmer, who squirms in his seat and reluctantly admits it. Mullaly reads from notes as he recounts Elmer's career at Boeing. His father worked there, and his son is now a Boeing employee. In fact, in true *This is Your Life* style, his son and his daughter are revealed to be lurking at the back of the room. Elmer is given a bright-green 777 ski jacket from a supply of goodies that cannot be bought in the Boeing shops – there are some things that you can only earn, not buy.

After this excitement the meeting resumes, with more reports, more bad news about delays and overruns, more discussion of what can be done to get back on target. To an outsider, most of the issues seem small, even trifling. Engineer Frank Rasmussen has brought to the meeting his need to get hold of twenty more chairs for his busy and expanding unit. There is a ripple of emotion as Brian Neal, the British propulsion engineer, raises the point that they have all been asked to save money and he has worked out that his division will save three-quarters of a million dollars if everyone travels coach class instead of business class between the UK and Seattle. It will save $3,000 per ticket. He recommends they all consider it, since it shouldn't just be left to just one division. There is a look of astonishment on the face of at least one of the participants, who turns to his neighbour and says, *sotto voce*, 'He expects me to do this? I spent 135 days away from my family last year. If he thinks I'm travelling coach he's crazy.'

The whole meeting is a demonstration of the unseen face of aeronautical engineering – the time-consuming, delicate and careful consideration of detail, dependent on an understanding of two complex types of behaviour. There is collected in this room probably the most comprehensive assembly of knowledge about the behaviour of materials, electronics, computer systems, aerodynamics and jet engines anywhere in the world. There is also as much management expertise as you will find in a large retail organization or a hotel-chain headquarters.

On this project, understanding *human* behaviour is as important as knowing the finer details of how a rudder behaves in a high wind when one engine is shut down. In the fiercely competitive world of plane-making, it is project management that Boeing hope will give their plane the edge over Airbus and McDonnell Douglas. And the underlying motive is to make a plane that is producible as well as being properly designed. As Henry Shomber explained, this had not always been the case at Boeing:

> Prior to the 777, the release of an engineering drawing was entirely up to engineering to decide. There was a signature from the designer who prepared it, the one who checked it, the stress man who certified that it was strong enough, and then the group's supervisor that was responsible for the part. There may also have been a Boeing materials-technology signature on it. But in addition we have now added a signature from the manufacturing engineer who planned how the part will be made. Now his signature means something different from the engineering signature. The engineering signature is a statement about engineering: that the engineering is correct. The manufacturing-engineering signature is a statement that it is *producible* – i.e. that we have incorporated to the degree we could the producibility suggestions that they've brought forward that we hope will make the airplane easier to build. This has been unheard of within Boeing, and in many ways was one of the most uncomfortable aspects when first proposed. Engineering's view was 'I'm responsible', and yet what we're trying to put in place is that this is a *team* responsibility and so this is becoming part of our culture.

For this culture to fulfil the hopes of the 777 team leaders, it had to infuse the working practices of every single member of the ten thousand or so people who built the plane.

No one characterized that culture better than Tom Gaffney, leader of the team that designed and built the passenger doors. He and his colleagues typified the benefits of CATIA and the design–build approach as they designed the best doors of any Boeing aircraft.

FIVE

Testing Times

'The data set you free.'
Alan Mulally

It was early evening on 16 June 1992. In a temperature of −50°F, two men in fur-hooded parkas were spraying water on the door of a 777 aircraft. They would be spraying on and off for several hours, until there was a layer of ice all over the door and frame. To someone unaccustomed to such low temperatures, the environment was surprisingly tolerable. It was certainly cold, but for a few minutes it seemed no worse than the average winter's day. Then, insidiously, more unusual signs began to appear. There would be a prickling in the hairs in your nose as the exhaled water vapour froze around them. A little later, a numbness began to creep up the fingers. At that point it made sense to move quickly to warmer surroundings. This was not difficult. A door led out of the cold chamber into the test bay where the 777 Passenger Doors team were monitoring the first low-temperature test to see if the door would open in some of the worst weather conditions it would meet.

The door that would be frozen shut was an isolated mock-up embedded in a piece of fuselage. Even though the overall design schedule was only 50 per cent complete, there was already a passenger door in existence, complete with all the attachments that were necessary to test its mechanisms. As with many other pieces of the plane, the design process required the drawing stages to be completed early enough for a prototype to be made and tested, so that any shortfall in performance could be rectified by changes in the design before the manufacturing treadmill started moving.

The 777 was to be one of the most tested planes ever, and the test in the cold chamber reflected the strategy that operated in such tests. The usual approach was to think of the worst conditions likely to operate in service and then exceed them by a comfortable margin. If the component, or indeed the whole plane, still performed under those conditions it was deemed to have a sufficient safety margin. With this door test, the condition being simulated was the worst combination of cold and rain the plane might meet, where it has been flying at an altitude where the temperature is −65°F and then lands in freezing rain. In this situation, it's just possible that an eighth of an inch or more of ice will form on the outside of the fuselage, including the area around the doors. It's important that cabin staff will still be able to open the doors with a normal amount of force, particularly in the event of some emergency that would require everyone to be got out of the plane as quickly as possible.

During the course of the evening, technicians stood in front of the door and directed a fine spray of water at it. Working in shifts, they sprayed through the night, until the following morning there was a layer of ice a quarter of an inch thick – thicker than would ever be likely to occur naturally. This was the criterion the Passenger Doors DBT had used when designing the door opening mechanism. Now, the quality of that design would be put to the test. One of the Passenger Doors team would step forward and have one chance to move the handle with a normal amount of force and hope to open the door.

It is difficult to convey the complexity of a large airliner's passenger door without showing it with its inner lining removed and all its parts exposed. When we're getting on or off a plane, we may be aware of the thickness of the door, but, since it is encased in a smooth plastic surface on the inside, we see little more than the handle and, when it is open, the hinges. Familiar as we are with house doors or car doors – and plane doors perform similar functions – it is not easy to appreciate why plane doors need to consist of hundreds of components, most of them of an individual design. Furthermore, in the past, each door on the plane had required different sets of parts with subtly different shapes and sizes, because of the different positions of each door in the fuselage. But doors are the weakest link in a plane, at least in a *pressurized* aircraft.

And that's the difference. When we enter or leave our houses we don't have to think about a possible pressure difference of eight or ten pounds per square inch between the inside and outdoors, and we are not faced with the possibility of our furniture, clothes, books and crockery being sucked out into the street every time we open the front door.

As an aircraft rises, it experiences a drop in air pressure of roughly 3 per cent for each 1,000 feet it ascends. If the cabin were not sealed and pressurized, above about 10,000 feet passengers would start to become short of breath and feel faint, since the pressure would not be strong enough for their bodies to extract all the oxygen they need

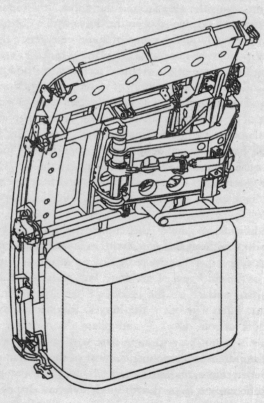

A 777 passenger door

from the air. In a modern airliner there is a sophisticated system to maintain a comfortable pressure in the cabin all the way to about 40,000 feet, where the air pressure difference could be as great as ten pounds per square inch on every part of the plane surface. Just one small window of about 150 square inches will then experience a force of two-thirds of a ton.

Think, then, of the size of a passenger door on a plane like the 777, with an area of perhaps 3,500 square inches, and you'll see that the first task for the door and its frame is to hold everything in place under a pressure of about fifteen tons, for many hours of a long flight. Not only must the door resist that force, it must also be sealed around the edges in such a way that there is no possibility of air leaking out of the plane during its journey. The next task is to devise an opening-and-closing system that makes it impossible for the door to open in flight but easy for flight attendants or airport staff to open the door on the ground. Because of all the associated strength and machinery, these doors are not light, and yet it has to be possible to open them by the easy turn of a handle. But opening them involves more than undoing a lock and pushing. The basic design is what is called a 'plug' door, a clever way to help prevent the door from opening under pressurized flight. In its closed position, a passenger door has projections around the rim that are pressed outwards against stops that are a fixed part of the door frame, 'plugging' the hole in the fuselage. In order for the door to swing open, it has to be lifted inward slightly and then up and out above the stops so that the door is clear of them. What this means is that the team had to devise a system that would allow the very heavy door to be raised on its hinge when the handle was turned, before it swung out, using a gearing that would convert the heavy weight of the door into a lighter force for the flight attendants.

There are further refinements that have to be incorporated in the mechanism to take account of the emergency escape slide that is an integral part of the door. During the period before take-off and after landing, escape chutes on the doors are activated so that, when the door is opened, the chutes automatically deploy on to the runway, allowing passengers to slide down and get away in an emergency. There is a lever in the door that deactivates the slide after landing, when the pilot says 'Doors to manual', and reactivates it before take-off, when he says 'Doors to automatic'. One small design problem that the Passenger Doors DBT hope they have overcome is the occasional tendency for flight attendants with long fingernails not to push the lever far enough because their fingernails scrape against the door behind the handle. This can leave the chute activated when the plane has halted at the gate, sending it flying out when the door is opened to let the passengers off. The traditional punishment for such an event is a week off with no pay.

There can be few passengers who have not wondered on their way to the lavatory what would happen if they gave the large and obvious door lever a yank at 30,000 feet. Tom Gaffney, the leader of the Passenger Doors design–build team is only too delighted to describe the way aircraft doors are designed to recognize that impulse, and to protect passengers from the consequences:

> What happens to the passenger who is disoriented and thinks he's going to the john and tries to open the door? If the airplane is at normal cruise and is flying along, the air pressure that's pushing against the stops is so hard that when you try to open the door you can't. The air pressure is holding it closed, and you can get the handle just a little way round and that's it. If it were during a period of flight where that full air pressure isn't there, we have a lock device that's down inside, and, when the airplane is going so fast that it's taken off and the doors must not be opened, the lock device comes down and you can open the door just a little way and that will let the aircraft pressure bleed if that were appropriate. But you can't open the door. And then when you land the lock device retracts and the door can be opened more and more.

Gaffney is a man out of the Alan Mulally mould, but with a harsher edge. Tall and perpetually smiling even when angry, he was ceaselessly active, thinking on his feet, cajoling, persuading and, unlike Mulally, occasionally threatening. Sometimes, it's difficult to tell whether he really is as dictatorial as he sounds, particularly in the warm friendly environment the 777 managers have tried to create. 'I allow a guy to pick and choose whether to join the group,' he says, in an apparently benign comment on how he builds up a team. 'Then I say, "This is the way we work, these are the rules. You can choose not to like them, in which case I can choose to find you another group to join." '

He revealed a little of his personal management style when he spoke of one early achievement of the team in improving on the traditional approach to door design. It arose out of the fact that, because fuselages curve, each door had been designed to be a slightly different shape, with slightly different fittings, including the hinges:

Early in the design process we realized that we were going to have three separate hinges, and they're rather complex parts. We also realized that if the hinge came into the door at a different place on each door all the mating parts would be different. Not only would manufacturing have to build all these parts, but in design I and my crew would have to design them all. What we recognized early on was that the key to make all the parts common was to make the hinge common, notwithstanding the fact that the shape of the body was different. And I put one of my best guys on it – put him in charge of hinges – and asked him to go and research and come back and show me how they could be common. He came back after two months and said they couldn't be common. I did a little management ploy. I said, 'Fine – who do you recommend to follow up on this and we'll let him give it a try?' And with that he said, 'Well, maybe there's something else I can look into.' And, lo and behold, it took him another month, but he had that dedication and he pulled it off. Unfortunately, after he was done we changed the contours of the airplane for better aerodynamic performance and he had to go back and do it again. But he knew he had done it once. The second time around it took him about four weeks, not three months. Then, of course, what do we do? We change the contour *again*, but by now he knew the techniques to use and he got the hinge to catch up in a week. And that was the key. Right now, not only is the hinge common but all the mechanism is common. Indeed, 98 per cent of all the mechanism of the door is common. What that means is that once you've made one door you've made 98 per cent of all the parts you need for all eight doors. This includes the opposite side of the airplane as well. So it was a critical design discovery, and fortunately the guy had the smarts to pull it off.

Gaffney was a firm believer in the potential of the new design methods planned for the 777 – CATIA and the design–build teams. Early on in the process, he and his colleagues looked back at records of what had happened during the design of the doors on a previous plane, the 767. They were particularly interested to see if there had been late changes or errors that would be avoided by the DBT approach, and, if so, how much money such an approach would have saved:

> We found that there were 13,341 changes, and we catalogued them as to what the cause was. But, more important, we looked at the new initiatives we've got on this airplane programme and we picked what initiative would solve that problem, obviate that mistake, make that mistake not happen. We also assigned a dollar value to that mistake according to some criteria we developed. That way we could prioritize our efforts. For instance, checking the drawing very thoroughly, having the DBT participating, doing our design work and solid modelling, and then putting all the parts together all in the computer – finding the problems where parts interfere with each other, and then removing the interference before releasing the part to manufacturing. On doors alone, according to our assessment, $64 million was spent just in changing the design of the 767 doors.

It's an astonishing figure when you bear in mind the fact that the basic asking price for a plane is of the order of $100 million.

The doors – passenger and cargo – were designed by two DBTs, and there were over 200 such teams. If the new working methods enabled them each to save a similar amount of money on building the 777 compared with previous planes, that would make a significant reduction in Boeing's development costs, and give the company an edge on competitors who did not use the same methods.

Gaffney was asked to predict how well the 777 team would do in reducing that figure of over 13,000 changes, errors and reworks:

> Oh that's a tough one, to predict my success. There were thirteen thousand changes before – seven or eight thousand of them were

on the passenger door; the rest were on cargo doors. My obligation is to produce a door with half the change, error and rework. So from that I guess I could say I can have three thousand mistakes. I don't intend to have that many. We've found on the test door that we had 95 per cent reduction in the number of errors we were expected to have. So we far exceeded the 50 per cent reduction we were after. It's extremely encouraging. I'd like to think from that that we can go ahead and build the production doors and when we're done we can have all the engineers go off and start designing a new airplane while we leave one guy behind to answer the phone. We'll see how that works out.

The role of the manufacturer's representatives on the design–build team was a crucial one in Gaffney's eyes. The passenger doors were to be made by Mitsubishi Heavy Industries in Japan, and, as an ardent Japanophile, Gaffney enjoyed his regular trips to set up the contract and he also liked having the Mitsubishi representatives around in Seattle, so that he could practise his Japanese. Just as the old 'throw it over the wall' approach used to apply between one group of designers and another, it was also the standard philosophy between designers and manufacturers on the earlier planes. Even in the first phase of the design work, where the only manufacturing work was making prototype doors for the crucial door safety tests, the CATIA/DBT approach was paying dividends. And as the manufacturing of production doors got into its stride there was an unprecedented closeness of collaboration between the designers and the manufacturers.

Gaffney and his team went back and forth to Japan, to observe how the doors were being put together.

We want to observe exactly how the door is in Japan and how the cut-outs are, and then, when they come together, measure it again to make sure that it adds up right. And then, when you rig it, meticulously keep track of what you did and then check the airplane-to-door relationship as it goes down the line, including when it's under high pressure and is supposed to blend with the body, and as you re-rig and re-rig and get things tweaked a little bit differently – with production feedback, data, information, all the way back to Mitsubishi – so the door is pre-rigged, and when it arrives you just pin it: that's it. When the customer gets the door, all of the rig fittings should be at the middle of their adjustability, not plus or minus.

But inevitably there could still be conflicts between the desire of the engineers to get it right and the need for the manufacturers to stick to their schedules. 'One of our clichés', said Gaffney in Mulally aphorism mode, 'is "One time, on time". The ideal engineering task would be completed on time with no mistakes.'

But it didn't always happen. The capacity of the new methods of designing in avoiding changes, errors and reworks was so great that it seemed to hurt Gaffney to release a drawing to the manufacturer when he knew that it could be 99 per cent perfect instead of, say, 95 per cent.

When it comes to the point of 'This drawing is due for release and we know there are errors in it', what do you do? Do you release it and change it, or do you delay the release and make the pick-ups now? So when one time and on time came into head-to-head combat, generally speaking we delayed the release date and we fixed up the engineering. And this was not done with manufacturing endorsement – they really wished we'd make the release date on time; they have a tremendous amount of recovery effort they have to do – but in the end correct engineering is much better than manufacturing heading off and then having to make a change. If we delay engineering for a month we can save twelve pounds of airplane weight over thirty years.

Gaffney's hope was that the pull of teamwork and a pride in getting it right would overcome some of the scheduling problems that could arise if engineering drawings were delayed:

Often we say that we're doing something for thirty years as opposed to 'I've got something I've got to get out by Friday and I don't give a damn.' . . . Once you've got people doing that and working together then all you can do is sit back. It's like wind-up dolls, you know – they just go. And then you give it to manufacturing and they say, 'Delay is one thing but good engineering is really appreciated.' And then they put the thing together in a month when the production schedule says four months.

If the Passenger Doors DBT is a microcosm of the way the whole plane is being designed, watching one decision being made by that team presents what you might call a nanocosm of this vast enterprise. One issue that was causing a lot of trouble in March 1992 was the design of an area of the door between a small window and a cut-out for the door handle. The window had to be in a position where a man outside the plane, a ground mechanic, could get his head up to the glass and look through. That need fixed the height, and then the horizontal position was fixed by the only area in the door skin at that height that was free of any of the mechanism inside. But this left an area of skin which wasn't very wide, and there was a query about whether this part was strong enough to withstand the stresses it would be expected to experience during the lifetime of the plane. Every issue to do with the endurance of a part was assessed in terms of the number of cycles it could be expected to experience, plus a safety margin of 50 per cent. 'Cycles' in this situation usually refers to the number of flights – 40,000 or so, plus a safety margin to bring it up to 60,000.

There were two separate issues.

First, would the area of door skin withstand the expected fatigue load? In other words, after 60,000 cycles pressurizing and depressurizing the fuselage – which would be expected to distort the door a little each time – would the material crack? Secondly, if the material did crack, would the stress it was under cause the crack to spread?

The calculations involved in assessing the safety implications of this design were subtle, and depended on the material the skin would be made of, whether or not the skin had what was called a 'doubler' attached behind it as a kind of reinforcement, and the nature and number of the fasteners that clustered in that area of the door. The team went to consult a couple a materials specialists who were familiar with the properties of the different materials they were using. But they came back with two different answers. One said that they should design the area so that it never experienced a force above

12 kps (a unit of stress – 1 kps is 1,000 lb per square inch); the other said it only mattered if the stress went above 27 kps. It turned out that they were both right. The 27 kps advice came from someone who was looking particularly at the need to avoid the situation where a crack that occurred accidentally or as a manufacturing defect propagated through the metal and become dangerously large. The material would have to withstand a stress of 27 kps in order to avoid an existing crack propagating quickly across the metal. The recommendation for 12 kps was from someone who was concerned only with the issue of whether a crack would form in normal circumstances under tension. For him, cracks in the material wouldn't arise if the material could withstand a stress greater than 12 kps (but he hadn't considered the 'damage tolerance' of the material to cracks that occurred for other reasons).

The team considered settling on a figure that was higher than 12 and lower than 27, such that the stress would never be high enough to *cause* cracks but if cracks did occur they would spread somewhat but not dangerously, and in such a manner that they would readily be spotted at the next maintenance inspection. But Gaffney pointed out to his engineers that, in early Working Together meetings with United, Boeing had promised the airline that they would keep the number of regular inspections for this sort of purpose down to a minimum. After five months of studying the problem, carrying out computer simulations, and testing different materials and ways of joining them together, the team decided that a new piece of metal would have to be fixed across the inboard surface of the door to double the thickness in the area that was narrowest and would be most under tension. It would add to the weight problems the team were experiencing, but they'd just have to find somewhere else in the door to remove an equivalent amount.

Even this description skates over the complexities of the final solution, which took hundreds of man-hours to solve, even though it was just one small element in the design of one part of the plane. Two things were apparent from the whole process. One was the immense amount of care given to a problem that would only *be* a problem if a rare combination of circumstances happened, involving excessive – but natural – wear and tear and accidental damage. The second was a more general point. In an understated way –

understated because it was taken absolutely for granted by every member of the 777 team – *safety* was the driving force behind the need to analyse exhaustively the few square inches of aluminium that flanked the window in the door, just as it lay almost obsessively behind every other decision that the DBTs took during the design phase of the plane, including the door freeze test.

Once the test door in the cold chamber had acquired its quarter inch of ice, Gaffney entered the chamber for the opening ceremony. 'Welcome to the Bahamas,' he quipped, as he stepped briefly out of the chamber to escape the cold (he was wearing a normal jacket and shirt at the time), then inside again to witness the important moment that would put the door design to the test. The signal was given to turn the door handle, and there was a pause as half a dozen of the team looked on inside the chamber and another small crowd stood outside staring through a thick window. With a sharp cracking sound, pieces of ice fragmented all round the edges of the door and cascaded to the ground, and the massive door swung slowly open. There was a cheer and a small round of applause. Gaffney walked forward and started inspecting the door's innards to assess how well the mechanism had worked. 'That's great!' he said, excitedly. 'Boy that's nice. This is a big key test and it worked great. I feel really good about it.'

The Passenger Doors team also benefited – or suffered – from customer participation in the design process. Even Gaffney's confidence could be shaken at times, as occurred when he experienced a minor public humiliation. He had organized a demonstration of the test door for representatives of the airlines, once he and the team were satisfied that it worked smoothly and efficiently. It was a carefully choreographed event, designed to put the door through its paces and impress not only the existing customers but also representatives of two airlines – Delta and Qantas – who had not yet decided to buy the plane. As the demonstration unfolded, Gaffney turned his back on the door and addressed the group of airlines reps. One of them said, 'Could you give us a hold-open device for the door?' Gaffney describes what happened next:

Proud papa that I was, I explained how this door did not require a hold-open device: that when the door is closed you can do certain work, and you can lock the door completely open and do other work, and that's really all the customer needs. Now what I'd just done was to redefine my customer's request and make it fit conveniently with my design. With that they said, 'Would you turn around?' And I turned around, and there was my own crew snapping a hold-open device in the door at an intermediate point of travel to go do work on the door. And all I could do was turn back to them and say, 'You've got it.'

The test programme for the 777 was reassuring and worrying at the same time: reassuring because of the wide and surprising variety of aspects of the plane that were already being tested in summer 1992, before the design work was even half finalized; worrying because the complexity of the plane revealed by the mere list of tests being carried out suggested that it was a never-ending task. Why should not every one of those '4 million parts flying in close formation' require its own testing programme? That this idea had occurred to the testers themselves seemed to be shown by a small rig in the corner of one of Boeing's test buildings labelled Toilet Test Rig. Taped to the side was a chart showing a lavatory bowl with the requisite number of boxes to be ticked off every 1,000 cycles, as the machine simulated a 200-lb person sitting down on the seat. In fact, rather than being an engineer's joke as it might have seemed, this was an attempt to get at an irritating problem in some of the lavatory seats that might have been due to some quirk of usage. As it turned out, there had been a production fault in some of the seats, but the rest, the vast majority, had no trouble sustaining the frequent inflight stresses of an international variety of bottoms of many shapes and sizes.

Next to this small but important test rig was a much more impressive set-up. The horizontal stabilizer was undergoing fatigue testing. This is the horizontal part of the empennage, sticking out either side of the plane at right angles to the fin. In the 777 this is made of carbon fibre bonded with epoxy resin. The 777 was to use more carbon composite than any earlier Boeing aircraft, and in more places – including primary structural components such as the tailplane and floor beams. The advantages of carbon composite lie in a combination of strength and lightness, although it can cost more than making the equivalent component in aluminium.

The stabilizer, designed like a pair of linked wings (although it was the size of the 737's whole wing), was held at a height of about twenty feet in a framework twice as high. It looked like a cross between a dying pterodactyl and a fairground ride of unknown purpose. Pistons, sometimes rhythmic, sometimes random, moved the ends and edges of the stabilizer with considerable force, producing gasps like a dying beast's death-rattle. It was the randomness that produced this almost biological movement, as it simulated the short pushes of gusts of wind and the longer more slowly changing forces produced by steadier air currents that the stabilizer would be subjected to for many hours on a normal flight. The stabilizer was covered with stress gauges that fed back data to computers hour after hour, showing which parts of the components were subject to what stresses, so that the engineers could check to see that the assumptions they had made when designing the components were borne out by this kind of endurance testing.

This was one type of test on one component of the plane – an attempt to make sure that, within the lifetime of even the longest survivor of the 777 fleet, the stresses and strains of regular take-offs and landings would not lead to cracks and structural damage due to

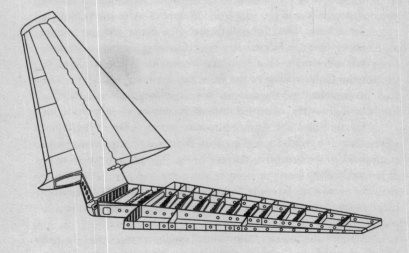

The 777 horizontal stabilizer

fatigue. In the same building there were parts of the wing surface, the landing-gear, the folding wing tip which might never fold and, largest of all, the pieces being tested at that time, a section of the fuselage. This cylindrical cross-section of the plane, about forty feet long, was constructed to be as airtight as the plane itself would be. It was a chamber whose air pressure could be increased regularly to create the pressure differences that the plane would experience as it went through the cycle of take-off, cruise and landing. By June 1992 it had been through two lifetimes without any damage. At the same time as experiencing the pressure cycles, the section had been subjected to strong and varying loads on the floor of the cabin to simulate the extra gravitational forces on the fuselage from the passengers and luggage each time the plane took off.

The ceaseless search for new materials is an important part of the attempt to build a brand-new plane that is more successful than its competitors. Alan Mulally explained the many different ways in which new materials can help:

In any business, and especially in ours, we constantly search for new ideas. We don't want to let any improvement in flying pass us by, and what that means to us is that in aerodynamics and in structures and in propulsion and in systems we're always looking for a better idea. In airplane design a better idea can be an improvement in functionality, or performance, or drag, or weight-efficient design, or a reduction in weight. When it comes to weight, the materials that we select are really important. The requirements on the material vary depending on where they are used. In some cases the material properties are important for fatigue where the airplane structure moves – like in the cabin, where we pressurize it to go up in flight and we depressurize it to land, so the structure's always moving. Whereas in the bottom of the airplane corrosion is important where water can get there, or condensation. So we're always looking for materials that satisfy many requirements – but in the most weight-efficient manner.

On one Boeing jet, maintenance engineers inspected the belly of a plane and found some unexpected corrosion in an area just below the galley. When they investigated, they discovered that the corrosion had come from a collection of discarded salt packets from passengers' meal trays. Sometime after they'd fallen into the bay, the paper had disintegrated and released the corrosive salt to attack the aluminium.

About fifteen years ago, Alcoa, the US aluminium company, came up with an alloy of aluminium and another metallic element, lithium, that looked as if it might have useful properties for plane-making. Boeing's materials-development people began testing it during the mid-1980s and so, when the 777 was in its early design phase, the team started to look seriously at it. It was to provide an example of technological decision-making at its most subtle, and to lead to a hiccup in the smooth process of designing the 777. As director of engineering, Mulally was closely involved:

> The materials division have been constantly working with this aluminium alloy to improve its characteristics – for example, its fracture toughness, so that when it's subjected to constant bending or sharp penetrations like foreign-object damage it's not seriously affected. They've asked various questions. Can you make it in sheet? Can you make it in plate? Can you make forgings? Can you make castings? Is it amenable to reliable processes, so that you get the same quality product time after time in its application? And all those things have to be researched in addition to its corrosion characteristics, its fracture toughness, its fatigue life.
>
> So with our research into aluminium-lithium we reached the point where the test results looked very good and it looked as if for mini-applications on the airplane it would be very appropriate. Now we were at a point in the programme where we wanted to take weight out, so we had a real nice match between some of the products and the aluminium-lithium. One was the in-spar ribs; another one was the stanchions that hold the floor beams.
>
> We had a couple of concerns still. One was that aluminium-lithium is still relatively expensive compared to the other alloys we could use. Now this was understandable, because it's a new alloy, the aluminium manufacturers had spent a lot of time investing in it, and the alloy itself it had more intrinsic value – it weighs less. It also had a long development cycle, so the manufacturers wanted to charge us a premium for it, which is understandable. We also had

to think about it in the context of the weight reduction and the value to the airline, because our airline customers would like weight-efficient design but they'd also like as low a price for the airplane as possible. So we thought this out and agonized over what the value of that would be, and we felt like this alloy was very close to providing value to the airline for the weight that it saved.

All the advantages. combined with a decision to accept the premium price, led the 777 engineers to design aluminium-lithium into the plane in certain areas. The design–build teams responsible for those areas fed data about the properties of the alloy, such as strength and weight, into their computers, and the alloy helped them to achieve the weight targets for those components of the plane.

As the designs for these pieces were finalized, the Boeing materials people continued their researches into the properties of the alloy, looking particularly at how it behaved when it was being carved and shaped and drilled into the pieces that would be part of the plane. To their dismay, they discovered that, when machined in the normal way, the material showed cracks – particularly where edges had been cut or holes drilled. Initially the research engineers felt they could find a way of removing the problem by adapting the tools that were used. But by March 1992 they realized that that would not be possible: if they were going to use the material, they would have to live with the cracks. It was this research that brought matters to a head in June 1992.

Every Tuesday, in one of the stark, faceless conference rooms at Renton, the five 777 VPs would meet for what was called the Muffin Meeting. Phil Condit would turn up carrying a 'Little Red Riding Hood' wicker basket covered with a homely gingham tea-towel. Deep in its recesses was a pile of home-made muffins, made by Mrs Condit and representing the note of informality that operated in this regular forum. It was one of many understated management tools that to Condit and his colleagues had an almost religious significance. The belief was that at every level the mode of communication was an important factor in determining *what* was communicated. Very few people outside the circle of five were ever invited to the Muffin Meetings, and the main rule of business was that there were no rules. There was no written agenda, and although Condit was the informal chairman – an honour earned, perhaps, through the supply of the muffins – there was no such thing as addressing remarks through the chair, putting matters to the vote, working to an agenda, or drawing up minutes. The nearest there was to a procedure was when Condit asked each of the VPs in turn to say if there was anything on his mind.

On Tuesday 16 June the group assembled punctually and sat round a conference-room table spread with coffee-cups and plates. Dale Hougardy, in charge of 777 operations, quietly deposited on the table several small pieces of metal with holes drilled in them – samples of aluminium-lithium. After some opening banter about the quality of the muffins, the group plunged into an assessment of how one particular training tool was working, called World Class Competitiveness Training. This led them to discuss how designers could be persuaded to be less proprietorial about their own parts of the plane and see that sometimes there were issues that cut across the priorities of any one DBT and affected the progress of the plane as a whole. Insulation blankets were raised as one of these issues. The group then discussed a purchasing decision that had to be made, where Boeing could either buy from one supplier, who would then be financially secure, and let two others go to the wall, or could buy a third of the components from each of the three suppliers. 'It's really important', said Mulally at one point, 'that we structure a business deal that works for the suppliers where they make money as well as support our schedule.' There were then some personnel issues, to do with moving senior managers around, followed by a safety issue that was worrying the team. The Federal Aviation Administration had changed the regulations applying to seats that were in the front row of a block, with a wall or bulkhead in front of them. They wanted some way of preventing passengers damaging their heads in the event of a sudden stop. This turned out to be a very difficult problem to solve technically, and the five vice-presidents discussed whether the research costs should be paid for out of the 777 budget or whether the team leader should go to the Boeing Commercial Airplane Group and seek funding there, since the problem was one that would affect all future Boeing planes.

There was also a moment or two of defensive banter about the appointment of a new FAA inspector for the region, someone whom the 777 team would depend on over the coming months to approve the myriad certification hurdles that the plane and its components would have to pass. 'Are you guys all wound up to cope?' said Condit to the group.

'We're going to try and make a new friend,' Mulally replied. 'I became very good friends with the last one,' he went on, 'and that was great until he moved on to McDonnell Douglas. We have three hours with him, and we're going to show all the issues and propose to him a partnership where we would work these off together and his quality of his life would be better.'

'I like that idea,' Condit said – 'that's great.'

'I'm going to wear deodorant,' Mulally continued, 'and put on a clean shirt.'

'Take a shower,' interjected Condit.

'Yeah,' said Mulally. 'He needs us and we need him, and somwhere in there there's got to be a partnership. Next Monday.'

Neil Standal then came in with a report on the forthcoming move that the 777 team would make thirty miles north, to new offices at Everett, on the same site where the plane would be assembled. The city of Seattle was keen that as many people as possible would sign up for car pools, to avoid huge traffic jams every morning as thousands more people headed north, and Standal reported that already over 1,500 people had signed up.

After a discussion of how well a couple of the other Boeing plants, in Philadelphia and Kansas, were doing in supplying components, the attention of the group was finally turned to the small pieces of metal that Hougardy had put on the table at the beginning of the meeting. Hougardy himself brought the issue up by referring to a meeting that had been called later that day of all the engineers whose components included aluminium-lithium. He explained to the group that, as they could see by looking at the samples, when holes were drilled in the aluminium-lithium there were little fractures of the material around the holes. 'It's really almost like a plywood,' he said, as Alan Mulally picked up one piece and Phil Condit another. Mulally referred to aluminium-lithium as having been described as a 'boutique' material, designed for a specialized task on the plane. Hougardy indicated that he felt the cracks would not interfere with the ability of the material to do its job, and described some of the techniques they could use that would minimize – but not eliminate – the cracks when the material was shaped into components. Then Mulally spoke, addressing his remarks initially to Condit:

> This is really a toughie, and before you get to this meeting this afternoon we both feel compelled to tell you what we think about the subject. I wasn't going to avail myself of this opportunity, but, since Dale chose to say what he thinks, it's very important that you hear what I think also.

Mulally had thought long and hard about the issue. He agreed with a number of the engineers who wanted to keep the material in the airplane that the cracks were not a problem – at least not in any physical sense. The metal would not have to bear loads which might tear the pieces apart, and he accepted that it would be possible to manufacture the pieces in a way that enabled them to do their job. But, as the senior engineer on the project, he had another worry – one that was psychological rather than physical. He did not want a plane where, in the future on some far-off airfield, a maintenance engineer could be inspecting the interior of a wing or of the fuselage and come across cracks in the metal, however benign they turned out to be. He explained his view of the matter to the group, and to Condit in particular, as team leader:

> All things being equal I would like not to pursue aluminium-lithium. We're going to be shown a lot of data at this meeting and we've been wading through it trying to make a judgement call about it. But there's some other things that bothered me about this, Phil. One is that we when we originally tried to develop this new material system we did it for all the right reasons. We did it because we thought it would save weight. We thought its fracture toughness would go up. We thought it would be more durable in service. We thought it would have wide application. We thought the customers would get a lighter and more efficient airplane, and at the time, with fuel dominating the cost structure, those all seemed like a good judgement.

The world's changed. It's expensive. The prices aren't going to change. This is a boutique material system. The competition between the aluminium companies didn't develop. The prices are still a lot. They still have low recovery rates with their big ingots. The application on the airplane is going down. The downside risk is that in some of the areas where we have it, like in the ribs and the wing, if we ever had a problem the exposure to the airline and ourselves to fix up is huge. In some of the areas where we have it, in the stanchions and supporting the floors, it's going to be subject to a lot of tools and changes and be damage-prone. So this is the way the future looks to me. We'll have to try to explain to the world that it's OK. And it *is* OK. I mean technically it's great. It's a great story – we can write papers on it, go to conferences. But it will look damaged. It will look like it has cracks. And we'll say it's OK. And it *is*. We have a little risk on the test programme, but all of the technical guys believe it's going to be OK.

Dale Hougardy interjected his confidence that the material could be worked and would do the job it was designed for, if they decided to leave it in. Mulally said that he wouldn't be happy to lose the material – Airbus had 30,000 lb of the material and had saved up to 2,200 lb of weight by using it on one of their planes, while on the 777 it was helping save just over 400 lb – but he nevertheless thought they had to, unless there were some really new data at the meeting that afternoon.

It was a subdued group of engineers who met later that day, with Mulally, Hougardy and Condit sitting in. As they gathered outside the conference room, they were already resigned to a negative outcome. One of them remarked that the suppliers would want a cancellation fee of $2 million if the alloy was taken out of the plane.

After various presentations of data by different engineers, the discussion was opened. Among the issues discussed was the impact on the manufacturing schedule if pieces had to be redesigned for aluminium. The in-spar ribs, some of the components affected, were being made by a Japanese company, Nippi, and there were concerns about whether they could respond quickly enough to the proposed changes. At one point the team discussed the fact that both

McDonnell Douglas and Airbus had aluminium-lithium in their new planes – Airbus in particularly large amounts. Mulally produced a piece of paper with details of all the components of the A330/340 that were made of the alloy, along with the weights used.

One contribution that eloquently expressed the dilemma they were all in was made by Rudy Schad, the senior structures engineer in the team, whose weight target would be most affected by the change. When the engineers had been considering ways of keeping the weight of the plane down, they had used a cost ratio of dollars per pound saved. This referred to the extra money that would have to be spent to save a pound of weight. With a very expensive new material that nevertheless saved a lot of weight, they divided the extra cost by the number of pounds weight saved to arrive at this ratio.

It might cost a hundred dollars or more per pound saved but that was the sort of cost the team were prepared to bear, in return for thirty or more years of benefit in the life of a plane that was lighter by that amount. The use of aluminium-lithium was calculated to save between 280 and 400 lb per plane in weight, depending on whether they decided to commit to all the possible uses. Schad was a broad, grey-haired man, with a serious demeanour and a slight European accent, and he spoke in quiet measured tones:

> You know, we worried about this back when we declared the weight emergency and we decided to go with it knowing it would be some risk. The fact is now that from a technical point of view I would not put this back on the airplane if I had a choice. Because we know more now than we did when we made the decision. On the other hand I do remember that 280 lb is still an extremely valuable weight saving for this airplane. But I can assure you we have approved a lot of things that were $600 a pound. If we take this 280 lb out then I don't know where I'm going to get it. We've worked extremely hard to save weight, and we're going to continue to work hard to save weight, and so it's a balance.
>
> While I'm reluctant to take it out this time, no matter what we do these releases are a critical issue. Nippi has told us in no uncertain terms that they cannot stand another day's slide on the releases of the ribs, so if we change this we're going to do it in an

orderly fashion and the chances are you're still going to have *some* aluminium-lithium stiffeners on the airplane as it is now. So you may have it and have to explain to some customers at the beginning anyways. Obviously if we declare it an emergency as such there'll be no aluminium-lithium on the airplane and somehow we'll find a recovery plan that may involve being late on documents for ribs and other components.

Schad's speech was more of a pouring out of his heart than a measured argument for or against a particular decision. But it crystallized the issues, along with the feelings that were involved, and seems to have given rise to a decision – to remove the alloy from the plane – that no one person really made but that Mulally clearly wanted to happen. On the following day, Mulally analysed what he thought had contributed to the decision:

On a decision to put aluminium-lithium in or a decision to take it out, you really want to use every bit of knowledge that you can, because there's not one right way. We all wish it would be that simple, but creating inventions and creating designs is a matter of balancing a whole bunch of objectives. Balancing objectives at one point in time when you are far away from the weight goal is a different judgement than when you get close. The minute we decided that to incorporate aluminium-lithium would mean the possibility of extra work to the airline and to ourselves it bothered us. So in the back of all of our minds on every decision we continuously review what has changed, and as things change we ask whether we should change the decision we made.

Now there are lots of things that change in a programme, some of which you can accommodate and some not. One of the things we had to talk about was, Could we release new parts with a more conventional alloy, and still be able to get it on the first airplane? Or would we deliver some airplanes with some aluminium-lithium and then only be able to get the new parts made to catch subsequent airplanes? These issues are so multifaceted that what I personally try to do is to orchestrate a meeting where the agenda brings out all the issues. The data really does set you free; the different opinions tell you what your alternatives are. So the way we try to get the best decision is to get all the pieces out on the table, see what's new, see what that means to us. Can we do something about it or not? And then usually that, through a discussion, leads you to the right direction.

And I think in the aluminium-lithium meeting we all had both opinions in our minds at the same time: It would sure be nice to just go ahead and get that weight in the bag and done, or It would sure be nice not to give the airlines and ourselves an extra problem. So we want it both ways in that case. And when I walked into the meeting I still wanted both. So you've got to be very careful not to make up your mind, and let all of the different sides of the issue get out in the open. And then you collectively use your strength to make the decision. It's not as if we're concerned about making the decision. What we want to do is to make the *right* decision. And, even after we've made a decision, if there's something new then we want to revisit it again.

The ins and outs of the aluminium-lithium decision would take a whole book to do them justice. What was most interesting about it was the fact that in the end, in spite of Alan Mulally's dictum, it wasn't really the data that set the engineers free – at least, not data in the narrow sense of figures and graphs derived from the physics of metals. *Those* data said, 'Leave the alloy on the plane – the cracks will cause no physical problems at all.' What set them free, or at least resolved the issue, was other data – the knowledge that, whatever the physics said, there would always be a human problem. The price of leaving the alloy would be a number of occasions in the thirty-year life of the plane when someone somewhere would insist that there was a problem with the alloy and have the power to do something about it.

SIX

ASAT and ASTA

On a rainy Friday afternoon in the middle of June 1992 the traffic on Interstate 5 had been bumper to bumper for twenty or thirty miles north of Seattle. People had started leaving the city about three in the afternoon, for a weekend that was forecast to be a frustrating mix of muggy warmth and total wetness. But in Building 40-04 at Everett the weekend was some way away as the afternoon shift was beginning to work on a machine tool that would play a key part in the 777. It was the tool that would drill the very first hole in the very first 777 airplane.

Most of us are not really familiar with the concept of a 'machine tool', even though we may know the phrase. In fact a machine tool is much more of a machine than a tool. It is a purpose-built piece of engineering that is designed to carry out some important machining task on a complex component. Typically a component will consist of several pieces of shaped metal which have to be connected in a certain way – usually by means of carefully placed holes and fasteners requiring a high degree of precision in the course of the drilling and fastening. While the pieces could be put together by hand, with the assistance of hand-tools like drills and riveting guns and so on, for the sake of speed, accuracy and strength – not to mention the avoidance of boredom and sometimes of vibration damage to the nerves of human operators – machine tools are designed and built to perform precisely the tasks needed for the particular component.

The typical machine tool in a car factory, for example, is a weighty piece of equipment, higher than a man, and designed to machine heavy components like axles, bearings, pistons and so on. The machine tool in Building 40-04 on that rainy Friday afternoon might have been described by Saddam Hussein as 'the mother of all machine tools'. It had been brought to Everett in parts to be assembled on the floor of the building over the previous six months. The parts had occupied ninety trucks on a thousand-mile drive from Wisconsin. Now most of those parts were joined together to form what was called ASAT2. 'ASAT' stands for 'Automated Spar Assembly Tool', and the tool was designed to join three long strips of metal making up the front spar of the 777 wing.

Nothing gave a more dramatic impression of the size of the 777 than this giant tool. It consisted of a row of C-shaped metal frames thirty feet high and stretching off into the distant reaches of the hangar-like building. The whole complex formed a kind of jig or template on which the components of the main wing spars would first be built up and then be fixed together by a drilling and fastening tool, the size of a compact car, that travelled along between the jaws of the Cs. This 'carriage' would hold a computer with instructions for where to drill holes, whether to insert fasteners or bolts, and which sizes to use. When completed the whole tool would resemble a giant zip fastener which would take a day and a half to drill about 6,000 holes in the various elements of the wing spar and zip these elements together. In fact the whole set-up was like *four* zip

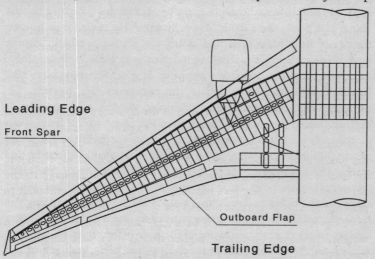

Wing structure showing location of front spar

fasteners, arranged in two pairs, each designed to take one of the four spars that make up the main support for the plane wings – left front and rear and right front and rear.

One of the members of the engineering team that afternoon was looking ruefully across at one of the four 'zipper' carriages that was standing on a pallet on the floor. It looked just like the other three until closer inspection showed some bent and damaged elements on the top of the frame. 'It came loose on the truck,' said the engineer, 'and it got all buggered.' Apparently, on some mountain pass between Wisconsin and Seattle the fastenings that kept the sub-assembly on the truck had come loose and the driver had had a fine old time trying to prevent the thing falling off. The engineer didn't know whether to be sorrier for the driver who nearly lost his load or the piece of equipment that was now sorely in need of first aid. 'Those drivers,' he said, 'they often don't know what it is they're carrying. They just drive between Wisconsin and here, drop their load, and drive back again. Sometimes I say to them, "Do you want to see what that thing is for?" and I show them into here.' He gestured across at the giant zipper. 'One guy could hardly believe it. I showed him all over it, and I gave him a couple of pictures to take away. He said it would make a great project for his daughter to talk about in school – he's from Massachusetts.' He pulled a picture of the device from his overall, and clearly got almost as much pleasure from contemplating it as some men derive from a *Playboy* centrefold.

Close to, ASAT2 was awe-inspiring. It was something over 300 feet in length, to accommodate the two spars side by side. To someone who had seen only drawings, posters and models, it brought home the immense wing span the plane would have. Two pieces each over 100 feet long either side of the width of the plane meant 200 feet from wing tip to wing tip. Like many aspects of this plane, ASAT was a first. It replaced men who used to do the same job in conditions of extreme discomfort and boredom. They would carry out the noisy, and noisome, task of drilling holes in exactly the right place and then hammering into each one a fastener that was slightly larger than the diameter of the hole before fitting a gripping washer on the end of it. The noise level was high, and one of the men had to use his physical strength to support the plate against which the other man used a tool to press the fasteners in.

In mid-June the ASAT tool was still in pieces. The carriages were in various states of disarray on the floor, although one was almost ready to be lifted on to the rail along which it would eventually run. In two weeks' time, the whole tool was meant to be ready for the first tests of its ability to do the job. The design and construction of ASAT had replicated the system that operated with the whole plane. ASAT had its own design–build team, with representatives of the plane engineers, the machine-tool manufacturers (an outside firm) and the people who would machine the parts that would be put together in ASAT.

As the leader of the team explained, there were all sorts of ways in which a decision made by someone who seemed to have little connection with the machine tool could actually affect their task:

> We have these tooling holes that are drilled in a fairly precise position to help line the pieces up for ASAT to work on them. Now the metal surface has to be shot-peened for strength. [Shot-peening is a process that batters the surface of the metal with tiny metal balls and changes the surface structure, making it stronger.] They were going to drill the tooling holes and then do the shot-peening, but the process could have shifted the holes just a little bit, away from the exact position they need to be in. When we heard what they were going to do, we said they should do the shot-peening first and then drill the holes. It didn't matter to them, but it sure did to us.

The man in charge of getting ASAT ready in time was Sam Behar, a calm enthusiast who drew a confident outline of the wing on a whiteboard as he explained how the various parts fitted together. Like all the other engineers responsible for actually making and assembling components, he was at the whim of changing designs in CATIA. Because he wanted to meet or even improve on his target date for ASAT to go into action, he would monitor the design of the wing spar every day, eavesdropping on the drawings in the computer and looking for changes since the previous day that might mean some adjustment to the jig layout or the computer program of ASAT. No one could hold his drawings close to his chest in this operation – all drawings were accessible to every member of the team who might need to see them. By judicious use of his computer terminal Behar kept abreast of changes in design before they were officially communicated to him, and so the precise settings of ASAT evolved in parallel with the wing spars rather than lagging behind. In fact Behar and his machine tool were so well prepared that Alan Mulally was heard to say to him at a meeting early in the schedule that 'If ASAT had been a plane it would be ready to fly now.'

With so much going on in and around Seattle it was easy to forget how much of the 777 was being made abroad – much of it on the other side of the world. There were the Australians, for example, who made two key parts of the empennage.

But the Australian situation was a puzzle. There were two companies – Hawker De Havilland (HDH) and Aerospace Technologies of Australia (ASTA) – making pieces which, to the naked eye, look rather similar and indeed to the probing ultrasound of X-ray *are* rather similar. They each use exactly the same materials – new light composites that replace the need for metal sheeting – and both companies have installed giant autoclaves to heat the materials under pressure so that the materials are transformed into hard strong surfaces and support structures. But it's a reflection of the way Boeing sets up, and then sticks to, long-term relationships with companies that when the 777 came along it was deemed perfectly appropriate for similar pieces to come from different companies in the same country.

HDH are making the elevators. These are the movable pieces of the horizontal stabilizer that sticks out on each side of the tail. Peter Smith is the commercial manager of HDH and has collaborated with Boeing for twenty years. After having a successful relationship with the company over parts of the 757, Smith was hopeful that HDH would get at least two parts of the 777 – perhaps an aileron or a flap as well as the elevator. He describes how he got the news that they were to be given only the elevator:

> The phone rang and I was told that we would get the contract for the elevator, and that was all. I was obviously disappointed, but then my contact said, 'Look at a picture of the 737. The elevator we want you to make for the 777 is about the same size as the *entire wing span* of the 737.'

During the years of design and manufacture, before parts of the plane are manufactured, it is often difficult for people to appreciate the scale of the plane, and the workforce have to be continually reminded by means of analogies and comparisons how huge the 777 is going to be. Another telling comparison gives an indication of engine size. The 777 engine and its outer covering are roughly the same diameter as the 737 *fuselage*.

The HDH contract is worth about $A200 million, which will provide about 500 elevators between 1994 and 2020. The actual composition and shape of the elevator hardly seem to justify the $A400,000 price tag, but, just as the Boeing Company have had to build an entire assembly building to make the plane, many of the contractors, like HDH, have had to invest a lot of money in new equipment and facilities, including a giant new autoclave, just to cope with the increased size of the pieces they are making. In terms of the technology involved, the elevator is not very different from the 757 elevator HDH make already – it's just so much bigger, forty feet tall, that it can't be done on existing premises. In June 1992, while the design–build team were working their way through drawing releases for the elevator, the last columns and beams of the elevator assembly building were being put in place on the outskirts of Sydney. At the same time, a container ship was easing its way along the north coast of Australia carrying the new autoclave from Germany that was so big that the task of getting it on to site was presenting major logistical problems.

It was a giant cylinder fifty feet long that would be needed to bake the surfaces of the elevator under pressure after they had been

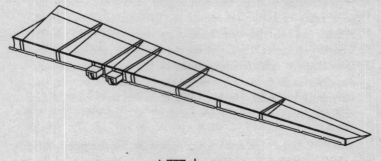

A 777 elevator

built up of layers of composite materials. The 777 elevator was making use of two main materials – carbon fibre woven into textile layers, and a honeycomb material called Nomex. In another display of the irrelevance of distance, the carbon fibre was shipped to Australia from the United States – in refrigerated containers to preserve its flexibility. Once out of the cold, the material would become brittle in about five hours. Before that stage it had to be cut into specific shapes determined by the designers and be laid, one layer upon another.

An identical process with identical materials was being developed four hundred miles away from HDH in Melbourne, in this case to form the rudder of the 777. ASTA is located by the Yarra River in Melbourne, and has established a good record with Boeing over the years by making rudders for earlier planes, notably the 757. They were delighted, but not surprised, to get the contract to build the 777 rudder. Although similar in structure to the 757 rudder, it was much, much bigger and would tax ASTA's engineering expertise to the limits. In particular, they too would have to build a very large autoclave – even larger than HDH's, because the 777's rudder is larger than its elevator.

Like many people in this business Al Tyler, general manager of ASTA, has been a plane enthusiast since a boy, and is tickled pink to be among one of the twenty or so contractors with whom Boeing have struck up a long-term relationship.

'You're a big boy now,' they keep telling me. If you're a big boy you've got to stand up and handle it like the rest of the big boys. It's interesting to think that they regard us in some ways in the same category as the Lockheeds and Northrops of this world. When I was a kid they were some of the companies that I used to write to in America. They were the big companies, and here we are – little ASTA in Melbourne, Australia. It's fascinating from my point of view to be in the industry. I always wanted to be in it, and sometimes I wonder whether I should stay in it, because of the pressures that come up. But it's good.

Tyler is a large man and moves bulkily across the plant, lovingly fingering the surface of a piece of airplane as he passes. Like the rest of the Australians on the team, he speaks an easy colloquial Australian English, with the odd 'bloody' and 'bugger' thrown in. Compared with the stiffly formal approach of most Boeing managers, Tyler is refreshingly honest and humorous, in a way which must have puzzled his Boeing contacts.

On this particular day, in early October 1992, he is worried about some threatened last-minute changes to the design by Boeing. As Tyler walks round the plant he stops and inspects a sticky black sheet of fabric lying on a bench, and what looks like some cardboard packing material tipped out of an empty packing-case. These are the famous 'composites' (pronounced 'com*po*sites' in the trade). The black sticky stuff is tightly woven fibres of carbon in the form of graphite, delivered in sheets and kept refrigerated until it is time to use them. For such a high-tech product it seems surprisingly cheap – $4.50 or so per square foot. But you have to multiply that many times to get the materials cost per square foot of the component, even before it is treated to harden it. There may be as many as twenty-five layers of the stuff, carefully placed by hand one on top of the other, in a configuration that has been designed in Seattle to get the best balance between strength and weight. The bottom layers may be made up of one large simple shape, but on top of these will be more intricate polygons with cut-out areas which will lead to the build-up of a large flat slab with up and down contours of an eighth of an inch or so – the thickness of a single layer. A square foot of the finished product can therefore contain 25 × $4.50 worth of carbon cloth: over $100 for the material alone. Multiply that to get two large surface panels about forty feet by six feet and you have $48,000 worth of carbon composite in one elevator or rudder. But there's more. The dips where there are fewer layers of carbon are designed to take an inch and a half layer of the honeycomb material called Nomex. This is made of a thin material that looks suspiciously like cardboard. In fact it *is* cardboard, with a plasticized coating. Weight for weight, a honeycomb of thick paper can support larger loads at right angles to hollow spaces than other apparently more robust materials.

The rudder of the 777 is a huge piece of carbon composite thirty feet tall. Its essential ingredients when assembled are a main piece reaching to the full height, a tab to help give extra turning power, and aluminium fittings that connect the rudder to the actuator, the device that moves it. The rudder is particularly large and strong on the 777 because the plane is a twin-engine aircraft.

The link may not be obvious, but in fact the rudder plays a vital part if one engine fails on take-off. Because the two engines supply all the thrust, the loss of one means that the other has to make up the difference. It is designed to do so, but such a huge force pulling suddenly on only one side of the plane will impart a large torque or twist to the plane, pushing it in the direction of the failed engine. In such an eventuality the 777 rudder will need to push the plane back into line so that take-off can continue normally.

The 777 has some extra refinements in the control system that make the plane more responsive in the event of an engine failure. Jim McWha, in charge of the plane's flight-control systems, explained:

> On this airplane one of the features that we have built in is what we call a thrust augmentation, which will sense the thrust from both engines and if there is a difference it will move the rudder in a direction to offset that yawing movement that's created by the differential thrust. During take-off an engine failure requires fairly rapid response to stop the airplane from yawing off the runway. We did in fact test this feature on a modified 757 a couple of years ago and got tremendous response from the various pilots – both from our own pilots and from certification agencies and from many of the airlines. And the neat thing about this feature is that the pilot doesn't have to react as fast. It's still important that the pilot is aware that an engine has failed, and we don't want to neutralize the performance totally, but it gives a little more time to react, because it does take time to assess exactly what may have gone wrong.

The leader of the Rudder DBT, Jim Simmons, was chairing a team meeting just about the time when ASTA were about to put their first rudder into the autoclave. The meeting culminated in some bad news that Simmons was going to have to take down to what he called the 'teeming masses' in Australia. The changes centred on the complex structure at the base of the rudder, where powerful electronically controlled devices would have to provide the force to move the rudder rapidly in the event of an engine failure. It's the worst possible place to have a source of force if you want to move a large, flat, heavy component like a rudder. Imagine trying to open a heavy door with a force that can only be exerted at the hinge.

One of the potential problems that can arise with rudders is caused by the airflow that swirls round the complicated three-dimensional shape of the empennage. With certain combinations of stiffness and eddies in the air, the rudder can develop a flutter. This flutter can be amplified to a stage where the rudder doesn't do its job and might even break up. Because the rudder is quite a complicated

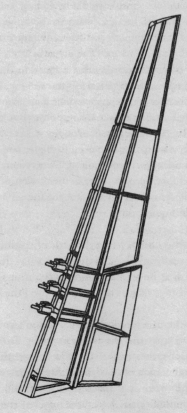

curved shape, flutter is difficult to predict, even in computer simulations, and so the design is usually put to the test in a wind tunnel.

To use an Al Tyler phrase, the rudder had been a bugger to design. Jim Simmons wearily summarized the story so far:

> We have a very unique rudder configuration in that a portion of it is double-hinged to provide the control power to handle the engine-out case [when one engine is shut down on take-off]. Because we're in a new area, about a year and a half ago we wanted a very careful review of the design to ensure we didn't have flutter in the surface. About last November we had determined that we *were* in a flutter condition, so we solved it by adding some weight, about seventy-five pounds, hung forward to the hinge line. The review also showed the minimum stiffness requirements both for the actuator and for the structure. The actuator is an extremely complicated piece of machinery. It takes a signal in the order of milliamps – a very, very small electrical input – and puts out about a fifty thousand-ounce force. It's an incredible gain factor. And the stiffer you try to make it, the slower the response. But you need a fast response time to handle our design condition – the engine out on take-off. Now, what has come to light in the last couple of weeks is that the actuator can't meet the stiffness requirement that we set out in November. So now we're in the process of stiffening up the structure of the rudder to account for the difference that the actuator couldn't quite reach.

Ron Ostrowski, who had become director of engineering for the whole plane, was not really involved in the day-to-day decisions about the rudder problem. But he was as concerned about it as anybody, although he put on a brave face as he contemplated the situation:

> I believe they're close to a solution. Frankly I don't know how it will be resolved. Do you make the actuators stiffer? Do you make the connecting mechanisms stiffer? Do you change the support structure? Or a combination of all of those? And in this case one of the things they're looking at is the rudder itself, and its ability, stiffness-wise, to transmit load. And there may be an impact, we

may have to add a little stiffness there. We may do something to
the actuators, the mechanisms themselves. It will probably be a
combination of all of those things. So it's kind of complex. And
the team is charged with figuring out the most efficient way of
meeting the requirements against the problem that they've
encountered.

It complicates schedules for certain, because we wouldn't have
anticipated having this problem this late in the game. We wouldn't
want it this late. So take ASTA in Australia, trying to produce the
rudder. If we have to reinforce it it affects them. If we have to do
something to the actuator [coming from an outside contractor] it
affects the vendor in that regard, and our own in-house stuff that
we're doing, the support system for the actuator. But these things
crop up, you know. There will never be an airplane that's perfect
right out of the shoot. It's too complex a vehicle to ever expect
that to happen, and changes do occur, and we just have to recover
from them as they happen.

Much of this was known to ASTA through Jeanette Collier, an
Australian engineer spending two years in Seattle to represent ASTA
on the Rudder DBT. But knowing that there were problems didn't
change the schedule for ASTA as they planned to bake the first
rudder. In fact, through Collier, who was aware of every stage and
put in her manufacturing expertise from time to time, ASTA played
a part in the design process. But all the design expertise in the world
may be unable to anticipate what's going to happen when a
component experiences the loads that it will find in flight. While
the Seattle team were trying to sort out the problem, Al Tyler and
his engineers – Pat Bogart, a one-legged ex-Boeing employee, and
Bob Ravarty – had to proceed with the old design, rather than lay off
workers and sit around waiting for the verdict from Seattle. Tyler's
patience was sorely tried. Neither profanity nor scatology was strong
enough to express his irritation, and he resorted to another
Australian expression:

I was cheesed off to blazes because of this. Now I'm not exactly
unhappy today, because we set out to achieve a whole series of
things with this particular rudder and we'll achieve most of them,

but probably the thing that worries me a little bit is that the configuration will change. And it's going to change fairly dramatically, and we still have to deliver on schedule. We've got a commitment to deliver this rudder in the middle of next year. And if we're late on that it puts Boeing in a bind. We don't want to do that if we can possibly avoid it. Our relationship with Boeing is excellent. It's top class. It's like a marriage. We have our arguments, but you've got to get back together again because neither of us wants to divorce each other.

In the factory in Melbourne the very first 777 rudder lay on its trolley ready to be loaded into the autoclave. At this stage, before baking, the material of the rudder on its rig was soft and pliable. After baking it would be as solid and tough as aluminium, but much lighter, if everything went to plan.

The rudder was to be baked at a temperature of 177°C for seven hours, and the temperature would be monitored by thermocouples – temperature-measurement devices – that were embedded in locations all over the rudder to make sure that every part of the rudder skin reached the right temperature for hardening and toughness. It was the first time ASTA had baked such a huge piece, and evenness of cooking would be essential.

Over the weekend of 3–4 October the rudder was baked and left to cool. Then, the moment of truth, it was ready to be wheeled out, covered in its plastic bag and paper coating. The key question was, Had it retained its intended aerodynamic shape with the required accuracy – a few thousandths of an inch?

Surveyors' instruments, theodolites, were used to measure the exact position in space of a series of target reference points. Some of the points that the engineers thought might have moved from their original position had hardly changed at all. But there was a problem. As the computer data from the baking become available, it turned out that four of the most crucial thermocouples had not worked.

Fortunately the thermocouple problem didn't seem to have affected the shape, although the success was academic, since everyone knew that whatever was being decided in Seattle was unlikely to leave this rudder with any useful function.

The following day Tyler congratulated his group of workers on a job well done, but in another meeting straight afterwards with his more senior colleagues he made no bones about his annoyance with Boeing. 'Now that we've got rid of the rest of the team we can talk about all these changes that have been put upon us by Boeing. Lovely company they may be, but they have given us a real problem in so far as building this rudder to schedule is concerned.'

After the meeting Tyler phoned Boeing to report on progress. His main contact there, Mike Voegtlin, was not pleased to hear about the broken thermocouples. With scarcely concealed irritation he said, 'Next time you might want to check them first.' With masterly forbearance, Tyler didn't tell Voegtlin, 'Next time you might want to design the rudder better.'

In late 1992, with a series of delivery dates looming ever nearer, the ASTA team adjusted the design according to new plans from Boeing, and set to work to try to catch up with the schedule. If the first plane was to fly in June 1994, it had to have its rudder in Seattle in August 1993, and ASTA had expected to be well under way with its manufacture by now. Instead, they had one rudder that would be useless on the plane, although it had shown them that their manufacturing methods were good.

In spite of occasional expressions of strong emotion, Tyler and his colleagues in Australia had been too long in the business – and were too dependent on Boeing – to let the design problem overwhelm them. But the fact that relations weren't as bad as they could have been was partly due to the careful cultivation by the 777 team of Boeing's Working Together policy. As Mulally explained at the time:

> To me it's a fundamental principle of our programme to have the designers and the makers work together. And it's one of the reasons we adopt as our fundamental theme 'working together' – because you're never done until you're done. You don't know it works until it works. And you're creating a solution and sometimes your solution doesn't satisfy all the objectives, and so our principle on the programme is that you share where you are and it's OK. If your idea didn't work out, share that. Share it early. Share it with the people that have a shared destiny in it, that are affected by your decision, and then let's just keep working

together. We all have a responsibility on that. The designer has a responsibility to do it in a timely manner. The maker has a responsibility to let the designer know what a timely manner looks like, and not to wait too long on the solution. I think sticking together is key.

SEVEN

'Without Us, They're Winnebagos'

Remark of a Pratt & Whitney communications manager

The Boeing people might have resented the status of their beloved plane being reduced to a glorified recreational vehicle, but they couldn't have argued with the central premise – that it was the engines that made the plane fly. And the engines were made by someone else, not Boeing. In 1990, Pratt & Whitney, General Electric and Rolls-Royce were the three companies still in the business of making large jet engines for commercial aircraft, and there were some who were to wonder how much longer Rolls would be around, given the small proportion of customers who ordered Rolls engines for their 777s. The contribution of an engine manufacturer to the 777 was far greater than that of any other single contractor. The engines cost about a fifth of the total cost of the plane – $10 million or so per engine. And, with fifty thousand parts, the development and production of the engines was every bit as complex as the Boeing designers' work on the plane. Some aspects of engine technology were more challenging than the design of the airframe. Parts of the engines had to withstand temperatures of 3,000°C during several hours of flight; other parts had to travel at supersonic speeds, and still others had to be able to withstand high-frequency vibrations for long periods.

All these characteristics, and the importance of getting an engine right, meant a special relationship with the plane-makers whose fate and reputation could be harmed by a bad engine. The relationship had evolved over the years, managed on the Boeing side by Granville 'Granny' Frazier. A tall, red-faced, white-haired man from Mississippi, Granny occasionally answered the phone by saying, 'Lee Marvin here', and there *was* a slight resemblance. Frazier stands out from the run-of-the-mill Boeing executives, by his loud, occasionally profane, and often humorous manner of speaking, challenging the listener to find something offensive or shocking in what he says. If you ask him a question, he will lean far back in his chair, in shirtsleeves and braces, and indulge in a stream of consciousness which, before it dries up, will probably contain the answer somewhere. Asked about his origins, he paints a picture of rural poverty and deprivation, over which, not surprisingly, young Granville triumphed by sheer determination and talent:

> I was born in Mississippi in an agricultural area, on a small farm, and only ended up in a modern school system by accident. My dad was the youngest of seven or eight kids, I forget which – eight or nine, there's so many of them – and moved to the big city during World War Two. While you Brits were playing with the buzz bombs, he was starting to help Dupont make powder for the big guns for World War Two, and that got me in a modern school system. And somehow or another as I went through high school, and proceeded to study and learn to read and write and eat with a fork and knife, instead of with a knife, I became interested in mathematics and physics, and when it came time to finish school I automatically went to the University of Tennessee, and I had had an older cousin who became a mechanical engineer, and without the least knowledge of what such a thing was I left and went to school, completed my studies – that span takes you from 1934 to 1952 – took five years to finish the study, and then came to work for Boeing in '57, and that's thirty-six years ago, and I've been here ever since.

Frazier was Boeing's linkman with the engine manufacturers. He left much of the day-to-day work on the 777 to a Boeing colleague, Rocky Thomas, and everyone knew that when Granny rather than Rocky was heard on the end of a phone call to Pratt or GE or Rolls, or appeared on screen at a videoconference between East Hartford and Seattle, then thunder would roll and lightning strike.

Granny's confidence, and his disdain for proprieties of language, sprang from his many years of successful work in the airplane business. To hear him speak was to wonder sometimes whether he actually had known Orville and Wilbur. And some of his directness probably suited the image he cultivated of a jumped-up Mississippi farm boy:

> When I used to go back home and visit my relatives who still work on the farm and grow cotton and corn and things like that, they used to ask me – and I'll try to lapse back in to my childhood accent – 'Granville, what yew dew out there at that Boeing?' And I'd say things like, 'Well, I manage the business in technical interfaces, between the Boeing Commercial Airplane Group and the various engine companies – Rolls-Royce, Pratt & Whitney and GE.' And invariably they'd say, 'Yeah, but what yew *dew*?' I finally learned to answer the question by saying 'I make airplanes.' And they'd say, 'Are yew a riveter or a welder?' and I told them, 'My job is more like welding.' So we have a lot of communication. You can hear somebody say occasionally, 'That Granville's got a nice job out there at that Boeing in Washington state – he's a welder.' As a matter of fact I have a plaque at home that I'm proud of from Pratt & Whitney that commemorated thirty-six years of welding at my last anniversary.

As Boeing's highest-paid welder, Frazier gives the impression of having observed a lot of the changes that have occurred in the relationship between plane-maker and engine manufacturer, although some of the events must have occurred when he was toddling around the farmyard in nappies.

> We used to sell airplanes the following way. Business deals were made with Juan Trippe of PanAm and Bill Glenn of Pratt & Whitney and Bill Allen of Boeing having a three-way handshake that essentially says, 'OK, we want to build a big airplane like the 747.' Trippe says, 'Allen, if you will build it and, Glenn, if you will make an engine for it, I'll buy it. We'll start off with twenty-five, or whatever it takes, and we'll talk some more details about price later.' Then we all worked away and started on it. Back in the old days, when we made guarantees, the engine guys went and guaranteed fuel consumption directly to the airline, we guaranteed drag, and the airline integrated this whole process together in

addition to being in the business of carrying people from one place to another. This is back when flight test was the king. Tex Johnson was really the leader of the gang. He took airplanes up, spun 'em around the sky, they counted the pieces that fell off, and then went and figured out why they fell off and put 'em back on again better.

Now we've changed things. One of the things that led to the change was when problems arose with the engine and neither party would accept the blame. Trippe would say 'Oh, by the way, you guys aren't running me back and forth between East Hartford and Boeing with one guy yelling 'It's TSFC'[1] and the other guy yelling 'It's drag.' Boeing, you take responsibility for guaranteeing the *total* performance from now on, and you pitch your relationship with the engine guy so that he's supplying you the performance guarantee.' So we moved from bi-comprehensive guarantees to comprehensive guarantees.

Now this was really tough. Here's the engine company, the rugged individualist, delivering something that probably cost just as much to develop as the airplane, a thing that you sell five times – once originally and four more times as spare parts, so the total revenue from it in the long run is probably about as big as the total revenue from the airplane – this rugged individualist moves to the role of a supplier. It's a big deal, and it was not done gently, and it's taken twenty-five years to complete that cycle.'

Frazier's remark about selling an engine five times was highlighted by a report in the US magazine *Business Week* about an Asian sales drive by two of the engine manufacturers for the 777.

A few months ago, China Southern Airlines in Guangzhou was trying to decide which engines to buy for six new Boeing 777 aircraft it had just ordered. Rolls-Royce had already dropped out of the bidding, leaving General Electric and Pratt & Whitney to fight it out. Pratt made its best offer – a discount of 96% on it $120 million asking price. 'We were giving the engines away,' says Pratt President Karl J. Krapek, who hoped to lock in twenty years of spare-parts and service business that might double the contract's

---

[1]Thrust-specific fuel consumption

value. Then, archrival GE did the unthinkable: although it won't reveal its winning bid, industry sources say it bettered Pratt's offer with concessions worth an extra $30 million.[2]

The first plane to fly in revenue service would be in the livery of United Airlines, and United had ordered Pratt & Whitney engines. Some said that United were bound to order Pratt engines, not least because of the long association with Boeing that went right back to the 1920s and 30s when Boeing, United and Pratt were part of the same company. But Gordon McKinzie of United disagreed. He felt that United considered equally seriously all three engine manufacturers before choosing Pratt:

I'd say all three of the engines were technically very, very comparable. The GE engine was an excellent engine, but a brand-new-technology engine. There were three parts of that engine that were virtually new technology. It had a new wide-chord composite blade, a new combustor design, and a very-high-pressure compressor which they had never tried before. But that engine also had a lot more growth potential than some of the others, and it had excellent fuel burn, so it was a real contender. The Rolls engine – also a great engine – a big core, a big engine, and we spent a lot of time in Derby looking at that engine. But we knew the Pratt engine very well, we were flying the core engine on the 747s and the 767s and we looked at the new engine they were looking at for this airplane, which was a kind of an extension of that design and we felt comfortable. But, in all honesty, all three engines would have worked for us.

The main characteristic that an airline requires from engines is the total thrust that will be available to achieve enough force for the plane to do what it needs to do with a sufficient margin of safety. The three engine manufacturers were required to deliver engines with thrust levels of about 80,000 lb. As an indication of how far engine technology has come, NASA's first manned space flight, the Mercury spacecraft, was lifted into space with an engine that generated 78,000 lb of thrust. Pratt's new engine for the 777 – an engine type called the 4084 – would deliver a thrust that was 30,000 lb above previous thrust levels.

The thrust required per engine in a twin-engine aircraft was not just half of what the whole plane needed: in fact the 777 would have to be designed so that it could take off and land with only one engine operating, in a situation where the other failed or was shut down. This excess capacity was standard on all large passenger aircraft – the 747 with four engines also had to be able to operate with one or two engines not working. But on the 747 two engines could go wrong before the situation became really serious. On the 777, if two engines went wrong, serious was too mild a word.

The 'twinness' of the plane certainly focused the attention of the designers on reliability as a factor that had to be established very early on, by good design, high-quality manufacture and convenient maintenance. All of these would help to prevent what were called 'inflight shutdowns' (IFSDs). These were not unknown in modern aviation. They happen, in fact, on quite a regular basis. The 767, for example, had experienced twenty-five inflight shutdowns after a million hours or so of engine life – a rate of 0.025 per thousand hours – although by 10 million engine hours the rate had dropped below 0.02 per thousand hours. This might seem worrying, but it wasn't nearly as worrying as an earlier generation of civil airliner engines – not those of the Wright Brothers era but engines introduced pre-1981, when the engines had inflight shutdown rates of 0.33 per thousand hours – 330 shutdowns after a million hours rather than twenty-five.

There were several factors that contributed to the inflight shutdown rate. Some of them had nothing to do with the core engine design at all – an engine might be shut down because of a faulty warning light, for example – but those that were due to an actual defect in the engine and its associated equipment could be a result of poor design, poor manufacture or poor maintenance.

Boeing carried out an exhaustive survey of every single IFSD on their planes over the previous twenty years, and analysed the causes into categories. They then set to work to learn the lessons of each category and transfer that knowledge into an improved design for the aircraft. Jim Johnson, director of large commercial engines for Pratt & Whitney, describes the results:

In one survey of every single incident that had occurred where an airplane had to deviate from its intended flight path, the answer came out to be that it often wasn't the engine itself: it was things like electrical generation, hydraulic pumps, communication systems. Over 50 per cent of all of the engine shutdowns in the world, in commercial aviation, have nothing to do with the core engine. They have to do with pneumatic systems or electrical systems or fire-detection systems vibrating and having a small leak which then lets the gas escape, which is the signal that you've detected a fire. So right out of the analysis came a very obvious issue. If we could improve the reliability of the items that are attached to the engine, or in the airplane, then you could assure the airlines that they could fly for a long period of time, over water, up to 180 minutes and be 100 per cent sure that they were not going to have a system failure that would cause the airplane to be diverted into another field.

For example, the investigating team looked at three similar incidents that happened to one airline between 1984 and 1987, when there was a high oil-temperature reading that turned out to be false. On two of the occasions, the plane either had to be diverted or turned back. Boeing and Pratt planned to use four separate steps, each introducing redundancy, or backup capability, in parts of the system to avoid problems like this that occurred with the traditional design of oil-temperature detection. The new engine would have dual redundant oil-pressure transmitters, dual redundant oil-temperature probes, dual oil-filter elements and software in the airplane's computer to discriminate true high oil temperature from false alarms.

This is just one tiny detail that arises from the complex structure of a modern jet engine. Deceptively simple from the outside – a bulbous cylinder with a rotating fan at one end and exhaust fumes at the other – the modern fan-jet reveals what seem to be most of its fifty thousand parts when the outer covering, or nacelle, is removed. And yet at its heart *is* a simple idea. Engineers say that the job of an engine is to suck, squeeze, burn and blow. Air is sucked in by a large rotating fan and is compressed in several stages until it enters a combustion chamber under pressure. Here, heated by burning

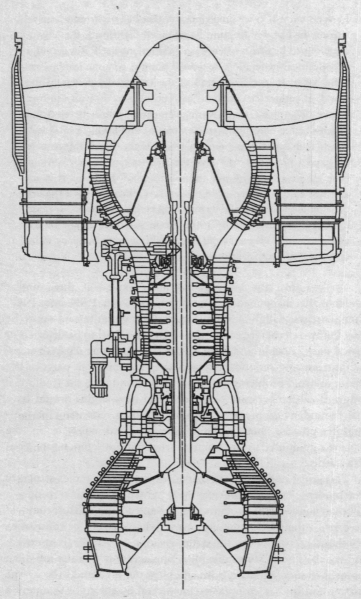

Cross-section of the Pratt & Whitney 4080 engine designed for the 777

kerosene, the air, bursting to expand, rushes out through turbine blades which are rotated at high speed by the rush of hot air. So far this is a description rather than an explanation. What is missing from this oversimplified picture is how it is that such a process will generate more than 80,000 lb of thrust in a 777 engine. The answer may seem surprising.

There is a popular view that jet engines work through some kind of reaction to the air rushing out of the back that pushes the plane in the opposite direction. Some people might be inclined to guess that the hot air pushes against the outside atmosphere to generate the thrust; the more knowledgeable, who remember that space rockets work without any air to 'push against', assert knowingly that the engine thrust comes from Newton's Third Law – to every action there is an equal and opposite reaction. Neither view is right. The first is entirely wrong; the second is 20 per cent right in the case of a large modern fan-jet. What generates the thrust in the engines that power a 777 (and a 767, 757 and 747) is the huge fan on the front of the engine. Effectively it is a giant propeller, and it pulls the plane through the air in exactly the same way as the much more feeble turbo-prop on earlier passenger airliners. (It's been calculated that the four fan-jet engines on a 747 would have to be replaced by eighteen piston engines with propellers to achieve the same thrust.) The significance of the 'jet' part of the engine is that the extremely hot, high-pressure air that is produced in the combustion chamber is loaded with huge amounts of energy to drive turbine blades that are linked to the axle of the fan. It's the high rotation speed imparted to the fans of the engines that gives the airplane the thrust it needs to take off.

The technology of a fan-jet engine tests materials to the limit. Some parts of the engine reach supersonic speed, and stay at that speed for many hours; other parts are bathed in hot gas until they glow cherry-red. The subtlety of shape of fan blades and turbine blades to achieve maximum aerodynamic efficiency challenges even the largest computers to design. Perhaps the least appreciated aspect of major airliner engines is the ability they must possess to run for hour after hour, at widely varying atmospheric pressures and temperatures, and extreme rotational speeds, without a hiccup.

Jim Johnson describes with loving pride the technological mastery that underlies a modern airliner engine:

If you can imagine the environment that a blade in a compressor of an engine experiences, with temperatures that can be as high as 3,000 degrees, with a very large quotient of the blade running at supersonic speeds, rotating in hot gases, with all of the thermal expansion, all of the distortions that come from all the variety of speeds on the engine, it gives you a sense of how really complex the environment is that these blades are operating in. Our engine that will power the 777 will eventually produce more than 100,000 lb of thrust, which will result from a fan that's 112 inches in diameter, with about 25 per cent of the fan, which is turning at about 3,000 r.p.m., at supersonic speed. So there's a whole lot of issues associated with something spinning at that speed, where each blade is fifty-five inches long rotating in an environment of ice and snow, or field temperatures of 100 degrees. The whole specification makes the design extremely complex.

Take the weight issue, for example – the lighter you can make the blade, the better it is from the standpoint of performance of the airplane. By the same token, if you make it too light, as the blade runs up to speed it begins to twist, because of very high loads, and that can destroy the efficiency of the blade. Our engineers are controlling blade angles for the fan of one-third of one degree – extremely close tolerances.

There are some other issues that are significant. We design our engines so that if there ever was a possibility of a blade departing the fan it must be able to be captured, and the engine continue to run until it can turn itself off. And when you lose a fan blade it's captured in a Kevlar[3] band that encircles the fan, that's about six inches long and about two feet wide. And to give you the feel for the kind of energy that that Kevlar containment ring must absorb, it's the equivalent of stopping a 10,000 lb automobile from seventy miles an hour, in five inches. So it's really marvellous engineering so the fan can operate in that kind of environment.

The exit temperatures of that combustor can be as high as 3,000 degrees. So the turbine blades are made of a very special material, which we call single-crystal blades, where we grow a single crystal of material, very slowly, so that it has a single crystalline structure,

[3]Kevlar – a very strong, synthetic carbon-fibre material

and then we machine that away in the shape of the blade that we want. That provides optimum strength, and eliminates any crystalline barriers that would provide fracture points. The blades are very sophisticated in that in the first few stages of the turbine they are cooled internally. And so each blade, as thin as it is, contains a whole series of cooling passageways so that air enters the blade from the root of the blade, and it escapes through very tiny holes along the trailing edge of the blade, and helps carry away the heat that's created by the combustor.

An interesting sidelight on the increasing reliability of jet engines emerged in an *Economist* article in 1988:

> With advances in aerodynamic design and the use of lighter materials, turbofan engines are being made more powerful and efficient. Jet engines are now some ten times more reliable than engines made ten years ago. Greater reliability means engine manufacturers now need to make more of their profits from the sales of their engines rather than spare parts.[4]

In other words, when engines were less reliable, engine manufacturers could rely on a significant income from the spare that the airlines had to purchase when the engines went wrong . . .

In June 1992 in East Hartford, Connecticut, two issues were being addressed that play a key part in establishing the ability of such engines to run for long periods without breaking down. One of them was on a computer screen in the office of Pratt engine designer Scott Hadley. He was using the computer to test the design of a component he had recently drawn. Pratt & Whitney were using a computer-aided design tool that was almost as sophisticated as CATIA but different. It was called Unigraphics, and the fact that there were two different CAD systems for the same plane didn't make things any easier. As is traditional, Pratt & Whitney design the core engine and Boeing design what's called the 'engine build-up', an array of hydraulic and electrical systems that form the interface between the engine and the rest of the plane. Boeing also design the

[4] *The Economist*, 3 September 1988

nacelle and the thrust reverser – the smooth, movable covering that is all that most of us see when we look at the engine.

One of the consequences of the engine's cycle of power up, cruise thrust and power down is the fact that the engine can pass through a whole range of different vibration frequencies, due to the speed of rotation of its parts. The vibration caused to the rest of the engine would be minimal if the engine were absolutely perfectly balanced. But during the life of an engine, several things can cause a slight imbalance, such as wear and tear or misadjustments during maintenance or the slight bending of a fan blade. In this case a small vibration can be imparted to the rest of the engine at certain rotation speeds .

During the development of previous Pratt engines, the engineers would test the engines in runs of 2,000 hours to simulate normal running. When they did this, they would make sure that the engine was perfectly balanced to start with, so that there were no excessive vibrations. With the engine for the 777, the test engines had changed standard practice, as Alan Jankot, a development design engineer at Pratt, explained:

> On these new test engines we purposely build in an imbalance on the rotors that's higher than a typical degraded field performance would see, and this extra vibration of the engine will excite and cause early failures of any suspect parts of the externals. So what we've done different on this engine is make a more severe environment in the development programme so that we can shake out any problems on these externals.

Scott Hadley had designed a tube that was attached to the turbine exhaust case and which was used to sense the air pressure inside the case. The tube followed a winding path around part of the engine. At certain points it was attached by brackets to the casing, but there were lengths of the tube that were free of attachments. Hadley was on the lookout for a problem that can arise when a length of tube between two fixed points is vibrated at its natural frequency. It's just like the way a stretched string will produce a musical note that varies depending on the length of string between two fixed points. The pitch of the note reflects the fact that the string

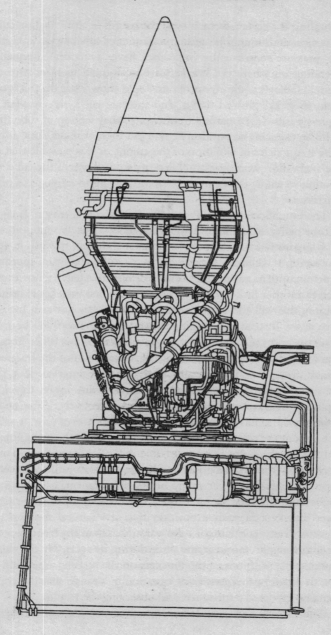

is vibrating at a certain frequency. If the length of string is shortened, the note sounds higher because the frequency of vibration is higher. The pressure-sensor tube will also have a natural frequency, depending on where the brackets are positioned to hold it to the engine. Hadley's computer program could show what that vibration would look like slowed down, and indicate on a screen what its frequency was. If the natural frequency of that section of tube fixed by the brackets in the position he had put them was the same as one of the frequencies of vibration of the engine, it was possible that the tube's vibration would be amplified, to a point where the tube was vibrating so wildly that it would snap off, owing to fatigue at a point of fixture.

This amplification would occur for the following reason. Imagine the tube being flicked midway between its two attachment points. It will swing away from the point of impact and back towards it, then away again, travelling a shorter distance, and back again, repeating the action until its natural tension will bring it to a halt. If, however, it receives another flick when it returns for the first time to its original position, this will add to the energy it already has just as it turns to move away. Instead of damping down, the vibration will be more energetic, and the tube may even travel further this time. Because extra force changes only the distance it moves and not the frequency of each cycle, it will still return after the same interval. If it then receives a *third* flick at exactly the same point in its travel, its amplitude of travel will get even greater. Effectively, if the engine vibrates at the same natural frequency as the portion of tube, it will be giving a series of carefully timed flicks to the tube at the same point in the tube's cycle of movement, and the tube will move more and more widely away from its rest position, putting a strain on the connection points and possibly, over many hours of vibration, causing metal fatigue until the tube snaps. Hadley's job was to make sure that he placed brackets in such a position that the natural frequency of vibration of any length of the tube was higher than any frequency that the engine could impart at any stage during its cycle. He did this by changing the positions of the brackets on the screen, subjecting the tube to different frequencies of vibration in a range that the engine would be expected to produce, and observing the results.

This process had to be followed for every single section of every single tube that festooned the engine. A leakage of air, the failure of a sensor, or a leak of oil or hydraulic fluid might not harm the engine irreparably but it could well lead to a need to shut down the engine in flight, just to be safe, with the consequent problems in a twin-engine plane of finding a diversionary airport, putting off the passengers, finding somewhere for them to stay, bringing in a maintenance engineer and spare parts, and coping with several hundred very angry people who wanted to be in New York rather than Newfoundland.

Computer simulations are used a lot in the design of complex modern artefacts, and the question naturally arises as to how accurate they are. If you are using a computer to design for some rare event, and if the computer data reassure you that, in that rare event your design will continue to function, it will – by definition – be a rare occasion on which that assumption is put to the test, in a real situation. In the case of Hadley's test, there was a way of testing the calculations without waiting until the first plane with a Pratt engine flew. There were in fact many hours of tests on the engine itself, running it in a variety of situations of temperature, pressure, thrust level and states of imbalance, and the effect of vibration on engine parts is such an important – and potentially dangerous – factor that Pratt have a special test chamber, called a shake rig, to observe the outcome at different frequencies of vibration.

The shake rig vibrates the engine passively, i.e. while it isn't running. It uses a metal arm, positioned against the engine case, which can be vibrated at any frequency. It is used to check for the kind of vibration problems Scott Hadley hoped he'd designed out of his part of the engine. The sort of frequencies of vibration that give problems are many hertz – one hertz means one cycle per second – so, even if a part of the engine vibrates excessively, this vibration will not be visible to the naked eye: it will be too fast. But the shake rig has a strobe light, a very bright light that can be made to flicker at any desired frequency. By shining the strobe light on the vibrating engine it is possible to detect any component that is moving excessively. If the strobe light is at *exactly* the frequency of a vibrating component, the component will look stationary. This is because the component will be in exactly the same position every time the light comes on. Then when the light is off the component will move through its cycle and will be back in the initial position when the light comes on. But if the strobe light is at a slower or faster frequency than the vibrating part the effect will be of a sinuous motion through the full width of the vibration, and this will enable an engineer to decide if this is likely to cause problems.

As well as getting final details of the design right in early 1992, the Pratt engineers were addressing the question of the *maintainability* of the engine. On a day in June 1992 a group of about forty maintenance engineers from United Airlines and American Airlines clustered around a mock-up of the 4084 engine. They were there to give their views of the maintainability of the engine while there was still time to take account of their suggestions. They would be encouraged by Pratt to swarm over the engine and pick holes in its design, by seeking out inaccessible lubrication points, fragile projections that someone might stand on, or components that could be seen but not touched or touched but not seen.

However well an engine works, it still needs maintenance work at each stage in its journey – replacement of oil or filters, for example, or regular checks to see that there is no damage from foreign bodies or birds. There has been a philosophy in the airplane manufacturing business that mistakes by maintenance engineers are no business of the plane designers – maintenance people should be trained not to make mistakes – but that approach is changing.

One small example from the engine that Pratt & Whitney made for the 747 illustrates this. There is an oil tank on the side of the engine that contains oil for the engine, kept under pressure to push it through to where it's needed. This tank has a cap. Sometimes the cap was left off or not tightened. The engineer would close a small door over the cap, in the nacelle, and nobody would know what had happened until the oil failed to pressurize and wouldn't lubricate the engine. The engine would heat up, register in the cockpit as a fault, have to be shut down, and delay the flight. There are about 100,000 occasions a year, counted across all 747s, when this sort of mistake could happen. Initially, when it did happen, the attitude among the Pratt people was 'What incompetent maintenance engineers!' and they left it at that. But then someone took a different approach. This unknown hero said, 'What if we find a way of making it more difficult to leave the cap unscrewed – won't our customers be pleased with us?' After all, many different airlines operated 747s, with many different standards. It might be reasonable to expect a United Airlines maintenance engineer on a spring evening in Chicago to put the top on correctly every time, but how about Air Ruritania's maintenance man on the ground in the depths of winter of Bogdig Airport, wearing thick gloves? So Pratt designed a cap that had a flange on it pointing up at an angle to the cap. This was designed in such a way that if the cap wasn't tightened the flange would prevent the nacelle door closing. If a maintenance man forgot to tighten the cap, he would probably notice when he tried to close the door. And if he left the door open, the pilot or copilot would probably notice during their pre-flight checks. In fact, even after this design change was made, there were still a few instances of engines being shut down because both cap and door were left open and no one spotted it. Now Pratt have designed an oil tank where there is a valve just under the cap so that the oil tank can be pressurized whatever the maintenance people do. It is this design that is being installed on the 4080 engine for the 777.

As the maintenance engineers climbed over the mock-up it was clear that they were rising to the challenge to find something that could be improved. For most of them their first reaction was to the sheer size of the engine. They were familiar with the 4000 engine, of which the 4080 was a derivative, but this one was eighteen inches wider. Among the crowd of airline engineers were some of the Pratt development engineers with clipboards and flip-chart pads, noting down every point that was made, even if it had already been pointed out by someone else. They were taking the process seriously, since past experience had shown real benefits from such gatherings, as Alan Jankot explained:

> Over the course of a year and half we've had three major airline conferences like this. At the initial conference we picked up 150 or 170 problems or ideas or suggestions for improvement: the second meeting showed up fifty or sixty ideas, and the final review showed ten or fifteen nits that they were still picking at.

At this stage in the development of the engine most of the design work had been completed. Plane-makers say that a new engine takes longer to develop than a new plane – about five years – but, since the 4084 was a derivative of the Pratt 4000 engine, it had taken Pratt rather less time to reach this stage. But having a fully designed engine was only the beginning: that engine had to be tested under conditions that would reproduce as closely as possible the conditions of in-service flight. And in the case of the 777, because it was a twin-engined aircraft, those tests would be given closer attention than any previous airframe–engine combination.

This attention clustered around an acronym that dominated almost every important design discussion but was particularly relevant to to the engines – ETOPS, standing for Extended Twin-engine Operations. It was a topic on which everybody, from pilot to poet, appeared to be capable of having strong views.

EIGHT

ETOPS – 'Engines Turn or Passengers Swim'

From New York Times article about the 777, 27 March 1994

During the winter of 1992–3 Vince Carroll of AlliedSignals Aerospace Company lived with a beeper attached to his belt, awaiting a call from a computer. The call came about every four hours, and often Vince ignored it. But occasionally he would drop whatever he was doing and drive five or ten miles to the airport at Fairbanks, Alaska, to keep an eye on his baby. Carroll was one of a team of engineers looking after the testing of the 777's auxiliary power unit, the APU as it was called.

Every passenger airliner has an APU, which is really an extra engine tucked away inside the back of the plane. But the APU has no propulsion role. Although it looks similar to the jet engine that propels the plane, its main job is to generate copious supplies of compressed air and power to provide for passenger comfort on the ground. So, when planes are waiting at the gate and passengers are settling into their seats, power and air are supplied by the APU, until the engines start up. The APU has a couple of other jobs too. It provides power to start the engines and, rarely but crucially, it can take over the supply of air and power in mid-flight if one of the engines malfunctions such that its generator fails or it shuts down entirely. The first occurrence is more frequent and less important, but having a functioning APU can make the difference between the plane taking off or the whole flight being cancelled. The reliability standards for the APU are rigorous, even though it is not strictly speaking a safety item. But, because of its possible engine-backup functions, it has to meet FAA standards of reliability and durability.

The APU was just one element on the plane whose reliability Boeing wanted to demonstrate before the 777 even went into service. As a large twin-engine plane, the 777 was designed to fly long distances, often over water and a long way from any airport. Before the plane would be allowed to do this it had to be certified for Extended Twin-engine Operations – ETOPS – by the various aviation regulators, such as the FAA, who must be convinced that the plane can fly for long periods on one engine – as it might have to do if one engine failed over water.

During 1992 and 1993 Boeing were pushing hard for their target of full ETOPS certification at time of service – a task not made easier by sporadic sniping from some who suspected that they were trying to go too far too fast. On the day that Carroll responded to his beeper for perhaps the last time in the current test cycle, the *Seattle Times* reported on a meeting that had taken place the previous weekend.

After a three-day Boeing aviation conference for airline representatives, pilots' groups and aviation regulatory agencies, there was an article about the 777 ETOPS issue. After interviewing aviation consultants and other journalists, the writer quoted a retired aeronautical engineer as saying, 'I don't think it is worth exposing 300-plus passengers to that sort of thing just to make a little money.' Faced with this disingenuous simplification, the Boeing 777 team could only throw up their hands rather glumly and get on with their job – now newly defined as 'making a little money'. The article was circulated to the senior 777 managers with a handwritten message from Mulally: 'This kind of reporting makes me feel so bad for all our customers, suppliers, team players, who are working so hard to produce a world-class product, and the travelling public.'

The Boeing people were no doubt frustrated at this kind of comment. It cast doubt on their own pre-eminent concern for safety above all other criteria, and it failed to recognize the deep and all-pervasive management structures that were responsible for the pioneering nature of the 777's design and manufacture. In a way that was not always apparent to outsiders, every part of this plane was at a much more advanced stage than any equivalent aircraft had been in the past. The tests that were being carried out on 777 components were often covering ground that earlier planes had not covered until they were in service. Whatever the reasons for the earlier design philosophy – inertia, lack of computing power, protectiveness of personal control – they were custom and practice in the industry, and it was considered regrettable but not unusual that small things kept going wrong with new planes, leading to costly redesign work and new planes being taken out of service.

But now, wherever a test that used to be done in flight could be carried out earlier, before there was a plane to fly, Boeing tried to make sure that it *was* done. With the APU, one key procedure that had to be as reliable as design and manufacture could make it was its start-up. Since the job of the APU was to start the engines, it was important that the APU was able to start itself, and in a range of extreme conditions.

If a prize were to be given to the person with the most appropriate name on the 777 project, it would have to be awarded to Roger de Rudder, the chief of the APU project. It cannot have been intentional that Mr and Mrs de Rudder's little boy grew up to be an aeronautical engineer specializing in activities that take place in the tails of aircraft. And it is idle speculation to suggest that the narrow avoidance of actually working on the rudder itself was deliberate:

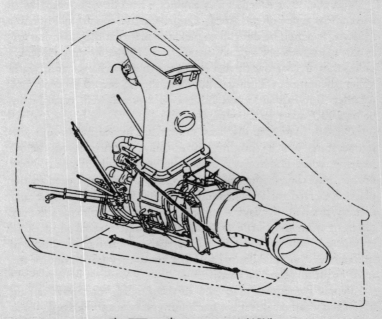

The 777 auxiliary power unit (APU)

that the young Roger, drawn irresistibly to aircraft design and manufacture, gritted his teeth and said, 'Let me not be sucked into rudder design, lest the world laugh.' For whatever reason, de Rudder's prime consideration over years of engineering work has been the APU which, in most aircraft, nestles just beneath the rudder.

As the APU testing cycle neared its end, de Rudder and two colleagues flew up to Fairbanks to join Vince Carroll in witnessing the final sequence of events. It was originally intended to carry out all the tests on the APU in Phoenix, either in the open air or in an environmental chamber that could be lowered to sub-zero temperatures. But then Boeing suggested that they actually put the engine somewhere that was cold all the time and really put the engine to the test. One of the tests that needed to be done was a 'cold-soak' test. This was not, as it might sound, a test in very cold water: instead, it consisted of letting every part of the engine reach the same low temperature and then seeing whether the engine would start.

Like the other AlliedSignals engineers who flew up regularly to within 150 miles of the Arctic Circle, Carroll was from Phoenix, Arizona. It would be difficult to pick two places in the USA that are as far apart meteorologically speaking as Fairbanks and Phoenix, unless they are Barrow, further to the north of Fairbanks, and Death Valley, the remote Californian holder of the US record for really hot weather. But Fairbanks and Phoenix did pretty well, occasionally being 100°F apart on the same day.

On 25 March spring was in the air in Fairbanks and the temperature was a sprightly 20°F, only twelve degrees below freezing, while Phoenix was basking in eight-six degree heat. Now on his third tour of duty in Alaska, Carroll was enamoured of the place. Deserted roads, a gentle way of life, fascinating wildlife and scenery, dramatic displays of auroras, all combined to make this very different from the bustle of Phoenix. It's not a place most of us choose to visit very readily, but, with an arrogance born of uniqueness, the inhabitants of Alaska know they live in one of the most beautiful places on earth.

People sometimes make fun of the English for always talking about the weather. But it is a truth universally acknowledged – or at least universally verifiable – that *everyone* talks about the weather wherever they live and however predictable it is. In Phoenix they talk about the heat all the time, and in Alaska they talk about the cold. There is a pride in extremes, and it was the extremes that had brought AlliedSignals to Fairbanks. It's one of the few towns where, when you put money in a parking meter, you get something in addition to the freedom to park. All the parking-meters have electric sockets to attach to the heaters that all the cars have around their engines. If there was any town that was appropriate to studying the problems of starting engines in the cold, this was it. And Fairbanks was happy that Carroll and his colleagues were there. When AlliedSignals first arrived there was a town reception for the company attended by every important person in Fairbanks, a town with fewer than 70,000 inhabitants and little indigenous industry.

By late March the AlliedSignals team had achieved over 450 cold-soak starts – a 100 per cent success on all first attempts – including one or two memorable moments when, at a temperature of $-50°F$ the engine started in under forty seconds. Another test consisted of throwing snow or rain at the engine for hours on end; even when there was a thick build-up of ice around the air inlet, the engine still started first time. As they headed south, the AlliedSignals team could feel satisfied that they had done their bit to help the 777 achieve its ETOPS rating.

There is a form of 'knowledge' that exists in the human mind that is more powerful than anything learned by rote, or passed on by teachers at school. This knowledge survives in the face of obstacles that, in other circumstances, would pose formidable contradictions. Call it 'intuition', 'common sense', or even plain 'obvious', it plays an important part in shaping people's attitudes to aviation. Indeed, the central premise of heavier-than-air flight is only grudgingly accepted by many people who find that the evidence of their own eyes and bodies is barely enough to overcome their fundamental belief that the whole business is impossible. In that form, this 'knowledge' that planes can't fly is harmless: they *do* fly, whether you believe it or not. The laws of physics remain unchanged by the massive weight of scepticism among the general public. Where such common-sense beliefs pose more of a problem is where they enter into subtler technical areas of safety or efficiency.

The most obvious example of this in the case of the 777 was the number of engines. Boeing had decided to go for a twin-engine aircraft. Economy was certainly one factor in this decision, but reliability and safety were others. These aspects were explored as thoroughly as any other in the early phases of the design of the plane, and everyone on the team was comfortable with the decision. But talk to any non-aviation person about it, describe this new plane and the fact that it had two engines rather than three or four like the other large airliners, and you would get an immediate furrowing of brows, a frisson of concern and a shaking of the head. 'Phew,' such a reaction could be summarized – 'I'm not sure I want to fly on one of *those*. Only two engines, eh? Compared with *four* on a 747, you say?' From being in a state of deep ignorance about the number of inflight shutdowns on a modern high-powered jet engine, such a person can turn instantaneously into someone whose wisdom dictates that *any* twin-engine aircraft must be less safe than *any* plane with three or four engines. In fact professionals sometimes shared this scepticism. One famous aviator was asked why he preferred flying planes with four engines; he said, 'Because they don't make any planes with five engines.'

But, so long as there were journalists who knew how easy it was to terrify the public about flying, the ETOPS issue was not going to go away. Clearly and obviously, any child can see that four engines are better than three, and three better than two. Indeed, you might argue for starting a campaign for five- and six-engined aircraft to make absolutely sure that, as each one failed in flight, there was another one available to take the load.

But you don't have to be a fanatical proponent of twin-engine aircraft to see that the number of engines alone is no guide to safety. A 100 per cent *guaranteed*-safe *single* engine would be fine if anyone could build such a thing. A plane with ten extremely unreliable engines would be no use to anyone. In fact a single event in an engine, such as a large explosion, can cause a catastrophic accident. On that basis four engines are worse than two. 'Maybe you shouldn't ever put more than two engines on an aircraft,' said one Boeing engineer, 'unless it is so big that you *need* extra engines.'

Ignorance is always irritating, but the 'common-sense' approach to ETOPS can also be harmful, since it embodies an implicit belief in the incompetence or corruption of the people who design planes.

For the argument must go as follows: 'If anyone – even I, who know nothing about aeronautical engineering – can see straight away that designing the 777 with only two engines makes it less safe, the people who design the plane must be able to see this as well. The fact that they are persisting in this course can only mean that, in return for higher pay, retaining their jobs, or making a more profitable airplane, they are ignoring the duty of care they owe to the public.'

This may not be the way most people outside the industry expressed their worries, but it was surely the inference to be drawn from their distrust of twin-engine aircraft. And on behalf of the general public, that distrust – or rather duty of care – was embodied in the official certification agencies in the United States and Europe: the Federal Aviation Administration and the Joint Aviation Authority.

Federal Aviation Regulation (FAR) 121.161(a) says the following:

> Unless authorized by the Administrator, based on the character of the terrain, the kind of operation, or the performance of the airplane to be used, no certificate holder may operate two-engine or three-engine airplanes (except three-engine turbine powered airplanes) over a route that contains a point farther than 1 hour flying time (in still air at normal cruising speed with one engine inoperative) from an adequate airport.

This is shown as the 60-minute ETOPS rule, and it would have applied automatically to the 777 when it went into service, if Boeing had not decided to apply for exemption.

Chet Ekstrand is a Boeing pilot who shared the task of helping the company get approval for exemption from 60-minute ETOPS so that the 777 could fly routes that took the plane up to two or three hours' flying time from a diversion airport. He sees the 60-minute rule as a hangover from a bygone age:

> The original rule in the United States was drafted in 1953, and that rule was based upon the reliability of the piston-engined airplane. The broad spectrum of today's airplanes, and not just ETOPS airplanes, has engines that are at least ten times more

reliable than those engines, and an accident rate related to engines that's at least sixty times better, and ETOPS airplanes have even improved reliability beyond that.

One early Boeing airliner, the Stratocruiser, powered by four Pratt & Whitney engines, experienced so many engine failures that it was dubbed by pilots 'the best three-engine airplane flying the Atlantic'. Nowadays, engineers point out, some engines stay in use for as long as 20,000 hours or more without removal for major maintenance, after which they can then last many more years. Rolls-Royce boasts of one engine that stayed on the wing of a Delta jet for more than 25,000 hours – setting a record.

The Boeing chief engineer for ETOPS in 1993, Lars Andersen, is a tall, gangly man with a big smile, and an ultra-polite way of dealing with queries that was in danger of wearing a little thin from the years of pressure that he and his colleagues had faced over the ETOPS issue. In any presentation that Andersen gave on the topic he started with a world map on which all the areas of the world that were more than one hour from 'an adequate airport' were shown in blue. On this map much of the ocean areas was blue, showing that a twin-engine plane couldn't venture into these areas with 60-minute ETOPS. There were circles of white all round the coasts of the major countries, and isolated circles in the middle of oceans, around island countries like New Zealand. There were also areas of Africa, Australia and Asia that would be forbidden to such planes. Clearly the 777 could not be a long-range world-class airliner if it could only fly in such a world, in which planes would have to fly two or three times the straight-line routes to get from one major airport to another, and would not be able to fly to some destinations at all.

The next stage up from 60-minute ETOPS was 75 or 90 minutes, but the map of the world got really interesting with 120-minute ETOPS. Then much of the area of the oceans was white, apart from a small diamond-shaped patch in the middle of the Atlantic and larger areas of blue in the Pacific to the west of the coasts of North and South America. But there was a second factor that made even 120-minute ETOPS a problem and 180 minutes preferable, as Ekstrand explained:

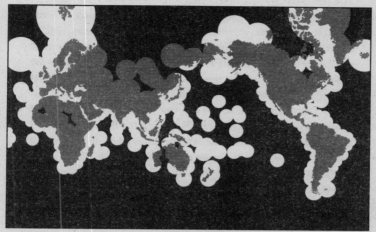

60-minute ETOPS

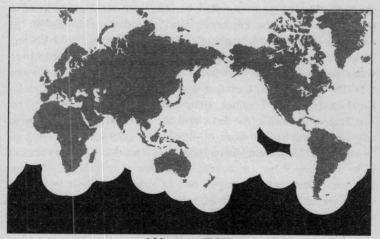

180-minute ETOPS

The ETOPS maps show how much of the world is within reach of suitable diversion airports. In the dark areas, a plane would be more than one or three hours' flying time from a suitable airport if one engine had to be shut down

120 minutes in essence causes fewer alternate airports to be available than 180. On a New York to London sector, for example, somewhat past mid-point on the route, two alternates become available, then one alternate, and then two alternates, and it increases again. But at some point you're down to a very small number of alternates on the North Atlantic, so if failure occurs the expectation would be that the pilot would have to proceed to that alternate. Under a 180-minute rule, at all points on a trip across the North Atlantic six, seven, eight or in some cases even more alternates are continuously available during the flight. Therefore I think increased diversion time actually offers a benefit to the pilot from a safety perspective. It gives more alternates to choose from in the event that a failure does occur. Certainly a pilot could choose, even under a 120 rule, to exercise his emergency authority and proceed to a different alternate, but he might have a bit of explaining to do.

Boeing was determined to deliver for the first time a plane that was certified capable of flying for three hours on one engine 'out of the box'. 'Out of the box' referred to the state of the plane when it was delivered to the customer, who would want to use it on passenger flights within days of delivery. Boeing had told United Airlines and the other airlines who needed to fly long routes over water that at the time of delivery the 777 would be '180-minute ETOPS' rated. When they first gave that assurance, it was a pious expression of hope rather than any kind of guarantee. The certificatory agencies, the FAA and the JAA, had refused to give any sort of exemption from 60-minute ETOPS for the 777 until Boeing presented them with a mound of data that satisfied them as to its reliability. What's more, the sort of data they had needed in the past had come from a year or two of flying the plane in regular passenger service under the 60-minute rule. If a twin showed an acceptably low inflight shutdown rate during service, the agencies would usually give 120-minute ETOPS and then, with further reassuring data, extend this to 180. But Boeing sought more than this. 'Out of the box' 180-minute ETOPS meant carrying out a much larger number, and a greater range, of tests before delivering the plane to the customers.

Although a lot of attention focused on the reliability of the engines – since the ETOPS criterion centred on the ability of the plane to fly with one engine shut down – there were several other aspects of the design of the 777 that Boeing had incorporated to enhance the case for early ETOPS. In addition to the APU, the 777 would have backup batteries with extra capability since the engines generated all the electrical power for the plane. The plane's autoland system would be designed to operate if one engine had been shut down. And there would be a fire-extinguisher system in the cargo hold that would be guaranteed to keep any cargo fire suppressed for up to 195 minutes. This last precaution anticipated the unlikely combination of an engine shutdown and a cargo fire – where the plane would normally head for the nearest airport, which might be 180 minutes away.

For Andersen, Ekstrand and dozens of other Boeing engineers in the ETOPS group, the facts and figures about the steps the company was taking to make the plane ready for 180-minute ETOPS-readiness were overwhelmingly convincing, and as the plane moved from design towards manufacture Boeing plied the certification authorities with the paperwork necessary to obtain the rating that customers had been promised. But the FAA and the JAA were cautious; they were making no promises. They had told Boeing the aspects of the plane's design that would be essential for the 180-minute rating, and they had also specified the tests that would have to be done on the plane before they would even consider this. But at no point did they say that, if these conditions were adhered to, they *would* certify the plane. It must have been very trying. Also very trying was the regular drip, drip, drip of criticism in the press and from some of the professional aviation organizations, such as the pilots' unions. Anyone who raised the topic of the 777 with working airline pilots would get an almost unanimously negative reaction to the idea that the plane would be certified for 180-minute ETOPS from day one of going into service. Not every pilot has experienced an inflight shutdown, but they all know that the consequences are more worrying in a twin-engine plane.

One indication of the seriousness with which Boeing treated professional concerns about ETOPS for the 777 was the hurried trip that Lars Andersen and Chet Ekstrand, along with John Cashman, the 777's chief test pilot, made to a suburban street near London's Heathrow Airport in June 1993. The British Airline Pilots' Association, BALPA, decided to hold an all-day high-level meeting for members of their airworthiness committee and other senior pilots to hear about ETOPS from the horse's mouth. They invited Boeing to send someone along, and they also asked someone from General Electric, who made the engines that British Airways would use on their 777s. Boeing's three senior ETOPS men arrived at BALPA's headquarters near Heathrow with bulging files of over-head-projector slides. They were joined by Kevin Mottram, the British Airways senior flight-operations manager for the 777, and one of his colleagues. Boeing and BA had a shared interest: both of them wanted to win the pilots over at an early stage, so as to avoid the sort of situation that had occurred with a previous innovation – when the unions were up in arms about plans to reduce crews from three to two because of a new inertial navigation system. But there was no disguising the nervousness and frustration at facing a battle, or at least a squabble, that Boeing and BA were not at all sure they were going to win.

To an outside observer the issue seemed to be this: pilots, like ordinary members of the travelling public, don't like taking risks. Furthermore, they are not used to complex risk/benefit calculations. If a new procedure or device has *any* risk attached to it, pilots do not want to have anything to do with it until it is no longer new – in other words, until it has proved itself in service for long enough for the predictions of the manufacturers to be shown to be accurate.

When jet engines were first introduced, pilots with many thousands of hours logged with piston aircraft approached the transition with suspicion and fear. There was a rumour among airline pilots that a jet flying at too high a speed would hit uncontrollable buffeting, and if you tried to slow down you'd stall. After the introduction of jets, one expert predicted 10,000 crash fatalities a year by the end of the century. In fact accidents *declined* with the introduction of jets, from 1 in 150,000 flights initially, through 1 in 1 million in 1975 to 1 in 2.5 million as the 1990s began.[1]

At the BALPA meeting, both sides behaved true to form. Within

[1] Serling, *Legend and Legacy*, p.155

moments of John Cashman starting his piece one of the pilots in the audience heaved a sigh and said *sotto voce* to his neighbour, 'It's the hard sell.' Boeing and GE spelt out in immense detail what they had done and would be doing *before the plane went into flight* to make sure that engine failures had a far smaller chance of happening on this plane than ever before. *And*, they went on, even if one engine did shut down, the probability of a second failure within the three-hour limit would be just so infinitesimally small as to be negligible. Charts and graphs of every known engine failure over twenty years or more of twin-engine flight were shown and analysed in different ways. The Boeing people even showed a graph – unnecessary you might have thought, for an audience of people who had spent all their working lives in aviation – of how many people are killed in a year in the USA as a result of different types of accident. (Deaths on bicycles are sixteen times the number of deaths in airplane accidents.)

The pilots, on the other hand, didn't attempt to argue with the evidence of what had been done, and what would be done before the planes went into service. The most vocal and concerned member of the audience, a laid-back, leather-jacketed cockney, put his views very clearly in a way that showed that the two groups were arguing from different premises. The way this pilot saw it, Boeing were introducing their planes using a *method of introducing new planes into service* that had itself not been tested.

To this pilot, all of Boeing's overhead charts and graphs, all the volumes of test data for the 777, were no different from the tests that were done on previous planes – they were just test results. The difference was that with previous planes there was a degree of caution when they first went into service which, he thought, would not operate with the 777.

When the twin-engine 767 received 180-minute ETOPS it had been flying for two years. Boeing's new approach with the 777 was effectively to devise such a wide range of tests, over such a long period before the plane went into service, that by the May 1995 delivery date to United Airlines they would have gathered as much data *as if* the plane had been in service for two years – even down to what they called the 'mini-airline' test, where the plane would fly ninety flights on a route that took in Washington, Chicago, Denver,

Los Angeles and Honolulu, carrying a crew and passengers and expecting normal maintenance to be carried out at each of the airports.

It seemed such a good idea at the time, but the ETOPS issue was to prove a real headache for the 777 team as the plane moved from design to manufacture and the delivery dates to the major airlines got nearer and nearer. The issue was to illustrate that all the technical knowledge and expertise and tests in the world are not enough to overcome the suspicions of people who are not aircraft designers but who will travel in the plane and who seek standards of certainty about technology that are rarely achieved in any walk of life. The Boeing people resented this, but they really didn't know how to counter it.

NINE

Flying by Wire

A joke told repeatedly at aviation industry conferences puts a man and a dog in an airplane. The dog is there to bite the pilot if the man so much as tries to touch the controls; the pilot's one remaining job is to feed the dog. Many aviation veterans have heard the joke so many times that it is possible to tell those in the audience new to the industry by their laughter.

Gary Stix, *Scientific American*, July 1991

There was a time in the history of air travel when it was the direct muscular force imparted by the pilot to the joystick or the pedals that caused the flight surfaces, such as flaps, rudder, elevators and so on, to move. These surfaces would then channel the airflow over the wings and empennage in certain desirable ways that changed the attitude of the plane and caused it to move in the direction the pilot wanted. This system was operated by cables that ran from the controls in the cockpit, over pulleys and along the length of the plane until they reached the attachment points of the flaps, ailerons or rudder. This era ended surprisingly recently: before the 747 came along there were many airliners that used the pilot's direct force to operate some of their surfaces. Then a new generation of planes had larger movable surfaces needing more force to move them, and hydraulic power was introduced. The pilot's muscular force was still transmitted along cables to the control surfaces, but the cable pulled not on the flap or rudder directly but on an actuator – a simple device that caused high-pressure hydraulic fluid to operate a piston to move the surface.

Jim McWha is one of the surprising number of British chief

engineers who worked on the 777. He is from Northern Ireland, a dark-haired, red-faced man with twinkly eyes, and he was project engineer in charge of a new flight-control system that Boeing had decided to install in the plane. The system is called 'fly-by-wire'. With fly-by-wire there are no long, taut cables carrying the tug of the pilot's arm from one end of the plane to the other. Instead, the pilot's instructions are turned into electrical signals in the cockpit, and those signals are carried by wire to the actuators at the movable surface on the wing or tail. This has considerable advantages over the old system. You only have to peer around inside the belly of a modern plane like a 747 to realize how vulnerable the long cables are to obstruction or damage. A large number of people were killed in 1974 when the door flew off a Turkish Airlines DC-10 and control was lost due to the disruption of the control cables by the collapsing floor. Although such planes have redundancy built into their cable runs, so that the loss of one or two cables is not disastrous, it's clear that sending the same signal along wires, without the need for taut pathways run over pulleys, conveys some safety advantage. But there is far more to the system than a different method of sending instructions. The use of electronic signals allows for computers to be introduced as part of the system, so that the input from the pilot can be processed and refined before being sent

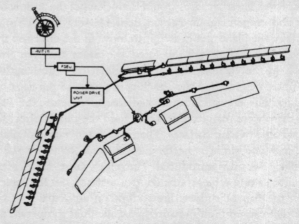

Signals from the pilot's control column can be adapted and transformed by computers before they trigger hydraulic movement of the control services

to the wing or tail, and the designers can also build in a flow of information in the opposite direction, from the surfaces themselves to the pilot.

The distribution of weight in conventional airplane design evolved to make the plane self-stabilizing in uneven airflow, so that it tended to settle back into a neutral position when tipped off balance. With fly-by-wire, which involves a sophisticated, computerized monitoring of every tiny movement of the plane, corrective movements can be automatically fed to the control surfaces moment by moment, leading to an equally stable plane but a lighter one.

Boeing had taken a tentative step in introducing fly-by-wire on some planes before the 777, but decided in the mid-1980s to take the plunge and apply the system to all the controls, as McWha explained:

> There are several advantages. We improve the airplane handling and we can add protection functions which improve the safety of the airplane. Also, once we are committed to fly-by-wire, we can take the opportunity to save a lot of weight in the airplane. In the older airplanes the wing had to be designed to withstand very strong gusts, and that resulted in quite heavy wings. In the newer airplanes we're able to take advantage of the system to make the gust seem smaller, and therefore we're able to reduce the wing weight by around 2,000 lb, which is considerable. We've also been able to take further advantage of the system in reducing the size of the horizontal stabilizer and the vertical tail. By moving the wing further forward it allows us to reduce the size of the tail also, and we save another 1,000 or 1,500 lb there. And all that translates into better performance from an operational point of view.

John Cashman, Boeing's chief test pilot on the 777, was instrumental right from the beginning in making sure that the fly-by-wire system reflected the views of pilots rather than relying on engineers -- even engineers as good at their job as McWha:

> You always have a certain level of suspicion when engineering tells you something. That's part of test pilot's self preservation, and it doesn't mean that you ignore what they tell you -- they're a great aid in telling you what to look for. But you're really looking closely

for the one unexpected event, or the anomalous behaviour that may in fact be more important than anything they warned you about. And that's always there, and that's really part of test work, whether you're a pilot or an engineer.

Cashman, unsurprisingly, was a supporter of the principle that let the pilot make the final decision, rather than the fly-by-wire computers:

From a safety standpoint, in our view one of the things that we do in the basic design is the pilot always has the ultimate authority of control. There's no computer on the airplane that he cannot override or turn off if the ultimate comes. In terms of any of our features, we don't inhibit that totally. We make it difficult, but if something in the box should behave inappropriately the pilot can say, 'This is wrong', and he can override it. That's a fundamental difference in philosophy that we have versus some of the competition.

Airbus were the true pioneers of fly-by-wire, introducing it into their A320 aircraft in 1988. An article in *Scientific American* explained some of the nuances of this control system, and of its reception by pilots:

In 1988 the introduction of the Airbus A320 took aircraft automation another step further. In some respects, the flight-control computers on this highly sophisticated aircraft tell the pilot how to fly the airplane. When a pilot pushes the A320's control stick to either side, the computers let the plane bank left or right, but only so far. In effect, the software spins an electronic cocoon that stops the aircraft from exceeding its structural limitations. 'This feature of the A320 sticks in the craw of most pilots,' says Samuel Don Smith, a captain on Boeing 737s for Delta Airlines. Smith, who is a member of the human-performance committee of the Air Line Pilots Association, the main pilots' union in the U.S., believes that a flight crew should be able to take any action, even stressing a plane beyond its tolerances, if it is headed toward a mountain or another aircraft. Airframe manufacturers, however, argue that the discomfort many pilots feel toward their electronic copilots is outweighed by a huge dividend in safety. Some of Boeing's newest and most automated airliners, the 757 and 767, have had one accident in nearly four million flights combined, compared with one for about every 200,000 flights for the Boeing 707, a 1950s airplane. But even as they applaud the remarkable mechanical reliability of the modern jet airliner, the entire aviation community has begun to worry about what flying a plane that flies itself does to professionals who are proud of their self-control in the most trying situations. 'I'm concerned that we may automate so fully that there's little or nothing left for the cabin crew to do,' says James B. Busey, administrator of the Federal Aviation Administration (FAA). Indeed, there does seem to be some justification for this concern. Last year, Airbus took the unusual step of issuing a notice warning pilots against overconfidence in flying its newest airplane, the A320. 'We got the idea that some crews felt they had God on their shoulders in flying the aircraft,' says Bernard Ziegler, Airbus's senior vice-president of engineering and a son of one of the company's founders. 'They do not. What we've built is an aircraft that is very easy to fly. But the laws of physics still apply. If you don't have enough energy to fly over an obstacle, you will hit that obstacle.' That was, unfortunately, exactly what happened to an A320 operated by Indian Airlines on February 14, 1990, when it made what is known euphemistically as a controlled flight into terrain. The crash, in which 92 people were killed, happened during a landing approach with the engines at idle, a setting for the plane's automatic throttle that is used at higher altitudes for making a descent but is never supposed to be engaged on landing. The accident followed by nearly two years another low-speed, low-altitude accident at a French airshow in which three people died. Following the Indian crash, Airbus changed software in the automatic throttle to prevent the plane from falling below a minimum authorized speed.[1,2]

[1] Gary Stix, *Scientific American*, July 1991

[2] The results of a recent NASSA Report entitled 'Pilots(sic) opinions on High Level Flight Deck Automation issues: Toward the Development of a Design Philosophy' were that A320 pilots in fact prefer hard limits for envelope protection

It is difficult to overstate the degree to which the 777 challenged the engineers who were responsible for designing the fly-by-wire system and its associated software. It was to generate the need for millions of lines of specially written software, all of which had to be tested to be bug-free, and the Systems team on the 777 was the one that was most often behind its targets as the plane moved inexorably down the assembly line towards first flight.

But this was one area where things just had to take as long as they took to design, test and finalize. As in other aspects of the plane, the Boeing engineering made great use of 'lessons learned' from the past. Walt Gillette was chief engineer in charge of Systems during the most intensive phase of the development of the fly-by-wire system. He describes one 'lesson learned' that is incorporated in the 777's control systems:

> A number of years ago there was a four-engined commercial airplane that was going down the runway for take-off and at the moment the flight crew pulled back on the column and the elevator in the back of the airplane moved up, so the airplane would take off, a very small rock was kicked up by the tyres and it happened to lodge in a certain part of the actuator back on the tail and jammed it. So the tail was in the nose-up direction, the flight crew pushed on the control column, and they couldn't overcome the rock, and the airplane stalled and crashed. The lesson learned from that is there's a clutch now between the two control columns, and the two tails are separate, so if the same thing happened again the pilot not flying could push on his control column and break the two apart – de-clutch it – and he then has enough authority to fly the airplane on his side. Now when we went to the 777 with fly-by-wire, we could have said, 'It may be difficult to put that clutch in between the two sides', but that is the lesson learned and it must not be forgotten.

But in addition to things that might happen outside his control, there is also the possibility that the pilot might actually introduce problems into a new aircraft – a possibility that Boeing was aware of when they first contemplated the change. As Jim McWha put it:

There's a sense of apprehension any time you change technology, and particularly when you switch from mechanical, which is visible, to electrical, which is not. So it's a kind of a paradigm shift. We've been challenged obviously to understand very clearly what all of the requirements of the system are, and to some extent we've taken a conservative approach to make the airplane fly like a conventional airplane from a pilot's point of view.

'Making the plane fly like a conventional airplane' is an intriguing process that effectively carries out a con trick on the pilot. Some of the computer software in the fly-by-wire system is designed to give the pilot the feel he would get from flying a plane with an older control system. One simple example is that the joystick on a conventional cable-controlled plane puts up some resistance as the pilot pulls it back or pushes it forwards. When there was a direct link between the joystick and the flap, say, that resistance would come from the resistance of the flap itself tugging against the cable. Clearly, if the signal is conveyed electrically, by a sensor under the joystick detecting how much the pilot moves it, there need be no feedback at all from the flap itself. In fact, as we've seen, the joystick itself is not really necessary, and could have been replaced by a much smaller control lever. But the designers of the 777 fly-by-wire system wanted pilots to feel at home, and they built artificial feedback into the system that gave useful information to the pilot about how far he had pulled the lever.

The con trick was carried further in part of the system that took account of where the centre of gravity was in the plane. Depending on the loading of the plane – how many passengers, how much cargo, how much fuel, and where they are all located – the position of the centre of gravity of a plane can vary in its distance from the front or the back. In a traditionally controlled plane, the pilot has to take account of this in the way he flies the plane. If the weight is towards the front, pulling the centre of gravity with it, the pilot will have to keep the control surfaces in a position that keeps the nose up. With the fly-by-wire software, many of these corrections and additions can be added to the pilot's basic messages as they travel from the joystick or pedals through the flight computers on their way to the wings or tail.

Taken to its limits, fly-by-wire could presumably be made to fly the entire plane from take-off to landing with little or no human intervention. But the 777 system fell far short of that – deliberately. The Boeing pilots who worked on the system tried very hard not to turn the 777 into a plane that is flown by *reading* things rather than feeling them. Most commercial pilots have spent all their flying life in planes in which forces felt through the hands and body combine with sights and sounds to give continual feedback on how things are going. If exploited to the maximum, fly-by-wire could replace all of those physiological cues by a series of figures and diagrams on a very stylish set of video screens. Boeing, advised by Cashman and his colleagues, stopped short of that and made sure that pilots were still regularly required to use the seat of their pants as an aid to flying.

There was an almost religious fervour about the way the system's designers left a degree of freedom for the pilot in the system, so that he still retained some autonomy in flying the plane. There were, for example, protection systems which tried to prevent the pilot putting the plane into an attitude where the airflow around the wings was disrupted and no longer supported the wings, or where the plane

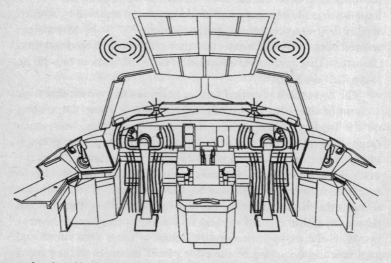

If a plane like the 777 were in danger of stalling – travelling too slowly to generate lift – the control columns would vibrate vigorously to warn the pilot

went at too high a speed for safety. Aircraft have a device called a stick shaker that vibrates the control column and sounds an audible warning when the pilot is in danger of getting into a stall. In the older planes, this couldn't actually prevent him from continuing to fly the plane to oblivion if he chose. The 777 designers had the possibility with fly-by-wire of making this part of the system prevent stalls absolutely, by taking over the control of the plane from the pilot. But this was not done. 'In an emergency situation,' said McWha, 'if the pilot feels like it's necessary to go beyond the program limits the ability is there for him to exert quite a bit of extra force and overcome the built-in protection.'

To a passenger this may seem an unusually liberal approach, particularly in a world where a pilot's sixteen-year-old son can be allowed to sit at the controls and switch off the autopilot, as happened in an Aeroflot Airbus in March 1994, killing seventy-five people. But there are also passengers who are fearful of handing control over entirely to computers, and they may feel more comfortable with a plane, like the 777, that has a human being making the final decisions.

During 1992 Boeing were constructing a building which would be dedicated to the task of testing the fly-by-wire system. Part of the building, called the Systems Integration Laboratory, would contain many computers, some of them prototypes of the flight computers that would run fly-by-wire. Other computers would feed data into the flight computers to simulate the sort of information that would be coming from many different areas of the plane, including the flight surfaces, but also simulating signals from temperature and pressure sensors on the surface of the plane, air-speed and attitude indicators, and other sources of information that would be integrated by the computers continuously during a typical flight. On the ground floor of the building was a laboratory to test the flight-control system. It was called the Iron Bird, and would consist of all the main flight-control surfaces – flaps, spoilers, flaperons, stabilizers and rudder – connected via the fly-by-wire computers to a 777 cockpit with joystick and pedals along with the other knobs, buttons, levers and glowing screens that would be in the real thing. When this was up and running it would be used to test the software that helped the pilot fly the plane.

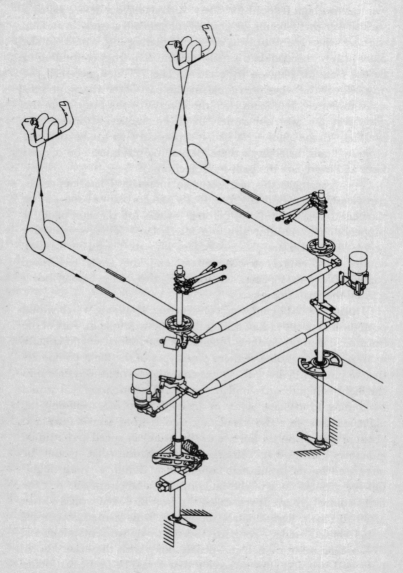

Movements of Control Column are transmitted to computers (but the system includes pulley and cable as backup)

When the pilot moves one of the control levers, such as the column, the following series of events happens:

● Under the floor of the cockpit and attached to the column there are three transducers – movement detectors. As the column moves, any one of these is able to detect the movement and turn it into what's called an analogue signal – an electrical signal that varies continuously, increasing as the column moves one way, decreasing as it moves the other. Since there are two identically moving columns, for the pilot and copilot, there are effectively six movement detectors, of which only one is needed to fly the plane.

● The signal from the column goes by wire to four boxes called ACE – actuator control electronics – which carry out an identical conversion on the signal to turn it from analogue to digital. There are *four* boxes so as to introduce an element of redundancy into this stage in the system – only one is necessary, but with four the system is robust enough to withstand the failure of one or more of them. The conversion from analogue to digital is purely because the primary flight computer, the one that does all the thinking, uses digital signals for all its processing. There is nothing mysterious about the conversion – it's rather like describing the profile of a mountain, an analogue signal, by a regular series of altitudes, from the foothills, up the main slopes, over the peak and down the other side. The list of numbers would allow you to reconstruct a pretty good profile of the mountain if you reinterpreted them as heights above a line.

● Once the movement of the column has been translated into numbers, these are fed into three identical computers called PFCs, or primary flight computers. Each of these computers has three subunits which act independently on the signal from the column, following exactly the same computer program, so if all goes well there will be nine identical outputs whose content consists of instructions to be sent eventually to the control surfaces. If all doesn't go well, and one of the computers disagrees with another in the same PFC, it will be voted down by the other two. If one of the PFCs disagrees with the other two, it too will be taken out of the system and the remaining computers will be used to fly the plane. But if they all agree, as they usually will, their responses will be in digital form which will have to be reconverted to analogue signals in the ACE. At this point, there will be two signals from the PFC. One of these is to be sent to the actuator that moves the control surface, telling it to move exactly as the pilot intended, or to move in a different way if the computer knows something the pilot doesn't. The other is to be sent back to the column to provide the pilot with the sort of feedback he's used to getting when he pushes on a conventional column.

At each stage in this process the PFC can – and usually will – change the signals according to the circumstances the plane finds itself in. If the pilot moves the control column in such a way that the plane might be heading for a stall, the PFC will send feedback signals that produce a force in the column that pushes against the pilot's attempts. If the PFC gets a message that the plane is flying through turbulence and is being made to change its pitch by the turbulent air, it may add something to the signal from the column to adjust for that change.

The design of the fly-by-wire system is a prime example of the 'hiding-to-nothing' principle that seems to happen quite often in plane-making. The system designed by Boeing had so many safeguards and backups that the layman might become suspicious that Boeing was not terribly confident in the reliability of the individual components. There are, for example, effectively *nine* computers, any one of which could be used to run the fly-by-wire system. On the other hand, if Boeing had just installed one computer to do the job, even if it had believed it was the best and most reliable computer in the world, nobody would believe that there wasn't some failure mode that might have gone undetected. Throughout the length of the plane, in the numbers of computers, the position of wires, the duplication of the actuators that move the surfaces and even – like a vestigial appendix – in the existence of some very basic old-style cabling, the engineers did everything they could think of to maximize the chances of the system working flawlessly throughout the lifetime of the plane. Once again it was an illustration of how the hazardous situations that engineers can imagine are far worse than the run-of-the-mill nightmares that most passengers have. In the case of two engines failing (once in 50,000 years), for example, although these normally generate the electrical power to run all the electronic equipment, while the pilot was addressing the problem of what to do about propelling the plane forwards he would have the comfort of knowing that his fly-by-wire system could be powered by the APU in the tail; and if that wasn't an option there was battery backup as well.

But when engineers devised the most unlikely multiple backup systems for the 777, they didn't always believe they were necessary. The rudimentary cable system that was left in the 777 was more for the leadership of the Boeing Company than because of any likelihood it would ever be used, and privately engineers expressed the belief that it would not be installed in future planes once the 777 had been in service for a few years.

There was a team of test pilots at Boeing who had helped develop the fly-by-wire system from the days before the 777 even had a number. As the project developed they stayed with the plane and would fly the first models to come off the assembly line. But years before there was a 777 to fly they helped to define and test the details of the system by putting in months of flying on other Boeing aircraft.

If you had wanted to cast an actor as a typical confidence-inspiring airline pilot you would have picked John Cashman out of the actors' directory, *Spotlight*, without any hesitation. He is a stocky, slightly greying figure with a walk that borders on a swagger, and he exudes a sense of being in control that would calm any passenger in a storm. In fact this characteristic is somewhat wasted as a test pilot, since few of his flights have passengers, apart from a team of engineers and computer specialists. Cashman seems always cheerful and has a good wit. Lining up at the counter in one of the many Boeing cafeterias, he said, 'We call this the food simulator.'

On Thursday 18 June 1992, Cashman and his copilot Frank Santoni were due to spend the morning in a specially adapted 757 plane, a smaller twin-engined aircraft than the 767 or the 777 but still a sizeable piece of engineering. It had been leased from Ansett Airlines in Australia specially to test some of the flight-control software. Today's test would compare several alternative ways of making a transition from the final approach of the aircraft to the actual position for landing – one of many 'control laws' as they are called – as the plane goes into a position known as the 'flare', where the nose tilts up level with the horizon and the plane 'drops' on to the runway.

The 757 had been adapted to fly in two modes – conventional and fly-by-wire. At 7 a.m. the two pilots assembled in one of the sophisticated videoconferencing rooms Boeing had built to make meetings easier between Boeing Field, where the 757 was based, and Renton, Everett and Boeing plants even further away. The room had a series of tiered levels of desktops, each with switchable microphones, facing six video monitors. This morning a dozen or so people arrived in person, while two slid into place on the monitor screen from a similar room in Renton. This remote attendance might seem unnecessarily extravagant, or perhaps lazy, since Renton is about fifteen minutes' drive from Boeing Field.

There were clocks on the wall showing the time in some of the other places that could hook up to the teleconference, and one labelled 'Zulu', the aviator's name for Greenwich Mean Time. Below these clocks, and looking a little like an afterthought, was another clock. On its face was the 757 test-plane team's sticker and a normal pair of hands. But closer inspection showed that every figure on the dial was an '8'. Bernie Green, the test scheduler, explained that this was a gift to the test team from the 757 maintenance engineers, who were continually being told by the team that they must have the plane ready to fly by eight o'clock. 'This way', the maintenance people said, 'we will always be on time.'

The meeting started with a run-down of the list of tasks for the day. The team would be flying for about four hours, over in western Washington state, at an airfield called Moses Lake. They planned to make twenty-five or thirty landings, testing different software programs and deciding which ones felt best. They would be taking a dozen engineers in the plane, each sitting behind a computer and monitoring the plane's performance and the operation of the software.

After running through the order of the tasks – which landings would use which software, what angle of flap the pilot would be required to select, and so on – the flight controller cleared the team to set for off the plane. It was a beautiful day, with clear blue skies and a light breeze. The 757 stood on the tarmac, unpainted, and reflected the sun blindingly off its silver fuselage. Cashman described from a pilot's perspective the purpose of the day's tests:

When you come down to land, the natural characteristics of
approaching the ground in an airplane are not there in a fly-by-
wire plane because the airplane doesn't know the ground is there.
In a conventional vehicle the fact that the wing is developing lift in
approaching the ground will cause the airplane to pitch down. The
pilot in a landing is anticipating that, and he pulls back to keep the
plane from going nose down into the ground. Then he pulls
harder to make a smooth landing. Now when that characteristic is
not there, in a fly-by-wire plane, the way the pilot lands would be
different. But we really want to keep the airplane flying just like
he's always flown it: we don't want him to have to learn new
techniques. So we have in our control law within the computer the
knowledge that the airplane is approaching the ground. And it
builds into the control of what he's doing with the elevator the
same characteristic that he would feel due to what we call ground
effect – the effect of the ground on the lift of the wing.

We're trying to keep the airplane so the pilot when he climbs
into it doesn't have to learn anything new. So today we're going to
choose one of these three flare laws to implement in our 777. So
far they all look pretty good. But this is something we've looked at
a lot, and I think we're very close to making a decision on it.

Four hours after flying east from Boeing Field, the 777 glinted in
the sun as it returned over Mount Rainier, the extinct volcano fifty
miles to the south of Seattle. They had completed their programme
of landings for the day and were ready to finalize just one small
element of the fly-by-wire software.

Regularly over the next couple of months the 757 set off to test
and refine the control laws. Although the Boeing test pilots did
much of the flying, they also brought on board other Boeing pilots
and some airline pilots – forty-six in all – to give their feedback on
how the plane would feel.

Cashman was pleased with the way the programme had gone:

We flew about 250-plus hours and I think somewhere in the
neighbourhood of 450 to 500 landings – it depends how many
times you hit the ground whether you call it a landing or not. We
call a landing one out of each approach. But we actually did some

where we touched down, lifted off, and touched down three or four times. We got the opinions of a lot of pilots, and from our standpoint we felt we had made some very good choices in our features that we offered, but we were very encouraged by the airline people themselves on how enthusiastic they were for the airplane.

TEN

First Assembly

On 31 August 1992, Phil Condit, general manager of the 777 team, was promoted. Alan Mulally heard the news when he was called in by his bosses and told that Condit was going to be president of the Boeing Company. Mulally reacted in his usual cheerful way:

> I was really excited that Phil was going to be the president, and I leapt to my feet, reached across the table, grabbed his hand, and said, 'Congratulations, Phil!' Leaped across the table the other way to Dean Thornton, who now works for Phil, who Phil used to work for, and shook his hand and said, 'Congratulations, Dean – great choice in picking your boss!' Then I sat down to get ready to leave, thinking all the time that it was really terrific that they would take the time in their busy day to let me know that my boss had been promoted. And with that they said, '. . . and Alan, we would like you to manage and continue to lead the 777 programme.' And my reaction was: 'What? I'm real busy.' And they said, 'Well, we hope you're not displeased.' And I said, 'I think I'm not displeased, but I'll have to think about this a little bit. But I'm humbled and I feel very gratified that you have the confidence in asking me to do it.' And that's how the conversation went.

As a man for whom 'leadership' is a quality to be rewarded in others, Mulally was clearly cut out for his new role. If it was possible for him to work harder than he had been doing, he now did so, taking on many of the broader functions of running the team and passing on the job of director of engineering to Ron Ostrowski, a quieter, more measured individual. If there was a good time for such a change in the programme management, it was probably then, with the design mostly completed and the increasing bustle on the floor of the main assembly building at Everett showing that assembly of the plane was about to begin.

Now that he was general manager, Mulally would get more involved in the sales and promotion side of things. In October there was a visit to Renton by Lord King, of British Airways, and Mulally showed him round the interior mock-up of the plane that King's airline had already committed to purchase. The mock-up was a full-scale interior of the 777, with a fuselage made of plywood and plastic, complete with overhead bins and three classes of seats, including some ten-abreast rows in the Economy section. As King and his party, including British MP Tony Banks, moved up the plane, from First Class to Business Class and then towards Economy, Mulally would take King by the shoulders or the arm, push him into a seat, swing him around to look at some detail he was particularly proud of, and generally delight in the presence of a real English lord. When they reached the Economy cabin, King looked around at the serried rows of seats and said, with no trace of irony, 'Ah, this is where the passengers sit.'

At the end of the mock-up, in a separate section, was an area known informally as the Dirty Pool. Boeing has had 'Dirty Pools' for some time, ever since it was trying to sell the 737 in competition with the BAC1-11 and the DC-9. Here customers could see in graphic detail how much better the Boeing cross-section was than any of its rivals. Mulally darted around, bending under the lower bins of the MD-11 and the A340 and then standing at his full height to show how much roomier the 777 would be. He showed Lord King into a seat and sat next to him to demonstrate how much more vertical the 777 side wall would be than the more curved walls of the rivals.

The mock-up was a very important sales tool. From the earliest discussions with the Gang of Eight, Boeing had given a lot of attention to the interior of the plane, building in flexibility in the position of the galleys, a wide choice of seating configurations and the overhead bins. In spite of the immense amount of engineering innovation that was going into such characteristics as the wings, the new materials and the fly-by-wire system, when it came down to it it was bottoms on seats that the airlines were most interested in – and preferably bottoms whose owners would be willing, unlike Brian Neal, chief engineer, Propulsion Division, to pay $3,000 a time. But closely behind bottoms came bins.

Mike Nichols was a design engineer who helped to design the bins, of which everyone was very proud. The bin team had a mock-up of their own, and Nichols would put on a *tour de force* for visitors which revealed that overhead bins had a terminology and a technology of their own. It would astonish the visitor to learn how much there was to say about an apparently simple object like an overhead bin, but, despite being one of the fastest talkers in the Boeing Company, Nichols was able to spend a good fifteen minutes revealing the ins and outs of the 777 bin – with a choice of words which showed American technospeak at its finest:

> We want to give the customer what he asked for, and that is volume – it's as simple as that. Give him as much volume as possible and give him operating forces that he can easily manage. That was our biggest challenge, and you'll see in our bin design the size of it is more than adequate. I think what we need to start with is the contour of the bin. A lot of designs have a shelf bin. This particular bin is a pivot type. And what it affords us is the kind of headroom where a person can walk comfortably under the end of the bin yet when it rotates down it gives us the kind of volume that we're looking for. Manufacturability as well as customer requirements are very important to us. We have changed our basic pivot design in several fashions. One of the most obvious customer-service-orientated changes was to get this snubber [here Nichols reaches up around the back of the bin, which, in the mock-up, is exposed] – this mechanism controls the rate of the bin – in a position where the customer, in the event that it fails, can get in and service that part. And those things are good for a hundred thousand cycles, but over the life of an aircraft those will wear and need to be replaced. Another thing we've incorporated in this bin is an end-frame casting unlike any other design we've had in the past. And this is a real manufacturability issue. It controls several key interfaces on the stow-bin design. It controls the latch strike point. It controls the pivot point. It controls an inboard track which offers us the opportunity to hang video across

the aisle. It also gives us overhead support for partitions if one were mounted.

So the end frame gives us a lot of opportunity to control interface which in the past we haven't had, and again that gets to our manufacturability issue: being able to create a product – and let's face it, it's assembly line in nature. We're spitting them out three, four hundred a week. So we need to be able to build the things very rapidly. Also, we've incorporated a lower outboard fitting that shares load, which we've never had in the past. This lower outboard fitting has a common tie rod, and we physically splice two bins together here. But the most important feature in terms of flexibility, which for the customer is their key interest, is being able to convert the configuration as rapidly as possible. And in order to do that we've incorporated an overhead rail which is tough to see but what it is is a fore-and-aft member that has interface holes or interface pick-up points for the stow bins. We have three sizes of bins, and those bins can be shuffled to any arrangement to sneak up to outboard monuments. (We call 'monuments' lavs, closets, galleys etc.) But, more importantly, in the past each one of those monuments was very static and had to be tied straight back to structure. In this design this fore-and-aft member allow that unit to be translated fore and aft in the cabin on one-inch centres anywhere in the airplane in prescribed flex zones that allow load-path capability in the overhead rail. So there's a lot of neat things on this bin design, and we've used benchmarking in designing this. We've looked, and we believe we have incorporated the best things in all the previous bin packages into this design.

We have had article-retention problems in the past, where the binned luggage tends to shuffle. The bin will open up and if you're not paying attention – you're in a hurry to walk out – they will come rolling out to you. We believe we've solved that by allowing a wide access to the bin but yet keep the angle of attack in such a fashion that articles, though they become dislodged, don't tend to fall out on us.

Nichols points to a small circular mirror on the back wall of one of the bins:

That mirror is our response to some of our customers who really feel the bins may be a bit too high. And these are quite a distance off the floor in terms of a pivot bin. And some of our passengers aren't as tall as myself. The problem is for both the passengers and the stewardesses to really see into the stow bin. So we've been asked to look at a concept. This is just that – a concept of a mirror in the stow bin which allows quick and ready access or vision into the back part of the bin to make sure it's completely empty and nothing's left behind.

Unusually, this concept is not something carefully machined in one of the Boeing factories:

No, this precision device I picked up at the drug store for about 98 cents, but in fact it works. I wish we could get away with it, but we've been asked – and we're listening to our customer – our customer asked us to put it all the way across so I can walk up and down the aisle and quickly glance. Here I kind of have to aim and look at that mirror. So they've asked for a full-length mirror so that she can or he can just rapidly go down the aisle and ensure that the bins are empty. This is an issue with our customers – more so with our Pacific Rim customers than, for instance, European customers and the American carriers . . .

It takes a moment to realize that the term 'Pacific Rim' in this case is more a physical description than a geographical one – it is a polite way of referring to the shortness of stature of people from the Far East. And in fact, once it's pointed out, it does seem that these bins are quite difficult to reach for people under five feet. As a tacit acknowledgement of this, there's a small step-like surface on the side of each aisle seat.

It's the ergonomics of the latch, and some of them feel that it's a bit too high. Now on a pivot bin it must be this high to reach the latch. But once it opens then the access to the bin is more than acceptable and more than appropriate in terms of a shelf bin – where the shelf bin remains static. You hit a latch that's quite low and the door swings up. And now I'm reaching up here to grab the door. So with the latch handle, though our customers have expressed some concern, they've all been through the mock-up and they understand our design, and to physically move it, that's something that would demand a lot of effort. And believe me we can do anything but we've planted our stake in the ground and believe ergonomically and demographically this is the right latch for a spectrum of population.

In spite of the depth and complexity of bin-related issues, Nichols and his colleagues have responsibility for many other aspects of the interior of the plane. He is equally eloquent, for example, about a phenomenon the engineers call 'rain on the plane', familiar to many passengers who find a steady stream of water dripping on to their filet mignon and wonder for a fleeting moment whether there has been some breach of the fuselage at 35,000 feet allowing rain to penetrate the aircraft. It's actually water vapour that has condensed out of the cabin air on contact with the cold skin of the plane. Nichols and his colleagues have developed a small green doughnut that absorbs the moisture at intervals along the plane and prevents such internal showers.

If you were surprised at the detailed design attention that a stow bin requires, you'd be even more astonished to meet Grace Chan, a slim young interior designer who has spent many woman-hours designing a coffee-cup-holder for the cockpit. She also played a major role in the interior design of the rest of the cockpit, choosing the two-tone brown scheme because surveys had shown that it didn't show the dirt. The design team carried out some mild industrial espionage by getting into Airbus and McDonnell Douglas cockpits and disassembling them in search of good ideas to adopt or bad ones to avoid. Pen-holders (replacing the conventional spring fitting with more upmarket leather), headphone clips, glare shields – everything required drawings and assembly instructions and some-one has to prepare those, right down to a small ball that hangs on a thread in front of the pilot. This turns out to be an eye reference point so all pilots sit with their eyes at the same level, allowing them to make the same judgements from plane to plane about distance from the ground, height of the horizon and so on. Shorter – Pacific Rim? – pilots can adjust the height of the seat until the ball hits them between the eyes. To avoid constant irritation for ten hours, the ball can then be hung up on a specially designed hook.

But Grace Chan's pride is the coffee-cup-holder, born of extensive market research and experimentation.

> There was a big demand from pilots for better cup-holders. Not all coffee-cup-holders hold every cup that there is. It's almost impossible to design a coffee-cup-holder for all the cups there are in the world, but we tried to collect all the cups we could from all the airlines – and not only cups, but pop cans, styrofoam cups: almost all the cups that we would think an individual would use – and then we tried to design an ideal holder for all those cups. It was hard, because everybody has their own idea how a coffee-cup-holder should look, and what different types of cups it should hold. We came up with concepts first in a drawing and then we made them out of cardboard, and after we finished the two designs we liked the best we started casting them. And then we refined them, so what you have in the flight deck right now is the refined version. And what's also nice, we came up with the idea that it could be removable because we know that over time the beverages would spill and it would stay sticky. We thought maybe some cups may have handles that may not fit, so we started to cut a groove in one of the prototypes. Now the groove takes the shape of the handle, so one design works much better than the other. We also had to take into consideration the height of the handles, just to make sure that it does fit into the holder itself. It was a team effort. If it wasn't for our engineers working with us – human factors people, draughtspeople, technical people – it wouldn't have worked. It was the team effort.

The efforts of Chan and her staff in designing the stylish 777 cockpit won them an industrial-design excellence award for commercial transportation.

By mid-December 1992 the ASAT tool was nearing completion. Originally the engineers had intended to start the first automated assembly of the wing spars before the end of the year, but then they faced some problems. As they tried to start the process of drilling holes in the front spar, the drilling head didn't work. Boeing got a manufacturer's representative on to the site and the machine then started drilling holes in the wrong place in the metal samples the engineers had put in the machine. 'Everybody that knows anything about drilling holes was there,' says Mulally. 'For a few days we had one of those normal development panics.'

Over the Christmas period, Mulally was in his office at seven o'clock in the morning on all days but the two he spent at home with his family. It was a quiet time in the gleaming new 777 office buildings in Everett, partly because it was Christmas and partly because some of the 777 engineering staff had not yet moved up from Renton. As Mulally sat in his vice-presidential office in the executive suite one January morning, it was still dark outside and he thought back over the the previous few days:

> It was kind of a nice time. It was almost like a time to reflect on the past year and think about the priorities for '93. I ended up walking around a lot and talking. We had quite a few people working – especially in engineering and in operations and planning and tooling, where they were supporting the first parts of assembly – so I talked to quite a few of the structures engineers and the planners and the toolers associated with structure. And I talked quite a bit with the systems engineers who are also thinking ahead to planning the flight tests, just to get a feeling for how they saw it, what their problems were and challenges and stuff.

But the immediate priorities for 1993 were overshadowed by the longer-term problems that the Boeing Company faced at the beginning of the year:

SEATTLE (AP) – January 4th, 1993 – The Boeing Co. said today it will drastically reduce production and cut employment by a 'significant' amount because many airline customers are having financial problems. The cutbacks were announced as Boeing, the biggest maker of commercial aircraft, reported earnings tumbled in 1992 to a third of what the company earned the year before. The company said output of model 737 jetliners will decrease from 14 a month to 10 a month in October, a drop of nearly 30 percent; 747 jumbo jet production will go from five a month to three in the second quarter of 1994, a 40 percent cutback. In addition, the company said it will accelerate a previous plan to reduce production of 757 and 767 planes. The company said development of its new 777 jetliner is on schedule. The company attributed the cutbacks to 'the sustained financial problems of many of the world's airlines'. U.S. commercial carriers have lost billions of dollars in the past three years because of higher expenses, fewer travelers and the harmful financial impact of aggressive fare discounting. Three big carriers – TWA, Continental and American West – are reorganizing under bankruptcy protection. Three others – American, United and Northwest – recently disclosed plans to cut back on operations and employment. 'While we remain optimistic about the longer-term prospects for our business, the present reality is sobering,' Boeing Commercial Airplane Group President Dean Thornton said in a news release. Boeing had not determined how much of its work force would be cut, but said 'it is expected to be significant'.

Although Mulally was not directly concerned with the fortunes of the company as a whole – that was now Phil Condit's concern – he was clearly worried about the current state of affairs:

It's an interesting time. You're designing a new product which is not going to be delivered till 1995, so your fundamental thought has to be that things are going to get better. On one hand you feel excited that you're working on the right product that's going to be delivered at the right time, to satisfy the airlines, who think they need it. And then your other thought that follows that is: 'My gosh, it's really tough right now. I hope it turns out well. I hope the airlines do OK, so that the airlines will be there, and we'll be there, and it will all get better a few years from now.' But it's so important for us that we absolutely not let the current events affect our intensity on getting this programme done, because this is such a long-term business, and these projects are big and they're made for the future, that we can't let the anxiousness and the ambiguity of today's environment in any way slow us down.

We talk about it: we talk about it openly – we talk about every cancellation, about every airline that gets in trouble, every airline that has to go into bankruptcy, and what it means to Boeing – and we talk about what's happening to Airbus the same way. And it's OK, it's really important that we talk about it. And then we move on to what our real job is, and that is to stay focused on developing the airplane for the future. That's our strength: to keep going. But it is worrisome.

Although the first assembly was starting, there were still outstanding design targets to be met. The team staggered the design process so that the pieces that were needed first in the factory were designed first, along with the tools to make them. They had completely designed about 48 per cent of the plane, and the pressure was on to keep up with a pace of manufacture that would accelerate over the next year. The first major assemblies of components to be put together were the wings of the first plane. And on 4 January 1993 the first part of the first wing was fixed into the ASAT tool for the wagon train to set off.

In Building 40-04 at Everett, Sylvia Leferer, a buxom Hispanic woman in jeans and T-shirt and dangly gold earrings, picked up a tube of grey goop and fitted it into the end of a rubber tube carrying air under pressure. She then pressed a lever to allow air to push against the tube and squeeze out the goop in a steady stream, like icing a cake. Nothing happened.

So began the first assembly of the 777 left front wing spar, a milestone in the plane-making process. The rig of the ASAT tool was loaded with three pieces of aluminium – a web and two chords, each about ninety feet long – and the first task for the team was to join the two chords to the top and bottom edges of the web. Before this could happen, Sylvia had to spread a layer of sealant – the grey goop – all along the surfaces of the two chords that would be in contact with the web. The sealant would stay soft for thirty-six hours, forming a sandwich between the pieces of metal that would be joined together by hundreds of rivets. It would help to prevent corrosion by keeping the surfaces and rivet holes airtight and free from moisture.

The tiny hitch in the air line was fixed after a fashion, although

Sylvia found that she could spread the stuff just as easily by squeezing the tube by hand. She had been putting sealant on Boeing wing spars for twenty-four years having started with the 757 and the 767, and she managed to contain her excitement about today's events, although the 777 was a more crucial step in plane-making than either of those planes.

There was generally a muted air about the events around the ASAT tool. None of the VPs was around for the milestone, although a few senior managers dropped in from time to time to see how their particular aspect of the process was working. Even the FAA man waived his right to inspect the sealant layer before these first three pieces were pushed together. But it was an important first, for the tool and for the plane. Taking the process more slowly than the eventual production target of one spar every three days, within ten days there would exist a complex piece of wing that would help to provide a rigid framework over which sheet aluminium would be laid to provide the airfoil surface.

From 8 to 11 a.m. Sylvia spread the sealant, first squeezing a squiggly line of stuff along the surfaces and then rolling it smooth to the edges. After she had finished, a quality inspector came in and used a small metal gauge to make sure that the layer was the right thickness. Crouching like Groucho Marx, he walked along the rig keeping his eyes at the same level as the chord and occasionally pointed to an almost imperceptible patch of sealant for Sylvia to adjust. When he was satisfied, Sylvia walked along the rig unpeeling two long strips of masking tape from the top and bottom of each chord, put there to leave a clear area that would be filled by the spreading sealant as the pieces were pushed together.

The next stage in the process was for five men to push stanchions holding the chords in a coordinated move that brought the chords almost in contact with the web. It took about ten seconds and brought the three pieces to within half an inch of each other, at most points. But the accurately placed jaws of the tool that would grip the pieces in exactly the right position while the hole-drilling and riveting took place showed some kind of mispositioning. One of the chords was out of position at various points. Knots of men clustered around the points where the problem was apparent. Robert Roush, one of the managers, explained that one of the clamps that held the spars in position was in the wrong place and preventing one of the pieces from moving into its final position. It was a fiftieth of an inch out of position. One helpful supervisor standing watching the process asked tentatively whether it couldn't just be banged into place; he was told firmly by a colleague that the machine had a purpose-built lever to make the adjustment.

The phases in manufacturing the plane are difficult to grasp. Why, for example, was the wing-spar assembly so significant? Why wasn't the assembly of other parts of the plane, like the passenger doors, of which there were numbers lying around at the Mitsubishi plant in Japan, taken as equally important?

There's really a hierarchy involved: at one end the daily manufacture of thousands of separate components, some of which are made up of separate smaller elements, and at the other the final bringing together of a series of sub-assemblies, of which the wing spar would be part, to make a plane that would, a year from now, stand on its own three undercarriages and roll around in a confident and self-sufficient way.

That week Seattle was threatened with heavy snowstorms. But on Monday and Tuesday, as the wing-spar assembly continued, the snow could barely manage more than a light dusting from time to time. It was cold, 18°F or so, and the skies were clear. Unusually, Mount Rainier was visible on most days, with the strange property of looking at one moment nearby and at another far away in a manner that bore no relationship to true distance. Like the moon effect, where the moon low down on the horizon can look much larger than when it's up in the sky, the size of the extinct volcano varied with its surroundings, looking much smaller when seen rising out of the surrounding terrain than when glimpsed half concealed by a building.

At Frederickson, an hour's drive south of Seattle, the wing skin panels were being milled and shaped in a building a quarter of a mile from one end to the other. One end received half-inch-thick flat slices of aluminium, cut thicker and longer than necessary, which after three or four important processes would emerge at the other ends of the building curvaceous, delicate, tapering and smooth. If you were asked to imagine the size of the workforce needed to operate a factory which emitted a regular stream of ninety-foot wing

Right: Phil Condit, leader of the 777 team when the project began, became president of the Boeing Company in 1992.

Below left: Alan Mulally, 777 director of engineering, who succeeded Condit as team leader.

Below right: Gordon McKinzie, United Airlines representative on the 777 design team.

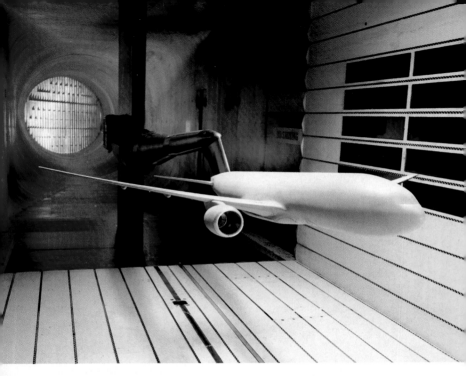

Wind tunnel tests at Farnborough and Seattle help to determine the best shape for the 777's extremely efficient wing.

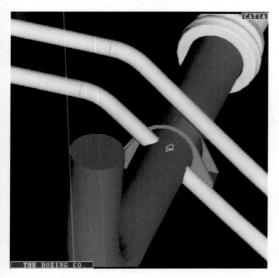

Left: The CATIA computer design process picked out potential interferences such as this situation where the white tube designed by one designer turned out to occupy the same space as another designer's larger purple tube. In previous planes this would not have been discovered until the parts reached the factory for assembly.

Above: The duct that failed. The clamp joining the vertical duct to the larger horizontal one failed on several occasions during test flights, leading to sudden decompression in the plane. Design engineer Neil McCluskey looks worried.

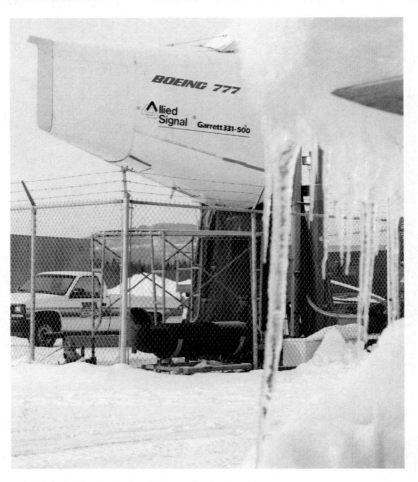

Fearing the worst. Every component of the plane, including the auxiliary power unit (above) and the passenger door (left), is put through the worst excesses of temperature it is likely to face, to ensure that the design is robust enough.

Right: Japanese companies manufactured about 20 per cent of the plane. Senior managers like Neil Standal made regular trips to monitor progress and take part in ceremonies.

Below: In the most active design phase, during 1992, dozens of senior project engineers met for many hours a week to monitor key characteristics of the evolving design, such as cost and weight.

Above: 777 pilots are trained in a fully movable flight deck simulator that reproduces the sights, sounds and forces of real flight.

Below: The interior of the 777 was designed in close collaboration with the airlines. It includes state-of-the-art overhead bins.

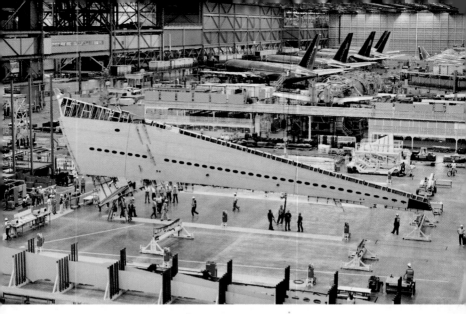

The birth and death of a wing. **Above**, the first wing emerges from the wing major tool. **Below**, the static test wing just before it snapped.

The Pratt & Witney engine emerges from the factory (above) to be tested in a Florida test facility (below) before being attached to the 777.

panels you might conservatively estimate a number in the hundreds. In fact on this January afternoon you could look around the Frederickson factory and glimpse only a handful of people. This huge building was working with perhaps a dozen workers. One would operate a milling machine, another would haul a wing panel suspended on rails into a paint shed, a third would cycle on a yellow Boeing bicycle down the aisle between two huge machines.

The first stage in the process was to grind metal away at various precise points on the panel, turning the dull, flat surface into a sparkling, flashing, iridescent layer of aluminium. The milling machine that did this was capable of reading the original CATIA design data and responding to instructions to abrade away forty-five thousandths of an inch here, cut out a rectangular hole there, create a taper somewhere else. It did this in a back-and-forth motion with a device that looked like the head of a large floor-polisher moving over the slab of aluminium until every part of the slab was accurately milled to ten thousandths of an inch in the shape determined by the designer six months before. The intricate patterns that spread over the finished panel reflected the conflicting demands of lightness and strength – at every point the skin had to be thick enough to bear its share of the maximum load that the plane would be expected to carry, plus a safety margin.

But the shaped panel that emerged was only the first stage. The panel was still essentially flat with indentations, but the final product would have to embody a gentle curve along its length, so that it looked like the subtlest of Ss, visible only when you looked directly along from one end to the other. The panel would be given this curve by a process called shot-peening.

The rounded end opposite the main face of some domestic hammers is called a ball-peen and is meant to be used for beating a piece of metal smooth and at the same time hardening its surface, although it must be a very small proportion of the owners of these hammers who ever indulge in a bit of peening or even know what the thing is for. The process also gives a measure of strength and of anticorrosion to a piece of metal, by crushing the crystals of metal together so that they are more tightly bonded and have fewer gaps for cracks to form. Shot-peening uses very small metal balls to achieve the same effect with a large panel of metal. After milling, the panel is moved into an enclosed chamber where hundreds of thousands of the metal balls are fired all over the surface at high speed, either by air or by small propulsive wheels. But the most extraordinary part of it is yet to come. In addition to treating the surface of the panel, the force of the shot actually shapes the metal, pushing some areas with more force than others so that the panel develops the twists and curves called for in the final design.

Next door to the wing-panel area, a new building with an area of 400,000 square feet was being constructed for the tailplane of the 777, the fixed vertical part of the tail that holds the rudder. On one side was an area of autoclaves for baking the parts of the tail, using the same technology the Australians were using for the rudder. On the other side was an area containing tools – huge frameworks – that would be used to hold and put together the various pieces of the tail. On a day when it was 18°F outside, these metal frameworks, designed with the exact measurements for the tail that was months away from being assembled in them, were being bathed in their own central heating. Hot air was needed to keep the steel jig at an even temperature of 70°F. Any change in temperature would soon lead to the jig, which had been fitted together very accurately using theodolites, becoming misaligned by many times the margin of error that was allowable for the tail.

The story of the rudder itself received a further twist about this time. On 6 January 1993 Mulally's aphorism number 17 – 'You're never done till you're done' – was borne out by the frustrating news of yet another hiccup in the saga of the rudder. One recent suggestion to solve the persistent flutter problem had been to shift the position of the hinge in the tailplane to make the rudder smaller and the tail larger. This might have cured the flutter, but it would have caused another problem: it would have raised the speed needed before the plane could take off with one engine shut down. This was a particular problem for the Japanese, whose generally short runways meant that the plane would have run out of runway in the worst case of engine failure before the plane had achieved the speed for a safe one-engine take-off.

So the never-ending story of the rudder continued not to end, when the Boeing engineers decided that the flutter problem had still not gone away, even though a day or two before an announcement had been made at a programme management meeting that at last the problem had been solved. Talking about it on the following day, Ron Ostrowski was both annoyed and composed. He knew the Australians would barely be able to contain themselves when they heard the news, and so fresh was the basic decision – to change the lengths of two pieces of the actuator mechanism – that he was unable to say what effect this would have on the rudders already piled up with the wrong design in Melbourne. All he knew was that the future rudders, in order to accommodate the change in the mechanism, would have to have a bulge on their surface near the hinge. This bulge would require a change in the template that was used to lay the carbon-composite layers, and would add a small amount of drag on the surface of the rudder. But this was the best solution so far, and Ostrowski's composure was due to his engineer's sense of inevitability. When you are working at the frontiers of technology and engineering, a problem like this is nobody's fault but nature's. This solution – or something with the same effect – *had* to be put into action if the plane was not to risk having a rudder that fluttered. And that was far more important than the ever more intense pressure it would now put on ASTA to stick to the deadlines.

In Melbourne, Pat Bogart summarized the situation: 'We've got a lot of major tools either completed or nearly there, and this last change is probably going to affect at least 65 per cent of our tooling programme – that's some 600 tools.'

Mike Voegtlin had appeared in Melbourne to soften the blow. As he arrived at the ASTA factory, fresh off the plane, he made a remark that emphasized the fast-changing nature of the rudder design process. 'I think we need to have a telephone conversation with Seattle,' he said to Al Tyler, 'to find out if there's anything that's changed between the time we left and the time we got down here.' At a meeting the following day with the glum-faced ASTA team, he tried to put a brave face on the situation:

> The good news is that our engineers have been working on this for about the last five weeks, and they now are confident that we have a good design fix. So John [a colleague of Voigtlin's] has brought the latest configuration, and in a minute he'll get up there and show you what the hardware's going to look like. Now the bad

news is, as you all know, we don't have a lot of time left. I've
looked at the schedule last night, and it tells me that we have about
five months and three weeks to complete this hardware, which is a
task that I would say under normal conditions would take about
eighteen months. So we have quite a challenge ahead of us.

After the meeting, at which ASTA's worst fears were confirmed,
Tyler described the team's feelings:

We all came back from the holidays and we thought we had a nice
smooth-sailing programme once again from the last change. They
told us, for instance, all these parts weren't changing – absolutely
not. And so we've rescheduled the programme based around that
particular assumption, and now we find out that some of those
major tools *are* changing. The addition of this fifth hinge, the
changing of those rear-spar mandrels and whatnot is a big impact.
It's going to be an interesting one to manage in the time-frame.

Tyler was in the traditional bind of someone who had pulled out
all the stops in the past and had succeeded against all odds – that was
then taken as the norm, and people's expectations were ratcheted to
a higher level:

We built the 757 rudder much, much quicker than Boeing ever
thought was possible. We've taken a few shocks in this particular
one, a little punch-drunk at certain times, but we keep coming
back. And we've been able so far to still live within their schedule.
But I think we're probably at the stage – although I said this last
time – where we've gone about as far as we can go.

Voegtlin agreed, and even he was concerned that ASTA might
not pull Boeing's chestnuts out of the fire this time. 'The problem is,
the magnitude of the workload is enormous. And the opportunity
for this to go wrong is great. And I am maybe a little more
pessimistic than what you might hear from ASTA.'

There was a lot at stake for ASTA. No one would really blame
them if they didn't complete the rudder by the due date, but if,
against all the odds, they succeeded, Tyler hoped it would lead to an

upwelling of gratitude on the part of Boeing that would ensure future business for the small company:

> Boeing has to have respect for a small company that has essentially – I don't want to say baled them out, necessarily, but certainly helped them out of a bind. I don't know that Boeing could get through one of these changes like this, this late in the game, in-house, on their programme.

By early 1993, two and a half thousand members of the 777 team had moved into the new offices at Everett, but the buildings were still two-thirds uninhabited. The cafeteria was blissfully empty and service was quick; car parks had many free spaces; and as you got out of the lift into the giant four-storey atrium you only occasionally glimpsed another human being gliding over the carpet at the other end of the building. The several silently moving escalators enhanced the impression of a department store that had very few customers, and the logistics of moving from one area to another were complicated by a bridge that was sometimes closed, floors that you were not allowed to exit on to, and a floor-numbering system of breathtaking inconvenience that should not be allowed to survive but, because of the nature of bureaucracy, was likely to do so for many months. As office floors were numbered from ground level but the numbers on the lifts started from the lowest parking level, if you pressed 4 in the lift, to visit somebody who told you his office was on the fourth floor, you would arrive on the second floor. This led to endless conversations of the type 'My office is on the third floor – that's the third *office* floor – you need to go to five in the lift.' And, when you'd had this sort of conversation, perversely the wrong number always stuck in your mind so that you ended up saying to yourself, 'Did she say she was on the third office floor or should I press 3 in the lift?'

The two buildings had different colour schemes to help people remember where they were. Building 40-88 had a blue speckled carpet, and 40-87 had red. Most people seemed to prefer the blue.

Between January and March 1993, the first wing spar that had been put in the ASAT tool acquired more of its eventual structure. It had been moved out of the tool to the other side of the building, where various projecting pieces were being lined up exactly in position to be bolted in place. Now it was in a clean room waiting to be thoroughly cleaned of all grease and oil and sealed by a similar process to the one that Sylvia Leferer carried out in January, squirting sealant into all crevices and dents. As well as preventing corrosion, this was designed to prepare the surface for its job as part of the wall of the fuel tanks. The hollow spaces within the wings are traditionally used to store jet fuel and are designed so that there is no separate fuel tank or inner lining that would just add weight.

Bill Richards, in charge of wing assembly, described an interesting discovery they had made after the first front spar had come out of the ASAT tool:

We found that the spar had expanded by 200 thousandths of an inch along its length. It's because when you put the fasteners in they're designed to expand the metal around the hole, and the molecules have to go somewhere so they push outwards. Because of the accuracy of the new tool we can now give instructions to Auburn, where they're made, to make them 200 thou smaller to start with. In the past this has presented a problem when we attach the skin, because that's made of much lighter material and it doesn't change size during fabrication, so we've had to use shims to make up for the difference. Now, with the next spars cut so that they'll expand to the correct size, there'll be no more shims.

Toward the end of the building was a jumble of pieces that had arrived by train from another Boeing plant, in Philadelphia. These were pre-assembled sections of skin with the familiar lines of rivets along the edges of the panels that you see as you look out of your plane window during flight. Everyone who passed ran a hand lovingly over the smooth surface or tapped to hear the firm hollow sound it made. Although they looked like painted aluminium, the skin panels were actually made of carbon-fibre composite and were backed up with some of the honeycomb that the Australians had also used for the rudder and elevators.

As Richards walked around the huge Wing Major Assembly Building he talked in a proprietorial way about 'his' pieces and what 'he' was going to do with them. 'That hanging crane up there will take my wing panel to the Gemcor fastening tool where I'll fasten the stringers.' And in fact the general absence of crowds in the building brought home the extent to which, if not assembled quite single-handed, major parts of this plane depend on only a handful of people to put them together: apart from the odd tool operator and an occasional walking figure glimpsed through the framework of a rig, there was no one to be seen. Even when the wings are being made at the rate of one every four days there will be two shifts of only thirty-five people each to make the huge and complex wing boxes, as they are called – spars, ribs and panels all fixed together.

Along one side of the building was a four-storey maroon framework where the wing boxes would be finally assembled. In early 1993 it was still under construction, but it was possible to imagine for the first time how huge just one wing of the plane would be. Some complex logistical planning would be needed to work out how to move the fully assembled wing box out of the framework and into the final-assembly building. Using a new four-hook crane, the wing, which is assembled horizontally, will have to be twisted into a vertical position before it can be extricated. Richards mused on what will happen with the next generation of even larger aircraft: 'Build 'em any bigger and technology says you won't be able to get 'em out of the damned tool.'

ELEVEN

The Bowing Company

While the first major assembly of the wing was taking place in Seattle, on the other side of the Pacific four large Japanese companies were getting to work on several other major parts of the 777. Mitsubishi, Kawasaki and Fuji, and a smaller company called Nippi, were contracted to make about 20 per cent of the plane between them. When it became known that Boeing were looking for Japanese collaboration in their new airplane, *The Economist* commented:

> When Boeing said it was hoping to recruit Japanese partners to help it build its next airliner, American protectionists thought their worst nightmares were coming true. After decades of trying, three of Japan's biggest industrial firms were about to gain access to the mysteries of producing big commercial jets, one of the few high-tech businesses in which America still leads the world. For America's growing band of techno-nationalists this looked like an industrial Pearl Harbor in the making – with Boeing supplying the blueprints for the bombers.[1]

In fact, the idea of a partnership with the Japanese didn't work out. Instead of an expected 25 per cent equity stake in the plane, the big Japanese companies became glorified subcontractors, making fuselage panels, floor beams and doors. One source quoted the Japanese companies as putting up 8–10 per cent of the over $3 billion start-up costs for the 777 for a smaller participation in the plane, which would bar them from marketing meetings between Boeing

[1] *The Economist*, 21 April 1990, p. 102

and potential customers, where details of the airliner's configuration and cost would be thrashed out. Boeing's explanation for the reduced role of the Japanese was that they couldn't afford the 25 per cent contribution – nearly $1 billion. But outsiders suggested that the Japanese were put off by strong anti-Japanese sentiment in America on trade issues.

Nevertheless, the Working Together philosophy that Boeing were following with their other contractors meant that Japanese engineers would form an intimate part of the design–build teams for the components they were manufacturing and become privy to a lot of information that was classified as 'Boeing Proprietary', a label that identified those aspects of plane-making that the company felt gave them a competitive edge over their current – or future – rivals.

Boeing people rarely commented in public on the incongruity of allowing in engineers from companies which in the future, if not today, might be rival plane-makers. There was a kind of 'make the best of it' attitude among people like Phil Condit:

> There is always the risk that somebody you're working with can decide they want to become a competitor. I think it's true in every industry. I am convinced that if you want to lead you have to run faster than your competition. A defensive strategy very rarely works.

Meanwhile, on the factory floor as well as in the DBTs, Japanese visitors could be seen taking a strong interest in everything around them. One factory worker commented, 'Everybody is warned not to take photographs around the plant, and yet these Japanese come through and they're snapping away, and they're the potential threat.'

A Japanese airline that was interested in buying the 777 would seek long meetings to which a team of managers would turn up, each with a separate brief to ask questions on a whole range of specialized topics. When they had pumped the plane or engine representatives dry, they would go away, equipped with a superb database on which to base their purchase decision, or – many people believed – with which to enhance the store of knowledge the Japanese aircraft industry was acquiring about how to make planes and engines. The openness of the American aircraft manufacturers –

and it applied to McDonnell Douglas as well as to Boeing and the two engine manufacturers – was dubbed by some engineers the 'open kimono' policy, as they saw themselves as required to open their kimonos and invite the Japanese to take their pick of the goods on display.

But there was little Boeing could do to keep the Japanese out, even if behind closed doors they were worried about the competition. They needed Japanese airlines to buy the 777, and they knew this wouldn't happen unless the Japanese were also allowed to make part of the plane. Mitsubishi started working with Boeing in 1974, on the 747, and by the 1990s it was making 15 per cent of the 767. In private, the Japanese often expressed their ambitions in the plane-making arena. The Japanese Aircraft Development Corporation is a grouping of the major heavy industries involved in contracting to make parts for foreign plane-makers. When Michio Daibo, JADC's managing director, was asked if they intended to make their own large airliner, he said simply, 'Of course.'

There were, of course, good technical reasons why the Japanese 'heavies', as they were called, made good contractors for the 777. They could, after all, do a very good job. Mitsubishi, for example, were to make the passenger doors. Tom Gaffney explained why:

> Boeing tradition is that the manufacturer who makes the body section that has the cut-out that the door goes in should make the door. That way, when they don't fit, we know who to say 'Go make it fit' to. However, experience has shown us that we'll have a different manufacturer making different segments of the body, and so we have different doors and the doors don't work the same. So, early on we decided – and this went up to the highest levels – that we would have all the doors built by one manufacturing facility. When this was coupled with our initiative to make all the parts common, we thought we would get the best door quality. At least they'd be all the same.
>
> We had several choices of who should manufacture the door. Ultimately we selected Mitsubishi Heavy Industries in Nagoya to do it. We have a lot of experience with Mitsubishi on the 767, and they are a major participant on this airplane programme, in the body sections as well. Twenty-five per cent of my workforce are

engineers from Mitsubishi. We also have from three to six manufacturing people from Mitsubishi here at any one time, depending on what the issues are. Sometimes tooling experts or machine-parts experts or casting and forging experts come over from Japan and join our design–build team for a period of time when we're solving those issues, and then they can go back to Japan and do their regular work.

In fact the participation of Mitsubishi in the passenger doors was just one example of their involvement in the 777. In the drawings of the plane that Boeing produced, coloured to show the national origins of each part of the plane, it looked as if the Japanese were making about half the plane; but Boeing people always hurried to point out that the drawings were deceptive, and that in terms of the whole plane, inside and out, the Japanese were contributing about 20 per cent.

Neil Standal, as Deputy General Manager of the 777 programme, was often delegated to deal at a high level with the Japanese companies. His combination of politeness, old-world charm and discretion suited the traditional Japanese reticence and the companies' desire not to be shouted at even if things went wrong. He often flew from Seattle to Tokyo for no other reason than to emphasize how much Boeing valued the relationship with their Japanese contractors. It marked the latest stage in an increasing understanding of the subtleties and importance of relationships with the Japanese, and a far cry from the kind of isolationism displayed by former generations at Boeing. Executives in the company have not always taken the sort of care that Standal took to attend to the Japanese.

In the mid-1960s, Everette Webb, an engineer responsible for much of the design of the 747, was asked by Joe Sutter, a legendary Boeing designer, to meet a leading Japanese engineer who claimed to be a fan of his – a certain Professor Ito. Webb said he was too busy, but he was persuaded to come to lunch. When introduced, Ito said, in English, 'Mr Webb, this is one of the great moments of my life. I consider you to be the foremost expert on the structural dynamics of large airplanes. I have read everything you have ever written on the subject, and it is a great honour to meet you at last.' Webb, who hadn't been listening very hard, turned to Sutter and said, 'Joe, you'd better tell him I don't understand Japanese.'[2]

In April 1993, as serious manufacturing work was under way in Japan, Neil Standal and Dick Blakely, Boeing's director of international business operations on the 777, flew to Japan for the latest in a series of regular monitoring and consultation visits to the Japanese manufacturers. The trip was a mixture of the ceremonial – to attend the opening of a new Kawasaki plant – and practical. On the practical side, there were plants to be inspected and schedules to be analysed. By the beginning of April each of the main Japanese manufacturers had taken the first cautious steps towards making actual parts of the first plane. But although it might seem like some kind of beginning, in fact it was the culmination of two years of working together, tracing the path from a component whose existence had only virtual reality – as an accurately described, rotatable, weighable mathematical entity in a computer – to a solid, shiny, cold-to-the-touch metal object which emerged from the workings of a series of purpose-built tools which themselves had to be designed to a greater level of accuracy than the components.

In and around the city of Nagoya, Mitsubishi had factories which made the passenger doors. Another pre-production door had recently been shipped to Seattle, successor to the door on which Gaffney and his colleagues had carried out the freeze-opening tests a year ago. Now, as Standal and his colleagues toured the plant, a small team of workers was assembling door 2 left, another pre-production door which would be used to carry out a slide test later in the year. Unlike the earliest pre-production doors, this one would have a fully working escape slide attached to it, and volunteers would be paid to escape as quickly as they could from an interior mock-up down the slide. But at the moment the door was in the earliest stages – a thin curved sheet of metal with cut-outs for the window and the door handle, including the newly designed doubler that the DBT had devised as a solution to their stress problem.

On Wednesday 7 April 1993, Neil Standal had a sleepless night.

---

[1]Serling, *Legend and Legacy*, p.309

The reason I couldn't sleep the other night was because I was worried about a meeting that we had scheduled with the general manager of one of the works, because he had made a commitment to Mr Blakely. About a month ago we discovered a problem, brought it to their attention, and they told us what they were going to do to resolve it. But things weren't happening. We met with them last week, they showed us what they were doing, and it was unacceptable. We expressed our concerns to them, and told them what was wrong. We had our people work with them on again, off again during the week, and we were not getting anywhere on resolving this. So we asked for a meeting with the general manager, and that meeting could have been very difficult. I couldn't sleep because I was worried about it. Mr Blakely was worried about it. Neither one of us slept well. And we did all our homework: we talked about it the night before – what we were going to do in this event, or if things took this course what would we do? And then we went in the meeting and had a good open Working Together-type discussion. Maybe it wasn't all positive, but we were able to have a discussion rather than a confrontation, and their general manager agreed that he would take the actions necessary to fix the problem. And he was apologetic – he was a gentleman about it. So we're relieved. But it could have been a matter of 'Where do we go next if we fail here?' If we had been whimsical and hadn't cared we would have gone to bed and gone to sleep. But we do care, for the benefit of the programme.

In another country this might be the insomnia of a man who was worried about his own job, but here Standal's worries were about how the Japanese would take the criticism and whether he could find a way to confront the key managers without them losing face and, of course, in such a way that the problems would be corrected. As it turned out, partly because the Japanese had become Americanized – or at least tolerant of American ways – in their relationship with Boeing over the years, the meeting went smoothly, the criticism was accepted, and amends were promised to the satisfaction of Standal and his colleagues.

But learning to deal with the Japanese was not easy, and things could go wrong in all sorts of small ways. They took offence at seemingly insignificant things, but it often wasn't possible to tell until you found out later – maybe through some more Westernized Japanese colleague (or a Japanized American one.) Politeness was all, from exchanging visiting-cards in the appropriate way to avoiding first-name terms at the point where you might adopt them with an American colleague. And, of course, making sure that you bow at the correct angle to reflect your social status relative to the person you were bowing to. By the end of such trips the Americans sometimes felt that they worked for the Bowing Aircraft Company.

Standal was a rather gentle individual, quiet-spoken and polite himself, so the abrasive qualities that might make it more difficult for other Americans to work easily with the Japanese were missing from his character. In a status-ridden society like the Japanese business sector, the visit of a Boeing vice-president had a symbolic value that added to its undoubted practical benefits at this stage in the project. And nowhere was symbolism and ceremony more obvious than in the events of Friday 9 April. Kawasaki had built a new plant to manufacture their contribution to the 777 – several major sections of fuselage – and there was to be an opening ceremony.

By ten o'clock in the morning the plant was festooned with red and white striped canvas booths and tents, and red carpet pathways. Tables under a striped awning by the main gate had trays of red and pink rosettes lined up, with meticulously prepared labels for each of the main participants. A dozen or so men in pale-green overalls and caps and white gloves bowed frequently and in all directions as guests began to arrive and were directed to parking-places. An equal number of young women bustled about, making sure that no guest remained ungreeted for more than a second or two. Worried senior executives scanned the horizon for anyone they would be required to pay respects to, in case they missed a key individual. A young woman stood with a tray which might have held canapés but in fact bore several pairs of white gloves. On a small table in a corner of the registration booth stood three telephones, and next to them was an ashtray full of barely smoked cigarettes – a sign that the stress levels were already rising so early in the day.

A clip-clopping sound marked the rapid approach of a Shinto priest in uncomfortable-looking Minnie Mouse shoes and a hat that looked like a miniature coal sack. He had arrived to conduct the religious part of the opening ceremony – an essential part of any major construction project, and a task for which, it was rumoured, priests could be paid 300,000 yen (£1,500) or more for a two-hour service.

The new factory was in spotless condition and, unlike many factories in the West, was likely to remain that way once work was under way, in a culture where door handles often had washable 'gloves'. Giant sections of fuselage – section 43 – were gripped in rigs that would be used to turn flat, single-thickness sheets of metal into curved, braced, riveted components that were recognizable sides of airplanes. In a far corner of the factory an area had been screened off from the rest and 200 or so chairs were laid out in rows facing several tables laden with fruit, greenery and gift-wrapped parcels, none of which, apart from the greenery, seemed to play much part in the ceremony that was to follow. Representatives of Kawasaki, the construction company that had built the plant, the Japanese Aircraft Development Corporation and Boeing were gathering for a ritual purification and exorcism of the building so that the work within would proceed error-free and on schedule, unhindered by negative influences.

The integration of the Shinto religion into everyday life has no real parallels in the West. There is an unselfconsciousness, combined with what appears to be genuine reverence, in the Shinto ceremonies and practices that punctuate personal and commercial life. In the centre of Tokyo, businessmen would be seen praying in the middle of the day at shrines like the shrine of the Fox. 'They are praying for more money' was the helpful Japanese explanation.

The nearest comparison in London or New York with the Kawasaki plant-opening ceremony might be the 'topping-out' ceremony for a new building, where a vague reference to propitiation of the gods might be seen in the green tree or branch that is hoisted to the topmost beam once the basic skeleton of the building is completed. And even in more directly religious public services in the West there can be a sense that many people are attending out of duty rather than reverence. But for the Japanese managers and bosses arriving at the Nagoya Seaside Plant the matter was in deadly earnest. From the sacred hand-washing, assisted by scrubbed and besuited Kawasaki middle managers, through to the final ritual smashing open of the sake casks by representatives of all the main participants, this was a serious business. Who knows – one wrong move might lead to the new automatic riveter breaking down at a crucial point in the schedule, or to an earth tremor disrupting the accuracy of the rigs that held the section-43 pieces in position to a few thousandths of an inch.

In their uniforms of dark suit and tie and plain shirt, the ranks of 'salarymen' found their seats – names and companies on beautifully calligraphed labels – and sat dutifully waiting for the ceremony to begin. They were displaying the Shinto virtues of unquestioning acceptance of one's position in a hierarchy, company loyalty and respect for superiors, and scrupulous observance of etiquette. To the Westerner in search of enlightenment about what was going on, the explanations offered by the Japanese were a little unsatisfying. 'He is reading from something like the Bible – it is very difficult to describe what he is saying' was one proffered explanation of a long chant by the priest in front of the best produce a fruiterer could supply. At one point, in an uncanny (and unconscious) imitation of a Pratt & Whitney 4084 engine revving up, the priest indicated his desire for any evil spirits to accelerate away from the place and fade into the distance.

The Boeing people were attending this sort of ceremony for the first, time, but they were unfazed by the participation required of them. At a certain point the various bosses of the companies involved came up in turn to the front and were handed a branch of a tree by the priest. Standal had had an impromptu lesson from two Kawasaki colleagues over breakfast:

> They said, 'When you go to the table, bow once.' Well the Shinto priest came to me with the branch and I never went to the table, so I bowed to him. Likewise, you bow twice when you put the branch down, and clap. Then they told me, 'Make sure you made it visible', so all my other Boeing friends would also clap.

As the bosses did, so did their workers – standing, bowing and clapping in unison. When it came to the four Boeing managers, they did not disgrace their company. Although the disparate genetics of the American population conspired to give them a much more ragged height profile than the ranks of the Japanese managers, they had been well-briefed, and the individual strength of their clapping made up for their lack of numbers compared with the other companies represented.

At one point the screens were thrown back to reveal a red carpet leading up steps to one of the giant machines purpose-built for the 777 project. The priest clip-clopped up the steps and, while saying further ceremonial words, showered the machine and its surroundings with what looked like cherry-blossom petals. (The blossoms turned out, more prosaically, to be small squares of white paper.) Then he returned to the makeshift shrine, and the president of Kawasaki mounted the steps and pressed a beribboned button to start the now purified and exorcised heavy-engineering equipment, to a round of polite applause.

The guided tour of the plant was as well-oiled and smoothly running as the machinery, as people were called out row by row and escorted round the factory floor to each significant piece of heavy equipment, already supplied with its appropriate component of the 777. At each machine, a Kawasaki engineer in cap and overalls addressed the dozen or so visitors through a megaphone, even though they were clustering round him, their ears three feet away. Then, like clockwork, he finished his piece in synchrony with the man on the previous machine and one group departed as another arrived.

Japan's role in the 777 was not very well understood by people outside the company. And even within the company there was sometimes a failure to see why Boeing – or any large plane-maker for that matter – *needed* to farm out so much of the work to foreign companies. One Boeing engineer who was part of the Working Together relationship with Japan had previously worked at Boeing's Auburn plant, and he spoke sadly of how, when he occasionally returned to the plant, his former colleagues didn't want to speak to him, believing that the Japanese connection was taking work away from them at a time when people were being laid off. But people have short memories. It might seem worrying at a time when competition has never been fiercer, and the Japanese are striding ahead in so many areas of technology, but the Boeing relationship with Japanese companies goes back twenty years, and is part of a continuing attempt to improve, improve, improve on design and manufacturing methods.

Two days later the Boeing group travelled to Yokohama, to the plant of the Nippi company, who were making the in-spar ribs. These were originally intended to be made of aluminium-lithium alloy, and Nippi had had to make major changes in tooling to cope with the change back to aluminium after the crisis meeting at Boeing back in June 1992. Dick Blakely described the tortuous series of events as they had affected the Nippi engineers:

> When we made the original decision in favour of aluminium-lithium, our friends at Nippi became rather concerned. They had not worked with aluminium-lithium before, and it has some characteristics in working with it that are difficult at best. And so one of their senior engineers came to Seattle and expressed his concern, and said, 'Are you sure you want to use aluminium-lithium, for these reasons?' And he had some documented concerns. And we said, 'Hey, we have a weight concern on the programme – we have to get the weight out. Our manufacturing, research and development people have looked at those concerns, and we think we can make it work.' So we continued to engineer it into the programme. And they worked very closely with us, overcome their concerns, and they understood in each area of application how we would apply it. And they actually became satisfied that they could use it. But then at the last minute we decided to not use aluminium-lithium, and it was pulled off the programme. In doing that, it put Nippi and us in a difficult situation, because we had to redesign aluminium-lithium out of the wing ribs. Now all of a sudden – when you take the aluminium-lithium out, put the new material in – you can't support delivery of the ribs on schedule. So Nippi took a look at the impact and they said they would be delivering the ribs late. We took a look in Seattle and said, 'OK, if they deliver their ribs late, what will that do to the assembly of the wing?' And we programmed it. And we do this all the time. You have changes that cause you to reprogramme. But Nippi then, continuing to take a hard look at the impact of that, said, 'No, by tightening our schedules and working considerable overtime, we can haul our

schedule back and deliver on time.' And now we've just heard that the wing ribs are in Seattle on time.

Such dedication deserves a reward, and the Boeing group were armed with a certificate of thanks which they presented to the Nippi programme manager who had been responsible for the extra effort to get the ribs completed on schedule.

After a week of plant tours, handshakes, bows, and giving the same speech over and over again, Neil Standal had to go through it all one last time at the Executive Programme Review. Held in the functional offices of Fuji Heavy Industries, this meeting was a final report of the Boeing group to the senior executives of the 'heavies' – Kawasaki, Mitsubishi, Fuji and Nippi heavy-industry divisions. There was an unusual degree of nervousness among the Boeing people about the fact that one of the heavies was not doing as well as the others, and some concern that this be put over in the right way. It was an illustration of the culture gap that existed between the two groups: such consideration for the feelings of others – and that's what it seemed to be about – rarely entered into Boeing's dealing with other contractors who might have slipped behind schedule. The ASTA people, for example, felt a little aggrieved from time to time when one of their little problems, such as faulty thermocouples, was picked on, when in their view it was Boeing's changes in the rudder design that was a far bigger problem. But there is something about the Japanese that encourages the view that direct criticism might not be the best way to correct mistakes. From the widespread custom of extra deference to those one is meant to be serving, to the expressions of dismay in hotels, restaurants or shops if some tiny detail is not to the customer's liking, the foreigner is led to believe that if he ever made clear his displeasure about something *important* the complainee would dissolve into an impotent jelly at the shame and disgrace of the accusation. And an expression of displeasure about one party in front of another could compound the potential damage to the errant individual's self-esteem.

Some of this might have been going through Standal's mind at the end of his April tour, when, in spite of much good news to report at most of the heavies, he and his colleagues were still unhappy with what they had seen. They had sent a fax back to Alan Mulally about some worrying delays on Mitsubishi's passenger doors, and there was some concern about the possibility that a small percentage of the brackets that were meant to carry the wire bundles through the fuselage might not be ready. But both Standal and Blakely, in their reports to the top Japanese executives, bent over backwards to shower them with effusive praise for the good things that had been achieved, and expressed the belief that Mitsubishi's problems would soon be solved and that they too would be awarded a thumbs-up sign on one of the traffic-light charts that the Boeing people used to summarize progress. It was a bit like awarding gold stars to schoolchildren for good work, and the Boeing people sincerely believed that by such transparent ruses they could avoid the offence they so dreaded causing.

But behind the scenes there was a close enough relationship between Standal and one or two of the other executives for a blunter message to be conveyed, not in front of their colleagues, to the Mitsubishi team. Daibo-san, for example, managing director of JADC, had first worked with Standal twenty years before, on the 747, and the two were old friends, and even drinking companions at Daibo's exclusive Japanese club. He served as a reliable channel through which the Boeing people could communicate their true concerns and rely on them being translated into whatever was the Japanese equivalent of a strong complaint.

But the Executive Programme Review was not only for Boeing to tell the Japanese what they thought of their progress so far: it was also for Boeing to give them a frank account of where the 777 stood as far as sales were concerned. Their 8 per cent share of costs allowed the Japanese a small share in the benefits if the plane became a best-seller, so they took a keen interest in the projected sales figures – particularly in the light of the rumours that had flown about a couple of months earlier that United was cancelling some of its orders.

With a mastery of the overhead projector, Standal showed a complex chart of his own devising which contained highly confidential information about each airline and the planes it had ordered and when they were to be delivered. Each plane was represented by a square, and Standal showed that, although indeed cancellations *had* taken place at the time United needed help with its financial problems, by shuffling the squares around to deal with the new situation the main impact appeared to consist of four planes being delayed for one year and four for two. To Standal, unless he was putting a brave face on the situation, this really wasn't very significant. Where the United changes *would* have a more serious effect was on the B model and the stretch versions of the plane, further downstream.

Standal also reported on the general cut-backs at Boeing that had led to the lay-offs earlier in the year. He warned the meeting that there would be pressures on the 777 team to save money, delay new tools, and generally tighten their belts as their contribution to solving the company's problems.

It was up to Dick Blakely to confirm the details of Mitsubishi's red traffic-light on one category, and then the chairman of the meeting asked for questions. Perhaps in a manifestation of extreme politeness, only one or two desultory questions were asked, and then the meeting broke up in a generally amiable way. Either the tact displayed by Standal and Blakely had softened their displeasure to the point where it was barely apparent at all, or the Japanese saw the force of the Boeing complaints but took them in their stride – as one might expect world-class engineers and manufacturers to do.

TWELVE

'Ticky-Tack, Snap, Snap, Snap'

Ron Ostrowski, describing events in the factory

There were two words to dominate all discussions of progress on the building of the 777 during 1993 and 1994. Those words were 'nominal' and 'guaranteed'. They referred to the characteristics that Boeing was aiming for when designing the plane – characteristics such as weight, cruising speed, length of runway that the plane could take off from, and distance travelled before refuelling. At the beginning of a project like the 777, the engineers would have months of discussion about what they thought they could get the plane to do. These decisions were all, of course, to do with money. Good fuel efficiency – 'miles per gallon', or in the case of airliners, 'gallons per mile' – the lightest weight, the furthest range, the highest speed, the lowest drag (the force of air resistance the plane would meet by virtue of its shape): all of these were targets for the designers. Their discussions resulted in a list of characteristics that they believed they could achieve – or rather that they believed they *should* achieve, years before they really knew whether they could or not. These were called 'nominal', so the plane would have a nominal weight, a nominal cruising speed, a nominal drag, and a nominal range.

However, when Boeing were selling the plane to customers, they would offer a different set of characteristics, all slightly worse than the nominal list. These would be the *guarantees* – the speed, range, weight and so on that the company would put into a contract and be bound to supply. If Boeing failed in any characteristic they would have to pay a penalty cost to the airline. They set the guarantees at such a level that they had an 80 per cent chance of achieving them, and the nominals at a 50 per cent level.

Jeff Peace, who was closely concerned with customer requirements on the 777, explained the significance of the two terms:

Our customers' expectation is the nominal levels, and so, while the guarantee is a legal requirement, the nominal is in fact a moral requirement, and we are very, very serious about meeting nominal, to make sure that we meet our customers' expectations. You sell an airplane on your credibility, and if you can establish the credibility which Boeing has over the years, of working everlastingly towards the nominal performance, then that's gold in the market-place. It's gold with this 150 or 200 customers that we have, and so we get real, real serious about meeting those expectations, even though the legal requirement is just the guarantees.

At the time when Boeing was guaranteeing all these character-istics to the airlines, the guarantee was a gesture of faith more than a firm engineering statement. Something like the nominal weight of the plane would be achieved only by the combined efforts of every single DBT to meet specific targets which the chief engineers had decided were achievable as much because they *wanted* to achieve them as because they knew definitely that they could. But during the most intensive design phase, as the aluminium-lithium discussion showed, every pound counted, and designers of the smallest components were entreated to save grams. As Alan Mulally put it:

Every pound of weight that we get out of an airplane is good for the airlines, and it's good for Boeing. We have to buy less material, and then they have to fly around less material. We both want the most efficient airplane we can, but they've based their business plan and their performance around what we guaranteed to them, because that's just prudent. You know, this is a new airplane, so it's real important that they base their business plan around the guarantee to them. But on the other hand they're pleased and we're pleased that we can meet that – that's why we always keep as our target getting to the nominal. Sometimes we even beat the nominal, and then there will be some areas on the 777 where we will do better even than nominal and we will give that airplane with that better than nominal performance to the airlines, and hopefully that will turn customer satisfaction into a delighted customer.

But there was always an overriding factor – safety. Every important characteristic of the plane that might lead to a safety problem was
overdesigned to allow for a margin. Alan Mulally explained the
principles:

> One fundamental is that we make all the parts stronger than they'd
> need to be for the normal operation. And the reason is that we put
> in margins of safety – extra material, extra speed, extra angles of
> attack. With everything about the airplane we have margins
> around its operation that are above and beyond the normal ways
> the airplane is flown. And that's why we see in the papers how in
> accidents where many airplanes have been abused or people have
> made mistakes the airplane has often been able to handle that. It's
> tolerant for that.
>
> The other fundamental in airplane design is redundancy. In
> structural design and in systems design, we have fundamental
> principles that allow us to tolerate failures. We assume the failure
> will happen, and we design the airplane to be able to tolerate that.
> And in areas that are used a lot, if they're flight-critical, then we
> build in more and more redundancy, more and more backup, to be
> able to handle degraded flight conditions. And that's where there
> are lessons learned, and every incident and every experience that
> we can gather in the field really helps us set those requirements for
> the redundancy and for the margins.

Every Tuesday morning the five vice-presidents and a number of
project engineers had a meeting called the Critical Issues Meeting.
On 30 March 1993 the main topics were the usual ones of weight,
drag and fuel consumption – all factors that were embodied as
guarantees in the contracts with the customers. For each airline,
these were defined in terms of a specific route and payload. So
British Airways might say, for example, that the plane had to fly from
Heathrow to Los Angeles with a full payload of passengers and five
tons of cargo. The characteristics necessary to achieve that flight –
weight, fuel consumption, drag, thrust of engines – were guaranteed
to BA, and it would be a pretty serious matter if Boeing fell short of
any of those promises when they delivered the planes. The issue was
complicated slightly by the fact that there were 'side letters' in the

contracts with BA and United that guaranteed them a weight that was nearer nominal than the main guarantee, and if Boeing delivered the less stringent guaranteed weight to them there would be a financial penalty to pay.

The meeting discussed one problem in terms of what it might mean to the customer. 'If we only deliver this,' said one of the speakers, 'it will mean a loss of 4,400 lb of payload on a sample trip. Over a twenty-year period, the loss works out to the cost of one whole aircraft.'

Today's meeting went over the figures, trying to get some sense of how the project was doing. Boeing engineers had tried to turn the art of prediction into a science. They would put up charts and talk in terms of delivering a first plane that had an 80 per cent chance of being 1 per cent over nominal, or of a 30 per cent chance of hitting the nominal target. Fortunately, the likelihood of being heavier than the guaranteed weight was off the chart, although there seemed to be a possibility that the BA and UA guarantees might not be met. There was similar discouraging news about drag. Clearly, the streamlining of the wings and body is one attempt to minimize drag, but, because drag changes with the airflow over the wings, there is no one design that can produce minimal drag. There is also a type of drag which is to do not with the actual shape of the wings or body but with the little bits and pieces that poke above it – air-speed detectors, for example, or door handles, or just general roughnesses on the surface skin.

On the factory floor at Everett there was a poster headed 'Cost of 777 Excrescence Drag'. It was a warning to anyone working on the plane that even small irregularities in the finishing process could have long-term consequences to an airline buying the 777. There was a set of examples based on the extra fuel that would have to be burnt to overcome roughness caused by poorly installed seals and fasteners, or gaps or steps at the junctions of components, or paint that was not put on smoothly enough. The figures were calculated in numbers of gallons of extra fuel burnt over a year by ten airplanes. So, for example, the poster showed that a square foot of paint that had been badly applied on ten planes, producing a rough surface, could result in an airline burning an extra twenty-one gallons of fuel in a year. So a badly painted area of, say thirty-seven square feet – the area of a couple of doors – would, over ten planes, result in 777 unnecessary gallons being burnt in a year. To bring the point home, the poster said that '777 gallons of extra fuel could mean that 25 passengers and their baggage get left behind.' And if this poster, with its eight examples of poor workmanship, did not supply enough information, the factory workers were encouraged to ring a dedicated phone number, 294-DRAG.

The Critical Issues Meeting was attended by about thirty people, mostly men in their Boeing uniforms of suits, plain shirts and ties. But there was a sprinkling of women, also in suits, some of them senior engineers. Alan Mulally slouched back in his chair, scanning each overhead transparency as it came up for news that he knew would be there but hoped would not. There was an air of relentless self-criticism that was to some extent deceptive: if you set yourself a high target, you're always going to be disappointed. 'This is the toughest set of criteria for a new plane there's ever been,' said Mulally afterwards, and his words were borne out by one of the overheads, which showed how far short of their nominal targets other airliners had fallen when they first went into service. There was no sense of crowing as they discussed a chart that showed Airbus and McDonnell Douglas's recent planes as anywhere between 4 and 8 per cent worse than their targets when they went into service. This is what happens in the airplane business, and they knew that they could be in the same position through no fault of their own.

But it was reassuring that, in spite of some of the unexpectedly bad projections for various elements of the 777, the bars on the graph showing the predictions for various characteristics – weight, drag, fuel efficiency, and so on – at Entry into Service, or EIS, was smaller than any of their competitors' actual figures. Nevertheless, there were aspects of the 777's current progress, particularly in the weight area, that generated a need for some action. One by one, the various possible areas of action were discussed. There was a list of 'big-ticket items' as they were called – single measures or approaches that could, at a stroke, save quite a lot of weight.

Changing door cut-outs – the holes in the fuselage – could save 400 lb; possible changes in the centre section could save another 400 lb; there was a whole list of fittings that could be redesigned to save 200 lb. And the team were worried that the thrust-reversers were coming in heavier than they should, and felt that another 200 lb could come off the design.

There was also an ingenious proposal to save some weight on the skin panels, not by changing the design of the panel but by altering the manufacturing method. Now that fabrication was under way, the manufacturing engineers could supply figures for the actual weights of panels as they came off the production line. In any manufacturing process there is a variability that leads to a range of values for the actual finished weight of the components. A skin panel designed to weigh, say, 200 lb may weigh between 199.9 and 200.1. This variation is due to the inbuilt tolerances of each step of the process that leads to the final shaped panel. At the meeting there was a slide showing the scatter of weights about a central point, the target weight. Boeing use a system called statistical process control which monitors such variations all the time during manufacture. Instead of just making sure that each part falls within certain limits of weight or size, SPC measures a much wider range of characteristics at each stage of the manufacturing process, on the lookout for new information that will help to improve the manufacturing process in the future. Here was an instance where SPC might be of some use.

In any batch of skin panels, there were clearly some that were heavier than they needed to be, due to natural scatter – what's called a Gaussian curve – about the mean (target) weight. There were also some that were lighter, but still within acceptable limits. If the curve could be shifted by a small amount to the left, all the pieces would be lighter, and this could save a useful amount when added up over the entire plane.

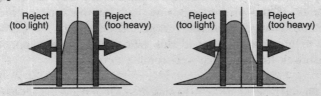

Reject (too light)   Reject (too heavy)   Reject (too light)   Reject (too heavy)

But there was one snag. If all the pieces were lighter, that would mean that more of the pieces on the left side of the curve, a small proportion of the total, would now be below acceptable limits – too light for the job – and they would have to be rejected. So the first question was, Should we change the manufacturing process in this way and achieve some weight loss, but at the cost of rejecting more panels? Or could we find some way of narrowing the curve, so that the central point – the mean – moved to the left but the right end and the left end moved closer together so there was not a significantly higher level of rejections?

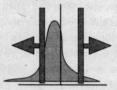

The meeting left this decision to be explored further and went on to consider other items, such as fasteners, paint, sealant and primer. Someone pointed out that the Airbus fuel-tank sealant was put on more thinly than current specifications for the 777 sealant – 'Their maximum is our minimum.'

There was also discussion of ways to make up for an overweight plane by increasing lift. It seemed a little late to be discussing such fundamental characteristics as wing span, for example, or centre-of-gravity position, or winglets, and yet no option was considered too extreme to be raised at this stage, as part of considering all the options, even if it was clear that it would be rejected. The wing-span issue, for example, was raised by an engineer who suggested that if the rake of the wing tip could be doubled it would increase the wing span by up to six feet.

But, to counteract the pessimism about the major guarantees on the plane, there was good news coming out of the factory about the benefits of the measures Boeing had instituted to prevent or minimize change, error and rework. Garnet Hizzey, whose job it was to monitor progress in this area, could barely suppress his pleasure at the results that were coming through:

> On this programme we've had instances where things literally have gone together like in an erector set. It's amazing, and yet, you might say, 'Well, this is digital definition. The methods by which we're building the parts in many cases are to a thousandth of an inch, so why shouldn't they fit?' But from our prior lives it is a surprise to see huge pieces of equipment and hardware, in many

cases married together for the first time from different parts of the
globe, just fitting together. Logic tells you that it should be that
way, but it still has a miraculous appearance that we can do this so
painlessly and effortlessly. Last Friday night I walked into the
factory and they'd turned over the section 46–47 body section,
the lower lobe, and I walked in there – it was probably about seven
thirty at night – and the mechanics were on their second-shift
lunch break.[1] I asked whether they had loaded the crown panel
which had come from Kawasaki, because they had anticipated that
it would take a full shift to do that task, and here they were at their
lunch break. It turned out that the job was already done. I looked
at the frames, and they all lined up precisely. In effect, they'd done
a shift's work in two hours. It was just incredible. I think that the
mechanics were surprised in themselves.

To Ron Ostrowski every shred of evidence looked positive. He
hadn't had an instance yet of disappointment about how the
manufacturing side was coming on. The original objective was 50
per cent less 'change, error and rework,' and the news coming out of
the factory was something like an 80–90 per cent reduction.
Whatever savings the new techniques had produced in design time,
they were more than matched by the manufacturing benefits. 'When
it goes to the shop it's ticky-tack, snap, snap, snap – it's all coming
together just like we had hoped it would, better than ever before,'
said Ostrowski. 'If we're going to make hay, it's out there in the
factory where the real money is.'

So pleased was everyone with the benefits of preassembling the
first designs of the components of the plane in the computer, which
had led to these reductions in errors and changes, that there was a
general injunction on the engineers not to talk so freely to the
outside world about the benefits of the new systems, in case their
rivals caught on.

Of all the regular 777 meetings, the Critical Issues Meeting
might be expected to engender the most heat as well as light. It was,

[1]'Lunch' in factories with three shifts bears only a probabilistic relation to the
middle of the day. It's the meal in the middle of a shift, whatever time of day that
occurs. It's similar to the astronomer's 'night lunch' that he eats at about two
o'clock in the morning.

after all, a forum to which particularly threatening problems were brought so that the combined wisdom of all the engineers could be brought to bear on questions like, How did it happen? What lessons can we learn for the future? And, How can we get out of this hole? And yet, the Working Together philosophy, with its maxims of 'no secrets' and 'the data will set you free' and a general respect for the views of everyone, seemed to turn these occasions into an exciting pursuit of enlightenment rather than a search for the guilty. This didn't mean that no negative criticism ever passed the lips of the participants, but when it did it was rarely directed at individuals. When Granny Frazier and Rocky Thomas were discussing how Mulally achieved this difficult feat, Frazier said:

> I can give you an example of one of the things that Alan does that's magic. As we were struggling with one of the engine work programmes, Rocky gave a status report to the Critical Issues team. When we got through, Alan said, 'Rocky, your plan sucks.' Now, he didn't say Rocky sucked; he said the plan sucked. So everybody turned around and looked at the plan and said, 'Gee, if this plan is bad then we'd better fix it.' There wasn't any personal reaction or any personal insult in the thing, although there may have been a momentary concern.

Thomas interjected with feeling, 'On my part, yeah.'

Mulally gave a modest assessment of his relationship to his colleagues at this stressful time:

> Sometimes the most important contribution I can make is to carry water for them. Once you have the plans laid out around a common plan, then the rest is helping. It's helping to remove roadblocks. It's helping people to make their contribution. And sometimes it's just saying thank you, just appreciating good work.

Neil Standal had been in Boeing long enough to see other ways of running meetings and achieving solutions, and he sometimes compared the new style with the old:

I've mellowed, because at times I sit in meetings and even now I get to thinking from time to time, 'Boy, back on the 767, or back on the 737, this is what I did and it worked', and I get impatient – I want to pounce. Yet, with the style we have and the team that we have, we are all in this together. We support one another; we don't pounce on one another. I can remember instances on other programmes where various functions would be just at each other – the parts weren't here and the manufacturing guy needed them, or the design wasn't done so the planners could do it – and they would be across the table at each other, just talking very loud. I've seen that many times in my career, and when you sit and look at the style we use – 'If he's got a problem, that's my problem, so let's go and work it' – it's working. It's magnificent to be able to sit in meetings and everyone be outward and honest and tell their every problem and there is no criticism. We don't shoot the messenger: we take the message, good or bad, and we work with it, and we're all here to help each other.

The public perception of Boeing in 1993 was coloured by two continuing processes. First, there was a trickle of stories about cut-backs in orders as the recession affected the airlines, including the 777's first and main customer, United. In February there was a flurry of press interest in a rumour first printed in the *Wall Street Journal* that United were going to cancel large numbers of orders for 777s, and there were confirmed cut-backs by other, smaller, airlines – although these were sometimes a cautious turning-in of options to purchase rather than cancellations of actual planes in the manufacturing order list.

The second indication that Boeing was having problems was in more announcements of staff cut-backs. These were not specifically in the 777 programme but across the board, and, in spite of the devotion of Boeing to good management techniques, within the company there was a degree of fear and worry among individuals about who would be next, and occasional mutterings that it was more to do with who you knew than how good you were as to whether you stayed or left. The atmosphere wasn't helped by the announcement of 12 per cent pay rises for Frank Shrontz and Phil Condit, among others, whose salaries were increased by amounts that would have kept on half a dozen employees.

A further sign of some kind of discontent was the rumour that two bolts fell 'accidentally on purpose' from a great height on to an All-Nippon Airlines 747 on the assembly line, causing damage costing about $50,000 to repair. Further bolts were allegedly found littered precariously on crane arms so that the vibrations of the active crane would send them randomly plummeting on to whatever was in its path.

But the air of pessimism was not strong enough to spoil the annual Boeing paper-airplane contest. On 30 and 31 March the atrium of 40-88 Building was put to the test and passed with flying colours. At lunchtime on both days the balconies that lined the atrium at each level were crammed with 777 staff, abuzz with chatter. From time to time a roar would go up and then a burst of applause that could be heard throughout the building. Normally, because of size, layout and good sound insulation, it was impossible to get any sense of how many people worked in the building, but the paper-airplane contest for Boeing employees had brought out the crowds – many in their green 777 colours. The rules determined that planes could be made out of one sheet of paper, with no attachments such as Scotch tape or paper-clips, and one by one the competitors came forward, ranging from secretaries to aeronautical engineers.

The design of the atrium was perfect for a test of navigation and range. From the top balcony at one end, on the fifth floor, you could see a clear route down to the third floor at the other end, where banks of escalators split in the middle of the building but left spaces on either side for the planes to fly through towards yellow concentric rectangles marked out on the carpet. One by one the planes drifted down, generating oohs and aahs at the ones that plunged straight to the ground or stalled and headed into the crowds on the balcony, and occasional cheers as one plane floated straight as a die to navigate past the escalators and on to the target.

In a nearby office, John Cashman experimented with a design he was making for the Boeing Communications Division. In spite of his years of flying everything from a Bonanza to a 747, his piece of paper did the usual predictable things, crashing into filing-cabinets or veering off into a corner. He created two flaps at the back of his

CATIA computer data (left) are an aid to designing the cockpit. A fully functioning cockpit simulator (below) presents chief test pilot John Cashman with realistic views of the outside and authentic flight data on the new liquid crystal screens.

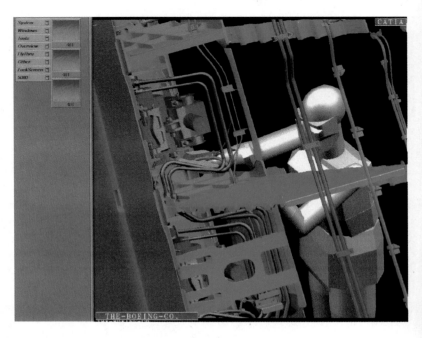

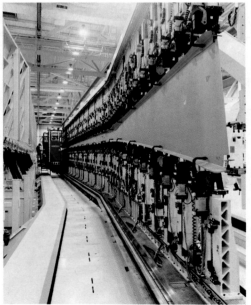

Above: CATIA computer design allows maintenance operations to be simulated, to ensure that parts are accessible to technical ground staff.

Left: The ASAT tool, as it begins the task of assembling the first wing of the first plane, in January 1993.

Above: 'Four million parts designed to move in tight formation' – but most of them are rivets and fasteners.

Right: At key moments in the 777 programme, such as the completion of passenger door design, engineers and support staff sign their names in indelible ink.

Above: Towards the end of 1993 the first 777 comes together in the factory at Everett.

Below: The slogan 'Working Together', a management style that contributes to the smooth running of the project, is used as the name of the first 777.

Above: On the day of the first flight, while the 777 awaits its flight crew, Phil Condit and his wife pose for the cameras of the assembled 777 team members and their families.

Below: The 777 team is ten thousand strong at its peak, and regular All-Team meetings have to be held in the world's largest building.

Above: Early morning at Edwards Air Force Base, California. Minimum unstick velocity (MUV) is the slowest speed at which a plane can safely take off. To maximize lift the nose tilts up and the bottom scrapes on the ground.

Below: After the maximum braking test the plane has to wait for five minutes before firemen are sent in to cool the brakes.

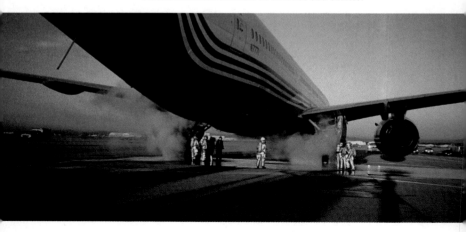

Above: 9 April, 1994 – Roll-Out, the day the 777 is unveiled to the public and the thousands of people who worked on the plane.

Below: Flight testing covers every eventuality on the ground as well as in the air. Here, one of United's first 777s brakes on a very wet runway.

Take-off and
cruise – the 777
begins its flying life.

Concorde-like design and tried again. It was getting better. 'You know,' he said, 'one of the most successful designs out there was just a cylinder of paper dropped forward from the balcony. It did really well. I wonder why?' He seemed to muse for a moment on the commercial aviation possibilities of a wingless fat cylinder.

On Sunday 25 July 1993 the first 777 wing to be completed moved in an upward direction, for a distance of five thousandths of an inch. It then stayed in that position for an hour or so, before moving a few more thousandths and then finally taking off for an assisted flight of thirty feet up in the air. The wing – a left-hand wing – took off from the framework in which it had been assembled in the previous weeks and landed a few feet away on the floor of Building 40-34. Its lift was provided by two brand-new cranes specially built for the job to lift one of the heaviest single pieces of the plane, at fourteen tons.

The move took place while the Puget Sound area was having one of its few sunny days of 1993, if you believed taxi-drivers and residents. Seattle's reputation for bad weather was summed up in the film that opened throughout the United States that month, called *Sleepless in Seattle*. When one of the characters talks of moving to Seattle, his friend says 'Seattle? But it rains there for nine months of the year!'

Plenty of Boeing people had given up the rare sunny afternoon to see an event that was probably the most significant so far in the manufacturing process that was rapidly gaining momentum. The event was about two months late, partly because some of the specialized tools needed to complete the assembly were themselves not ready. Making a brand-new plane carries with it the essential tasks of making brand-new tools to build it – and, indeed, brand-new buildings to house the tools to build the plane. As the managers looked at their schedules during the first half of 1993 there was sometimes a question in their minds as to whether the tools would be ready when the parts arrived or even whether the buildings would be ready for the tools or the parts.

The wing had been assembled component by component in a four-storey framework. There were four of these in a row, and when production was up to its full rate they would all be in use, holding pairs of wings for two planes. There had been a slow build-up over the previous weeks, starting with the wing spars that had been assembled in the ASAT tool. Then, as further pieces arrived they were fixed in position to form a hollow wing ninety feet long which would serve as a 10,000-gallon fuel tank as well as a source of support.

This first move would set the pattern for future ones, and was taken very slowly. There were perhaps thirty manufacturing staff working as a team, each with a position and a task. The first five thousandths of an inch was the most difficult. The cranes had to exert enough force to support the wing but not enough to pull it upwards until each of the bolts securing it to the base of the tool had been loosened. It was impossible to tell by eye whether the wing was supported by the cranes or not, so small weight gauges were used to indicate by how many thousandths of an inch the wing had been raised. The wing was positioned with its thickest edge, the leading edge, uppermost. In the wing major, the tall jig in which the wing had been assembled, there were four galleries where the wing-builders worked, one above the other, although most of the initial activity was on the lower two, where the main attachments were being freed. Occasionally there would be loud bangs as recalcitrant fastenings refused to come free. There was a particular problem with something called a Texas tower – a derrick-like structure to support part of the wing as it would swing from vertical to horizontal. There was a flurry of panel-removing to get at the Texas tower and free it from the framework, so that the wing could begin to rise.

Three hours after they had started, the team were ready to move to the next stage. The wing was now five thousandths of an inch up in the air, and the signal was given to accelerate the pace of lifting. Imperceptibly the wing moved, restrained at each side by horizontal supports called pogo sticks. The next half inch took another two hours, and then there was no stopping it. Over the next twenty minutes, accompanied by the warning 'parps' of the klaxon that sounds when the cranes move, the wing rose out of its framework until it was suspended thirty feet above its original position. As its path turned from vertical to horizontal it moved away from the tool towards a clear area of floor that had been prepared to receive it. To the people down on the factory floor, most of them sightseers, the wing became clearly visible – looking like a large submarine, down to the oval 'portholes' on the underside of the wing skin – and a cheer went up.

By the end of the day, the wing had been turned from vertical to horizontal and was resting on stands. The next task would be to seal the inside so that it became a liquid-tight fuel tank, and to paint the outside, before it took its place connected to the fuselage and the right wing in three months' time.

THIRTEEN

Summer of '93

On Saturday 24 July 1993 Terry-Lynn Thomas, the interior designer for the final-assembly building, spent five hours with a colleague, laboriously sticking down white and yellow tape to show the shape and size of the 777 in the position from which it would roll out of the factory. On the following Monday there was to be an All-Team Meeting of the 777 team, and it was Terry's bright idea to show the team how big the 777 really was. She had lived with its size for a year or more, as she had helped to design the interior of the huge assembly building and to fit each of the stages of final assembly into the available floor space. She had chosen the colour scheme for the building – a blush-peach colour in two shades.

The outline on the floor was a simple idea, but a good one. Because of the ordinary, familiar appearance of the plane, the small models that dotted the lobbies and offices of the Boeing Company gave no idea of its size. Short of a life-size model, or the real plane, there had been no way to sense how big it was. But here, drawn out on the floor at Everett, looking rather like police tape marking where a body had been found, was an airplane of awesome size. Standing at the point where the nose would be, you could just see the outline of the tail of the plane, 201 feet away, far off in the middle of the factory floor. And standing on one wing tip you peered a similar distance into the factory to see the other tip, one inch less than 200 feet away. But Terry Thomas's idea rather misfired as six thousand members of the 777 team drifted into the factory and covered the outline without really realizing what was under their feet.

Plans had gone a little awry. The public-address system had worked fine when it was tested in the closed factory, but then the fire authorities had come into the act and decided that there were not enough exits if all the team had to be evacuated, and insisted that one of the huge sliding doors be left open. This rather spoilt the acoustics, and some members of the team heard the proceedings only fitfully or with a disruptive echo as the meeting got under way.

In the middle of the floor was a platform hoist, forming a small stage about ten feet above the ground. Promptly at 8.30 a.m. the slim figure of Greg Hunter, a Boeing public-relations employee, climbed up a ladder and bounced on to the stage, microphone in hand, for all the world as if he was about to burst into song. Then he burst into song.

A few days before, Greg had kindly offered to sing 'God Bless America' to get the All-Team Meeting off to a rousing start. Such an offer, however generous, had been treated with caution by the 777 Communications Division, who were organizing the meeting, and Greg was made to demonstrate his talents in the office of Donna Mikov, director of 777 communications. He passed the test and, accompanied only by a musician on a small electronic keyboard, he filled the factory with many verses of the song. It was an astonishingly confident performance although after six or seven minutes with no mention of the 777 the assembled audience could be forgiven for wondering exactly what function the song was performing. Even the hearing-impaired members of the team were included in the fun, as the words were 'signed' by a woman at the foot of the platform.

In a small group, to one side of the platform, were the five 777 VPs uniformly white-shirted, along with Gordon McKinzie. Alan Mulally had joined them last, working his way down a cordoned-off passage through the huge crowd. Like an archetypal presidential candidate, he stopped from time to time for a word with someone near the cordon, squeezing his arm or patting him on the back. He might not have known every single member of the team, but he certainly gave a good impression of doing so.

Part of the purpose of the meeting was to give all the people working on the plane an opportunity to ask questions of the management, by writing them down and handing them in beforehand. Mulally clasped slips of paper and read out individual questions, or grouped them if they covered a common theme. The most critical questions addressed the issue in everyone's mind, about lay-offs. One team member asked whether the same process would be applied to management as to people on the shop floor. Mulally read the question out and then looked out at the assembled team. 'What do you think of *that*?' he said, as if he were slightly taken aback at the questioner's impudence and wanted the audience to share in his reaction. All he got was some whistles and a sympathetic murmur – sympathetic to the questioner, that is. Mulally justified the lay-offs with a rapid summary of the world downturn in aviation commerce and said that the same scrutiny would be applied to senior management posts.

Each of the vice-presidents gave a summary of the project from his point of view. Dale Hougardy gave some of the astonishing figures coming out of the factory for reductions in change, error and rework, in response to a question about EPIC. And McKinzie talked about how wonderful the plane was and how his airline wished they could get their hands on it sooner.

Whenever Boeing did anything like this it was difficult not to be impressed and cynical at the same time. The management team made supreme efforts to show how approachable, human and just like everyone else they were, and yet in fact they weren't. They may have been approachable and human, but they were also the people in charge, equipped with knowledge that the other ten thousand were not. It would not have been surprising if there had been very good reasons why they should not lay off senior management in the same way as the rest of the staff. There might have been all sorts of things going wrong with the plane that it would have been impolitic to announce to the crowd. But anyone in the crowd who saw the All-Team Meeting as only a management ploy would have been taken to task by Mulally and the rest, who believed that doing this sort of thing was better than not doing it, even if, in the end, it *was* a management ploy.

It probably was beneficial, although the managers might have been working too hard to convince people who either already felt members of a team, because of the way their more immediate managers and colleagues worked together, or were having a bad time in their own workplace and were unlikely to be convinced by the razzmatazz.

But there was an interesting demonstration of Mulally's sincerity, never really in doubt, when he was approached by a welder as he walked away from the dissolving crowd at the end of the meeting. This man had a complaint – a very specific one. He said that people with his skills had been laid off at the same time as similar craftsmen were hired by Boeing from outside. Mulally said that he knew nothing about this but on the face of it it sounded wrong and he would look into it. Six months later, when asked without warning if he remembered the exchange, he said that he remembered it very clearly, and had looked into the man's complaint:

> We found out that in parts of the company we declared some skills as surplus and in another part of the company on another project we needed those skills, so we went back and tightened up the communication between the different parts of the company, and so he was right in that respect. On the other hand we had followed the procedures, so we were pretty integrated on that specific skill, and I even sent him a note back myself and then I had another person give him a call and he was very pleased to respond. And I think it was a better business deal for Boeing because we straightened it out.

Six miles down the road from Everett, isolated from the rest of Boeing buildings, were the offices of the Materiel Division. It was here that Mike Voegtlin worked. Voegtlin was the man who had contributed to Al Tyler's becoming 'cheesed off to blazes' in the previous year, when he had said rather sourly that ASTA should take a little more care over their thermocouples. On the day of the All-Team Meeting, Voegtlin was preparing to fly to Melbourne for a further, and perhaps final, episode in the soap opera that was the story of the 777 rudder. As he sorted out his papers for the trip, his secretary brought in a cardboard box and a brown-paper parcel. The box contained 200 baseball caps with 777 logos on them, and the brown-paper parcel held a plaque, another of those tokens of Boeing's gratitude that they were fond of bestowing on foreigners who carried out tasks above and beyond the call of duty. In a way, the circumstances were rather similar to the Nippi efforts with the in-spar ribs: faced with a situation that was not really of their making, a foreign contractor had pulled out all the stops and had managed to complete the contract on time.

> We're very proud of what ASTA's done for us, and so we want to recognize that rudder down there, and we put together this little plaque. We actually had this plaque ready about six months ago, and Al Tyler kept telling us that he was going to make this 5 August delivery right here, so we actually engraved 5 August right on the plaque, and that was somewhat of a risk. As it turns out, they're going to make it.

It was now 29 July and the rudder would have to leave Melbourne in the next couple of days if it was going to go into the Iron Bird test rig on schedule and thence on to the plane. This could be a high spot in the Boeing–ASTA relationship if everything went well; but if there was another snag then Voegtlin would not be a popular man with the Boeing engineers who were waiting to get their hands on the rudder. But he had known high spots and low spots already:

> The high spots were when we kicked the programme off and we all had very high hopes and we knew we had a great airplane – just a matter of designing it and building it. As we went along, we met some of these challenges, some unexpected things, and we had to make some changes. Six months ago, if you had asked me if we were going to deliver this hardware on time, I would have been very sceptical. In fact, ASTA doesn't know this but I reported to the programme that we were going to be late, and we put contingency plans in place up here to work around having this hardware into our factory late. And as it turned out, working together with ASTA in a very close relationship, they were able to achieve almost the impossible.

Voegtlin didn't know that there were still one or two tiny problems. Several small components of the rudder were missing. They were fasteners which Al Tyler *believed* were in mid-air as the team in Melbourne began to prepare the crate for the completed rudder.

As if the pressure hadn't been enough, Boeing had asked ASTA if they could ship the rudder three days earlier than planned.

'My mother used to say I had a disposition like a cow and the face to go with it,' Al Tyler was fond of saying when people asked him how he remained so calm in the face of adversity.

Some people think you can get away with ranting and raving, but that doesn't work. A lot of people didn't believe that it was ever possible to meet the delivery date, and we could have made a fortune if we could have bet on it. But once people realized we were not going to change the delivery date nobody came to me and said, 'Oh look, we've slipped here or slipped there, therefore we must change the date.' Instead they said, 'We've got a problem, but here's our recovery plan.' And we never changed the delivery date.

Until Boeing asked for it 'just a few days earlier'.

In the Iron Bird test rig, the engineers were using a wooden mock-up of the rudder to test the flight-control system, but they were concerned that they were not getting accurate results, in the light of the complexity of the aerodynamics of the final design. So crucial is the overall skin shape of the rudder that the final tests have to be carried out after the rudder is painted, and before it is put on the plane, since adding the thickness of a coat of paint after the rudder is installed could throw off all the results. To accelerate its arrival, Boeing had decided to pay for the rudder to be flown across the Pacific on a 747 freighter instead of it being shipped by sea, which would have taken about five weeks.

When Voegtlin arrived in Melbourne he spoke to a small ASTA group, including Al Tyler, who were packing the rudder.

'One, we want to congratulate ASTA for the tremendous job they've done,' Voegtlin said. 'Two, we have some issues that we have to clean up this week . . .'

'Money,' Tyler interjected in his cheery no-nonsense way – looking forward to the contractual discussions that would now ensue with Boeing about this and future projects. 'We've gone through this production development, we built them, we delivered them on schedule, which can't do us any harm. And the potential for more work for all of us might come from a task such as this.'

As the rudder was crated up, Tyler added his considerable bulk to the task of closing the lid, clearly elated now that ASTA had achieved the impossible in the face of the continual design changes.

There was an excited gathering of people at Melbourne Airport to see the end of the rudder saga. On a blustery, rainy day, they gathered on the tarmac undeterred to see the 747 land and taxi to the loading-area. One of the freight contractors was a little nervous about the tightness of fit. As it was, the thirty-nine-foot-long crate would have to go into the plane at a forty-five-degree angle, since they had been told that the crate had to fit within a 96 by 96 inch cross-section. As the shipping contractor said:

> We have achieved that, even though with timber you have to make some allowance for the variations in timber over such a long length. We end up in actual fact with a half-inch clearance within that envelope height-wise, and then we have a further two inches of clearance to the underside of the ceiling of the flight-deck of the aircraft. But a lot of airlines have the habit of altering the designs slightly, and I've just been up to the plane to check that the original height factor was still being maintained on this aircraft. They have done so, much to our pleasure.

The freighter opened its hinged nose with a big grin, and the crate was hoisted up and slid slowly into the hold. It was indeed a tight fit, and required half a dozen men to negotiate the final inches across the floor of the hold. In spite of all their care, the final rebellious gesture of this rudder was to gouge an inch-deep hole in the ceiling of the hold as it was shoved into its final position.

With a loud roar, the plane sped down the runway and took off into a cloudy sky. It was rather a solemn moment, but a happy one too for Voegtlin, Tyler and the ASTA team, as if the pressures of the last two years rose into the air with the Cathay Pacific 747 and its cargo of ruddy rudder. After it disappeared into the clouds, the group turned away with a general air of relief and Tyler and his colleagues set off back to the factory for twenty years or so of work, starting with seven rudders a month for the first 200 or so 777s.

FOURTEEN

To Fly or Not to Fly

John Cashman couldn't resist a wide smile as he confirmed that there *would* be a flying test bed for the 777 engines. The final decision – an important one – had been made early in 1993. As he and his colleagues had hoped and argued for, a 747 – the first to be built, called RA 001, which had been borrowed from the Museum of Flight – would be converted so that one of its existing engines, the inboard left, would be replaced by the new Pratt & Whitney 4084 engine designed for the 777. This would be connected to controls on the 747's flight-deck so that Cashman and the other test pilots could take the plane up in a series of flights to put the engine through its paces, with one or more of the other engines turned off.

Some in Boeing believed that the test was unnecessary – that the engine was being so thoroughly designed and tested on the ground and in an atmospheric chamber that you wouldn't learn much more in a flying test bed, and what you could learn could wait until there was a real 777 to fly. But pilots were born to fly, and Cashman just didn't believe that all the conditions of flight could be covered in ground tests, however thorough:

> The more interesting testing is where you're doing the outside corners of the envelope so to speak, because you're loading the engine to a very high power and taking it to very critical airflow angles to the inlet, and at that point it's somewhat unknown exactly what it will do. The engine has never been there before. In putting that in a ground simulation, they try to simulate it, but they can't quite get it the same as you can in flight. And the events that can happen when the airflow separates off the front of the engine as it goes into the engine can make the engine very unhappy. It can

bang and you can get what we call surging, where the airflow over
the blades of the engine separates and the engine fires forward.

Cashman had spent the last six months on the ground since
finishing the 757 fly-by-wire control-laws tests last autumn. He had
been involved with the necessary but surely less exciting work of
sitting in the flight-deck simulator and putting every wrinkle of
AIMS – the Aircraft Information Management System – through its
paces to test the enormous amounts of software that a fly-by-wire
plane needs. That work was proving a little troublesome, and was
slipping behind schedule, and the decision had already been made to
leave one facility, the electronic checklists, out of the first plane so
that the rest of the system could be perfected in time. The nearest
Cashman had got to flying one of the new engines was when he
helped with the ground tests, as the engines were put through the
cycle of take-off, cruise and landing many times a day in a Pratt &
Whitney test chamber. Most of the time during the test the Pratt
engineers would operate the controls, but, as Cashman explained
with graphic and delicate gestures, 'The engineers move the throttle
like this – slowly and lightly. Pratt wanted to get pilot input so that
the engines were subjected to the kind of treatment they'd get in
practice' – and he thrust an imaginary throttle forward with firmness
and a touch of bravado.

So a date had been set for the test bed to fly, 15 November 1993,
and there was now six months of work for the test team to adapt the
747 while Pratt pushed ahead on preparing the engine for the tests.

The strength of feeling among some of the propulsion engineers
over this issue was illustrated by an overheard conversation between
two of them – let's call them A and B. 'B,' said A, in a mock naïve
tone, 'why are we testing the engine on a flying test bed?' 'Because
we're fucking stupid,' said B. Certainly the decision was a finely
balanced one, with very senior figures in the team arguing that the
time had come to abandon this costly method of testing a new
engine now that wind-tunnel and laboratory testing facilities were so
good. Granville Frazier put the arguments in his usual robust way:

Let's see, how do I approach this? History has shown us that you
can't fully test an engine on a ground test rig. You need to fling

one about the sky, and have the rotors and the case work their clearances out, and you need to see how the engine's going to operate when you're pulling a rapid wind-up turn in an avoidance manœuvre, with air loads on the fan case pulling it towards the tips of the fan. So in the past – *in the past*, right – we have always decided you should go have a flying test bed and take the engine up and fling it around the sky.

Well, our design and test techniques are becoming better and better and better. The two engine companies, Rolls and Pratt, decided that Tullahoma, the engine development centre in Tennessee, had reached the stage where there was the size and the ability to put loads on the engine that are typical of what you get with different manœuvres, plus the fact that you can control the temperatures and the environment precisely, by turning a knob, where with the test bed you have to fly around the sky and hunt for it. They concluded that they could do a better, more reliable, job of wringing the engine out in the altitude facility than they could in the flying test bed.

Now in the contract I wrote I required all three engine companies to fly a flying test bed. They came to us and said, 'We want to not do that.' Well, Boeing is a conservative company and it's got people in it my age, and it's got young guys in it. We decided that we didn't want to make that big a change at once. So we agreed with the engine company that if they would add their testing in the Tullahoma wind tunnel it would calibrate Tullahoma as a facility to use in the future. As a matter of fact, our plan is to proceed that way. We will fly the engine on the airplane this fall, and we'll fly it in the wind tunnel, and if we check the tunnel out, Rolls won't fly the flying test bed. I would for my own standpoint have been ready to make the decision to go to the wind tunnel without the back-to-back test on the airplane. There were people who were not willing to do that. Those people happened to be in a position to make the final decision and I wasn't.

He laughed a full, throaty laugh, suggestive of long and not always polite arguments.

It was interesting to hear of the discussions that had taken place between Boeing and the different engine manufacturers. GE, too, had decided – or been persuaded – to fly their 777 engine on a flying test bed and had actually bought a 747 for the purpose. It was a cut-throat business, and, considering the amount of investment needed to supply these large thrust engines for a new plane, it was surprising that all three engine manufacturers were still in the race, with an inevitable diluting of the number of engines any one manufacturer was likely to sell. Each manufacturer eyed closely what the others were doing during the testing of the new engines, and, as one industry observer reported, 'Executives at Rolls-Royce and Pratt freely discuss a GE90 engine that failed during a test flight, forcing the pilot to land using his other engines. GE responds with details of a Pratt engine that fell off during testing.'[1]

Ron Ostrowski put the argument for making this sort of change sooner or later, rather than clinging to traditional techniques for the sake of it:

> You know, technology moves, and so does our ability to capture data in different ways, and do it more efficiently. As long as we don't jeopardize safety or reliability – as long as we satisfy the regulatory agencies, and our customer base and ourselves and the public – we will always move towards better ways of doing things. So that's all we're trying to do here. It's a first step, but we won't take it until we're sure it's for real.

In fact, in the long and exhaustive discussions that took place about the issue, Ostrowski was one of the voices that argued in favour of abandoning the flying test bed, as he explained a year after the decision:

> To be quite honest with you I recommended we were ready to do that. Now, in hindsight, I had a lot of advice from others, and it was good advice, because given where we are today – somewhat behind in the schedule relative to the validation of the engines themselves – if we had not gone ahead with the flying test bed we would be concerned about our position now. So, the broad-based expertise and experience level that we have within the company

[1]Dick Beveridge, 'Jet Engine Race', AP Wire Service, 3 May 1994

came forth, and, as a result of that, the decision a year ago was that we weren't ready to take that last step yet.

As usual, it was Alan Mulally who held the ring and tempered the rush to innovation with a blurred but effective compromise:

> We all listened and we all talked about it and we decided 'Well, you know, it's a big development programme, and it's a big change, and so why don't we go check it out on the airplane, and then we'll validate that correlation between the ground facility and the flight test?' And if it turns out we really do understand it from the ground facility, then we won't fly subsequent engines on flying test beds. So I think both people will be right. Kind of. And we'll learn a little bit. But I think most of the knowledge we'll have known from the ground testing.

The hindsight that Ostrowski referred to was sharpened by an event that happened early in the programme of flying-test-bed flights in November 1993. The first problems they had were to do not with the engine but with the fact that the venerable 747, somewhat the worse for wear, lost all the electrical power to the instruments in the right seat, the one John Cashman was sitting in. Fortunately, the pilot who was flying the plane, Boeing's chief 747 test pilot, still had instruments and it was a clear enough day to rely on visual references, so they pressed on.

It was on the third flying-test-bed flight in November 1993 when Cashman's worries about an engine surge turned out to be prophetic. As the plane took off, the crew heard two large bangs and the plane moved slightly to the left. They were all too aware of what had happened, and Joe Macdonald, the pilot, throttled the engine back to idle. After one more surge, the engine stabilized and the crew continued to test. From the ground, it looked more fearsome than it was, with flames and smoke belching out of the engine.

Although an engine surge is not a disastrous event, it is not something you want to happen regularly, particularly on take-off, which is precisely when it will happen if it's going to. At a point when the plane is flying very fast under full power at an angle to the airflow and right near the ground, the conditions all combine to increase the possibility of a disruption to the airflow as it goes into the engine. But the engine depends on a continuous flow through from front to back, and if disruptive eddies or vortices occur around the inlet or, a little further back, around the fan blades, the pressure drops in the front and there can be a momentary reversal of flow as the hot air in the back of the engine comes forward, producing a momentary loss of thrust as the engine effectively backfires. This is what was happening on RA 001.

In the various post-mortems that took place about the event, it became clear that there were all sorts of reasons why this particular engine had surged. For one thing, it had already undergone a rigorous series of ground tests, including attempts to produce surges by suddenly varying the fuel flow to the engine. Tom Davenport, in charge of the programme for Pratt, gave a graphic description of the engine's earlier career:

> The engine that was installed on the 747 had been through a very severe series of tests, including a number of stalls, where we intentionally forced the engine to act abnormally. And a stall on an engine is a very severe and violent event, and it does create the possibility that we could open up clearances and degrade the capability of the engine to operate in normal circumstances. We lose surge margins, we wear out seals, we open up clearances. Every time you stall an engine you run that risk. We had stalled this engine over fifty times before we flew it on the 747. It's intentional – it's part of gathering the data – but it takes the goodness out of the engine for future tests. We did that on our development programme before we went to the flying test bed. So when we flew on the 747 the engine was in a degraded state – it wasn't a new, representative engine: it was a damaged engine that had been worked very hard. And we got an answer from that test programme that said, 'That's not a wise thing to do.'

The situation was complicated by the fact that the engine used on the test bed was what was called a baseline engine, used for development and flight testing but without some of the refinements of the engine design that would go on to the first customers' planes, the production engines, also called EIS, or 'Entry into Service' engines. It turned out that the test engine had a more flexible case around the blades than had been specified for the EIS engine design, and one of the reasons for the surge might have been that air was flowing around the blades as well as through them.

The surge worried everyone on the propulsion team. 'People at Pratt were leaving meetings and vomiting in wastebaskets,' said one observer with a picturesque turn of phrase.

After the surge event, Boeing and United began to think that it would be better for all concerned if they had EIS engines on all the first planes to fly, although the ground testing and some of the RA 001 flying-test-bed tests could still be done with the baseline engine. They also decided that they would need more flying-test-bed tests after the problems that led to the surge had been overcome by Pratt, and scheduled some for March. March was only two months away from 1 June, when the first flight, scheduled for that date since the beginning of the programme, was due to happen.

Perhaps the main lesson that Pratt learned from the surge event was less to do with engineering than with public relations, as Tom Davenport commented ruefully:

> There was a lot of discussion in the media about that flight-test effort, and the fact that the Pratt & Whitney engine had stalled. We ran a test programme that damaged the engine, and we got an answer in the public eye, flying out of Boeing Field with the 747, with some of our competitors and some of our customers observing, where the engine stalled and recovered and we continued on the flight. But it was a very visible signature that we had to explain over and over again, first to ourselves and then to our customers, as to why it happened and why it's not representative of the production article.

Meanwhile the flying test flew on, with a succession of tests that had been scheduled months before the surge events.

One of the tests RA 001 had to perform was a test of the engine's ability to operate under high crosswinds – winds that flow across the wide opening of the engine rather than in the direction of movement of the plane. In particular, the plane-makers needed to know that, if there were strong crosswinds while taxiing or taking off, the engine wouldn't surge or the fan blades vibrate in an inefficient or dangerous way. This test was not scheduled on a particular date because it depended very much on being able to find crosswinds naturally on some windswept airport or another. It also had to be an airport that could allow a 747 plane to straddle one of its runways for a couple of hours with a clear area behind the plane that would not be affected by the force of the 4084 engine running at maximum thrust.

Pratt were only obliged to test the engine up to a wind speed of ten knots, but they decided to find thirty-knot winds to put the engine to the most severe test they could. After the week in which the first four flight-tests had been completed, the plane was brought back and left standing on the edge of Boeing Field. Thanksgiving was looming, and the test-flight team were juggling with various options that would still allow everyone to spend their holidays at home. Also, changes in the engine installation were needed as various detectors and monitoring instruments that were no longer necessary were removed and others were fitted.

On the morning of 22 November, Seattle awoke to a sudden burst of severe winter weather that in an instant, it seemed, paralysed many of the main roads around the Puget Sound. Emergency news bulletins reeled off lists of schools that would not open, and television helicopter teams sent back pictures of long streams of traffic locked solid, jackknifed buses and twelve-car collisions. Boeing Field itself seemed an oasis of calm, as RA 001 stood out gleaming in weak winter sunlight, and a chill wind turned the fans of the 747's own engines with a regular clanking as each blade shifted in its socket on every rotation. The Boeing staff there listened smugly to horror tales relayed by their colleagues in Everett of ten-mile freeway journeys taking three hours or more.

The decision was taken to 'hunt crosswinds' and find somewhere in the United States that had the requisite thirty knots. Although it was pretty windy at Boeing Field itself, the airfield was no good for the test – there was no suitable position for the plane to sit undisturbed. Although the team would have been willing to go anywhere, nearer would obviously be better. One of the nearer airfields that was used a lot by Boeing for all sorts of test and training flights was Moses Lake, over in the east of the state. During Monday

morning, the Boeing meteorology department had established that
the winds at Moses were fifteen or twenty knots and rising. There
was a high-pressure area moving towards it that was expected to
generate winds of up to forty knots some time later in the day. This
looked like a good time for the test. As part of the monitoring
process, engineers started to fit pressure-detection devices around
and inside the inlet of the engine, while other technicians started to
check the plane for airworthiness. Each time the plane was prepared
in this way it was given a 'release' with a validity period of twenty-
four hours. After that time a new series of checks would have to be
carried out to ensure that it was still all right to fly.

By the middle of the afternoon the test looked more and more
likely. The winds were still strong at Moses Lake, and Dennis Floyd,
the test operations manager, decided to call a pre-flight briefing for 7
p.m. with the aim of taking off soon afterwards if everything seemed
OK. Some people were called from home, as their shift had finished,
and a small crowd gathered shortly before seven, in one of the flight-
test conference rooms. The Pratt representative on the team
distributed khaki Pratt & Whitney baseball caps to everyone while
they waited.

What they didn't know was that Floyd had been phoning Moses
Lake at regular intervals since it was decided to go ahead with the
flight, and was getting the gloomy news – for Boeing – that the
winds were dropping almost by the minute. The trough of high
pressure had clearly not had much strength or staying power, and
looked as if it had already passed over Moses Lake. At 5 p.m. the
winds had dropped below twenty knots, by six they were down to
fourteen, and two minutes before the briefing they were only ten
knots.

'This is going to be a very short pre-flight,' Floyd announced,
giving the team the news of the drop in wind speed. 'It looks as if
Moses Lake is not going to have the winds we need. But we could
wait another hour or so just to be sure. What do people think?'
Floyd looked over to Bob Silman, the Pratt representative on the
team and therefore representing the client who would pay for the
flight.

One of the engineering team who had been installing the sensors
reported that one sensor wasn't working and would be impossible to

fix. There was a discussion of whether the test would be valid with one sensor too few, and people agreed that it probably would, although there was also some talk of getting a new one.

Having ruled out Moses Lake, Floyd produced another option. 'Now we could wait till tomorrow and go to Cheyenne, Wyoming. We've checked the forecast there and they do have winds gusting to forty knots, but they also have other hellacious weather.'

Joe Macdonald, who was scheduled to fly this test, pointed out that to fly to Cheyenne involved flying through snow or rain that might damage the sensors. If they *were* going there, the sensors would have to be removed before the flight and reinstalled when the plane got to Cheyenne.

With a little more of the consensus-seeking that Boeing people were so good at, Floyd nudged the group towards the conclusion that (a) they would not try to go anywhere that evening and (b) they would check the forecast for Cheyenne at seven in the morning and if it looked good they would take the plane there as soon as possible after that – maybe as soon as eight thirty or nine if they could get people together.

The following morning the right course of action was still not clear. There were two windy places in Kansas that looked possible. One of them, Salinas, turned Boeing down because they couldn't provide the right space and position at their airport. The other location, Wichita, which has an airfield shared with the Boeing plant, accepted them. The wind at Wichita wasn't quite as strong as they needed – twenty-one knots instead of the twenty-five knot minimum they required – but there was a chance that it would increase, though nobody had great confidence that it would. Still, as Floyd pointed out, in the past people had waited six months for the right condition for this particular test. If they *did* get it today, it would be good to have it under their belts. As the morning briefing continued, there was an almost imperceptible move from doubt to decision, although Floyd clearly didn't encourage that decision until he knew that Silman, on behalf of Pratt, would accept it. Pratt, after all, would be paying the $10,000 dollars or so that the trip would cost.

Once the decision was made, everybody's name was taken down on a list for insurance purposes and then people were told to report to the plane as soon as possible so that they could set off while the winds were still good in Wichita. The nearest the test flight had to a stewardess was flight-test manager, Bob Moretto, who gave everyone a safety briefing before take-off and distributed forty lunches in Boeing Proprietary cardboard boxes. There was a choice of beef, chicken, turkey or vegetarian. The beef box contained one beef and cheese sandwich, a small container with macaroni salad, another container with two slices of tomato, a packet of Frito Lay crisps, a huge impenetrable apple, and a piece of banana cake. There were also supplies of drinks – vacuum flasks of coffee, and an icebox of 'sodas'.

RA 001 certainly showed its age. The 747 cockpit looked very old-fashioned compared with the liquid-crystal displays that all recent Boeing planes used. Everything inside the plane had a knocked-about feel. The upper lounge just outside the cockpit had, in its former life, been a haven of luxury for first-class passengers. Now the sofas had torn upholstery, the ceiling was missing, revealing pipes and cables, and some of the wall panels had been ripped out.

Down in the main cabin, everyone took his seat as the plane took off about 2.15 p.m. The plane flew south over Mount Rainier, snow-covered and glistening in the sun. The activity of the 4084 engine on the left wing was observed by a small video camera. Most of the people on the plane were Boeing test engineers, but along for the ride was a team from Smith's Industries, the English company which had been contracted to make a new type of fuel gauge for the 777. It was intended to be more accurate than any previous fuel gauges and was supposed to measure the density of the fuel and its level in the tank so that the mass could be calculated – the characteristic that really tells you how much energy you have left. With the less accurate type of fuel gauge, pilots have been known to switch an engine off and divert to an alternative airport in the belief that they have run out of fuel when in fact there has been some left.

As the plane headed west towards Kansas, the light faded surprisingly quickly. Dennis Floyd held a briefing meeting in the first-class lounge and then went into the cockpit to watch the final rays of the setting sun. In the red glow, he talked about the difficulties of arranging this kind of test:

The weather conditions were just marginal, and we still had to find a location that's suitable to do the testing, a large enough airport for a 747 to operate in and then be able to allow us to position the aircraft in any manner such as we can bring up this test engine to 90,000 lb thrust without blowing half a county away.

I would put it at 50 per cent at best for the weather to come through as predicted and give us over twenty-knot winds. The goal is to have twenty-five-knot winds, but we've made the commitment that anything over twenty knots we'll go for it. Right now the airplane is looking in good shape, the engine's looking in good shape, we've got the facilities lined up – all that had to come together in the space of about two hours and we've got past that – so our only remaining constraint now is hoping that mother nature's going to co-operate.

It was dark by the time the plane landed in Wichita and pulled up to a corner of the airfield operated by Boeing. There was a sense of the power of a company like Boeing and a project as vast as the 777 as the front left door swung open, steps were rolled up to the plane, and people materialized with rental cars and news of thirty-two rooms which had been found and booked at the Wichita Suites hotel since the decision was made a few hours ago. Already Floyd had realized that he hadn't got time to organize thirty-two packed lunches for the next day's flight back, and he told people to have a good breakfast at the Wichita Suites in the morning.

It was certainly windy at the bottom of the steps, and people were generally pleased that the weather forecast had proved correct – so far. But was it windy enough? Floyd decided to try a crosswind test straight away, with the opportunity to have another go the following day if it didn't work. Engineers came down from the plane and clambered into the engine inlet. With some force they slowed down the fan blades, which were windmilling quite fast just because of the wind. They then removed the protective foil coating from the probes that would detect the pressure of the air as it approached the fan blades and measure whether a process called 'inlet separation' had occurred – an indication that the engine had not been able to sustain the airflow in a high crosswind.

Two members of the team were meteorologists, and they set off to set up a small weather station so that the actual wind speeds and direction could be relayed to the test team in the plane during the test. All meteorologists in flight-test programmes are called 'Windy' and addressed indiscriminately by that name. 'Windy's just gone down to the other end of the airfield,' someone will say, and it won't matter whether it was Bob or Chuck or both of them, or someone else filling in. Nobody called the pilots 'Jetty' or the maintenance people 'Fixy' or the firemen 'Flamey' – only the meteorologists have to put up with the anonymity and interchangeability of a single label, whoever they are.

The wind was still quite strong as the two Windys struggled to set up the pole with the wind-speed and direction indicator. There was then the fiddly business of getting ink to flow in a surprisingly low-tech pen recorder.

While the weather station was being established, the plane taxied to a corner of the airfield, to a position at right angles to the wind direction where there was nothing behind that might get blown away. Just to be sure, two security cars were parked two hundred yards back, to stop anyone approaching.

When the pilot was ready to start, Bob Moretto remarked on the onset of 'visible moisture' – rain – and said that the engine was not supposed to test under those conditions. But a few minutes later the shower passed, and they decided to start the engines. The pilot asked for a wind reading, which was greeted with disbelief in the plane. They also had airport meteorology data on radio channel, and the two contradicted each other. It turned out that Windy was reporting the wind direction as where it was coming *from*; the plane people wanted where it's going *to*.

Finally everything was ready and two engines revved up on the 747. They ran the normal 747 outboard engine on the opposite wing to the 4084, to prevent the plane twisting under the 88,000 lb thrust. For several minutes, there was a loud roar from the engines, while the weather men charted the wind conditions in the hope that there were gusts that were consistently strong enough and in the right direction. A small cheer went up when one gust reached thirty knots.

A minute or so into the first test run, two loud bangs close together signalled a surge. But in fact, it was the old 747 engine protesting about the conditions. There was a series of tests covering acceleration and deceleration, and steady runs at different thrusts, but they were all in vain – the wind was just not doing its stuff, hovering around fifteen to twenty knots.

Finally the decision was made to stop the tests, and the plane taxied at a surprisingly sprightly pace back to its parking-place. It was 11 p.m. in Wichita, 9 p.m. Seattle time.

There was no strong sense of disappointment among the team. It would have been good if they had obtained the winds they required. It would also have been a miracle to complete the test first time. Floyd called the team to the front of the plane for a briefing. He had discovered that four vans and eight cars had not material-ized; instead there were five seven-seater minibuses. He gave directions to the Wichita Suites hotel, and the convoy set off to spend the remainder of the evening in the Cafe Chicago eating Wichita wings, prime-rib sandwich or chicken and curly fries, or in the Cowboy Bar, drinking beer straight from the bottle.

On the following day the team tried again, but the wind still wasn't up to the task and they flew back home for Thanksgiving. It was to be another six weeks of regular monitoring of the weather over the United States before they found their winds, in Montana, and the engine passed its crosswinds test.

It's an obvious point, but one that flight test people were to find themselves explaining over and over again in the following months, that things that go wrong aren't necessarily bad news. They are, after all, what the tests are designed to bring to light. Even the infamous engine surges were seen by Alan Mulally in a very positive light:

> The engine surges were a gift, they were good news. It was a good piece of data. It provided a perfect example of why we laid the plan out the way we did. Eighty-five to ninety per cent of all the things that we validated by flying the engine supported what we thought from analysing the engine ahead of time. We were surprised and Pratt was surprised that we had an engine surge where we did on take-off. After we analysed the data we also realized that we had not run that condition during our test programme, so we went back and ran that test condition and it also surged on the ground in our test cell. So we got some really valuable information about

that, in that it told us another thing to look at in our validation testing with the engine on its own, and also it told us the value of testing the engine with the airplane. Because we had that knowledge, Pratt could modify the engine, put in some design changes to not have that happen.

So I think it's a perfect example of what you have to do – include all the lessons learned, do the best design you can, but then comprehensively test it on the ground, in the test facilities and on the airplane and learn from the data, and then be able to deliver an even better quality engine. I think Pratt is really pleased with the engine now, and I think the airlines feel real good about and I know that we, the Boeing Company, feel real good about the quality of the Pratt engine.

FIFTEEN

From Boardroom to Factory Floor

The door to the 777 executive suite in Building 40-88 is usually open. Anyone can wander in, and if he's looking for the men's room or the cafeteria he will be sent on his way by the executive assistant nearest to the door, who works for Ron Ostrowski. There are many square yards of space stretching diagonally from the door past the offices of successive vice-presidents to end, with Alan Mulally's office far off in the distance. Between Ostrowski at one end and Mulally at the other are the offices of Dale Hougardy, Fred Howard and Neil Standal, stretched out on the right, each with windows making a projecting corner. Down the left side of the diagonal are a kitchen, a couple of meeting rooms, and offices for other support staff – people like Dick Blakeley who don't qualify for an expansive spread of windows, or indeed any view of the outside world at all, but are better off then those who work in the open-plan areas of the rest of the building.

There is more public space, so to speak, than office space, and it soaks up every sound with the help of its carpets and large stuffed armchairs, so all that can be heard most of the time is the occasional distant murmur. Such a murmur might have started as a shout in one of the offices or conference rooms, but it will soon disappear into the soft furnishings before any hint of raised emotions can be detected.

But blazing rows probably don't go on very often in these rooms. The VPs know each other too well to indulge in histrionics every time they want to make a point, and they seem to embody in themselves the management style that they try to use with others. In fact in late October 1993 they could have been forgiven for momentary lapses from good nature and calm forbearance. There were signs of gloom and doom everywhere. In one of the cafeterias a coffin was placed next to the salad bar; hanging above the grills counter was a small, white-sheeted ghost and every few seconds it let out a moan; office doors and partitions were festooned with skeletons or bats. It was, of course, Hallowe'en, but these emblems could hardly be expected to cheer up the engineers, designers and programme managers who queued up for their roast beef and cheddar sandwiches – if they had time to go to the cafeteria – in the midst of the type of pressure that put into the shade the previous year's rush to get the design completed. Alan Mulally showed signs of weariness as he laid out the current preoccupations the team faced:

> The thing that's pushing us the hardest is the schedule, because it is relentless. Every minute counts, and every day there's a different event, and so just getting the things done on schedule, so that you don't end up with a bow wave of activity that's hard to manage, is really important. It's almost like you want to pay special attention to every event, every day, every design release, every digital pre-assembly, every new piece of knowledge that comes out of the test programme, and to get out in the open and fix it, and get the supplier involved that made the part, or the designer, or the manufacturing engineer. Just keep going, day in and day out, getting every one of them done, so you can have time the next day or the next week to handle the new knowledge then.

On the factory floor the inexorable progress of the plane could be witnessed, still meeting its major milestones, sometimes at the expense of extra shifts and the dedication of the people building it.

One of them kept particularly busy in October was Ed Kacalek. It's difficult not to make him sound like a commercial for the Boeing 777 – or at least for the digital-preassembly concept:

> I think digital preassembly is. . . well, the word that I can describe the best is 'perfect'. It's just amazing how well the parts and the components on this airplane are going together. There has been virtually no trimming of parts, or having engineering to redesign parts to make them fit the airframe. It's working extremely well.

For meeting after meeting every week for two or more years the 777 teams had been trying to design plane parts that wouldn't just work but would be easier to build and maintain than in any other Boeing plane. Kacalek himself had been a member of twenty-seven design–build teams in his time. He was the manufacturing representative on the all-important centre section of the plane, where the wings came out of the body, and if he and his team were going to get this section assembled properly he had to be alert to every possibility for improvement, as enthusiastic engineers in the various DBTs produced their elegant, functional and unmanufacturable drawings. Kacalek would lean over the table, covered with progress charts, design drawings, overhead projection slides and electronic calculators, and make some point, his small red moustache bristling, about what would happen in the factory once this elegant design met with the combination of unyielding metal and only-human plane-assembly workers.

Often the need for the improvements that he suggested arose from pure inertia. Most parts on the 777 corresponded with components of earlier planes, and you can't blame the designers for occasionally doing what they'd done before, and presenting a design for a part that was essentially the same as that part on a 767 or a 737, scaled up to fit.

The wing-strut fairing, for example, is a common or garden cover for the back part of the strut that holds the engine to the wing. It's a shaped framework looking a little like a boat, and in the past it had two small doors in one side to allow access for maintenance. Inside the fairing is a lot of equipment to do with the hydraulic-pressure system, the electrical controls, and so on. When Kacalek was one of the manufacturing representatives on the team designing the fairing he helped to draw attention to the fact that, in the past the limited access through the small doors had made it necessary to remove the whole fairing to get at any of the larger units that might need maintenance or repair. He suggested much bigger doors, on both sides of the fairing, so that anything that had to be removed could be with much less effort and delay. Now the fairing has become a framework holding six doors, giving easy access to all the equipment inside.

On a Saturday in October 1993 the fairing was lying on the factory floor waiting to be fitted around the strut, on which the engine hangs. But Kacalek had other things to think about that day. The plane-makers had reached the stage where two wings had been assembled and now had to be attached to the centre body section, and it was his responsibility to see that this task, planned for the following day, was achieved successfully.

At 6.18 a.m. precisely, determined by the complicated shift pattern Boeing workers followed, the factory team had arrived at the 777 assembly building. It was dark outside, and raining, but inside the building all was glaring brightness. Rows and rows of bright mercury vapour lamps high up in the ceiling illuminated the working surfaces, assembly tools and interior office buildings, all coloured in cream or pastel shades of pinky-brown. The two wings and the body centre lay in the position they had been in for several weeks while the factory team had installed an intricate network of hydraulic tubing, bundles of wires and actuator mechanisms that would move the flight surfaces – flaps, elevators and so on. The whole set-up was about twenty feet above the main factory floor, on a giant platform that was shaped to allow easy access to the wings for the teams who had been installing the systems. From a central well that held the body section, two gracefully curved floor sections rose like shallow sand dunes towards the tip of each wing. The curvature was necessary because the wings were held at the angle with the horizontal that they would retain from now on. For the best flight performance these wings were tilted upwards from the inboard end, as well as being swept back.

The wings and centre section were in position at the beginning of the assembly line. From this point onward they would travel together in increasingly close proximity as they acquired the rest of the plane, in front and behind. Today they were to be moved to the position where the wings and the body would actually be joined together. Ed Kacalek knew there would be problems. As with all the 'firsts' on this project, part of the purpose of the day would be to learn by doing. No one had lifted this weight before, and the specially designed four-hook cranes were experiencing some bugs in their computer software.

Even the cranes, those mere magnifiers of manual strength, had entered the computer age with a system that was designed to give an accurate account of the load on each of the four hooks. These hooks hung from a turntable that allowed the load to be rotated. And the cab that held the turntable was suspended from a bridge that moved along the factory ceiling while the cab could move along the bridge. This complex arrangement meant total freedom to lift a piece in any orientation and deposit it anywhere else on the vast factory floor at any other orientation. Theoretically.

Just in case the crane system didn't do what was required of it, Kacalek had thoughtfully arranged for a pile of bags of lead shot to be standing by. They would turn out to be essential. The wing was much heavier at one end – the wide or inboard end – than at the other, the outboard end. Attachment points consisted of a yellow bar attached inboard, and two eyelets outboard. By eight o'clock the crane had brought over a suspended horizontal grid with hooks that matched the attachment points and had exerted enough lift to sense what the loads would be. Over the wireless intercom, the crane team – four men in the cab poring over their computers – gave details of the loads that each of the four hooks was lifting. The news was not good.

Since the wing was last weighed it had acquired a lot of extra weight in the form of hydraulic systems, fuel tubing, wires and movable components on the trailing and leading edges. In addition to adding to the weight, which wasn't such a problem, the additional loads had changed the centre of gravity of the wing. The crane was meant to be able to deal with this situation by adjusting the tension on each of the four hooks. But the software had a cut-out command to prevent lifting if the imbalance between the four hooks was too great. Although the distribution of weight in the wing was perfectly acceptable, the cut-out kept operating whenever they tried to lift. The engineers could have overridden it, but it was decided to do things by the book and even out the tensions by putting weights near the hooks that had the lowest tension, as well as hanging large concrete weights on the grid.

Soon after eleven o'clock the wing lifted off for its last solo flight. With an incongruous pile of canvas bags on one end, it rose about fifty feet, moved forwards about twenty, and settled into the next position.

There were about fifty people scattered over the floor of the assembly area. Centre stage were the crane team, but there were other assembly workers charged with seeing that the pieces carefully settled into their new positions on the jacks that were part of the rig. There were also safety superintendents, scuttling around like mother hens, persuading rebellious chicks into line. One of them was festooned with blue and yellow waistcoats to identify those who were allowed into the working areas. He also made sure that hard hats were worn where necessary. Another safety supervisor tutted as he saw a worker walk along the surface of the wing to adjust the lead-shot bags. 'That wing is more than four feet above ground. That guy's got to wear a safety harness,' he said, and rushed off to see to it. Boeing could be fined up to $25,000 dollars for that sort of safety violation, and it was a source of pride to the supervisors every time they prevented that sort of penalty – and, of course, injury to one of the workers. But for some workers in an industry where hard physical work is a component there is an inevitable aura of wimpishness about hard hats, safety harnesses, ear-plugs and safety spectacles.

Today was another of those days – increasingly frequent now the plane was actually being manufactured and there was something to see – when people who weren't essential to the process drifted in to watch what happened. A few weekends ago Phil Condit had been seen wandering around the factory with his wife, obviously missing the plane whose team he no longer led on a day-to-day basis. Today Ron Ostrowski walked around, talking to some of the people who were controlling the operation. Garnet Hizzey was also there. As production engineering manager, he was ultimately responsible for the development of the sequences of . events by which the components and systems of the plane all came together. Both these senior Boeing engineers wore casual dress. It was a display to the world that, although today was not an official work day, they had detached themselves from American family life, abandoned such tasks as putting the gas-fired barbecue into mothballs for the winter or helping little Kenny with his basket shots in the backyard, and had come to lend visible support to this plane on which their and the company's future depended. Such neglect of family life was, in fact, a regular occurrence with many of the 777 engineers and managers. They were more visible at milestone events like the wing–body join, but on Saturdays and Sundays they were to be seen walking the corridors and open-plan areas of their workspaces in the same polos, chinos and boat shoes.

After the first wing was in position, a similar weight problem had to be solved for the second wing. It too required a combination of lead-shot bags and weights on the sling, but the ratio of the weights was different. More consultations took place between the crane operators and the team below, and more calculations were done before the moment of lift-off. But the process eventually went smoothly, and in a few minutes the wing was being lowered into position. The final phase was a matter of manœuvring by inches, signalled by intercom instructions and some hand waving.

On the underside of the wing there were several sockets for the jacks that would hold the wing in its final position, and the crew were guiding the wing so that the sockets were directly above the jacks. At one point it looked as if the wing in its final position would clash with a small electrical switchbox, and the final manœuvring was extra careful to avoid a nasty collision.

With the two wings in place, the trickiest part seemed over. Unlike the wings, the third piece to be moved, the centre section of the plane, was symmetrical and so there was no need for counter-weights, lead-shot or tricky calculations. Four canvas straps hanging from the turntable and hooked to points on the fuselage were enough to support the load, and the green cylinder moved easily up, across and down into position. The same final finesse was needed to lower it on to its jacks, but here a minor snag became apparent. Two metal plates a few inches wide projected from part of the platform that would surround the fuselage. As the crew tried to move the section vertically above its jacks, it was discovered that the plates were in the way by an inch or so. With a shower of sparks, a man with a power saw severed the plates from the posts they were attached to, and the final descent continued to a successful conclusion.

For someone not used to the inevitability with which detailed drawing was followed by accurate manufacture and finally – usually – predictable function, the sight of a finished wing, with a coat of paint and all systems installed, was a breathtaking statement of confidence. What blind acts of faith were embodied in thin-walled aluminium tubes following a precisely engineered path from fluid reservoir to flap actuator, in bundles of many wires of many colours parting and joining with other wires, from and to many other parts of the plane?

None of these pathways – for hydraulic fluid or electric current – had ever conducted its medium at the correct pressure or voltage, flow rate or amperage. Now that they were installed it was probably impossible for anyone physically to trace their paths. Any attempt to do so would be frustrated by bulkheads and metal skin, floor segments and insulation blankets. The act of faith was invested in the three-dimensional computer data where such paths could be traced if anyone wanted to, but computer simulation had not reached the stage where the hydraulic fluid could actually course through the imaginary tubes, or current flow through the prettily coloured wires.

The limitations of design engineering, and the extent to which the final nuances of performance had yet to be verified, were shown by the red labels littered along the trailing edge of the wings. The words 'Defective part' were printed at the top, and the dozen or so such tags on just this visible part of the plane were enough to make anyone wonder at whether these engineers were as good as they were cracked up to be. How had they reached this advanced stage of design while still producing so many defective parts?

In fact the labels were misleading: they indicated components which had been made exactly as intended but had not yet been tested in flight. The first flight tests might well lead to improvements on changes in the design, and it was only after they had been shown to perform in the most appropriate way that the components would get an FAA certificate and lose their red-tag status. Until that point they were to be treated as defective in the sense that they were not the final version certified for use on the production aircraft.

It's only when you see a part going through its paces in the factory that you begin to appreciate the layers of complexity that in the design phase were merely hinted at in the person-years of discussions, mile-high piles of overhead transparencies and football-field areas of drawings. At first the only surprise is the size. Everything is large – the building itself, of course, with its 200-foot-high ceiling sprinkled regularly with star-like piercingly bright lamps; the parts themselves, particularly the wings, but also as you approach them the tubular sections of fuselage looming like train tunnels; the four-hook cranes like circular space-ships, each with its crew of four or five glimpsed through the iron-mesh floors of their cage as they stare at the computer screens which control them. And then it strikes you that there are other even larger objects here – the tools that are used to manipulate the parts. One is a cylindrical framework larger than a fuselage whose sole purpose is to turn over a section of fuselage when work is completed on its bottom. It's obvious when you think about it – to try turning over a huge cylinder with hooks and cranes would be a tricky business, but putting it inside a purpose-built cylinder that rotates the whole thing in a twinkling clearly makes sense. But then you realize that somebody had to design and build the rotation device. Was there a design–build team for that too? And were the pieces of this tool made with other tools that had to be designed specifically for the task by yet more engineers? An infinite regress opens out, and you wonder where it stops – perhaps only when it reaches ordinary tools like hammers, drills and screwdrivers that you buy in a hardware store.

If you look carefully around the main areas in late October 1993 you can see almost all of the first plane still in a dismembered state, along with parts of planes 2 and 3. Entering by a door on the east side of the building you walk up a wide passageway, passing a section 41 – the nose of plane 3 – recently delivered from Wichita. Straight ahead and ten feet up is the wing–body join area stretched out like the wings of a seagull, curved in a mid-glide, and 400 feet across. There are the wings and centre section of plane 1, just recently joined together. Over to the left are two front sections of the plane – plane 1 and plane 2. Today, in the midst of the knitting that seems to be going on as sheaves of coloured wires are threaded through preplanned paths along the fuselage wall, a small knot of important visitors looks at the cockpit area. Lyle Eveland, the genial general manager of the factory, along with Ron Ostrowski and Jeff Peace, are showing someone around. He seems to be important, and they defer to him with traces of awe. The visitor turns out to be Joe Sutter, legendary chief engineer of the 747 who was also helpful in the early days of 777 design. Also around today are two of the doors engineers, coming to look at the handiwork now it's installed.

Behind this area lie the rear sections of the same two planes but without horizontal stabilizers, fin or rudder. In the next assembly hall, parallel to this one, the two parts of the horizontal stabilizer are being joined as it stands upright and fanning outwards like a giant butterfly. Meanwhile, in a separate but adjacent building off to the right, a wing with a difference is propped up on the floor, having various extra pieces attached to it after its main assembly process in the wing major. The difference lies in its outboard end. About twenty feet in from the tip is a sudden disruption in the smoothness of the wing's underside. A series of massive hinges marks the point where the folding wing tip will fold. This is the first folding wing tip to be built. It may also be the last unless some airline responds with the sort of enthusiasm that evaporated from American Airlines along with its desire to buy the 777. At the moment its destination is an ignominious one: it will go on what's called the static test airplane, an oddity of an aircraft with one folding wing tip and one normal one, destined for destruction before it's ever given a chance to fly. Its wing will be bent up in the same way that a cruel schoolchild will bend upwards his playmate's middle finger. Like the finger, each wing will take the strain until it has moved through about eighteen degrees. Then, as the relentless hydraulic jacks push ever upwards, it will snap somewhere along the join, never to be repaired or rejoined.

Every few minutes, it seems, an electronic signal sounds through the factory. It indicates an impending shift change, or the shift change itself, for either the 747, 767, or 777 crew. Such moments are part of the choreography of Boeing working life, essential to avoid the simultaneous spilling on to the freeways of 26,000 people.

These working areas never seem crowded, partly because they dwarf the workers. The actual tools and jigs are home to individual mechanics or engineers, often heard before they are seen as they rivet, tighten or drill. Two legs dangle from a hole in the underside of a wing, a disembodied hand pokes out of a horizontal stabilizer and waves a signal. If you look carefully, you can see the corresponding disembodied feet resting above another hole. It's like the two ends of a lady who is about to be sawn in half by a conjuror. And along the wide painted passageways cyclists meander from one area to another.

In the space of ten months this area has turned from an empty, echoing stadium into a twenty-four-hour-a-day creature, consuming parts at one end, assembling them in its innards, and in six months' time beginning to disgorge them and take in more 'food'.

But where does the 'food' come from, and how does it get

there? Only Dennis Sieminksi knows the full story. He is transportation manager for the 777, and has at his fingertips the origins and
sizes of every single large component of the plane, and will tell you
with little hesitation the routes they all take to get to Everett and the
problems they might face on the way:

> Pratt & Whitney engine? Yeah, that's, of course, being produced
> in Connecticut. It'll go on a truck at the Pratt factory and it'll cross
> the north-eastern United States and the Midwest and then
> through Wisconsin, cross the Interstate 90, most of the country,
> directly into Seattle, or it'll go first to our Propulsion Systems
> Division facility which will put the cowling parts on it and then it'll
> be trucked from there to the factory.
>
> Because the width and the height are so big, things like that are
> restricted in every state in the United States to one degree or
> another, although each state is a little bit different. So there are
> certain times of the day you can move it over the road and then
> you have to stop and then start the next day, so you have to think
> about things like that when you have very restricted transit and no
> flexibility to recover.
>
> We've gone into enormous detail for the Pratt & Whitney and
> the General Electric engines, looking at every single state, every
> single road, every single route, how long it takes, what are all the
> restrictions. We've looked at things like road-construction projects
> for the next ten years and weather conditions, to know exactly how
> long it's going to take and how reliable the transit is going to be.

Even local Puget Sound transport needs a certain degree of
planning, since the parts can be quite large. On 27 October 1993 a
shipment of wing spars was due in Everett to be fitted together with
the ribs in the ASAT tool. These were made down in Frederickson,
not far from the lowest slopes of Mount Rainier. At about 100 feet
long, these were among the longest individual pieces of the plane.
They were typical of the problems of transportation that faced the
plane-makers. Frederickson is about fifty miles from Everett and for
most of the way the two sites are linked by good stretches of freeway,
so road transport was the cheapest and most obvious way to deliver
them.

At nine o'clock on the foggy autumn morning, Bill Foster, Gary Longman and Lenny Lombardi gathered to move that morning's load. The vehicle they were using looked from a distance like an ordinary truck–driver's cab over front wheels, and, a few feet behind, a set of back wheels. But, when Foster got into the front cab and drove it forward, the back wheels stayed where they were. Between the two sections stretched a couple of tubes – power cable and hydraulic pipe – entwined round a cable. When the bundle was taut, the front cab had moved about 100 feet away from the back wheels. Meanwhile a long yellow container had been pulled out of the factory by a tractor. The container was almost like the fuselage of an aircraft itself, with the cross-section of an arched door and a length of 130 feet. It was deposited on the ground alongside the extended truck, and then two fork-lifts dexterously hoisted it into the air and moved forward in unison. In barely a moment, the three drivers had helped to lower it on to the front and back wheels, locked it into place, and were ready to set off. It now became clear why three drivers were needed. Nestling in front of the back wheels and attached to their small chassis was a second driver's cab. Today Gary Longman was to sit in the rear 'steer cab' as it was called. His sole job was to steer the back wheels in coordinated manœuvres as the truck negotiated various bends and a few corners between Frederickson and Everett. There was a comical contrast between the size of the load, the massive chrome-gleaming front cab and the small, low box at the back.

Lenny Lombardi would drive the pilot car, a pick-up truck with flashing yellow lights on top and a notice saying 'Oversize Load'. As the three of them finished the task of loading up, they ribbed each other with an easy familiarity. Asked how low an overpass they could get under with their huge load, Gary said, 'As low as we like if we go fast enough,' and chuckled.

Once the container was loaded, the truck set off at a fair lick towards the factory gate and the first stretch of road, an ordinary suburban four-lane highway, but mercifully straight. The procedure at each change of direction was balletic. Over the intercom that linked the three drivers, Bill in front would describe what was coming up. If it was a right turn, Larry in the pilot car at the rear would swing protectively into the outside lane. No cars behind could overtake now, and, while the front cab stayed in the inside lane, the back wheels swung out so that for a few seconds the truck was driving in two lanes at once, with the load describing a long diagonal across the lanes. As Bill kept going in the new direction Gary would realign himself in the same lane and Lenny would tuck himself back in behind them.

In spite of the size of the load, the truck proceeded at a fast speed – the maximum allowed – along the freeway. Many drivers sped past, or were overtaken, without noticing that the truck had two drivers. The ones that did notice always took a second look. At first sight Gary looked like someone who had been driving a compact car that had got stuck under the truck. He always gave a cheery wave, particularly to children, although he was less well-disposed to the driver of the Porsche who once tried to cut underneath the truck from one lane to another. In fact, he would have been able to do – there was space to spare – had it not been for the cable and tubes that hung below the container, which he noticed just in time.

The fog varied from very thick, when the front wheels were barely visible from the back, to gently misty, but it didn't hinder the steady fast pace of the truck. The intercom dialogue was a mixture of businesslike sharing of information and camaraderie. As the truck neared Everett, not much more than an hour after leaving Frederickson, the sun broke out, revealing the snowy peaks of the Cascades that lie between Seattle and Vancouver, further to the north. The truck curved in a wide sweep off the slip road from Highway I-5 and off to the west to the Boeing plant. It swept past the new 747s, gleaming with fresh paint and awaiting delivery, and turned into the plant gate where, released from the narrow constraints of public roads, the back and the front took a few elegant liberties in their relationship with each other and behaved more like the two vehicles they really were.

Once they had parked outside the 777 assembly building, within minutes two fork-lifts had appeared from nowhere and taken off the load. With barely a pause for a pee, the drivers set off back to Frederickson to repeat the trip with parts for the new 747s that were being built next door to the 777s.

SIXTEEN

Finally Assembled

Wednesday 12 January 1994 is a mild day at the Boeing plant at Everett, but in the 777 conference room people shiver under the rather erratic air-conditioning. At least it makes a change from the sweltering heat that had greeted people in their offices when they first moved into the building a year ago, as the heating and the air-conditioning behaved equally erratically.

There are about seventy people in the room, to participate in the weekly Programme Review Meeting. This will last a modest three hours – a far cry from the Mega-Meetings of 1992, six-hour marathons that used to make grown men sleep. About sixty-five of the people attending are men, and there are about half a dozen women. As usual with Boeing meetings it is dominated by overhead slides, slapped efficiently on to the screen at a breath-taking pace and often containing closely packed figures, words or symbols. Schedules dominate the slides in one form or another, as graphs show how people are sticking to – or falling short of – the targets which have to be met if the planes are to be delivered on time. Alan Mulally has a set of 'Principles and Practice' that are meant to govern these programme reviews. They are put up on a slide at the beginning to remind people of the ground rules. They include:

> Use facts and data
> No secrets
> Whining is OK, occasionally
> Prepare a plan, find a way
> Listen to each other
> Help each other, include everyone

Enjoy each other and the journey
Emotional resilience

It is during this week that the American magazine *Business Week* publishes an article about Boeing's management style entitled 'When the Going Get Tough, Boeing Gets – Touchy Feely', and much that goes on in these meetings does smack of an invasion of psychotherapists. But there is no doubting the genuineness of the reaction of one guest at today's meeting who says how surprised he is at the non-adversarial nature of the discussions compared with most other meetings he goes to in other companies, where there is usually blood on the floor by the end.

One sign of the way these people work together is the high standard of repartee that erupts from time to time when the tension needs relieving. When John Cashman slips into the meeting a few minutes after it starts, someone says 'John Cashman – never late, seldom on time.' Only occasionally does a more critical note creep into the meeting's reactions to the succession of reports. A man delivers a report about progress at a Boeing sheet-metal plant. 'How many parts do you make?' says Mulally. 'Three hundred thousand,' the man replies. 'How many do you deliver?' says another man, with some feeling, and not quite *sotto voice*.

The content of the meeting covers every aspect of the plane, from sales and orders to progress on maintenance manuals. Alitalia, the Italian airline, have suddenly appeared as potential purchasers, and the sales people are clearly jumping to supply the paperwork, cost breakdowns and possible deliveries that the airline wants. One of the senior sales people gives a graphic account of one recent sale he helped to complete. He is God's gift to the 777 programme as his own enthusiasm for the plane bubbles out during his report. 'This airplane is dynamite,' he says. 'We have the MD-11 killer. And once they see the interior it's irresistible.' He shows photographs of the official contract-signing ceremony, set up for the local press. Representing the customer, an impressive ministerial figure from the board of the purchasing airline; for Boeing, the salesman, with an uncomfortable expression on his face: 'This was the point where the guy turns to me and says, "Can't we change this?", pointing to a clause in the contract about training. I said, "But we've already discussed all this." "But we want to change it . . . " And there's all these press guys taking their photographs as we're having this conversation. So I turned to my colleague from Boeing and we had a quick conversation. "How much would it cost to do what this guy wants? $100,000 a plane? Well, I think we'd better do it." And the contract was signed. So you'd better make the plane cost less to make.'

The salesman describes some of the ploys that he uses to persuade potential customers that the 777 is better than its rivals. On one occasion he went into the meeting-room before the session at which representatives of Airbus, McDonnell Douglas and Boeing were to make their pitch and put up a full-scale drawing comparing the cross-sections of the 777, the MD-11 and the rival Airbus plane. Of course the facts were incontrovertible – the 777 is five inches wider than its closest rival – but it didn't make it any easier for the other salesmen to tolerate. But things don't always go Boeing's way. One night a Boeing salesman was having a drink with one of his rival counterparts. The other salesman said, 'Have you ever wondered why you lost that deal when we undercut your price so effectively?' The Boeing man said that, yes, he had wondered whether they knew Boeing's price by some means. 'Well,' said the other salesman, 'we were all staying in the same hotel, and we bribed the receptionist to show us all the faxes you were sending and receiving.'

Many of the progress charts have the usual traffic-light symbols to indicate whether something is good, unsatisfactory or bad. At today's meeting many of the reports that relate to the Pratt engine are red, but the nearest Mulally gets to expressing criticism or concern is when he talks about the engine schedule being 'tight'. The other major culprit is AIMS – the Aircraft Information Management System – which is presenting a number of headaches and slipping further back in the schedule. Many of the other aspects of the plane, including the production schedule, are bang on target or even better than forecast. Praise abounds where it is due, and the meeting is punctuated by occasional rounds of applause, triggered by such Mulally remarks as 'Is Joe our man or not?', followed by the sort of 'whoop' that is more usually heard from the audiences of late-night TV chat shows. But it does the trick, and makes everyone feel motivated to strive even harder to make this plane the 'preferred aircraft' rather than just another plane.

At midnight on the following day, an expectant crowd stood around on the floor of Building 40-25 at Everett. They were looking at plane 001 in its final body-join position and waiting for it to be moved to its last position in the factory before it went out of the door. Ron Ostrowski was not among them, although he had asked to be called out of bed when the move was imminent. The plane had wings, a tail, horizontal stabilizers, and, most important of all for the evening's events, landing-gear. The only key components that were missing were the engines, and their absence was emphasized by the contrast between the smooth contours of the rest of the plane and the messy struts, with wires and tubes hanging out of them, looking a little like the stumps of severed arms.

The man of the moment was a driver called Dennis Lavalle, who spent his working hours moving planes from one position to another. He was one of three drivers who might have moved the first 777 to its final-assembly position, and he had been told the night before that he would be the one. The momentousness of the event appeared to leave him unaffected, although he may have had a moment's pause when he saw the number of people gathered to watch his efforts. The third shift at Everett is often conducted in an atmosphere of funereal calm as the rest of Puget Sound lie asleep in their beds, but tonight there were about 200 people willing to forgo their sleep until dawn if necessary, just to see their plane move on its own wheels for the first time.

Earlier in the evening, the various platforms and access stairways had been moved away from the plane, leaving the front half unencumbered. The wings were still suspended over the giant dune-like work platforms, but the safety rails had been laid flat to allow the wings to move forward. Under the big belly of the plane the wheels of the landing-gear hovered an inch or so above the floor of the building. The plane was still supported on jacks and jigs, but slowly the gear was lowered by hydraulic pressure so that the wheels began to take the weight of the plane. A rubber chock under one of the wheels began to buckle as the wheel came down, and one of the technicians realized that it shouldn't be there. It took two men to heave it away from under the lowering wheel.

Although the 777 was a very big plane, comparable in some of its dimensions with the 747, there was something about its conventional shape that made it impossible, from a distance, to get a true sense of its size. Only the tiny dots of people clustered at its feet gave some sense of scale. In an empty hangar, it might have been mistaken for a 767.

Among the dots, Lyle Eveland, the factory manager, watched, standing alone in the crowd. If this could be said to be anyone's evening it was Lyle's. He was the guy who ultimately answered for the manufacturing process at the high-level team meetings, and he was the man who currently was getting the most plaudits for a largely snag-free operation. A quiet man with a perpetually beaming smile and an occasional disarming wink, he was someone who didn't force his personality upon people but just observed and monitored and occasionally intervened in events, if he could see that his years of experience might be useful. In some senses Eveland was the unsung hero of this year of manufacturing. While Dale Hougardy was, of course, ultimately responsible for this aspect of the project, Eveland was in day-to-day contact from his office high up over the assembly floor, where he could see the whole sweep of manufacturing activity, and he seemed to carry in his head the complex matrix of which plane was at what stage of manufacture.

The details of tonight's move were being managed by Willis Clark, a large, prematurely grey man with an easy smile. With many of these major procedures, the people in charge seem to do very little other than hover, ask questions, and occasionally cajole. But success in a situation like this clearly depends much more on the planning than on decisions made on the spot, at the time. Tonight's events would go as well as the interaction of the plane, tools and building would allow. Someone, in the design phase, had had to make sure that the complex three-dimensional shape of the plane would not bump into anything on its hundred-yard journey from final body join to final assembly. The heights of platforms, the gap between one plane position and the next, the actual height that parts of the plane would reach once it was on its own landing-gear, taking account of the inflation of the tyres, for example – all of these had to be calculated carefully. For Dennis Lavalle, the nerve-racking part of the job was trusting the 'wing-walkers', equipped with walkie talkies and electronic alarms, whose job it was to watch out for any unforeseen obstacles as the plane moved and turned along the path between the two positions. One reason tonight's move was likely to present Lavalle and the rest of the team with fewer problems was that he had a clear run from the final body-join position to final assembly. Since 001 was the very first plane in line, there were no other planes to be manœuvred around on the way.

But there was an almost palpable sense of pressure from the other planes in various stages of undress throughout the rest of the plant. One of the many thousands of charts the Boeing people issued every day to keep track of progress showed which plane was in which position and in which stage of manufacture. The chart issued at the beginning of the week showed floor plans for seven buildings. In Building 40-25 – final assembly – there were five positions occupied and ten vacant. In each occupied position was the number of a plane – 00-something if it was destined to fly, 99-something if it was one of the static test planes. In the final-body-join position was 001; behind it, in the seal, test and paint position was 997; then in the wing-to-body-join position, where 001 had been in December, was 002. There were six positions for systems installation – one was occupied by the front end of 002 and one by the front end of 997. Working back to earlier stages of the assembly process, the wings of 998 and 004 were being assembled in the wing-major tools, and the lower lobe of plane 004 was being assembled upside down nearby. In one corner of Building 40-34, where the assembly process had begun for plane 001 almost exactly a year ago, it was now plane 005's turn to have the components for its wing spars fixed together by the automatic riveter of the ASAT tool.

In carrying out this combination of processes for the first time on plane 001, the plane-makers had learned a lot about how to do things better, and the planes that followed behind were benefiting from all sorts of refinements and improvements. The pace with these first planes was much gentler than would be necessary once – as everyone hoped – they were making three planes a month.

Once the fourteen thick-tyred wheels were supporting between then the full weight of the plane, the remaining obstacles to the forward move were cleared away, while men with brooms swept up an untidy mess of papers, screws, bits of plastic and paper cups that had gathered under the plane's belly. Willis Clark had one important act to perform before the plane could move – bureaucratic but necessary: his signature was required on an official piece of paper to signify that the plane was passing out of his hands and into the hands of people who would look after it during its final assembly.

Dennis Lavalle got into the seat of his squat, sparkling-white, brand-new tractor and started the motor. The exact moment that the plane began to move was almost undetectable, so slowly did it start. But it gathered momentum as the wings cleared the wing tools, watched closely by the wing-walkers. There was a burst of applause as the plane broke free – metaphorically – from its bonds and headed down the centre of the assembly building. On the right side of the plane, away from most of the onlookers, one of the passenger doors swung open as Lavalle turned the plane slightly to point it towards its final position. 'You can tell Alan Mulally the doors open real smoothly,' someone commented, although Clark, as he watched, made a mental note to latch the doors closed when they moved the next plane.

Lavalle stopped the plane halfway through its journey for photographers to take pictures of the event, then, barely twenty minutes after it had started moving, plane 001 eased smoothly towards the final-assembly position at an angle to the balcony from which the people working on the final installation would enter the plane. This balcony had movable platforms that would extend right up to the doors when the plane was in its final position, although there had been a small ruction the day before the move when it was discovered that one of the platforms just would not extend as planned. It turned out that someone wanting to run a vacuum-cleaning tube from a ground unit into the plane's interior had decided that it would be a good idea to pass the tube through a hole in the platform. Since there wasn't a hole, he made one, effectively blocking the platform's movement.

In the final-assembly position, just where the main landing-gear would rest, there were two large hatches, covering pits into which the gear could be raised and lowered once the plane was supported on jacks. As the wheels moved on to these platforms, there was a sharp, crackling, rippling sound, as if the tyres were rolling across a pebble beach. The hatches bowed slightly under the weight, but held, as they were designed to. Lavalle manœuvred the plane back and forth to get its nose and tail in exactly the right position along the line painted on the floor. Then, his main task for the night achieved, he switched off the motor and got down from his cab.

It was about 12.30. A few minutes after the plane was in position, Ron Ostrowski hurried into the building. It was all over so quickly he hadn't had time to witness the event. Willis Clark hovered near the plane, watching a new team of people start to prepare for the mountain of work that still had to be done on the interior and on the systems that would only now, in this final position, get electrical power. A fork-lift truck brought some wheeled steps towards the plane, 777 painted on the side. Like everything else in this area, the steps had been specially designed for just this plane and they gleamed with new paint. Another fork-lift towed a triangular framework underneath the tail to begin the task of supporting the weight of the plane. It towed it away again when it was discovered to be the wrong height.

By now, most of the sightseers had gone to bed. At about 1.30 Willis Clark got into his red pick-up and drove out of the plant into a night that was dank and misty. As the night shift set to work a thick fog descended on the Everett plant, and the illuminated Boeing sign high up on the side of the factory could barely be seen.

On 19 January 1994 it had been foggy all day. John Cashman sat in the Jet Deck restaurant at Snohomish Municipal Airport inspecting – without much optimism – the menu that included hamburgers named after every one of Boeing's airliners, including the 777. He ordered a turkey club sandwich and looked out over a still, silent airfield. He was on his way to meet a couple of other Boeing pilots who were to help him with a secret Boeing project. At one o'clock Cashman set off slowly around the perimeter of the airport to the far side, keyed in a security code to an automatic gate, and drove past military lorries and a couple of helicopters dimly visible. The fog seemed thicker on the airfield itself, free to lie heavy and flat across runways and taxiways. Even if Boeing hadn't wanted to keep it secret, their LAGOS project was shrouded from anyone's view in this far corner of the airfield under its security blanket of fog.

When Cashman got out of his car, another pilot was waiting for him. The two men talked for a few minutes and then walked over to a structure looming above them. They climbed a set of metal steps and through the door into a cockpit with two seats for pilot and copilot, a primitive steering-column and the usual tiller for turning the nose-wheel. An engineer and another pilot followed the two pilots into the cockpit, and the stairs were moved away. Cashman spoke on the radio to the airport control tower and to other Boeing people in a converted recreational vehicle on the ground. He then turned to the other pilot and asked him to drive backwards for a few feet. With barely a jolt, LAGOS – Boeing's Large Airplane Ground Operating Simulator – was on its way.

The idea had been around for a couple of years, from the time Boeing decided to market a stretched version of the 777. It was realized that the wheelbase of the new plane – the distance between the nose landing-gear and the main gear further back – would be longer than in any other airliner. Furthermore, the cockpit would be a long way ahead of the nose landing-gear. This could present problems for pilots as they manœuvred around the taxiways and runways of the airports the plane would be likely to use. How would the pilots learn to drive the stretched plane while it was on the ground? They couldn't rely on their abilities learned on existing aircraft, since nothing would have a nose-wheel so far back from the pilot's window or main wheels so wide apart and far away from the front. Without adequate training, pilots could find themselves involved in embarrassing and costly foul-ups as they ran off the tarmac on to soft grass and had to be towed out. Not even pilots who had been trained on the A- and B-market 777s could transfer across very easily, since the stretch added another thirty-seven feet to the wheelbase. But Boeing's customers would appreciate any way of avoiding expensive retraining, so Working Together led to a commitment to come up with some solution that would make it as easy as possible to drive the new plane with the minimum of fuss and the least amount of new learning.

An early idea was to use a Boeing 757 as a sort of 'scaled-down' 777, and try steering it around a shrunken airport layout, painted on the airfield at Moses Lake. The thought was that the difficulties of turning a plane with a wheelbase of 140 feet on a 150-foot-wide runway could be reproduced by painting a 100-foot-wide runway and trying to turn the 757 with its smaller wheelbase. But it was decided that this would never reproduce closely enough the stretch 777 situation, and so LAGOS was born.

Few people who had seen LAGOS could talk about it, without a smile playing on their lips. Cashman had described it as a praying mantis, and it also had affinities with some of the longer, slimmer dinosaurs. The oddity of its shape – a long tube with an angled tail at one end and a cockpit on a stick at the other – was a result partly of its severely functional role as a support device for the wheels and the cockpit and partly because of the expectation generated in all of us by decades of industrial design that a vehicle – any vehicle – should incorporate some aesthetic qualities: streamlining, perhaps, or colour or decoration. But LAGOS was not meant to be looked at. It was a tool, purely and simply, and the fact that it looked for the most part like some corner of a deep-sea oil rig that had become separated from the rest of its parent structure was neither here nor there.

At a Programme Review Meeting the week before, when LAGOS was mentioned, someone had asked whether it had 777 painted on it. 'No,' said somebody else, in a cruel disowning of the ugly vehicle – 'it says Airbus 350.' Even earlier today, at the latest Programme Review, the 777 Communications Division had mocked up the front cover of a fictional magazine called *Seed and Irrigation Review* with a picture of LAGOS and a photo of Cashman seated at its controls. It was another humiliating metaphor for LAGOS – this time drawn from the resemblance to those rotating horizontal irrigation tubes with a wheel at one end. But more seriously there was praise for the vehicle as well, as Cashman told the meeting of a successful series of test runs at Paine Field, also known as Snohomish Airport, where experienced pilots tried to steer their way through a series of complex test turns and manœuvres and then told Cashman and his training colleagues what they thought could be done to improve things.

One of the things the team were looking at was whether to build video cameras into the stretched 777 so that the pilot could look at the nose-wheel or the other landing-gear and see how close they were to the edge of the runway. There were arguments against this apparently sensible idea. First, it would be expensive – both in the cost of the technology and in the weight it would add to each plane. Second, in Cashman's view, it could make the pilot less reliant on his own knowledge and skills. The Boeing philosophy, as embodied in the fly-by-wire system for example, was to leave the pilot in ultimate control of a situation rather than trusting too much to equipment, measuring devices or monitor screens. It was much better to train the pilots to develop a sense of where the wheels were than to let them rely on visual information that, by its dominance, might lead them to ignore other, subtler, cues. But it wasn't easy. LAGOS was fitted with three cameras, two on its 'tail' looking forward at each main landing-gear, and one underneath looking at the nose-gear. But during today's test run, as LAGOS lumbered out on to the runway, Cashman would sometimes switch the monitors off and leave the training pilot, Jim Wallace, to his own devices. He did pretty well, producing some accurate 180-degree turns between lines painted to represent the 150-foot runways that could sometimes be expected. But afterwards Wallace said that he felt uncomfortable without the kind of established visual markers that experienced pilots develop for themselves. Just as reversing a car into a parking-space can be easier if it's done with reference to the nodding dog in the rear window, so a good pilot can tell a lot about how a plane is moving by using the corners of windows, or tips of the wings. In the case of the 777, the swept-back wing tips would not be visible from the cockpit, and anyway LAGOS didn't have any wings at all. And the whole thing was made more difficult by the nose-wheel being so far back, some way behind the cockpit.

For an hour or more Cashman and his colleague crawled their way along the runways and taxiways, with Cashman questioning the other pilot closely according to a questionnaire that was being used to help Boeing make the right decisions about the ungainly device. Then the winter gloom set in and they called it a day.

'One infallible rule of making planes is that planes are always weighed in the middle of the night.' Allen Bailey was echoing the complaint that was also made about line moves, a stage in the assembly process when the plane moves one position down the line towards final assembly. It was probably something to do with the fact that the processes involved were not really labour-intensive and therefore would need a smaller night shift to carry them out. But every 'first' with the first 777 always attracted a large crowd. Anyone who had even a feeble excuse for being around would turn up and watch.

Considering how important the weight of the plane was, it was surprising how late in the day it was before anyone actually checked to see the outcome of all the calculations made at every level from individual designers trying to lose a few ounces to the chief engineers' Mega-Meeting working out how to get another ton off the plane. In fact no customer would know the absolutely impossible-to-doubt weight of his aircraft until a few days before delivery. Until then, it was a matter of believing in the careful weight calculations that were an integral part of every single component.

But for the first plane there was to be a weighing of sorts, in March 1994, and Allen Bailey would be in charge. Having supervised, cajoled and worried for four years about a target that had been set more by guesswork than anything else, he would have a personal stake in seeing how near the real plane was to that target. The test plane was not an ideal candidate for judging how successful the weight-control team had been. Although its overall structure was the same as the other planes, it contained a large amount of extra weight in the form of test equipment that would be needed on all the first test flights. If you added together small add-ons like the ejectable windows in the event of an emergency and the twenty or so linked barrels of water to adjust the centre of gravity for some of the tests, there was about 35,000 lb of extra weight. But since these add-ons were not designed and calculated with the same accuracy as the rest of the plane it was impossible to be sure. So any attempt to weigh this plane would give only a rough idea of the true empty weight of the 777. Nevertheless, on the night of 18 March the crowd gathered, and Allen Bailey, relaxed in bright yellow sweater, slacks and sneakers, was there to see the result – 'Not, you understand, that it will tell us anything at all about the true weight of the plane.'

The weighing was needed in preparation for a test called the ground vibration test. The plane with its long wings and complex empennage could be considered as a giant tuning-fork – or rather a collection of several tuning-forks fixed together. It would vibrate if struck or buffeted, and the engineers had designed the plane so that the 'modes of vibration' under normal or even abnormal wind stresses and gust patterns would not shake the plane apart or damage any component. It was a similar problem to the vibration modes of the metal tubing on the engine that had been tested with the Pratt & Whitney computer system. The 777 team hoped they had checked that the whole plane would not inadvertently have a vibration mode that would shake it apart, but the ground vibration tests were another example of the essential checks that were needed to make sure that the world of the computer and the real world were in tune. The tips of the plane surfaces – wings, horizontal stabilizer and fin – would have force generators attached to them, moving the ends back and forward in a random pattern for several hours at a time. These movements would not be large – it wasn't intended to damage the plane as in the static tests on the other side of the factory – but they would cause the plane to experience an overall pattern of random shaking. Several hundred accelerometers were fixed all over the surface to measure any small acceleration at the point of attachment. The signals from these accelerometers were then fed back to a computer that built up a picture of how the plane was vibrating. Different frequencies of vibration were introduced to produce computer data to compare with the predicted patterns of vibration at each frequency.

But, before any of this could be done, the plane had to be weighed. The expected patterns of vibration were based on a calculated weight for the plane, and the team needed to know both the actual weight and the position of its centre of gravity – the point in the plane where you could balance it on a pivot and it would not tip over. Those data could then be incorporated into the computer model of how the plane should behave.

So how do you weigh a plane? One way is to weight it in bits, and this had been happening during the manufacturing period. Each piece designed on CATIA had assigned to it a calculated weight, based on the volume and the density of the material from which it would be made. Once the pieces were made, the actual weight could be checked against the prediction. Not surprisingly, the predictions were remarkably accurate – any discrepancy was usually due to some manufacturing problem. In this way, maybe 60 per cent of the plane had been accurately weighed by early 1994. For the rest of the plane, the engineers had to rely on the original design calculations and add them in to the measured total. This brought the expected weight, without the test equipment, to 271,000 lb.

But the best way to weigh a plane is to put it on some scales. Boeing's seal and paint shed had purpose-made scales for weighing anything up to a 747, and these would be used for the completed ready-for-service planes. But the flight-test 777 was still in the final-assembly area, and so it had to be weighed on six sets of scales, two under each of the three landing-gear assemblies.

Shortly after 10 p.m., the plane was pushed slowly back about forty feet. Several of the weighing crew brought over jacks barely larger than the sort a garage mechanic uses to lift a car. Each of these was wheeled under the axle of a pair of wheels and lined up with a jacking-point. With each jack there was a blue cylinder, the actual measuring device. Inside the cylinder was a pressure-sensitive plate, a transducer, that converted the magnitude of the pressure into an electronic signal. These cylinders were about the size of a family tin of baked beans, and six of them would support and measure the weight of the plane – nearly 120 tons. To continue the culinary analogy, the cylinders would be put in position and 'left to cook', in Allen Bailey's words, for twenty minutes or so with the plane jacked up. They were linked by cables to a briefcase placed on a trestle table under the left engine. When the lid of the briefcase was lifted it revealed a control panel with keypad, buttons and a digital read-out. Printed on the panel were the accurate but prosaic words 'Aircraft Measuring Equipment'. The keeper of the briefcase was Winston Metcalf, a serious middle-aged man with a well-groomed head of greying hair. Metcalf was called a load-master, and had been weighing Boeing planes for thirty years.

It took about ten minutes to get the jacks into position and start the transducers 'cooking'. Meanwhile, the team had to be sure that the plane was level. As far as the weighing was concerned, this didn't really matter – whatever angle the plane was at, the weights measured at the six transducers would still add up to the total weight of the plane. But the centre of gravity was a different matter. If the plane wasn't level, the calculations of the centre-of-gravity position, based on variations in the transducer readings, would be wrong. For Boeing's newest and highest-tech airplane the device that measured whether the plane was level or not was a throwback to five-thousand-year-old technology. Suspended in the main landing-gear was a plumb-line with a shining new brass plumb-bob. During the course of the next hour or so, the plumb-bob would be consulted each time the jacks were raised, and shouted instructions would ensure that the heights of the six jacks were adjusted to keep the plane level. Each time the team took a measurement they had to spin the wheels to make sure that the whole plane was off the ground by half an inch or so.

The process was not without hitches. One jack leaked oil from its pressure cylinder and had to be slid away, leaving a snail's track of oil behind it which had to be covered with sawdust and swept up. Another jack refused to lift the wheels off the ground. Although the lifting power came from a combination of high-pressure air and oil pressure, there was also a bar for operating the jack manually. Disgusted with the lack of movement on the wheels, one of the team wrapped his hands round the bar and pumped away energetically before exhaustion set in. No movement of the plane was visible while he did this, but that wasn't surprising, since he was trying to lift about 50,000 lb of airplane. Jacks are designed to convert a small force over a large distance into a large force over a small distance. The many feet travelled by the man's arm pushing the bar up and down were translated into a fraction of an inch of plane movement. When he'd had enough, the first man handed over to his colleague, a young man in white T-shirt and red braces. With a few strokes of the jack handle the giant rubber tyres of the undercarriage could rotate freely and the problem had been solved.

Over at the trestle table a small crowd had gathered to observe the results. There seemed to be several people doing the calculations: at least two calculators and a pencil and paper were in evidence, as well as the aircraft weighing equipment. Although the equipment had the ability to add up the separate transducer figures, nothing was left to chance. Orders were given to raise the jacks, and one of the team checked the plumb line, occasionally calling for tiny adjustments in the height of one or other jack. When the aircraft was level and entirely off the ground, the calculators set to work.

Lying on the table next to the computer was a sheet of pencilled calculations carried out earlier in the day, when Bailey and his colleagues had tried to work out what they expected the weight to be. To the predicted empty weight of the plane, based on design predictions and measured component weights, they had added various extras. These were the best estimates for the weight of the test equipment, metering cables and water barrels, as well as one or two subtractions for pieces of the plane that weren't attached that night. Their prediction for the weight of the test plane was 290,206 lb. As the computer digital display flickered with the pressures of the individual transducers, Winston Metcalf noted each figure on a form and solemnly added them up with a pocket calculator, although the aircraft measuring equipment was doing the same thing in a millionth of the time. Both totals agreed. The weight of the plane was 297,678 lb. Although this weighing wasn't – as Allen Bailey kept reminding anyone who would listen – of any relevance to the true weight of the final in-service aircraft, he was clearly a little puzzled as to why the plane and associated test equipment was three tons heavier than expected. It was always possible that something in the jacking process had led to a transducer sticking or being pressured at an angle, and so each reading was usually taken at least twice. The signal was given to lower the plane to the ground and then to raise it again. Fifteen minutes later, with much hissing of high-pressure air, the plane was up on the jacks and the weight was calculated again. This time the figure was 297,734 lb – entirely consistent with the first. A difference of fifty-six pounds was well within the margin of error.

Associated with each of these readings was a calculation of the plane's centre of gravity, important data for the ground vibration tests. The first reading showed that the centre of gravity was within half an inch of the predicted value, and the second was within a tenth of an inch of the first. The close agreement between all these figures suggested that the test so far had gone extremely well. Whatever the reason for the unexpected weight, it was unlikely to be equipment error. Bailey and his colleagues planned there and then to make a more thorough estimate of all the test equipment on the plane during the following week, to find out about the extra three tons.

SEVENTEEN

Run-up to Roll-out

In February 1994 Ron Ostrowski was showing signs of pressure, as he sat in his office and looked at the picture of his boat, which he hadn't seen in a while, on the wall:

Well, it's really a critical phase. The fact that little time remains if you encounter severe problems makes it a tense time, relative to everyday business and moving your way through the plan. I feel better today than I did three months ago, because I see that we're still on that plan to achieve what we want by 1 June and there haven't been new problems developed that jeopardize that plan. It doesn't mean to say I'm relaxed, because any day in this complex business new things come up. But I do feel better, so every day is a new day.

Ostrowski, as director of engineering, lived from day to day by the plan – or rather by a whole slew of plans, each of them relating to a different process, system or target, and all of them having to converge on the date of 1 June, when the first flight was due to take place. Any one 'delinquency', as problems were called, and the plane couldn't fly. If the plane didn't fly on 1 June, or soon after, the schedule of tests would be set back, the ETOPS tests would start later, and the delivery date to United in May 1995 would be threatened – an almost unthinkable eventuality, since the airline was already building the planes into its worldwide schedules.

In fact the team had stayed remarkably on target for much of the time, although when you talked to Ostrowski about how that was achieved it appeared that sometimes when he said that they were sticking to the plan he meant that they were sticking to a different plan from the one they started with – a plan that had been changed to allow them to work to a delayed target or a changed objective:

> A couple or three months ago, we put a plan together to recover from a delinquency in the software as it appeared in our test programme here, and that allowed us to achieve the objectives we needed to before we flew the airplane. That compression isn't any different today than it was two or three months ago. We're on that replan. That's the point – we're on the replan. And it's tough. We watch it every day. We've been reinforcing constantly, wherever we needed to. We're very close to precisely what we wanted to do at that point, three months ago. So if I was to index from that point, as opposed to the original plan, we're on plan – we're on the replan, and so we're pleased with that.

He understood very clearly what he was staying, but it sounded a little like moving the goal posts – doing a replan so you could say you were still on the plan. In fact the key word was compression – the overlapping of some tasks, the intensifying of others, even dropping elements that were desirable but not essential for the first flight and picking them up later for the production aircraft.

Meanwhile the plane was acquiring more and more of its essential systems and components. In mid-January Alan Mulally had switched on the power system in the first plane and for the first time the liquid-crystal screens in the cockpit glowed purple and red and green, although they had not yet the final software installed to run the full navigation systems.

Towards the end of January the plane was pressurized for the first time, in a test that, predictably, took place late at night. The pressurization system is designed to keep the air pressure inside the plane at a suitable level for people to breathe. On the ground, no pressurization is needed at all – although planes still have to be air-conditioned rather than condemning people to sit in stale air. But as the plane rises to higher altitudes it gets into thinner air. Above about 10,000 feet people would start to notice breathlessness as the air they breathed in failed to satisfy their bodies' needs for oxygen. For the plane itself it is essentially the pressure *difference* between the inside and the outside that is the important factor. At higher altitudes, the thinner air outside the plane means that the normal atmospheric pressure inside the plane causes ballooning of the fuselage as the whole plane tries to expand. Windows and doors are crucial elements in the pressure-containment system. With the normal pressure difference of about eight pounds per square inch (p.s.i.), a surface the size of a window can experience a force of half a ton and the correspondingly larger doors up to about twelve tons.

The early passenger planes were not airtight, so they could not fly above certain altitudes unless pilot and passengers wore oxygen masks. Then Boeing built the first pressurized passenger airliner, with two essential ingredients: a completely airtight interior – except when the door was open – and a system to pump air in and out of the plane through valves that prevented the higher-pressure air inside from leaking out. That plane was the Stratoliner, and like any airplane nowadays it had to go undergo a test during assembly to prove that the fuselage was capable of holding air under pressure. One Boeing engineer who used to work on the Stratoliner described how the test worked:

> All the skin joints were covered by what we called 'paw' tape. You fit the skin, then you trimmed it, put the paw tape on, and covered it with kerosene to soften the tape. Then you drove the rivets through, which supposedly sealed it. To check for leaks, which generally occurred when you got a bum rivet, you covered up the joints with Ivory soap suds. If you saw a bubble come up you had to rerivet the area.[1]

When, on the night of 21 January 1994, the 777 was taken up to pressure for the first time, the procedures were rather more sophisticated.

First the plane was draped with rope mesh and plastic sheet covers over the areas that would fail if the pressure difference led to some kind of blowout. A team of engineers stayed inside for the first phase of the test, taking the plane up to about five pounds per square inch, just to check that there was no major leak in the system – a hatch left open or a valve stuck. At the briefing beforehand, anyone

[1] Serling, *Legend and Legacy*, p.44

with a cold was told not to go in, and people were also told not to wear ear-plugs. This was because blocked ears would lead to a pressure difference between the inside and the outside of someone's head which might be painful.

Air was pumped into the plane from outside, and all was well as the plane reached a pressure difference of 5 p.s.i. Then the air was let out, engineers left, and the pressure rose again, this time towards 8 p.s.i. Although this was the pressure difference that the plane would experience in normal conditions, as with all tests like this the engineers had designed in a margin of safety of about 50 per cent. This meant that the plane had to be able to sustain a pressure difference of 12.1 p.s.i. – much higher than it would ever be likely to experience in service. As the pressure rose, Tim Schmitt, the engineer in charge, expressed quiet pleasure at the way the plane was behaving, as seen on dials and gauges at a small workstation outside the plane. Among the other observers was John Mahoney, the door designer who had been working on CATIA two years before and who had followed his handiwork through the design and manufacturing phases to this crucial test.

The test was almost completed – the pressure had reached 12 p.s.i. – when there was suddenly billowing plastic over the rear door on the left-hand side of the plane. The seal had failed on the door, and air was escaping through a small gap. This was disappointing but not entirely surprising. If anything was going to fail it would be the door seals first, unless there was a major fault in some other component. It is a difficult technical problem to calculate the forces that the seal will experience at every point around the door, not least because the door and the fuselage change shape under pressure in ways that are quite difficult to predict. The seal has to be compressible in the available gap when the door is closed under normal pressure but must expand to fill that gap effectively when the whole plane expands like a balloon. Because of this demanding task, the door seals have a complex structure, made up of silicone rubber containing a stainless-steel insert with slits that can act like fingers and accommodate the local distortion of the door.

Two years beforehand, Tom Gaffney had talked about the difficulties of designing door seals:

In our original design, put in EPIC, the seal was judged by experienced people to be very leaky, and we came up with a new design. Interestingly enough it was judged to have probably the same risk but it weighed forty pounds less, so this is what we went with.

When the door seal blew, Tim Schmitt decided at first to keep the air pumping in, in the hope that the plane could reach the required pressure of 12.1 p.s.i. This would still be a useful test of the rest of the plane and would reassure them that only one seal needed fixing. If the air could be pumped in much faster than it was leaving through the rear door, the pressure could still be maintained.

But it didn't work, and the plane was depressurized so that the door engineers could go and take a look. They knew they would have to redesign the seal in the area where a gap had opened up, but for now their main task was to make a temporary fix so that the plane could be taken up to pressure again to test the rest of the plane.

With the help of some sticky tape and plastic tubing the door was sealed, the plane was taken all the way up to 12.1 p.s.i., and the rest of the fuselage passed the test.

Ron Ostrowski could have done without this further small problem, but he put a brave face on it:

It was a fairly simple problem really. It occurred on the aft door, which is in the most severely contoured area of the body. The seal just didn't have enough length to sustain the pressure load. What we've simply done is redesign the length of that seal so it would bridge that slightly larger gap and maintain pressure. It's going to take a slight modification to the seal design that we had in place.

But of course that 'slight modification' would have to be fitted to the rear doors of all the planes now coming together in the factory. Plane 001 was no longer the only 777 that was recognizably an airplane: as Lyle Eveland explained, looking out from his corner office with the panoramic view, there were now several more to be seen on the factory floor:

The number one airplane 777 is in final assembly – you can see it over my shoulder – and we're currently doing functional tests on the airplane. The static test plane, which is the second airplane we built, will come in to final body join during the night. The first airplane we built for United Airlines, WA 002, is in systems installation. The wings have been joined and the body systems are being installed. The second airplane we built for United Airlines is in body structures, and a piece of it is over in clean, seal and paint. Wings and spar building is going on for British Airways' first plane at this time, and so the process continues.

But a major component missing from all these planes was the engines, which had been experiencing a few problems of their own that were a real test of the 'Working Together' philosophy.

Late March 1994 was not a good time to be pushing the Pratt & Whitney workforce to stay on schedule and stick to the plan. A recent pay rise of about 90 per cent, to $1.9 million, for one of the senior executives of the company did not mesh very well with the fact that another 150 employees were to be laid off that week and who knew how many more in future weeks. There was a union-organized protest march outside the headquarters of United Technology, Pratt's parent company, and workers on the shop floor were openly contemptuous of the way management was behaving. There were posters around the plants appealing to workers to 'Call Karl', with a toll-free number on which they would be able to have a conversation with the company president, Karl Krapek, during a regular period every few weeks. But this kind of worker–boss relations did little to defuse the situation, although it might have given the individuals who did call Karl a chance to let off steam, if they weren't worried that they would be victimized for doing so.

The pressure was on Tom Davenport, leader of the 4084 team, to get the two engines for the first plane finished testing and across to Seattle as soon as possible. Davenport, like several senior Pratt executives, had worked for Boeing in the past, and when the initial phase of the 4084 project was not going too well he was moved across from another engine programme in the company. On his

office wall was a picture of his boat and an aerial photograph of
Mount St Helens, the volcano in Washington state that exploded:

> When I get irritated, I look up at Mount St Helens, and for a
> moment I blow my top. And then I settle down, because I look at
> my boat and I go for a ride.

Davenport is a tall, charming individual with a raffish moustache
and an air of relaxed competence. He did sometimes blow his top,
particularly on the 777 programme, but he also knew that such
responses had their limitations:

> Emotion and ranting and raving, while it has an impact, it doesn't
> last very long. And sometimes it can be a negative. It can take away
> from the focus, and it can create hurt feelings, and people react
> with a change in their attitude that's not positive but negative. So
> we're much better off to have a plan to make sure the people are
> there, the parts are there, and that we support the plan.

Regular, almost hourly, conversations with Rocky Thomas in
Seattle analysed the situation backwards, forwards and inside out,
checking that every tiny detail that could hinder the operation was
being supervised and any snags were anticipated. Occasionally, with
news of a potential slippage of a few hours, Rocky would ask
plaintively, 'Why did that happen?', as if the mere act of asking would
somehow prevent such a thing happening again. The irritated,
sometimes profane, tone of such conversations sounded like fierce
criticisms of Davenport and his team, and someone listening in
might wonder how the two of them could ever talk amicably
together again. But this was 'Working Together', and that meant
that they both understood the rules. Whatever the disappointment,
frustration or irritation, each was there to help the other solve the
problem, not to fight over who was to blame.

Behind Rocky Thomas was Granville Frazier, and they are both
people – perhaps all propulsion people are like this – who explode
from time to time, on the principle that to every action there should
be an equal and opposite reaction. Two months after the crisis, to
hear them talk together about Working Together as it operated

when the engine programme was in trouble is to get a flavour of the careful line they both try to tread between the old and the new management techniques:

The first two engines for airplane 1 [Rocky Thomas says] were probably four weeks behind their scheduled delivery date to the Boeing company, and that's my responsibility, so I was the one that not only had to tell Granny but I had to tell Alan. It's created a lot of problems for us, and we had to do a lot of work around, and it disrupted a lot of our other schedules. But it comes with the job, and I still think that, as managers, we have to control what we are responsible for and that there'll always be instances where people need to be given direction. It's *how* you give the direction or how you look at somebody that's bringing unfortunate news that I see changing a lot.

Frazier joins in:

But we did it. We took the teams, and we took the people that had practised Working Together and brought their unique talents, and we corrected the schedule deficiencies, and without compromising anything on the programme we got the engines where they were supposed to be, when they were supposed to be. It was an almost superhuman effort, because people wanted to make it work.

'We're still behind schedule,' Thomas added:

Pratt's still behind schedule, and we've accelerated the first flight of airplanes 2 and 3, so I kind of got mashed from both ends. The changes Pratt made in the compressor after the surge were tested, we flew again in December and validated the design changes, and the engine has handled and performed quite well.

'The question is,' Frazier said, 'As these things come up, do they impact the working together relationship?'

Well, the honest answer is 'Of course.' Sometimes there's a short-term reaction where you respond with one definition of stress: the terrible feeling you have when you need badly to strangle somebody to death and you can't. Then there is the fear you have for a moment that the problem you've run into is insurmountable and you won't be able to find a way through the labyrinth to get that thing done which you need to do. We get through those first two pretty quickly, and the whole team goes to work. So far, without exception, we've found the way through the labyrinth without compromising anything on the programme.

Thomas then said, 'I think in any programme where you're developing something as complex as a jet engine you're going to have to be very fortunate to have everything go perfectly from the day you set out.'

'However,' Frazier chipped in, 'there are some of us that think it would be fun to do that.'

'Yeah,' said Thomas thoughtfully, 'I would love to be on that programme. Very much.'

The Connecticut river used to be a main artery of communication and transport in the nineteenth century and was lined with bustling ports that have now become small, quiet towns, and factory buildings that have either decayed or been converted to other uses. When local industry was at its peak, the river was so polluted that nobody built at the water's edge, and today the unimpeded access to the river has turned the banks into a popular boating and picnicking area.

Along the Connecticut river lies the small town of Glastonbury. Water from the streams that run into the river used to provide power for the Glastonbury tannery, until it closed down. In the 1950s the building, a single-storey brick and wood construction with an elegant clapboard house attached, was acquired by the machine-shop company run by the Flanagan brothers. A rushing stream runs past the windows, after falling eight feet or so from the old mill-pond nearby, used today as a trout pond for the employees to fish in once a year. Nowadays the smell of stinking leather is replaced by the aroma of heavy machine oil, as the company makes a crucial part of Pratt & Whitney's 4084 engine for the 777.

Today, 23 March 1994, although the sun is shining and men are walking around in shirtsleeves, there are dirty snowdrifts round and about – remnants of the eighty or so inches of snow that have fallen in New England this winter. There is something miraculous about snow's ability to survive the temptations to melt presented by a day or two of hot sun. Snow still lies under the trees in the many wooded areas of this region, and some ponds have a coating of ice.

Jim Flanagan is part-owner of Flanagan Brothers, a family firm that employs his three sons and a daughter. He is nearly seventy, about six feet tall, with a slow, measured gait. As he walks round the plant he bends his balding, grizzled head to peer into the bowels of a grinding tool. Flanagan is under particular pressure at the moment because Boeing are shrieking at Pratt for timely delivery of the next engines in the pipeline, and Pratt are shrieking at him to warn him to make sure that he delivers the promised turbine exhaust cases according to their agreed schedule. 'There's a rusty knife at Pratt with my name on it,' says Flanagan, 'and they're going to cut my balls off if I don't deliver on time.' This is Working Together Irish-American style. Although the general idea of Working Together is that Boeing or Pratt and its subcontractors should share problems and schedule changes, old Jim Flanagan keeps back a few things from his paymasters. 'We're going to finish this piece a day ahead of schedule,' he says with a smile, 'but don't tell Pratt or they'll get all excited.' He is also rather cagey when asked how long it takes to make one of these pieces. 'A week or two,' he says. 'If I was any more precise Pratt would find out how much profit I make.'

Flanagan has been in the machining business all his life. He claims to have started the company as a boy of fifteen, to make copper fruit-bowls. As he talks, he shows an example of the sort of thing he made, looking remarkably like a copper hubcap that has got a little battered after falling off a car. Soon the company consisted of 'thirteen guys pounding copper in my mother's basement'. Flanagan shows no signs of panic or rush. He's been in the business long enough, and doing work for Pratt since 1952, to know that panics come and go, and that if you do the best possible job you can, in the time that it takes, no one can – or should – complain. But then he will not have witnessed the screaming match the day before, between Granny Frazier at Boeing and Tom Davenport at Pratt, as

Boeing made clear its displeasure at the time it was taking to make the revised engines that Boeing needed to replace what were meant to be the first production engines on the first flight-test plane. However much of a figure of fun Frazier might seem when in full – and profane – flow, his wishes and his concerns had the full might of Boeing behind them.

There were all sorts of changes that had emerged from the engine test programme, including the redesign of the compressor after the surge. Jim Flanagan had not been at all pleased when Pratt told him that the design of turbine exhaust case he had been contracted to make would have to change. This particular change had been decided as a result of a blade-out test on one of the experimental engines. With an explosive bolt, the Pratt engineers severed a blade during high revs, simulating the kind of event that can occasionally happen in flight. They were interested to see whether the engine contained the pieces of the blade, as it was designed to do, without exploding. It did, but one consequence was that the now unbalanced engine transmitted a twisting shock wave back towards the Flanagan exhaust case. Measurements of that wave with strain gauges showed that in some circumstances it might cause the exhaust case to buckle, and so the engineers redesigned it to be stiff enough to resist that force.

To see the exhaust case being made, it was difficult to believe that any force could buckle it. It arrived at the Flanagan factory as a 5,500 lb solid metal piece shaped like a giant bottomless fruit-bowl, forged from a much cruder ring-shaped metal billet in California. It was impossible to lift it, or even raise one side of it, by hand. In a journey through a series of machine tools, the crude bowl with roughened surface was subjected to a series of drilling, grinding and carving operations that removed 5000 lb of metal chips, leaving them scattered on the floor or in bins looking from a distance like silvery candyfloss. When standing on its smaller end, the bowl tapered in a series of steep terraces, with slots and grooves that had to be accurately machined under computer control. These opera-tions could take several days, as the case rotated slowly under the cutting edge of a machine tool, with milky coolant constantly pouring down the inside to prevent the cutter and the metal overheating. By the time the case was finished, two men could lift it comfortably between them. In spite of its size, it was a precision object, and Flanagan was proud of the high standards he and his shop were achieving. But for him this was not a primary consideration. 'Pride of authorship may be great,' he said, 'but I prefer money.'

The Flanagan operation was one example of how a project like designing and building the 777 can sometimes seem like an inverted pyramid, in this case resting on a point in a small sleepy town in Connecticut. Late delivery of a turbine exhaust case could delay the delivery of the engines that would go on the first United flight, with consequences in terms of finance and contract that would make grown men wake up in a sweat at night. But for Jim Flanagan, looking forward to retirement in a year on the coast in Maine, the screams and shouts in Seattle were as unnoticed as the rushing of the mill-race outside the window of his office under the eaves of the old tannery.

Whenever Glenda Barnes was in danger of passing near WA 001 in its final-assembly position, she took another route. Along with fifty thousand employees who had worked on the plane, she had been invited to the roll-out ceremony, scheduled for 9 April, and she wanted her first sight of the finished plane to be a unique experience,

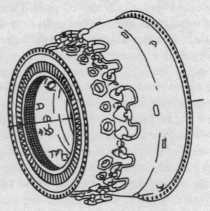

The Flanagan turbine case

its impact sullied by previous glimpses. She was a wing-sealer for Boeing, and had moved on to the 777 programme in 1993, at the beginning of the assembly of the plane. Like all the invitees, she was allowed to bring one guest to the ceremony – a condition which some employees saw as unnecessarily restrictive. Why couldn't they bring the whole family? After all, they had lived with the pressure and the excitement as the plane neared completion. Surely it was the least the company could do. But fifty thousand plus one guest meant coping with a hundred thousand people. Add a couple of kids and maybe an in-law and Building 40-25 would have to host maybe a quarter of a million all in a day. Glenda was fortunate in that her husband was also a Boeing worker and so received his own ticket, so she could invite her father, Reuben Holliday, who lived in Michigan but had himself once worked for Boeing.

There was never any doubt that the 777 roll-out would make an impact. For months before the event its planning, scheduling and logistics activity were as intense and detailed as for building the plane itself. Like many other design and engineering milestones, this one was met smoothly and efficiently. But, unlike the other milestones, it was an event whose symbolism was far more important than any specific set of achievements in the construction of the plane. What was important was that on 9 April 1994, the first 777, in some form, should be unveiled in front of employees and the media. It could have been an empty shell for all the visiting crowds would know (not that there was any danger of that). Almost whatever the state of the plane on that date, the 'roll-out' would have gone ahead: invitations had been sent out to a party, and could not be withdrawn.

It was not a roll-out in the original sense of the word: the ceremonial part of the event would involve no movement at all on the part of the plane. To make it possible for 100,000 people to see it close up in the space of a day, WA 001 was to be left in the final-assembly area and groups of 7,000 or so would be allowed in in shifts. There were to be fifteen roll-out ceremonies, one per hour from 6 a.m. to 8 p.m. In the middle of the day journalists would be brought along and given interview facilities and photo opportunities.

Donna Mikov and an enhanced communications team drawing on every part of the Boeing company had lived with the roll-out ceremony for the last six months. It had loomed ever closer in the midst of her daily task of answering, usually for the tenth or hundredth time, questions about the 777 from the world's press. Mikov was appointed from the Boeing Air and Space Division when the 777 was no longer part of project development. She is a tolerant woman who tries her hardest to deal with any query, however stupid, without making the questioner feel uncomfortable. Her role and responsibilities showed how seriously Boeing took the PR on the plane. She was in and out of the 777 executive suite on a daily, sometimes hourly, basis, and was taken completely into the confidence of Condit and Mulally, who knew how one PR slip could do immeasurable harm to the new plane.

Mikov and her team were given the task of organizing the roll-out, and they had hired a company called Dick Clark Productions, based in Los Angeles, to orchestrate and choreograph the plane's entry into public life.

There was an eerie silence in the south end of Building 40-26 at about 5.30 a.m. on the morning of 9 April. It was before sunrise, and the area was in near darkness, apart from the spilled light from two large video projection screens. No one would have believed that 3,500 people could be so quiet. Here was the first stage of the roll-out ceremony, the pre-event area, where people invited for a particular showing could wait during the hour beforehand. All eyes were watching the video screens with the rapt attention of people watching news of the Second Coming. In fact they were being shown a corporate video, the first of two specially made for the roll-out, including at intervals a series of trivial facts about the plane.

At 5.30 the room was already nearly full with half an hour to go before the people would be shepherded into Building 40-25. The plan was that at 5.55, Alan Mulally would step up to a podium about forty feet above the crowd and welcome them to the roll-out. While he was doing this in Building 40-26, Phil Condit would be doing the same thing on the other side of the roll-out area, in Building 40-24. Strangely, perhaps because of some imbalance in the delivery points for the buses that brought the guests from the car parks, Condit's area was half empty at 5.30. Mulally claimed to Condit that this was indication of the relative attractiveness of the two of them, which Condit denied fiercely. Both men were in Saturday domestic wear –

open-neck shirts and sweaters: Condit in dark green, Mulally in pale blue.

At 6 a.m. precisely the introductions finished, and people were allowed to file through to the final-assembly area. If they thought they were going to see the plane when they got there, they were disappointed. Its time had not yet come. What greeted them was another large darkened factory area, lit here and there by festoons of red and blue coloured lights suspended from the factory roof. The people lined up facing a 300-foot swathe of projection screens, on which slides of Boeing-related images were projected while music played. Moving 777 logos were projected on the floor, rotating in swirls of light while small children danced around them. It took about fifteen minutes for everyone from both pre-event areas to assemble, and again there was that unexpectedly low level of noise from such a large number of people, although here there was at least a low murmur of expectation.

At 6.20 the music changed and moving images started to run on the screens – a combination of black and white videos (a clever move to avoid pre-empting the all-colour vision of the plane itself) and colour slides with one-word attributes of the plane and its manufacture, such as 'teamwork' and 'trust' (although for a moment, because of a darker T, this almost looked like 'rust'). Frank Sinatra sang 'Come Fly with Me', a narrator spoke about the 777, interspersed with comments of workers and managers, and time-lapse cinematography of the assembly of the plane was run. The music got louder and grander, and black drapes behind the white ones rose, revealing a dim image of the 777. It could almost have been another projection, since it was only dimly lit, with a criss-cross pattern. Then the white drape lifted and the plane was there, still not quite real, bathed in coloured lights. The whole area erupted into gasps and rapturous applause, with whoops of excitement. Many people wept. Lights went on in each of the plane's interior areas in turn, starting with the cockpit, where a fake pilot and copilot were seen to be waving like Disney animatronic hominoids. The music reached a climax as the plane was bathed in very bright light and the narrator instructed the people to 'Come on up.'

If there was one image that dominated people's memories of this event it was the moment when 7,000 people surged forward to see the 777 for the first time. Whether by design or accident, it recreated compellingly the moment at the end of the film *Close Encounters of the Third Kind* when the waiting masses walk forwards into the bright light emanating from the spaceship that is going to take them away. Seen from the back of the crowd, as the first people arrived near the plane, their silhouetted heads became lit up and almost too bright to look at.

This sequence of events – gasps and applause, tears, and a reverential surge forward – was to be repeated at half past the hour until 8.30 in the evening. Mulally, Condit, Jeff Peace and other senior Boeing figures, including Frank Shrontz, talked themselves hoarse, as they introduced each session and were interviewed by innumerable journalists from all over the world. Many other senior 777 figures were compulsory volunteers, available to journalists to talk about their aspect of the plane – Jim McWha on fly-by-wire; John Cashman, accompanied by wife and three sons, to talk about the flight tests; Lars Andersen, weary with the pressure of supplying ever more test data to the certificatory agencies, to talk about ETOPS. Local television stations produced what were sometimes hourly live reports about the event, largely celebratory and with little evidence of the occasional critical media coverage the 777 team had resented in recent months. Two Reuters journalists took colour stills of the event, processed them in a small box, dried the colour negatives with a hair-drier, scanned them with a computer, and sent them by telephone to newspapers, all in a matter of minutes.

Fifteen people fainted and one had a heart attack, and everyone took away a small commemorative 777 nylon bag with a snack in it. At about midnight, observed by only about a handful of night-shift workers, the true roll-out occurred, when the first 777 left the assembly building and was towed across the bridge over Highway 526 to the refuelling area, for its giant wings to be filled with fuel for the first time.

EIGHTEEN

All Systems Nearly Go

On 25 April, with the success and excitement of the roll-out still ringing in people's ears, Frank Shrontz, Boeing's chairman, addressed the company's annual meeting. The company would weather a period of long-term decline in the aerospace industry, he told the shareholders, as he announced a fall in the first-quarter net income. He also expressed concern at current efforts to prevent renewal of Most Favoured Nation status to China, just as the country was on the point of ordering some more Boeing planes – including, it was believed, fifteen 777s.

So far the company had 147 firm orders for the plane, plus 108 options. An order for another fifteen would be very welcome, since total sales so far were below the great expectations expressed when the plane was first planned. But as figures on paper they failed to convey the full significance that new orders would hold for Boeing. That only became concrete in the assembly building at Everett and on factory floors in Auburn and Wichita, Melbourne, Nagoya and Philadelphia. The monster was up and running and needed feeding. It was fine at the moment, and current orders would keep everyone busy for four years or more, but this was a long-term project – to be measured in decades rather than single years. The orders had to keep flowing, and fifteen planes would keep people busy for another year or so.

Bob Cullen was a foreman in the section that made the floor beams. He had worked at Boeing for fifteen years and was well aware of the cyclical nature of his type of work. At least on the 777 he felt slightly more protected than people working on some of the other planes. He was also proud to be working on such a large Boeing plane. 'Those of us who work on the 777 call the 737 and the 757 "ultralites",' he said.

Cullen was in charge of the floor beams of the plane, made of carbon-fibre composite. He had now seen the benefits of the DBT approach in action for a year or more as he looked after a huge framework that would become the basis of the floor of the 777. Over in one corner a group of men were bending down, looking at a junction point of several components. 'Look at them,' said Cullen:

> Before, I couldn't find an engineer. Now, today, I have to ask them to leave so we can build. They are manufacturing engineers working with the mechanics. These guys are from the office building, and they're coming out talking to the mechanics – something you would never have seen in the past. The mechanics have been absolutely amazed, because we're getting changes done in a matter of one airplane, so it really works well.
>
> A lot of times I have a tough time getting the mechanics to understand how important it really is. And they just don't comprehend that. They come to work; they think it's just a boring ho-hum job. But they don't realize what they really do. I love this job. This is the best job.

Another benefit of the new design approach that impressed Cullen was the fact that two components of the floor beams that came from two entirely different factories had arrived at Everett with the holes drilled in them registered to four places of decimals so that when they were brought together they fastened with no trouble at all.

The floor beams stretch across the plane from one side to the other, and support the seat tracks that have to hold the seats in place under a force of sixteen times the force of gravity in an accident. They also have other tough technical criteria to meet. Because of the corrosive effects of wine, Coke and beer, the tracks in the galley area are made of non-corroding titanium rather than the cheaper aluminium that stretches across the rest of the floor.

There are numbers and letters written on the side of the floor beams that relate to the reference system used to build the plane. It's an interesting hangover from shipbuilding, and the floor beams are used to set the reference level for the whole plane. The floors of all Boeing planes are designed to be at 200 inches above what is called the water line, rather like a ship's deck. There is no part of the plane that is actually on a water line – it is an imaginary level some feet below the bottom of the fuselage.

All measurements in a vertical direction are referred to this water line. All measurements from front to back are referred to as stations measured in inches back from an imaginary point out in front of the plane. So the forwardmost part of the plane, the tip of the nose, is station 92.5, and the rearmost, the strobe light above the APU exhaust, is station 2,570.3, from which it is possible to infer that the plane is 2,477.8 inches long. And – in a reference to human anatomy that is accepted as a matter of fact by plane-makers – all distances in a horizontal direction to left or right of the centre of the plane are referred to a mid-line called the buttock line, named after the point in the body often visible over the top of a pair of jeans – what is called 'builder's cleavage'. And, just to complicate things a little further, the fixed line in each plane to which all the other horizontal measurements are related is called LBL 11, because it's 11 inches to the left of the buttocks line.

On 31 May Alan Mulally chaired a meeting called a Special Attention Meeting, the new name for the weekly Critical Issues Meeting. There was, as usual, a whole list of things to talk about,

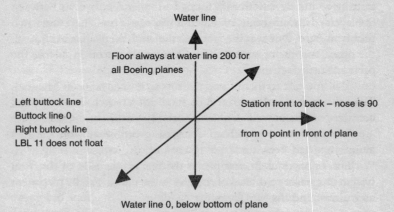

Baselines for different measurements during
manufacture of plane – all figures in inches

none of them dramatically worrying but all of them needing quick solutions. As the first flight loomed, the team divided problems with the plane into those that had to be fixed before first flight and those that would only really be necessary on the final production planes.

One problem related to a crack that had been discovered in the horizontal stabilizer that was undergoing tests in the laboratory. The stabilizer had been moved around a lot in the previous months, and no one was sure whether it was a fatigue problem, in which case it wouldn't affect the first flight, or a load problem, where the piece had cracked under a force that shouldn't have affected it. When it had first been noticed the previous week, Rudy Schad, in charge of Structures, had gone into the lab over the weekend and subjected the piece to forces way above what it would experience in normal flight. There were no further cracks, so it seemed that it was a fatigue problem. At least, then, they needn't worry about the stabilizer on the first plane, although in the medium term they had to do something about it so that the customers' planes had a redesigned stabilizer with enough extra material to avoid the problem.

A second 'Special Attention' item was something called spar-web delamination, where a particular component, the spar web, was arriving at the factory from a foreign supplier with spaces between the layers, or laminations, of which it was made up. There were two problems here. One was the fact that the voids were appearing at all; the other, that the company hadn't detected the problem before the parts left their factory.

'Will you talk to them?' said Mulally to his colleague in Materiel. 'Yes,' the man said. 'In Spanish or English?' There had clearly been broader communication problems with this particular company.

The third item concerned continuing problems with the fuel gauge that had been undergoing tests on the crosswinds flight to Wichita. In previous Boeing planes the fuel gauge used an electrical system to measure the level of the fuel in the tanks. The 777's system uses ultrasound. As Mulally put it:

It's really simple and it's really neat, but they have to finish the design, because you have to account for a slosh in the fuel in little waves, so when you send down the ultrasonic signals you're bouncing off the top of the wave or the bottom or the wave, and so you have a mathematical algorithm that measures the difference between the top and the bottom and averages it out and it does it in different places in the tank. And they had some reflection problems where they were reflecting off the waves and not getting a real clear signal back, and that's the issue they're working on with it. But the technology looks really good, and we really believe in it and it's really simple. But we would like to have had it worked out before now, because it means we have to have some work-arounds for the first flights.

But the biggest problem the team faced, and had done for some months, was delays in the aviation electronics, or avionics, that would be needed to supply all sorts of services to the plane.

It would require another whole book to do justice to the stories of the 777's electronic system – not just to the problems the engineers faced, but to the complexity, ingenuity, innovation and versatility the systems displayed. Like so many aspects of the 777's initial overall concept, the need for these systems in quite the volume and variety that they ultimately assumed came out of initial discussions with the airlines. Now the question is, Did the airlines really know the implications of what they were asking for? Sometimes customer satisfaction can be too much of a good thing. Granny Frazier summed up its drawbacks in one conversation:

I used to never understand customer satisfaction, because if a customer comes in and tells you he wants something – if he comes and tells you he wants your product for free, for example – well, we aren't going to satisfy him, so what does this foolishness mean? Then one day a gentleman from one of the consulting companies looked at me and said, 'Wait a minute, we're addressing the customer's *needs* not his wants.' So that really helped me, because when you start concentrating on what he needs then you can work customer satisfaction. Now when you deal with my wife, when she *wants* something it very quickly becomes a need, so you have to watch that.

Walt Gillette was the chief engineer in charge of systems during the year before the first flight of the 777. He described how the 777 systems emerged out of discussions with the airlines:

First, for their passengers, they wanted more inflight entertainment – television sets for every seat, interactive video, ability to play games, those kinds of things – and that established the need for a large number of avionics. In addition, for their passengers' comfort they wanted to make sure that the temperature control is nice within plus or minus two degrees – no hot spots; no blasts of air in their face. And will the lavatories work for the whole flight? In other words, have the waste tanks been emptied? Or is the plane going to run out of drinking water? Those kinds of things. So there came some more avionics units for that part of the function. They also wanted more capability for years out into the future, so we had to do this in modules that could be easily upgraded over time.

The next thing that they wanted was an aircraft that was much easier for their maintenance people, in that it would not provide misleading information about which particular piece of system had failed and would point them directly where to go to a repair if some part *had* failed. They also wanted the design to not fail nearly so often. So that brought up the idea of fault-tolerant equipment. Let's suppose a certain function needed two computers to ensure the safety level, then we would provide a third unit so that we could drop down to two units and still be safe. In some of the main systems in this airplane we actually added a fourth, so that the airplane can go into service with four, have one unit stop operating, and it is now at the original design level. That's fault-tolerant. And so the fault-tolerant idea spread to several other units, the ones that control the primary flight computer, some that tell the airplane where it's positioned in the skies, those kinds of things – items that are very important, and in the past have required quite a bit of maintenance.

Now the third area where they wanted more capability was for their flight crews. And they wanted two kinds. They wanted to make the flight crew's load even easier when they fly the airplane, so the flight crew would have just the information they wanted, would only concentrate basically on flying the airplane and doing the navigation. And so that brought out a whole host of new capability, and so we had to add many kinds of computers to the aircraft – computers that do the primary controls, computers that control the electrical power distribution in the airplane, computers that control the hydraulics. So that would provide the flight crew with a much more agreeable airplane to fly on a daily basis.

They wanted another capability, connected with the fact that navigation and the airplane environment will change quite a bit over the next twenty years – global navigation, enhanced vision so that they can see the mountains in the clouds, those kinds of things will come on line – and they wanted the capability to be able to easily upgrade this airplane, without having to make major changes to various computers in the airplane.

It would be wrong to suggest that the airlines were like Frazier's caricature of his wife, a little confused about the difference between their needs and their wants, but, from Walt Gillette's account, the early discussions with the airlines and Boeing did sound awfully like somebody in a hi-fi shop saying, 'I'll have one of those. Oh, and I've just spotted one of those – perhaps I'll take that too. And what does this do? Oh, really? Well, I've never heard of one of those, but it would probably be a good idea as well.'

To a certain extent the figures that describe the size and complexity of the systems that were eventually designed to fulfil these needs (or wants) are meaningful only if you've got past the initial stage, that most of us haven't, of being amazed at what ordinary little computers on our desks do in the batting of an eyelid. But Gillette and his colleagues rightly saw the 777 avionics as somewhat out of the ordinary:

We had to create a computer called an Airplane Information Management System, or AIMS for short. It's a very massive computer. It does about 140 million calculations a second and it looks at about three-quarters of a million words of data, and each word of data can have up to thirty pieces of information in it, each second. It takes that information and distributes it throughout the aircraft on a series of eleven major highways of information called

ARINC 629 data buses. These are just highways of data flowing throughout the aircraft to keep all this coordinated.

This airplane has over 2 million lines of software – what you might call sentences to the computer – which are created uniquely for this airplane. And when we add in sentences or computer code that's off the shelf, there's about 5 million lines of this kind of code. But what was really crucial were the 2 million lines of new code. So, to compare it with other comparable systems like the air traffic system that's being redone for United States, that uses 1.6 million lines of code. The modern military fighter has about a million and a half lines of computer code in it for its flight systems and its fire-control systems. A submarine warfare aircraft has all kinds of radar systems and it's about a million and a half lines. So the 777 was a very substantial undertaking in terms of the amount of new computer programs and lines of instructions that had to be done.

One almost unbelievable fact about the computing power on the 777 is that about 40 per cent of it is taken up with the passenger entertainment system. Each seat has a telephone, a video screen with a choice of up to twenty different channels, some interactive computer games, and 'in-the-sky' shopping facilities by credit card. Just to provide these needs alone required 1,700 computers per airplane, compared with 180 for the rest of the avionics.

A small hint of the challenges faced by the people working on the plane's systems was contained on a sticker in the laboratory where the flight-control systems were tested. It said, 'Yesterday is just a memory; tomorrow is only a vision; but today's a real bitch.' And in another electronics laboratory, where the passenger entertainment systems were tested, a notice on the wall said, 'A design will always be changed so that something unwanted can happen.' A larger hint came in a newspaper article in a Seattle paper in early 1994 that had a reputation for reporting regularly on problems at Boeing. The story was headed 'Programmers Scramble to get Glitch-free Software, Hardware for Boeing 777 off the Ground', and included the following paragraphs:

We went with some new technology and really didn't schedule enough time in our program to take into account the learning curve,' said Honeywell program manager Morrow. 'So we went downstream a little farther than we wanted.'

By late last year [1993] the AIMS development effort had become what one company insider described as a 'hairy white-knuckle situation.'

A major milestone had to be met in early January. In order to power up the No. 1 777 for the first time in the factory, Boeing needed the first level of AIMS software – maintenance codes assigned to monitor the health of all the jet's computer systems.

'We had hardware we were using in the lab that did not include all the features of our final production hardware,' Kelley [another Honeywell manager] recalled, 'so it was that transition to the real hardware that was difficult.

'We just knew we had to get it there. We were looking at power-on in the airplane, in early January . . . we had to have a lot of maintenance functions in because Boeing had planned to use the maintenance computer during fabrication of the airplane.'

Honeywell resisted the inclination to throw teams of software engineers at the problem – about 750 Honeywell engineers were already working on the 777. Instead, about a half-dozen of the company's brainiest engineers, led by Dennis Prestholdt, a military programs guru, were drafted.

'It wasn't that we didn't know how to do it, it was just that our plans upfront were too optimistic in what it was going to take us to do all the tasks you have to do,' Morrow said.

Boeing powered up the 777, with the AIMS maintenance monitoring feature running, more or less on schedule, Kelley said.

There was a whole additional set of electronics required for the test flights that the first five planes would carry out. Each of these would be festooned with 120 miles of distinctive orange wire. In a continuous diagnostic check, every important component of the plane would be festooned with gauges to measure temperature or force or air speed or vibration, and the data would be fed back to yet more computers to be stored and analysed to check back later if anything anomalous occurred.

Take for example, the fuse pin – a metal rod that holds the engine to its strut and is designed to break if the engine develops an uncontrollable vibration in flight. In the test planes the hole through which this pin fits – a hole three-eighths of an inch wide and two inches deep – contained sixteen strain gauges. These were tiny slivers of plastic with wires that were thinner than a hair. When the wires stretched, they changed an electric current flowing through them and this could be calibrated to measure what forces the pin and its fitting were experiencing. There were similar clusters of such gauges on the wing struts, the wing spars, the landing-gear struts, the landing-edge flaps and the trailing-edge flaps – all components where it was important to check that the specifications for the forces they were designed to withstand were not being exceeded.

As the date for the first flight approached, the Boeing people were concerned that they would not be able to load and check all the software in time for the original date of 1 June and it was quietly shifted to 12 June, well within the buffer that most of the schedules still had in them. On the airplane, now parked on the flight line at Paine Field, the airfield next door to the Everett plant, there was daily feverish activity in the electronic bays that held the computers.

On 30 May the plane was ready to move under its own steam – not yet to fly, but to taxi. Although the main taxi tests would take place on the day before the first flight, now that the plane had everything it needed to move under its own power Cashman and the test team couldn't resist just trying it out. Mulally watched the first taxi tests from the airfield, while Ron Ostrowski went along for the ride. The following morning Mulally held a staff meeting, and memories of the day before kept bubbling up. 'And then it started moving all of its feet around, and then it was going up and down the runway at 100 m.p.h. . . . John was ecstatic.' The tension and the excitement were building up in the team, and much of the content of that day's meeting was devoted to aspects of the forthcoming first flight. At one point Donna Mikov, director of communications, raised the issue of publicity and the importance of Boeing not concealing things when they went wrong. 'Tell them what we know when we know it.' That way, the frequent good news about the plane was more likely to be believed.

There was to be one more taxi test on the day before the first flight – the high-speed taxi test, where John Cashman would take the plane up to – but not past – the speed the plane needed for take-off.

NINETEEN

Like Kids in a Candy Store

- 'And they talked the moon out of the sky
But will the 77 fly?'

Graffiti in Park Ave bar and grill, Renton – *1 June 1994*

The weekend of 10–12 June presented an unsurprising mix of clouds and blue patches over the Puget Sound area. From mid-afternoon on Friday, the 777 Communications Division had been phoning journalists to confirm that the first flight of the plane was scheduled for Sunday. But they tried to emphasize that this did not mean that it *would* take place on Sunday, and they were surprised when television and newspapers failed to catch the fine distinction and told their audience that the test flight would happen then. Underlying the Boeing team's concern was the desire to avoid making promises that could not be fulfilled and being at the receiving end of critical stories about schedule delays and problems with the plane. This caution led to the often-expressed statement within Boeing that 'This is not an event', as if events were things that were defined by the organizers. In fact, of course, it would be an event – there was no way round that. There was no better way of describing the first flight than as the event that marked the culmination and justification of three years' work.

But perhaps it's true to say that Boeing did everything to avoid it becoming an Event with a capital E. Employees were not formally invited, for example, although Boeing were prepared to welcome any employee who wanted to turn up at his workplace on a Sunday and wander over to Paine Field. They had, of course, made

arrangements for the media to see this non-Event, but with a
remarkably low-key programme concentrating mainly on access to
viewing-points at the airfield and a press conference after their flight.

One reason the Boeing people were cautious in their Friday-
afternoon calls was because there was one final hurdle to be
overcome before the first flight. Although two weeks beforehand
the plane had spent a short period taxiing for the first time, there was
a further and more systematic series of taxi tests that had to be
carried out before the plane could actually be allowed to lift itself
from the ground. Like a fish out of water, a plane on the ground is
subject to a different set of physical laws from when it flies, and needs
different operating technology to move it around. Taxiing tests
involve checking all those parts of the plane that are there partly or
solely to help the plane move – and stop – on the ground, the
landing-gear stresses and vibrations, tyre pressures, brakes and, in
particular, brake heating. Then there was steering the plane on the
ground, using the tiller that operates the nose-wheel and the
differential force of the engines. The test would also be used to try
moving down the runway at near rotation speed and getting the feel
of the first phase of take-off, when the nose lifts off the runway.

The diagnostic data about every single operation of the controls,
and a huge range of characteristics of the plane's response to those
controls – temperatures, pressures, strains on individual components
– would be fed back to a telemetry room thirty miles away, in the
flight-test centre, where a roomful of engineers would be following
the stages of the test closely on computer screens and carrying out a
continual dialogue with the pilots. There were specialists from every
team that had built the plane, ready to try to provide a quick answer
to any problem that might come up during the taxiing, and indeed
during the flight itself.

At 7.30 on Saturday morning a small room on one side of the
flight line was crammed with engineers and flight-test workers. They
were there for the pre-taxi briefing, when John Cashman and Ken
Higgins, his copilot, would run through the tasks that would have to
be achieved during the taxi tests. Engineers overflowed into the hall,
and into the adjacent office of a manager called Bob Fisher who
'owned' the plane at this stage of its progress, after the factory had
finished with it and before it was formally handed over to flight test.

Cashman and Higgins were late, strolling in at about 7.40. There was a bright-eyed jauntiness about them as the first flight approached, although Cashman's rock-solid competence and confidence was always in evidence as each item on the list was discussed. For the rest of the weekend Cashman and Higgins would perform the same double act, with Cashman doing most of the talking while Higgins occasionally interjected a quiet remark.

After about three-quarters of an hour the meeting had covered the agenda and people stood up. The usual small knots of unfinished business clustered around the room, and Cashman perched on the edge of the table with his airline pilot's bag open. As he took off his glasses, one of the side arms parted company with the main frame and he spent the next few minutes discussing the 777 taxi tests while wrestling with one of life's universally insoluble problems – how to put back a screw the size of a pinhead armed only with a pocket knife (and, incidentally, wondering why technology could not invent a pair of screwless – or at least screw-unlooseable – spectacles).

The two pilots walked across to the plane about 500 yards away and 'kicked wheels' in a final visual check for obvious defects. Then everyone but essential test personnel was moved away from the plane to allow space for it to pull forward and turn right along a taxiway. Most of the senior flight engineers were there, although there was no sign of Alan Mulally. But he was there in spirit, as he called Donna Mikov for progress reports at intervals from his Proton speeding up Route 5 from his home on Mercer Island. In the period before the taxiing began there was an important task to be carried out by the assembled audience: they had to perform a FOD walk along the length of the taxiway. FOD – foreign-object damage – can be caused by debris sucked into the engines, and Boeing didn't want even the slightest possibility of that during the taxiing out to the runway.

Like spectators pressing divots after a polo match, or police searching for bodies in a field, a long straggling line of engineers, family members, vice-presidents and anyone else who happened to be around walked slowly across the concrete slabs of the taxiway, occasionally stooping to pick up a tiny stone or a screw. In a display of commendable but perhaps unnecessary zeal, one man was seen energetically pulling several inches of rubbery grouting from between the concrete slabs – grouting that would probably have been perfectly happy to stay in place as the plane rolled by.

While the FOD walkers did their stuff, the two pilots were carrying out various checks in the cockpit. Then people drifted back to the viewing-area opposite the plane and waited for the engines to start. The steps were driven away from the door, and a mechanic stood on the ground beneath the nose of the plane, connected to the cockpit by a phone line.

The left engine was started first, with a smooth whine. After a few minutes checking revs, thrust and other characteristics, the right engine was started. Parked in the viewing-area was a van full of test engineers in radio contact with the cockpit, and Mulally, who had arrived by now, divided his time between working the crowd and putting his head into the van to keep a check on the messages going back and forth between the cockpit and the telemetry room. A burst of conversation from the cockpit followed by replies from the telemetry room heralded a problem. The engines powered down and a few overalled figures approached the plane. What had happened was that the pilots had got a message in the cockpit implying some kind of leak of hydraulic fluid somewhere in the area of the left wing. But was the message genuine or was it just the result of a faulty indicator? It was soon apparent that the message was correct: a pool of liquid lay under the wing near the point where it joined the fuselage. By the time the crowd of observers had been allowed back around the plane, wads of absorbent material like giant paper tissues had been laid over the wet area, which was also sprinkled with something like kitty-litter. Two mechanics were on a scissors lift unscrewing a panel on the underside of the wing. Knots of engineers stood around looking up, and an anxious Bob Fisher – it was still 'his' plane – kept a sharp lookout for anyone who strayed too close. He was particularly concerned that no one went downwind of the leakage as the mechanics probed around inside the wing, looking for the source of the leak – hydraulic fluid is a mixture of chemicals, none of which is particularly nice to receive in the face. In fact conditions inside the wing were too inhospitable for the maintenance engineers to explore very far. There was a mist of hydraulic fluid which had to disperse before they could look any further.

The steps had been rolled up to the plane again, and Cashman and Higgins had come down to the ground, more curious than concerned. They stood around talking to Alan Mulally.

After about an hour, when the engineers had investigated deeper inside the wing, the cause of the leak was found. A seal had ruptured in a pipe that carried hydraulic fluid away from one of the actuators. John Cashman looked with interest at the flexible black O-ring, less than two inches in diameter, that was now missing about a fifth of its circumference, shredded away as a result of faulty installation.

The pilots went back to the cockpit while the seal was replaced and the hydraulic reservoir filled. A small commotion near the nose of the plane was caused by the sudden appearance of Cashman through the open cockpit window, wearing a giant joke pair of pilot's goggles. This turned out to be part of a plan to make a funny video commemorating the 777 tests to be shown to the flight-test team. As the crowd was ushered back into the safety area, Alan Mulally lingered in front of the nose of the plane and performed a small routine for the same video. Starting with the sort of conventional arm-waving manœuvres that are used by ground staff to guide the plane on the taxiway, Mulally moved arms and legs ever more wildly in a dance for the Boeing video cameras.

It was an astonishing piece of informality, but entirely consistent with Mulally's style. It reflected a degree of confidence in the plane and the test programme that Mulally and all his senior colleagues were to display over the next thirty-six hours. It showed that to all intents and purposes the first phase was over, bar the shouting. Who would play the fool like that if there were any danger that the test might fail, or that Cashman and Higgins would be taking their lives in their hands when they took off on Sunday? It was the sort of confidence that dominated the events of the weekend, and prompted one of the Boeing minibus drivers to say to Mulally, admiringly. 'You know, it's pretty ballsy of Boeing to do it all like this, so open and relaxed.'

Soon the engines were powered up again, first left and then right. The ground man disconnected his phone line and stepped back; another member of the ground staff held up both his arms with their bright orange batons, and the 777 moved forward under the power of its engines, led by a Boeing police car and a fire engine. The onlookers barely had time to register the beginning of the move

– and to cheer and applaud – before the huge plane swung right in a wide curve and then turned left down the long straight stretch that had been cleared of FOD two hours before. 'Sporty' was the word that came to mind to describe the quick, sure movements of the plane. Cashman wasn't wasting any time.

The crowd turned away from the plane, before it was out of sight. Because it had to travel a tortuous route to the end of the runway, everyone now moved to a good viewing-position for the next event, leaving the plane to make its way unobserved.

There was a wait while the plane stood at the far end of the runway, barely visible over a gentle rise in the ground. The pilots talked to the telemetry room while they checked each of the key parameters to be sure that everything was OK. Then, when Cashman said over the intercom 'One, two, three', indicating that he was releasing the brakes on 'three', the plane accelerated down the runway until it was level with Mulally and a crowd of flight-test engineers.

At this position in the run the speed was 140 knots – around the speed when, in the right wind conditions, the plane could take off. Nobody will confirm what many people suspect: that all the wheels lifted off the ground for a moment as Cashman pulled the nose up. It was clearly a view shared by most of the small group of engineers watching and by Mulally, who said, 'Now, say after me, "First flight is *tomorrow*".' And they solemnly did. (Cashman afterwards said that the instruments showed that there was always at least one set of wheels on the ground and that people were misled when he rocked the plane from side to side to lift each main set in turn off the ground.)

Cashman and Higgins did two runs, and at the end of the second the plane stood in the distance at the south end of the runway, its backside pointed ignominiously towards the spectators. The radio van crackled with more conversation. Cashman was inviting a select group of people to ride back down the runway to the parking position. Mulally went up to a handful of people who had been closely connected with the plane and asked them if they would like a ride. Like boys on a camping trip they piled excitedly into a van and drove down the taxiway. Among them were Tom Davenport of Pratt & Whitney and Mulally himself, riding the plane for the first time. Because the plane was at the end of the runway, away from any steps, the group had to clamber in through a small hatch on the underside near the nose, after climbing up a stepladder that was slightly too small for the task. It was a tight squeeze, and one that involved twisting through two or three layers of electronic equipment, eventually to emerge through the floor of the cabin just near the forward door.

With a revving of the engines the plane swung in a circle and pointed north up the runway. Everyone inside the plane commented on how quiet the engines sounded, although, without many of its internal furnishings and with few passengers, the plane had less sound insulation than it would in passenger service.

The plane taxied back to the office building and disgorged its proud passengers for a post-flight briefing, at the end of which John Cashman said plaintively, 'We can't test any more on the ground!' This time tomorrow, if all went well, the 777 would have flown for the first time. Cashman and the rest of the team pushed their chairs back, stood up, and, after a few final exchanges, left Paine Field and headed for home. John Cashman had determined to have an early night tonight.

First flights are not necessarily trivial events. In fact any test flight has the potential for serious problems, as the history of Boeing planes shows.

In 1938 the second Stratoliner to come off the production line disintegrated over Mount Rainier on its first flight when an engine was shut down to test the plane's low-speed stability; all on board were killed. A flight engineer called Mike Pavone was scheduled to be on the plane, but was then switched to another assignment and survived. In 1943 a B-92 on a test flight crashed after an engine fire, killing the crew and eleven test engineers. Believe it or not, Mr Pavone was also scheduled to go on this flight, but this time there weren't enough parachutes to go round and he had to stay on the ground. Two of the crew who tried to use their chutes died when they didn't open.

More recently, but less tragically, first flights of other Boeing planes have also had their share of problems. On the first flight of the 757 it took several minutes to relight one of the engines after it had been deliberately shut down in flight. On the first flight of the 767 it proved impossible to raise the landing-gear after take-off, and the flight had to continue with it down. Also, when the pilot went to the lavatory during the flight, he flushed the toilet and there was a loud bang 'as if a twelve-gauge shotgun went off in my ear'. It turned out to be due to a faulty valve in the vacuum flushing system.

On first flights there was always a minimum crew – a captain and a copilot. On WA 001, the first 777 test plane, there was a feature that showed how the company still took seriously the possibility that anything could happen. On the right-hand side of the plane there were four windows which had rather unusual oval frames projecting into the interior of the plane. These frames had explosive charges on them that could be fired in a grave emergency, if Cashman decided that the plane had to be abandoned in mid-air. The explosion of the charges would release the pressure inside the plane and allow one of the doors, specially adapted without hinges, to fall out of its frame and permit the crew to jump. All this would happen after Cashman and Higgins had donned oxygen masks and parachutes, supplied as part of the first-flight kit.

On the day of the flight the weather had got worse. Grey, angry clouds hung over Everett, and gusts of rain swept the tarmac at Paine Field. At 6.45 a.m., in the media centre that had been set up in the lobby of Building 40-88, the cellphones were crackling. A small crisis, one of the few of the day, had cropped up: not enough coffee had been delivered – two orders had got muddled, so that too much coffee had been sent to the VIP centre and not enough for the sixty or so journalists who would arrive in a couple of hours. Over in the VIP area a room had been set aside for Frank Shrontz, Phil Condit and their guests, and another room nearby was allocated to the families of Cashman, Higgins and other key figures in the test programme. The first room had a loudspeaker that would relay the conversation between the plane and the telemetry room. It had been rigged to give Jim McRoberts, a senior Boeing test pilot, control of how much of the conversation would be fed to the press and to the families' room. If anything suddenly went wrong, the relay could be cut off by the press of a switch.

Over the other side of a corridor, electricians were putting up television lights in a room that would be used for the post-flight press conferences. Gordon McKinzie of United Airlines and his wife and children arrived bright and early, looking very smart. Shortly after, Frank Shrontz turned up, in a blue blazer that some saw as his trademark. 'You're looking smart,' said Shrontz to McKinzie. 'It's only because we've come straight from church,' said McKinzie. '*Touché*' said Shrontz.

In fact, as befitted a non-Event, most people were dressed smartly informal – few suits and ties, but not many sloppy jeans and T-shirts either. At about 10.30 Alan Mulally led the assembled VIPs out to a small bus and they were driven over to a position opposite the plane. A crowd had gathered, and was being herded away from the plane as the time approached for take-off. An elderly man in a flat cap was among the VIPs and was greeted effusively by a succession of senior Boeing executives. He was T Wilson,[1] who joined Boeing after the Second World War and rose to become the last chairman before Frank Shrontz.

Mulally's hand barely stopped shaking for a moment – seized by a succession of Boeing people, past and present. His arm would go round someone's shoulder if it were a man, and there would be a kiss on the cheek and a hug for a woman. Occasionally men got a hug too.

John Cashman and Ken Higgins climbed the steps, and on the platform at the top, Cashman stopped, turned to the crowd with a wave, and raised his hand with index finger extended and pointing straight up to the sky. Then he was gone, into the plane. There was quite a strong tail wind out on the runway, and there was some concern among the flight-test engineers. After a delay of three-quarters of an hour, with the wind at twelve knots it was decided to give the go-ahead.

Mulally's wife and children were there, and when the time came for the plane to taxi and take off, they jostled like anyone else for a good position on the edge of the runway.

It would be wrong to use the word 'anticlimax' about an event that clearly wasn't so in objective terms, but for people on the ground the event to which the last four years or more of hard work had built up was, of course, over very quickly. Only for John

[1] Never known by any other first name than 'T'.

Cashman and Ken Higgins was this more than two brief moments of tension and exultation combined – at take-off and landing.

When it happened, the take-off was quick and surprising, helped by full engine power and a tail wind. Somehow you felt that because it was done for the first time it should be done slowly and carefully. But of course it's the speed that produces the lift, and so there were only seconds between seeing the plane start its take-off run in the distance at the end of the runway till it lifted off the ground with a roar, headed a mile or so north, and then banked to the left towards the Pacific. But for those seconds Alan Mulally didn't take his eyes off the plane. Hands clasped in front of him, apparently oblivious of the crowd around him, he willed *his* airplane up into the air, and clung to it with his eyes until it was safely on its way. 'Oh my gosh! Isn't that something?' he said, as Phil Condit and then Frank Shrontz came up to share an emotional embrace, followed by Gordon McKinzie. As Condit's wife lined them all up for a photograph, Condit, Shrontz and McKinzie looked at the camera, but Mulally couldn't help taking another look at the plane, now a dot in the distance. 'Didn't you think it was pretty?' Mulally said to McKinzie, his hand on the top of McKinzie's head. 'They should get the gear up,' said McKinzie, inconsequentially, looking over at the plane. 'Get your order book out!' said Mulally, not missing a trick.

Thinking back later to the moment of take-off, Mulally was thoughtful:

Everybody has their own personal thoughts on an event like that, where you have so much of your life and your creativity dedicated to something, and everybody feels that satisfaction of accomplishment in different ways. I thought it was neat that some people jumped up and down. I thought some people looked reverent, and some people looked in awe, but they all had a deep sense of respect for what everybody had done together

I just didn't want to miss any part of that moment, because at the end of the day and in your life you go around once, and we've all dedicated our lives to make the best airplane in the world and I just wanted to make sure that I didn't fail to appreciate that accomplishment.

The plane turned west towards the Pacific, the crowd broke up, and the VIPs and the press went back to the building where a press conference was to be held. By the time they arrived, the telemetry room had already been in communication with the plane and established that all went well, although Cashman had decided to turn east over eastern Washington to escape heavy cloud.

Condit, Mulally, Shrontz, Wilson and assorted family members retired into their conference room for lunch and listened to the back and forth of messages, largely routine, between the cockpit and the ground engineers. For a short period the plane was out of radio range for the test equipment, because of its change of route, and so the flight was lengthened from a planned three hours to nearer four, so as to repeat the tests nearer to Seattle. In the words of flight-test director, Charlie Higgins, who happened to be Ken Higgins's brother, the point of the first flight is just to 'wring out the plane for the first time', and the pilots had a long checklist of systems and components to try out. They flew at near-stall speeds, raised and lowered the gear, checked the APU, and even tried to land on a cloud. The only thing they don't appear to have tested on the flight was the valve in the lavatory's vacuum flushing system – or at least they didn't report such a test.

Much of it did not feel like 'the first time' for the pilots. There had been so much work on flight simulators, including more than 2,000 hours in the Boeing Systems Integration Lab, that the controls were beginning to have a familiar feel. The pilots even felt comfortable enough to switch off one engine during the flight and restart it – without any trouble. In the words of one industry analyst, 'You don't shut down an engine on a two-engine plane unless you're very confident things are going well.'

But the things which seemed impossible to anticipate, because of the unpredictability of the behaviour of air, were the responses of this huge two hundred and twenty-five ton, three-dimensional metal solid as it moved at 250 knots through the atmosphere. The rudder problem had been one small foretaste of how the interaction of geometry and fluid dynamics can surprise even the most experienced engineers. Now, on the first flight, there were a couple of similar, but less serious, examples.

First, there was some kind of vibration that occurred when the landing-gear was raised. During the flight the team could establish no precise cause, and it was left as a problem to solve on future test flights.

There was also a buffeting problem which occurred on landing, when the trailing edge of the wing was fully extended. 'It's not uncommon to have some buffeting of the flap on landing, but this plane has a little more than we would like.' With his habitual understatement Cashman highlighted a problem which required several weeks of engineering ingenuity to solve.

A third problem, of no significance at all, was visible to all when the plane landed. In the rear of the plane there is a huge wheel carrying a coil of tubing which is threaded through to the outside of the plane to measure air speed away from the turbulence caused by the plane itself. This had proved impossible to wind fully in, and as the plane did a perfect landing, to the cheers of the spectators, the tube trailed behind like a length of thread hanging off a new garment.

TWENTY

Peeling the Onion

From 12 June onwards there was rarely a day when there wasn't a 777 in the sky. The flight-test programme had taken off now that it had a plane to fly, and soon there were two planes as WA 002 took off for a five-hour-long first flight in mid-July, then three as WA 003 followed in August. There was still a huge amount of work to do. Alan Mulally described how the programme worked:

> It's almost like peeling an onion. You start out at a system level – hydraulics, for example. After you've checked out that the hydraulic system is working, the engineers will go deeper and deeper into the system to try every possible situation that they've designed for, whether it's normal operation or abnormal operation or something that could happen to the airplane, and then just keep checking it out in more and more detail. Then they'll do this for all the systems on the airplane.

John Cashman flew WA 001 for nearly 100 hours a month during June, July and August to start to get beneath the skin of the onion and to push the plane further and further into the corners of the 'envelope'.

The concept of a flight 'envelope' refers to the extremes of speed or altitude that the plane explores, and a plane is designed so that it can safely fly out to the edge of the envelope even though that edge is set to be further away than would ever occur in everyday flight. But the design still has to be tested by flying out to those extremes. So the plane will carry out a series of manœuvres at an altitude above the highest it is meant to fly, say 42,000 feet in the case of the 777, and the same manœuvres at below 10,000 feet, where the denser air will produce very different results. And those manœuvres might consist of flying as slow as possible, just above the point where the air over the wings loses its smooth flow characteristics and the plane stalls, round about 110 knots, and as fast as possible, such as the speed of a fast dive that a plane might have to make in the case of a rare event like a sudden depressurization.

Engines have envelopes too. An engine may have to operate in outside temperatures from 110°F down to -60°F and be capable of generating thrust up to 85,000 lb at any temperature within the range. Most of the time the range of characteristics will be much narrower than the full envelope. A plane may not experience maximum temperature on a particular trip and, because of a light load, may not have to generate maximum thrust. But the designers must always give it the potential to explore the envelope right out to its edges. At the extremes of the envelope there lurk what some engineers called 'coffin corners' – combinations of speed, altitude and temperature which you stay away from if you possibly can.

While the test flights in June and July were 'peeling the onion', they were also being used to look more closely at the problems that John Cashman noticed on the first flight – the vibration linked to the nose-gear and the trailing-edge flap buffeting. On the second and subsequent flights the same problems occurred.

When engineers went up in a chase plane and watched through binoculars they were able to see quite clearly that there was a major vibration of the nose landing-gear doors. What seemed to be happening was that, of the two sets of doors – forward and aft – the aft doors closed before the forward, leaving a lip that vibrated as air flowed around it. It was a design problem rather than an installation problem, shown by the fact that exactly the same thing happened on the second 777 on its first flight. The team had to do something about it quickly. The buffeting was very strong, and if it had been allowed to continue it could have shaken the door off its hinges. And until it was fixed the plane had to fly at a lower operating speed when the gear was lowered. It just showed how, even when you've thought of everything, something comes along to surprise you.

'We missed it,' said Ron Ostrowski, in the midst of trying to find a way to fix the problem:

We just missed it. The door either isn't stiff enough, the actuation system isn't located properly to support the loads it's going to see, or there's things we might do aerodynamically internal to the wheel well, and in fact that's where we're going. We're putting some baffle plates to change the flow distribution within the wheel well, to change the load that gets applied to the door, and hopefully that'll take care of it. At the moment we won't change the structure of the door itself. But that's another option if we choose to go that route.

The other buffeting problem, on a trailing-edge flap, which occurred when the plane was coming in to land at low speed, also generated quite a lot of attention, because the team wanted to solve it before the plane flew down to Edwards Air Force Base in California to carry out some low-speed take-off and landing tests. It was quite a complex problem to solve, and involved wind-tunnel tests to see why the air was breaking up around the existing shape of the flap and to test out slightly different cross-sections to try to solve the problem.

As the tests continued, there were inevitably other undesirable events that occurred, some of them reaching the press and triggering more fits of concern in Boeing about the negative approach of the media.

During 1993 and 1994 the Boeing public-relations people became increasingly irritated by the writings of Byron Acohido, the aviation correspondent of the *Seattle Times*, one of the two main Seattle newspapers. He sometimes gave the impression that the 777 was stretching the envelope of safety too soon and too fast, and he wrote a number of stories about three main areas, all of them very familiar to the 777 team. He forecast that early ETOPS was going to be difficult to achieve; he wrote about difficulties with the Pratt 4084 engine; and he harped continually on the dangers of fly-by-wire and the risks Boeing was taking by plunging into service with a system that had not been tested long-term in flight. Acohido also drew attention to what he saw as a cosy relationship between the FAA and the company in the various mechanisms for monitoring standards and certifying safety.

Without ever expressing more than a disciplined disagreement, the Boeing people were clearly irritated, annoyed and angry at the activities of Acohido and other reporters who, they believed, seemed to look only for bad news (although this is a complaint anyone written about in the newspapers generally utters about anyone who writes about them).

Said Granny Frazier:

Some newspapers have an adversarial approach to the Boeing Company that actually nauseates me and I've stopped reading them. I spent fifteen years on the Boeing crash-investigation committee, and I learned first hand the difference between what gets reported in the paper and what the facts are. I concluded that there was almost no relationship between what was written there and the facts, and it made me nervous about reading anything else. I just quit taking the papers.

Acohido's was quite a lone voice – or at least a lone tone of voice. On the whole, Boeing got a good press in the Seattle area. Even when the rare aircraft accident happened that was clearly in some sense Boeing's 'fault', superb public relations gave the impression, probably correctly, that the company had done and was doing everything it could think of to correct the problem and make up for its effects.

But it was disingenuous of the Boeing people to protest as much as they did. Every scientist, technologist and engineer must understand the deep and seemingly unalterable ignorance of the public about matters that he or she finds transparently obvious. As with the ETOPS argument, so it is with every other aspect of flying that is unfamiliar to the public. If a new and complex control system such as the 777 fly-by-wire software is being used for the first time, there *might* be some unforeseen set of circumstances that would cause it to fail. If something goes wrong in a test programme it takes a great deal of understanding of the issues to see it as a 'gift' in Alan Mulally's terms. What goes along with the public's folk wisdom is the belief that for some unfathomable reason the engineers themselves have not thought of the arguments that are so obvious to the public – or at least to journalists.

Unfortunately, Acohido was given more grist for his mill by

something that happened on one of Cashman's test flights towards the end of August:

PANEL FLIES OFF IN 777 TEST, CUTS LANDING-GEAR LINE

A loose panel knocked out part of the Boeing 777's hydraulic systems during a recent test flight, forcing the pilot to return to Boeing Field and use a flying maneuver to lock the landing gear in place to manage a safe landing.

The Aug. 21 incident started over Eastern Washington as test pilot John Cashman attempted to retract the 777's landing gear at high speed. A small access panel protecting a hydraulic-system filter flew loose and severed a nearby tube. Hydraulic fluid swiftly drained out of the system.

The 777 has three separate, overlapping hydraulic systems, which supply pressurized fluid used to move parts. The hydraulic system damaged by the flying panel powered the landing gear and some wing panels.

Boeing spokeswoman Donna Mikov said it was the third time that particular access panel had torn loose in test flights although this was the first time the hydraulic system was damaged as a result. In one instance, a panel fell into the ocean and washed up on the Olympic Peninsula. The panel lost in Eastern Washington has not been recovered, she said. Around the time of the Aug. 21 incident Boeing officials decided not to fly the 777 to the Farnborough '94 Air Show, which begins at an airfield outside London Monday. Mikov said the incident was not related to Boeing's decision to keep the 777 home to focus on flight tests.

Boeing is flight testing three 777s. The mishap occurred on the No. 1 airplane, painted in Boeing company colors. That plane has had more than 40 test flights. Why the access panel breaks loose is not clear. Mikov would say only that the problem is being fixed.

Federal Aviation Administrator spokesman David Duff said 'the problem must be fixed before the basic airplane can be certified' as safe for commercial flights. He said if the problem is fixed, Boeing could still win special approval for its controversial proposal to immediately fly the 777 on long overseas route. 'This is one of the reasons they do this [flight testing],' Duff said. 'To identify problems and fix them before the airplane enters service.'

As the incident unfolded, pilot Cashman found he could not retract the landing gear, nor use normal procedures to deploy and lock 'side braces' necessary to keep the gear from collapsing upon landing.

So Cashman flew back to Boeing Field with the landing gear extended. As he approached Seattle, Cashman performed a 'sideslip' maneuver, using gravity to lock the side braces in place for landing.

Industry sources said Boeing officials stood by nervously, concerned about the possibility that the landing gear might not be securely locked in place by the maneuver. If the landing gear had collapsed, and the airplane had belly landed, the 777 program could have faced a major problem and a costly delay.

But Cashman landed safely. With no control of the nose wheel, also powered by the breached system, he used engine thrust and brakes to ease the 777 off the main runway over to an adjoining taxi way. The crippled jet came to rest at the south end of Boeing Field, its rear sections coated with leaked hydraulic fluid. A tow-tug vehicle was dispatched to haul it back to company hangars at the north end of the field.

Cashman notified Boeing Field air-traffic controllers only that the 777 had 'hydraulic problems', and might take a little longer than usual clearing the runway after landing, said Federal Aviation Administration spokesman Dick Meyer. Had a similar problem occurred on a passenger-carrying jetliner flight, the airline pilot very likely would have declared an emergency, alerting all available emergency crews to stand by for a possible problem landing, Meyer said.

Mikov said Cashman considered the problem minor and handled it in a manner he considered routine. She said cockpit instruments indicated the gear was locked after Cashman performed the sideslip, and that the veteran test pilot was 'absolutely not concerned' about the possibility of a belly landing. Generally, the captain of any flight has total discretion in determining when to declare an emergency.

'If he [Cashman] was being perfectly safe, and faced no political repercussions, he probably would have declared an emergency,' said Leo Janssens, president of Aviation Safety Institute, a Worthington, Ohio-based aviation-safety advocacy group. 'He was betting that things wouldn't compound; that's why he didn't declare an emergency.'

Cashman was exasperated by this coverage:

You know, we're trying a somewhat new thing on this programme of being more open with the press, giving them more updates – not just on the initial idea of the airplane, but how it's going throughout the test programme. And from my standpoint it's a little frustrating – probably for them talking to me as well – but it's a world that most people are not exposed to unless they're directly in the business. And I'm sure for the press it's hard to understand that failures of any kind are acceptable: that to us, at this stage of the game, that's success. When people take that information and blow it out of proportion, or misinterpret it, or try to make a creative, dramatic story out of it, I get frustrated, because I view it as somewhat of an attack on the pilot community. But also it's a break in the trust that I think should exist in both directions. And the information is there if somebody would just ask us instead of going writing a story about it. But at the same time I understand that it's a different world to most people. They relate to what these things would mean in the airline world with them flying as a passenger, and that's a totally different environment. We're looking for different things, and the goal is to solve the problems before we ever get to the airline world.

But of course the real question is not so much whether the report was suggesting that these pieces were going to drop off all the time from planes once they get into service but whether it was news *even though* the piece dropped off a test plane.

I wouldn't want to say it was totally trivial. But the fact that we found it is the important thing. And they made a big story out of it like there was some conspiracy or cover-up of it, and that was not the case at all. So that, for me – from my standpoint – was frustrating.

To someone else it may sound pretty dramatic, but at least to us it was pretty routine, because I knew what was involved – I knew what the failure was. It occurred when the gear was starting to come up, and it was the process of the landing-gear coming up, at high speed, that led to a vibration that caused this door to come loose, and then, flopping around, it cut a hydraulic line. It was a little door behind the landing-door gears.

The gear then dropped down again but didn't lock, because of the related hydraulic failure:

After that occurred, we knew that the landing-gear would probably not lock into place, and we knew already how to make it lock. So I did this little manœuvre, rolling the airplane a little bit, and the gear popped in and it was fine. Basically, the only function that I lost was the ability to bring the landing-gear up. And all the sensors that tell me whether it's up or down are the same ones that are there in every other landing I do, when everything is totally normal. So I wasn't greatly concerned about it. I was trying to be a good neighbour and allow other traffic to land at Boeing Field ahead of us, because we would probably have to be towed off the runway.

The only thing that really affected the landing was I had no steering in the nose-gear, because that's hydraulic. And so I landed and rolled out without steering. And we thought we might have to be towed from the runway. As it turned out, I was able to get it off the runway without the tow truck.

The differences between the two stories seem to be difference of emphasis as much as anything else. The newspaper story writes of the 'crippled jet' and reports on the decision not to send the plane to Farnborough as if it was related – there was, in fact, very little likelihood of the Farnborough trip, since it would have taken one test plane out of the series for a week or more. There is the quote from the FAA spokesman saying that it 'must be fixed' before the plane can be certified, as if anybody was suggesting it wouldn't be. And so on and so on.

What probably really riled the Boeing people was that the incident was reported at all. And the feelings of people like Cashman and Mulally and the Boeing communications people were based not on one story but on a drip-feed of coverage, some of it based on quotes from unnamed 'aviation experts'. On one occasion Mikov was rung up by a journalist and asked if Boeing had asked permission not to fly a proper three-hour single-engine diversion flight as part of the ETOPS tests but to fly with two engines and see if one of them failed. She checked this extraordinary idea and told the journalist that it was not the case – in fact it would have implied such a lack of faith in the engines that the company would be being almost criminally negligent in allowing them on the plane. Nevertheless the story appeared, ascribed to 'industry sources'.

As the flight-test programme proceeded, Boeing began to get some sense of whether the plane was meeting the guarantees or nominals they had worked so hard to achieve. The drag – the air resistance generated by the plane's shape – was lower than all expectations, meaning that the plane could fly at a faster cruise speed. Its target had been 0.83 Mach[1] but because the plane slipped through the air more smoothly it could go slightly faster, at 0.84 Mach.

Alan Mulally was very pleased – because the customers would be pleased:

> On a ten- or eleven-hour trip that's probably twenty-five to thirty minutes of savings and time because your plane flies faster. That's a tremendous value to the airlines. In a way you can say, 'Well, boy, these guys have got these really really smart aerodynamicists and they designed the airplane for 0.83 Mach number and it goes

[1] Mach is the speed of sound – about 760 m.p.h at sea level, and slower at higher, colder altitudes. Designating speeds by Mach number, rather than by miles per hour, gives a more accurate representation of the conditions experienced by the plane in air of different temperatures and density.

faster than even what they thought.' And then we must say, 'It's still an art, and even we can be pleasantly surprised.'

As one of the aerodynamicists, Ron Ostrowski was pleased too:

It's a clean airplane. We went to great detail to understand precisely what all the bumps and bruises were on the airplane, and to minimize what we call excrescence drag. We just managed ourselves very carefully from day one, relative to the airplane capabilities in drag. And the difference of 0.01 Mach number has some real benefit to the customers in terms of their route planning and their competitive advantages relative to the other craft on that same route system.

The final weight of the plane was not quite on target. When WA 004 – one of United's planes that had a proper interior without tons of test equipment – was weighed at the end of August, it weighed in at 297,400 lb – 100 lb less than Allen Bailey's prediction at the beginning of the evening, based on a careful adding up of everything they knew about the weight of the individual pieces. The team had started out designing a plane that was 17,000 lb heavier than their nominal target and had managed to get down to 4,000 lb heavier than nominal but 2,000 lb below what they had guaranteed the airlines. And, because of the lower drag, the plane still met its fuel-efficiency targets – a slightly heavier plane pushed against slightly less resistance ends up burning the same amount of fuel.

In the heat of August, WA 003 flew down to Phoenix, Arizona, to carry out tests on the heating and air-conditioning system. The plane sat on the runway for eight hours with the doors open until every element of the plane had reached the ambient temperature: 100°F or so. Then the test crew checked all the systems to see that they would still operate under those conditions. Among the engineers was Sharon Macdonald-Schramm, one of the comparatively few women engineers on the 777 project. She is English, from the Midlands, and is an advertisement for how well girls can do if they are not dissuaded from doing science and engineering at school. Small, slim and feisty, in an English sort of way, she describes herself as 'naturally bossy' and says that having an English accent has some advantages at Boeing, 'because everyone tells me it makes us sound more intelligent'.

There are multiple tasks for the plane's heating, cooling and ventilation systems to perform, involving a mixture of mechanical engineering, electronics and fluid dynamics. In addition to heating and cooling the passengers, the equipment has to heat the cargo bay (in case you're shipping your dogs to Alaska), deal with anti-icing, run smoke-detection systems and carry out several other jobs.

The temperature-control functions all start with hot air from the engines which is then cooled down in huge air-conditioning packs in the belly of the plane. The 777 has a more controllable temperature system than any other Boeing plane, with separately controlled individual zones to deal with differing passenger needs. This also helps to get over a problem with the central part of plane cabins, over the wing box, which contains more metal than the rest of the fuselage and therefore tends to be colder than the rest of the plane unless the system works very hard to prevent it. The 777 cabin staff will use touch-panel computer screens where they can find information about the plane in flight that they've never had access to before, down to the state of the lavatories.

Macdonald-Schramm described the eventful journey of an air molecule through the plane's air-conditioning system, as vividly as if she'd travelled that journey itself:

The air goes into the engine as we're flying along, and then we have what we call the bleed system, which is where we actually bleed air off the engine, and that's our source of air. If I want to melt ice on the engine cowl, I would stay right there at the engine and go to the cowl of the engine and melt any ice which might have formed, if we're in icing conditions. Along a similar path we go to the leading edge of the airplane, where we have some heated slats where we take the hot air.

For the air coming actually into the cabin, we would come from the air-supply system in through the air-conditioning pack and along a whole system of ducting. Then the air would come out of air-supply grilles which are above head height. The way our flow pattern works is that it goes across into the middle of the cabin and then circles back round, and we have a return air grille, which is on the wall at about foot height. We have fans drawing the air through, which helps the uniformity of the heat. And then, depending on whether this is some air that's going to be recirculated, we'd go through a filter. Eventually the air gets exhausted out through outflow valves which let the air leave the airplane. The airflow valves are part of the pressurization system of the airplane, and so, depending on what altitude we're at, we control the rate at which air enters and leaves the airplane in order to maintain the pressurization of the airplane.

One thing many people 'know' about planes, thanks to recent publicity, is that the air-conditioning system cleverly accumulates germs from all the passengers with colds or flu and distributes them fairly among the other passengers. Macdonald-Schramm indignantly denies this rumour:

> I think what happens is that people get hold of a story and then it's a media frenzy and so everybody gets very excited about it and it becomes a huge issue. We have very, very strict standards for the quality of the air. In the airplane we have to have carbon dioxide and carbon monoxide at certain levels, and we obviously keep it well below the allowable levels; we have a filtering system on the recirculation fans that is equivalent to the best operating room in the country, so that the talk of spreading germs is really not all that well founded, we find. The fact is that the air comes down and goes round in a lateral cycle, so that the air's not really going forwards to backwards very much, and we don't feel there's a lot of bad things being spread around a cabin.

In the shimmering heat of Phoenix, the team found one of those problems that flight testing is so good at throwing up when you think you've thought of everything:

> We found that the flight-deck was getting too warm when we were sitting in the sun with the door open, and we went round and round in circles trying to find out what the problem was. And it turned out that when we'd done all our original design and analysis we'd had the flight-deck door closed, and having the door

open totally changed the airflow patterns. All the cool air was coming straight out of the flight-deck and wasn't actually stopping to cool anything – it was just going right out of the door. In doing so, it was drawing hot air up from the electronic-equipment bay through the rudder pedals, and making the front part of the flight-deck very warm. So it's an incredibly complex situation when you look at all the places where air is coming in, going out, and moving around.

Engineers have found no better way of tracing air currents than with smoke – sometimes cigarette smoke, which can send the engineers home reeking, to spouses who might be suspicious if they didn't know any better. Once they'd traced the pathway of this disobedient air, the engineers had to fix the problem with a couple of changes in the design of the system:

> The displays in the flight-deck give off an enormous amount of heat – the surface temperature is about 125 degrees. So, in addition to the warm air coming up through the rudder pedals, we actually have heat being radiated in the flight-deck. We've made a design change so that we're going to be actually blowing cold air across the front of the displays. Also, some of the air from the electronic equipment bay goes into the cargo heating system, and we're going to increase that flow so that there's less chance of the rudder-pedal air coming up through the flight-deck. It's involved several changes – software as well as the actual hardware change.

The compensations of sitting on a sunny runway with the doors open were to be replaced later in the year with a flight to Sweden where the engineers were required to sit in the plane while it cooled to −25°F and then turn on the heating to see how long it took to warm up.

In August 1994 Alan Mulally prepared to set off on holiday with his family. It was two months after the first flight of airplane WA 001. Airplane WA 002 took off for its first flight on 15 July; airplane

WA 003 on 2 August, Phil Condit's birthday. By 23 August the 777 had built up 500 hours of flight time on the first three test planes. On that date Mulally stopped being general manager of the 777 programme and was given a new, more senior, post in Boeing.

Ron Ostrowski was flabbergasted:

> Alan came in one day to my office and said, 'Ron, this is what's being considered.' And he asked me what I thought. And I was in shock – I said, 'What?' It just didn't seem right at the time. I mean, here we are, very close to the end in terms of the certification process we're going through, but a very critical time in the programme. And the programme was stable, going well, we have had no serious, significant problems, everything was pretty much on track. And it just didn't seem like the right time, from a company point of view, to pull the leader out and put him elsewhere.
>
> Now the job that Alan has taken on, in my opinion at the time, didn't seem to justify taking him from this programme, because we just felt we needed that leadership. But it was kind of a shock thing really at the time, and my advice – and he asked for it – was, 'Alan, I don't think this is right, and I don't think you should do this.'

Mulally also has memories of that encounter:

> When I told Ron that I might be leaving, he said, 'You're kidding.' And I said, 'I'm not.' He said, 'You're *kidding*.' And I said, 'No, I'm not.' And then we both looked at each other for a while, and then we said, 'It'll be OK. We'll figure out how to make it OK.' But in a way something I feel really good about is that we talked about it way before it ever happened, and not just me but all of the members of our team. Because life's about change and being adaptable, and we tried not to make it a bigger deal than it really is. We are in different situations at any given time, and in the next day or a few days it'll all change. And so I think that the sense we had was that this was something we all had to deal with. We did the same thing when Phil left, we did the same thing when Neil left,[2]

---

[2]Standal had left the 777 team to run one of Boeing's fabrication plants.

and, as we've been redeploying the engineering team, people that came in and added their tremendous creativity and left – Tom Gaffney going to China – every one of those, it's kind of like we've gotten pretty good at it. You miss your colleagues, and the transition's always tough, but you know it's the right thing to do. You just have to make it OK.

The Boeing Company has a surprising number of senior posts. Just when you think you've understood the hierarchy there turns out to be another layer. This is very convenient when people who are already senior have done a good job and need to be rewarded. In Mulally's case he was promoted to replace the vice-president of engineering in Boeing's corporate headquarters charged with trying to decide which new airplanes and derivatives to make and when to bring an engineering perspective to the task, based on the perceived success of the new approaches on the 777. But Boeing were at pains to point out that Mulally would not be doing the same job as his predecessor, and that he would have increased responsibilities.

That left the question of who would lead the 777 team in the post-Mulally era to consolidate the flight-test programme, incorporate the lessons learned, and produce the first in-service planes. Dale Hougardy, vice-president 777 in charge of manufacturing, was Boeing's choice. He greeted the news with a little fear and trepidation:

You know, you can never replace a guy like Alan. What a charismatic leader! So I think that that was a significant issue. The things that I needed to emphasize are (1) stability, so that people don't feel like, 'Oh, we're in a dramatic upheaval here' and then (2) just continue to foster the teamwork.

The Farnborough Air Show, held every two years about thirty miles south-west of London, was originally set up as a showcase for the British aerospace industry. With the effective demise of the British aerospace industry, the show has turned more and more into a rag-bag of exhibitors of everything from 'bone-domes' (pilot headgear) to plastic airplane kits. Of course the major players in the world aviation industry are still there, but represented as a pale shadow of their former presence. Right up till a few days before the 1994 show opened, on Monday 5 September, there was the hope that the 777 would appear. Some of the sales staff believed it *would* come, and had even prepared plans for it to arrive at 1.30 p.m. on the Monday and depart for Seattle twenty-four hours later.

About a week before the due date, the decision was made not to go. The flight tests were in full flow at that point, and a plane would have to be taken out of the test programme for six days to allow for its twenty-four-hour guest appearance. Although the tests were going well, the pace was still a punishing one, and Boeing decided to forgo the publicity benefits in favour of continuing to tackle some of the problems that were showing up.

In the absence of the plane, Boeing sent Alan Mulally instead, and he held court in the Boeing chalet, mingling with journalists and visiting airline representatives. At a small press conference, Mulally reported on the flight test programme and answered some generally rather bland questions from the aviation journalists present. Fortunately for Mulally, none of them was a regular reader of the *Seattle Times* and so the issue of the flying access panel didn't come up. After an upbeat summary of the test results, a journalist asked what things had gone wrong, and Mulally gave an open account of the main problem areas that had been identified. He didn't mention the access panel either. Either it had slipped his mind or he didn't think it important enough, or both.

By contrast with the pit-bull tendencies of some of the American journalists who cover aviation, some of the Europeans were a docile lot. There was also the occasional suspicion that they didn't know as much about airplanes as they might have been expected to. One Boeing executive described with astonishment a press conference earlier in the week where, among other information, a Boeing spokeman had described the fact that the 777's fuel consumption was lower than expected. Apparently the following exchange, or something like it, had occurred:

JOURNALIST: Apart from the fuel-consumption problem, where there any other problems?

BOEING PERSON: What do you mean, 'fuel-consumption *problem?*'

JOURNALIST: Well, you said it was lower than expected.

BOEING PERSON: That's good, the airlines like a lower fuel consumption.

JOURNALIST: (*puzzled*) Oh. Well, how do you make it lower? You use less power, I suppose . . .

TWENTY-ONE

VMUs and RTOs

There is a mural in the flight-test building at Boeing Field that represents some of the themes of flight test. It includes images that are of significance only if you have been part of the tightly knit group of pilots and engineers who have tested Boeing's new planes over the years. In addition to eight nude women (you have to look very hard to find them), the artist has included an image of the Desert Inn in Lancaster, California. Outside the hotel is the sort of lettered sign that usually says, 'Welcome Palmdale Buick Managers' or 'Congratulations, Chuck and Doris Horowitz Silver Wedding'. In the mural the sign says, 'Welcome Boeing Manager Dennis Mahan'. It refers to the time one of the senior flight-test managers was promoted. In September 1994 Mahan was back again in Lancaster, along with more than 100 flight-test team members spread between the Inn of Lancaster, the Desert Inn and the Valley Inn, each known by its initials.

Everybody said that the flight-test people were different. Alan Mulally affectionately called them 'cowboys'. As individuals, they were probably no more unusual, and covered no wider a personality range, than any of the other teams working on the 777. But, as a team, they predated the design–build teams. They had always had to work together with a mix of disciplines, each with a different specialism and a different objective. They had always had to try hard to submerge personal differences and objectives in the task of ensuring that a new model of plane was safe to fly. They had always had to find ways of reflecting and accommodating the differing objectives of pilots, engineering, maintenance, and safety officers. They had developed a closeness that led to an easy good humour as they flew to various parts of the United States to carry out the huge number of tests that were designed to stretch the 777 design to its limits.

But the highlight of the test programme was always the trip to Edwards Air Force Base, about 110 miles from Los Angeles. There Boeing tested its planes in a number of manœuvres that required a long runway in an isolated location. Edwards is one of a number of military bases that seem to take up much of southern California inland from the coastal strip. Its runway is part of a dried-up lake bed, which means that even if a plane runs off the end of the runway it can go for miles before it runs into anything solid. The base also contains a NASA facility, used as part of the Space Shuttle programme. In the early days, when the Shuttle had not settled into a routine, it would take off from Cape Canaveral but land at Edwards, with plenty of room to manœuvre. But it then had to be flown back to the Cape on the back of a specially adapted 747. By 1994 the Shuttle landed routinely on the East Coast, with Edwards kept for emergencies, such as bad weather at the designated landing-site.

In September 1994 the 747 Shuttle-carrier had been joined on the tarmac by the first 777, WA 001. By then the first three planes – WA 001, 002 and 003 – had flown between them more than 110 long test flights, as well as many more take-offs and landings for shorter test conditions. The attention given to the first flight only three months before had been replaced by a comfortable acceptance that, sure enough, the 777 could fly, as it was designed to, and now there were too many other things to get on with to spend time gazing open-mouthed as two hundred and eighty tons lifted from the ground and confirmed the laws of physics yet again. On one morning alone during the summer the plane had taken off and landed thirty-two times.

The weekend of 10–11 September marked the beginning of two weeks or so of specific take-off and landing tests that would lead eventually to a mandatory test in front of the FAA in October or November. There were two main types of test to be carried out. They were connected with events that can happen during take-off that sometimes challenge the plane to the limits. The tests centre on three figures which every pilot needs to know every time he takes off. These figures describe certain velocities that are a function of the weight of the plane, the length of the runway, the altitude above sea level and even whether the runway is wet or not.

V1 is the decision speed which determines whether a plane should take off or abort if it has a problem. Below *V1* the pilot will stop for most major problems. If he tries to take off below *V1* with an engine failure, say, he will need more runway than he has available. Above *V1*, if he tries to stop for a major problem he will not have the runway space available to stop.

'With most incidents that happen on airplanes above *V1*,' John Cashman said, during the tests at Edwards, 'you're far better to go.'

> It would have to be a major failure to ever try to stop above *V1*. An example of that might be if you hit something and you don't know if your wing's there, for instance. Or you run into a massive flock of birds that wipe out both your engines. There have been a few events like that. But what most pilots have found over the years is, even if you're near *V1*, it's better to continue and go.

There are two other important speeds: *VR* and *V2*. Ken Higgins explains:

> Let's take the case that you have accelerated to *V1*, and up till *V1* nothing is wrong, so you decide at *V1*, 'I'm going to go.' After *V1*, suppose the engine fails. Then you have to begin your rotation at *VR*, the rotation speed, and aim for *V2*, the take-off safety speed. And if you target *V2* and fly *V2* you will meet the take-off performance numbers and the take-off will be safe.

The Edwards tests that began in September were called VMUs and RTOs. VMU stands for Velocity Minimum Unstick – the absolute minimum take-off speed. Once the VMU test has determined this speed, this in turn can be used to determine the safe take-off speed, *V2*. There are various situations in which a pilot might need to use the minimum speed, though he should never plan to do so. The most likely situation is if an engine fails during acceleration to take-off and it's too late to abort the take-off. The plane has to fly, and can, on one engine, but the pilot suddenly has to generate enough lift from less total thrust. The way to do this is to angle the wings at a greater angle to the horizontal, by putting the nose higher. But because the plane pivots about the under-carriage, under the centre of the plane, putting the nose up means that the tail will go down. In the worst case, the tail will scrape along the runway.

RTO stands for Refused Take-Off. It is a stringent test of the plane's braking systems to ensure that they can stop the heaviest 777 before the end of the runway when the brakes are slammed on at or just below the take-off speed. The crucial factor in an RTO test is the tremendous amount of heat that is generated and the ability of the brakes to absorb the heat without setting the plane on fire.

It was the VMU test that the team were due to carry out on the Saturday morning. They had to calculate what the VMU was in various situations, covering different airplane weights and extremes of runway conditions, and then check that the plane performed as expected. Sometimes at what the pilot thinks is a suitable take-off speed the engines don't lift the plane at all, and that's where the long runway at Edwards comes in handy.

This test first became part of flight testing after two Comet accidents in the 1950s when pilots who were afraid they were going to run out of runway tried to take off too soon and didn't have enough lift because of the high altitude of the airfield and warm air.

All the 777 flight tests were graded for risk, and by definition nothing was 100 per cent safe if it was being done for the first time, even if it was just an apparently routine increment in procedures that had been shown by previous tests to be OK. This was another advantage of the Edwards airfield: since it was a full-time test facility the pilots didn't have to worry about the possibility of disrupting other traffic if they had to declare an emergency. It also, of course, had efficient and alert emergency services.

The base was located in a deserted area of California and covered hundreds of square miles. About ten miles after passing the sign on the threshold of the base you would come to the first signs of aviation – a cluster of test aircraft from the past, out in the open air, forming the nucleus of a planned flight-test museum. At 3.30 a.m. on Saturday morning, 10 September, the road between the town of Lancaster and the Edwards base was sprinkled with a couple of dozen cars making their way from the three hotels to the flight-test centre. The first to arrive at the base would be the maintenance people, whose job it was to prepare the plane for the morning's activities. Following some miles behind were the project engineers, including Dennis Mahan and Dennis Floyd, the two flight-test directors, who both thought they had one of the rarer American Christian names until they met up. Last in the straggling line of cars were the pilots, John Cashman and Joe Macdonald, who had had the luxury of a lie-in fifteen minutes longer than the others.

It was pitch dark, with high scattered cloud and bright stars shining through the gaps. There was little traffic about apart from the occasional mile-long goods train, its three bright headlights piercing the night from miles away along the line that ran parallel with the Sierra Highway. The route to the base was along a straight road north for eleven miles before turning right at a road junction called Rosamond on to the twelve miles that ran through the base. The only lights were the odd petrol station and the occasional all-night store, lit by a fitfully flickering sign. Over on the right, past the entrance to the base, and invisible in the dark, was the Pancho Barnes Ranch, which used to be a sort of base brothel in the 1930s and was now a ruin, although still used for barbecues. There were no other cars on the road, and when the team arrived at the base there was no one else around, since it was the weekend.

WA 001 was visible from a distance, its '777' on the tail brightly lit by the built-in spotlight shining from the horizontal stabilizer. The previous day a plan had been confirmed for the morning's tests, and another for further tests in the afternoon, after a change-over of pilots. There were just three Boeing pilots at Edwards that day – Cashman, Macdonald and Frank Santoni – and so one of the pilots, Macdonald, had to fly both the morning and afternoon sessions.

At that time in the night there was still a summer warmth in the air. The plane was ready, and the pilots climbed up the steps. Inside the plane there were already a dozen or so engineers, helping themselves to coffee and doughnuts from the improvised galley or sitting by their computer screens.

After a short pre-flight briefing, John Cashman wrote some figures in ballpoint on his hand. They were the empty weight of the plane without fuel – so that if the plane's computers went down he could still feed in the data to land properly – and the number of 'souls' on board, so that he could be sure that everyone was out if they needed to evacuate the plane in an emergency.

A tow truck prepared to pull the plane out of the confined area to a section of taxiway where it could start engines and make its own way to the runway. A small van raced off ahead of the plane, carrying the team's meteorologists, Windy and friends, to set up a wind station at that point on the runway where the plane was due to take off.

As the 777 taxied towards the runway, jack rabbits and coyotes bounded away into the desert scrub. The first glimpse of sunrise was visible in a dull red glow on the eastern horizon. The plane would make its first VMU test as soon as it was light enough for observers beside the runway to observe the plane. The Edwards runway was about 15,000 feet long – far longer than at a conventional airport – but for these first tests the plane used maybe a third of it. As the plane stood at the end of the runway, the dark red of the eastern horizon had spread upwards to illuminate the high clouds and produce a mottled pink across most of the eastern sky.

When Windy had spoken, and the 'one – two – three' of the flight controller, Bernie Green, had echoed Cashman's countdown to releasing the brakes, the plane roared down the runway. At about

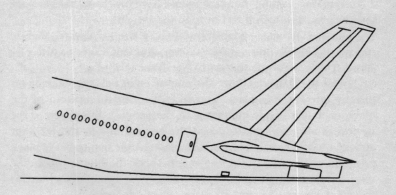

The tail of the test plane has a block of oak which scrapes along the runway and prevents damage to the fuselage

the 5,000-feet marker the nose lifted up quite sharply and then held at an angle while the plane ran a further 500 feet or so with the tail dragging along the runway.

To prevent unnecessary damage to the plane's underbelly, the 777 was fitted with a piece of equipment called a tail skid – a protective device fixed under the rearmost part of the fuselage. The tail skid had two components – an oak block on top of a compressible pad that acted as a final protection if the pressure was strong enough to push the block into the skin of the plane. The oak block touched the runway and was dragged along as the plane prepared to take off. It was this that established that the tail of the plane had actually scraped the runway – an essential condition of the test. The friction would add drag to the take-off, slowing the plane slightly.

As the plane reached VMU the plane took off. Although the angle of attack was sharper than a normal take-off, the plane took a very shallow path off above the runway. The team were interested in the minimum take-off speed under these conditions, and so the lift generated by the plane's velocity was only a little more than that necessary to support the weight of the plane. Because the runway at Edwards was so long, and the dry lake bed extended for miles beyond it, there was no problem with the very shallow climb, but at a conventional airport the plane would have had to fly dangerously low for several thousand feet beyond the airfield.

The two Dennises – Mahan (moustache, even-tempered, slightly ruddy) and Floyd (taller, smiley, boyish, diffident, eager to please) – stood at the side of the runway to watch the take-offs.

Twice the plane slid down the runway on its tail before taking off directly into the rising sun. To make sure that the bottom of the plane really had made contact with the ground, there were three devices: a long rod that touched the ground first, a shorter lever attached to the wooden block, and a laser. After two tests the plane returned to the side of the runway to check the block, which had worn down several inches. A new block was brought forward to replace the worn one, and the plane taxied out again.

By mid-morning the 777 had done a carefully recorded programme of VMUs under various circumstances and the plane now stood out in the warm sunshine. On the left side of the fuselage there was a rectangle of silver sticky tape, covering the edges of the access panel that had twice departed from the plane in the earlier tests. The test engineers were taking no chances until the part had been redesigned to move more consistently in formation with the other 4 million parts.

After a change of crew, the team started a graded series of RTO tests. During this visit to Edwards, the tests covered stopping with various weights of payload, different percentages of brake power, and different runway conditions, including wet. They started with a heavy plane and lightened it to the next test weight by burning up fuel in a series of circuits around Edwards. For environmental reasons they were not allowed to dump the fuel, and burning it up seemed simpler than bringing the plane back to the airfield and extracting 10,000 gallons. The fuel cost 15 cents a gallon, so the process of lightening the plane in this way cost about $1,500, plus the flying time on the world's newest aircraft. The circuit around the California skies also helped to cool the brakes.

John Cashman described how the brakes had been designed to carry out successful Refused Take-Off manoeuvres:

It starts with the very early definition of the airplane, when you size brakes for a vehicle. You really have to look at the weight and the speed and how it relates to runway length and altitude. The higher you go in airfield altitude, the air speed at which the wing makes lift is actually a higher and higher speed on the ground. What that means is that if you want an airplane to fly out of Denver on a hot day, which is a mile-high city, basically you have to size the brake such that you don't limit the take-off by this energy capability of the brake. You have a lot of parameters to look at. If you want to fly a mission to Tokyo, say, you have to be able to get a certain weight off of a given length of field, and when you decide what that is it helps design the wing and everything else. But part of the process is to look at what the brake has to be able to do and not limit the performance, because you mustn't take the airplane off if you can't stop it. You have to be able to stop up to the decision speed that the pilot uses to abort the take-off.

Now when you do all that, in this particular airplane – as in most modern airliners – it uses a carbon brake, which is a multiple disc assembly on each wheel. And the beauty of them is, well, they're very expensive – which I suppose is a beauty to the brake manufacturer – but the beauty of it is they're lightweight, compared with large steel brakes, and they have enormous heat-absorption capability. So they can take all this kinetic energy in stopping the airplane and turn it into heat. After a maximum-energy stop on most airplanes today the brake is intact – it doesn't break up as the old steel brakes used to do.

The steel brake would actually start melting small pieces of itself before it stopped in a maximum-brake-energy test. And, before you stopped, the brakes actually welded, and that was it – you were stuck. In recent tests, on all of our airplanes and probably the competition, you can do this test and taxi off the runway. And when the brakes cool they look like new brakes. It's absolutely phenomenal.

So, when you size all of that for this given design, you want that energy to be more than the other factors that limit the take-off, so the brake design never restricts what you can do. And any additional margin that you build in above that is just extra safety in being able to stop.

Everyone knew that these September RTO tests, which showed up no serious problems, were only steps on the path to the test that people called The Big One. This took place several weeks later, after the team had returned to Seattle to collate the data on the first Edwards run and had then flown back in mid-October.

When British Airways decided that, in order to fly their 777s out of Dallas, they needed the brakes to absorb a slightly higher energy level, they certainly didn't think of the effect that request would have on the flight-test team at Edwards Air Force base. The forty-five Boeing engineers and support staff were just nearing the end of a second successful but demanding series of tests which had begun on 13 October. Step by step they had built up to the essential 100% RTO test. This was to be the last test in the series, and one that was attended by representatives of the FAA, including an FAA pilot, Dick Paul. The plane had to pass this test, simulating an event that was one of the most extreme imaginable in normal service, a situation that might arise if a pilot flying a 777 with the maximum load it could carry reached take-off speed and then had to abort the take-off and put on the brakes with maximum force.

There were two important parameters that would establish whether the 777 could safely cope with the most extreme aborted take-off. The first was, Could it stop before it ran off the 15,000-foot runway? The plane would accelerate with an engine thrust of 84,000 lb and the brake would be slammed on after it had travelled 8,200 feet. The plane was designed so that it should travel no further than another 6,000 feet or so after the brakes were put on. In fact there was only 2,000 more feet of the runway before the terrain changed to the packed sand of the dry bed lake. During this 6,000 feet, the carbon-fibre disc brakes would be squeezed together with such tremendous force that they would be heated until they glowed. At this point, the next important question would arise: Could all this heat be contained, without benefit of firemen, for five minutes after stopping? This would simulate the sort of time period that could elapse at an average airport before firemen arrived to cool down the brakes with water.

And the matter was more complex than it might seem. Once the plane stopped, the heat that had built up in the disks would be transferred through the metal brake housings and the axles to the tyres. These are filled with nitrogen, and if there were no way of releasing the suddenly expanding gas they would explode like a 500 lb bomb. On an RTO test on the 747 the heat built up so quickly that all sixteen tyres exploded. Those tyres were fitted with fuse plugs, which were designed to melt and allow for quick release of the gas, but they weren't quick enough. Now the 777 was to go through the same test.

Although there would be firemen standing by, they were forbidden to intervene before the five minutes were up unless it was absolutely essential. And if it did turn out to be essential the plane would have failed its test.

The team had approached this Everest of flight testing through the foothills of lower levels of braking. Sixty, seven, eighty per cent of the full braking capability had been tried out in the previous weeks, with a successful 90 per cent test on Sunday 30 October. Now they were poised for the final test.

On the morning of Saturday 5 November the team met for a

post-flight briefing after some take-off performance tests they had done earlier that morning. The meeting room had rows of seats all facing a couple of tables at the front. As the members of the team filed in, John Cashman started turning some of the chairs around to form an impromptu circle, as if he anticipated that rather a lot of group work was going to be necessary in the next hour or so. The bombshell was dropped by Dennis Floyd, who had been seen in a huddle with Cashman by the doughnut and coffee counter in the front end of the plane. A message had come from Seattle to ask if Sunday's 100% RTO could be done with an increased brake-energy level. It was precisely the level that BA required for a Dallas take-off, and, although no one knew precisely where in Boeing the message had originated, words like 'sales' and 'marketing' were muttered by some of the engineers present. There were several puzzles associated with this request. BA would have 777s powered by General Electric engines and using brakes designed by a different manufacturer from the ones under test on WA 001, which was a United Airlines plane. Why, then, did this test have to be done at all on this plane? Somebody at the meeting reported that it was because Boeing wanted to have a common flight manual for the plane – at least as far as the brakes were concerned – and therefore they needed to know that these brakes could sustain the higher forces of the kind of thrust that would be required only on a plane fitted with different brakes.

Cashman was clearly worried. His customary easy-going cheerfulness in the face of all challenges often concealed the concern he felt about taking unnecessary risks. RTOs were somewhat risky, and 100% RTOs were 100 per cent risky. The crew would be kept to a minimum – eight, including the two pilots – because of the dangers of sitting for five minutes on top of twelve glowing carbon disc brakes. He started to ask questions, addressing them one by one to representatives of each of the special interests around the room. How much extra speed would that extra thrust produce? About 1 per cent, someone hazarded. How much more runway would be eaten up by that extra 1 per cent before stopping? Supposing the ground-speed indicator failed and they had to use 'ship speed', a less reliable indicator of the speed of the plane? He might then not put on the brakes until the plane was going faster than he thought and more runway would be eaten up, bringing the lake bed dangerously near. Did anyone know if these brakes had undergone lab tests that took them into the new range? Was it really necessary to have a common flight manual for the brakes? Who exactly in Boeing had made this suggestion in the first place? Dick Paul, the FAA pilot, looked on, apparently amazed by the turn of events. It certainly seemed unlike the usual Boeing meticulous planning, and it was clearly important that Paul, representing the FAA, agreed with what was done and how it was carried out. He did venture an opinion at one point, suggesting that the team should stick to the original plan.

An additional concern of Cashman's was the small chance that he might be faced with a genuine engine emergency during the test. One of the engines had suffered ten fuel cuts during the previous weeks' testing – a normal procedure to make the engine shut down and simulate engine failure. But this procedure took its toll of an engine, which became, in engineers' parlance, an 'abused' engine. No normal engine would suffer that many deliberate shutdowns, and it was a source of pride to Boeing and Pratt that they could still operate the test programme perfectly happily with such engines. Nevertheless, engine abuse did increase its chances of hitting higher than permitted exhaust-gas temperatures during the tremendous thrust of take-off. And if the thrust was to be increased beyond what the team had expected, that, Cashman felt, might just be one factor too many to worry about.

In the end the meeting was adjourned, and Cashman decided to call Ron Ostrowski at home in Seattle and find out whether the test really had to be done the way they had been asked to do it.

At the end of the working day, which finished at lunchtime because it had started so early, the team were urged by Dennis Floyd to go off and 'sacrifice' – a traditional procedure before an important test. This probably came from a desire to propitiate the gods and consisted of going off and having some beers at a nearby bar called 'A Wing and a Prayer'.

In semi-darkness, the flight-test engineers sat round a long table eating hamburgers and drinking pitchers of beer while the management ran videos of nasty crashes that had happened during test programmes at Edwards in the distant past. John Cashman joined in with the rest, sitting under a plaque that said, 'Old pilots never die, they just go on to another plane.'

The Desert Inn was accustomed to generations of test engineers coming down from Seattle to use the Edwards test facilities, but its welcome didn't extend to breakfast at the unearthly hour of 3.30 a.m. on Sunday 6 November. Instead, the engineers got up and dressed in the silent darkness, deprived of sustenance. If they turned on the television, however, they found a programme on almost every one of the forty or so channels, from Laurel and Hardy films to a course in business forecasting on the Mind Extension University channel. One Boeing test engineer was to be seen outside the hotel lobby wielding a bent coat hanger, desperate to open his hire car, which he had accidentally locked, key inside and engine running. The others turned up at the base between 4.30 and 4.45, to be shuttled to the plane, which was parked on Pad 14, after being towed there earlier in the night.

It was the day of The Big One. No pilot likes the thought of fire in contact with his aircraft, and yet today Cashman and his crew of seven were going to sit on top of – or at least above – twelve glowing brake discs until the tyres deflated as the fuse plugs melted from the heat. That was guaranteed. What was less certain was whether other things might happen as well. Would the tyres deflate in a disciplined way, or might one or more explode, sending flaming shards of rubber in all directions? Might flames spread upwards in some way into the landing-gear wells and thence to the plane?

The 100% RTO test was just another illustration of how the plane-makers explored the far corners of the envelope in their attempts to make the plane safe. What happens when an engine fails on take-off had to be explored to the full, ensuring that the plane could survive the worst imaginable combination of factors. This scenario would be bad enough in a plane that had a good set of brakes, an average load of fuel and passengers, and the thrust of one engine (the other having failed). The test could have been done under such conditions – the ones that were likely, on average, to apply in normal service. But the designers went further than that. What if, they said, the brakes were at the limit, or even just beyond the limit, of wear and tear? Could the plane still stop safely then? To add that ingredient to the day's test, they ground down a set of 777 brakes by 100 per cent – that is to say, they removed all of the safety margin, so that the brakes had enough carbon left to stop the plane but were at a point where the airline would normally be required to replace them. Next they made the plane as heavy as possible, using fuel as ballast, so that it actually represented the weight of the B-market plane, which hadn't yet been built. For the A market, this meant that the plane was heavier than it could ever be in service. Being heavier meant that more force was required to stop it and therefore more heat would be generated in the brakes. The third element that made the test more challenging than the designers could imagine happening in real life was the fact that, at the point the brakes were put on, the plane would be powered by two engines. This meant that the thrust was greater than would be likely if this manœuvre was ever to be used in the heat of the moment, since it was most likely to be needed in the event of an engine failure. This extra thrust just added to the amount of force that would required to stop the plane – something over 9 million foot pounds of energy, all of which went to heat up the brakes.

Now, however distrustful you might be of the competence or even of the intentions of the plane-makers, it is difficult to see a need here for even more stringent combinations of events to be tested. But, who knows, in some future aborted take-off of the 777 all the above conditions might operate, along with – heaven forbid – spilt fuel on the runway, debris sucked into the engine causing it to shed a blade which cuts off the hydraulic pressure to some of the brakes, and a bird strike on to the windshield that knocks out the pilot. Should the plane be tested under these conditions also, just to be sure? This is the dilemma of the chimera of 100 per cent safety.

The test team had been blessed with good weather for much of the October test period. They were a group of men used to seeing the sunrise, and Sunday's was as spectacular as many of the previous days'. At 6.23, almost exactly at sunrise, the huge airplane, weighing 632,500 lb, appeared as a dot at the end of the runway, revved its engines up to full thrust, and headed to the east, growing in size until it was level with Windy and the knot of Dennises at about the 8,000-feet marker. Then, at 183 knots (210 m.p.h), Cashman slammed on the brakes and the plane rolled another 4,000 feet or so, the anti-skid brake disks rotating against the fixed carbon disks in the wheel and building up heat as they went. The plane came to a halt and all was quiet in the desert air. Then there was an excited hubbub of conversation and the crackling of radio messages on walkie-talkies as the observers ran back to their vans to drive to the taxiing point where the plane would go after five minutes.

Over on the runway, the brakes were now glowing fiercely and a little smoke was rising, from the burning-off of stray grease. They had been almost white hot as the plane was rolling to a halt, and now they glowed a duller but still impressive red colour. Inside the plane the crew sat and waited. The gauges in the cockpit showed that the tyre pressures had peaked at 290 p.s.i. and the brake temperature had gone off the scale to about 3,000°C

Waiting by the reception area for the plane were several Boeing fire engines, surrounded by firemen in silver protective suits. They had been on the runway when the plane taxied and then raced back for the next phase of the test. The plane slowly taxied in, its brakes still glowing, and waited for the five minutes to elapse. The first fuse plug had gone three seconds before the plane stopped. After five minutes the firemen then waited for the other plugs to melt before they poured water on the wheels – to spray them while the fuse plugs were intact would risk the tyres exploding. One by one, fuse plugs melted, clouds of steam billowed up from the firemen's hoses, and the plane slowly sank down on its wheels.

Nearby were trucks with replacement wheels and tyres, and by 8.30 in the morning two wheels had already been replaced in a smooth operation. One by one all sixteen wheels were taken away for inspection – three-quarters of a million dollars' worth of equipment deliberately destroyed – and by eleven o'clock the plane was ready to taxi back to base showing a clean set of wheels. They *had* carried out the more stringent test that Boeing had asked for at the last minute, putting 9.7 million foot pounds of energy into the brakes instead of 9.2, and the 777 design had passed triumphantly.

TWENTY-TWO

Troublesome Cycles

Between December 1994 and March 1995 the 777 programme was firing on all cylinders with five aircraft. There were two deadlines that had to be met. One was the delivery of the first plane to United, planned for 15 May; and the other, upon which that delivery depended, was a series of flights which, Boeing hoped, would demonstrate to the FAA that the 777 should qualify for 180-minute ETOPS from the moment it entered into service. They were planning to fly 1,000 cycles on WA 004, one of United Airlines' first planes. This meant 1,000 simulated trips, consisting of a take-off, some period of cruising and then a landing. But before they were allowed to start the 1,000-cycle airplane test they had to be sure that the current engine design was capable of running regularly and problem-free. The criterion they needed was 3,000 engine-cycles without major problems. And those tests were being carried out on the ground in Florida.

Friday 9 December was a humid eighty-degree day in the Florida swamps inland from Palm Beach. Rain fell from the sky in short bursts, requiring the highest speed of windscreen wiper for a few seconds. So localized were the showers that it was raining on one side of Interstate 95 but not the other. When a shower stopped, the water would begin to disappear almost immediately from the hot road surface.

In a pond in the middle of the vast Pratt & Whitney test plant, an alligator lay three-quarters submerged. Every eighteen minutes a terrifying roar would issue from the rear of a 4084 engine suspended about fifteen feet above the ground. The normally placid water of the pond would be transformed into a miniature storm at sea as the exhaust from the engine at full thrust spurted about 200 yards across the surface, bending trees on the other side that had lost many of their leaves and smaller branches in the face of the regular onslaught. The alligator was either deaf or so inured to the noise that the full thrusts of the engine no longer had any impact on its life. In fact, it would be interesting to see how the creature reacted on those rare occasions when the tests were stopped. Did it look around and wonder, at the time when full thrust should have started again?

Friday was one of those occasions when the tests were stopped. The engine test had reached a halfway point in a scheduled endurance test designed to show that the engine could operate effectively over a long period of normal in-service flying without major problems. With all the attention focused now on getting ETOPS certification, everyone was eager to see proof that the chances of an engine going wrong, particularly after months of normal operations, were very slim.

Of course, by now Boeing had acquired a large number of flying hours on several 4084 engines. 777s were now flying all over the place. By early December each of the five test planes was flying regularly in a series of flights that first established that particular plane's characteristics and then tested some aspect of the generic 777 design. WA 004, for example, before it set off on its ETOPS flights, had been used to test the inflight noise levels on a flight around the USA. But in terms of flying hours, and more specifically in terms of what are called flight cycles, the total amount of activity was nothing like enough to establish the endurance of the engine and its ability to work effectively, day in, day out, in a pattern of regular flights on routes which might involve up to four or five take-offs and landings a day.

Bob Mazurkivich was the Pratt test engineer who ran the team in Florida. Tall, thin and only thirty years old, he headed a group of half a dozen engineers who sat around in the bunker-like control room, about 100 feet from the engine. Through the window, they could see in the warm and humid outdoors a large test rig holding a 777 engine, with its associated coverings and framework. Because the whole engine assembly was under test, there were some parts that Boeing had designed, festooned around the Pratt engine, and so there were also Boeing engineers in attendance in the control room. Around the room were computers and monitors, including a bank of equipment called the 777 Engine Health Monitoring System, showing a whole range of characteristics of the engine during every phase of the test. From time to time Mazurkivich would be called over by a colleague to look at a reading or deal with a query. The room had the quiet hum of electronic equipment and low-level conversation, but every eighteen minutes or so the sound levels would rise sharply as the loud roar of full thrust penetrated even the robust sound-proofing of the control-room building.

The set-up was one of a number of engine test rigs that Pratt had installed out in the Florida swamp. Most of them were for defence purposes – new fighter-plane engines, for example. They tested the Space Shuttle engine here, which produced a far more deafening roar than the giant 777 engine. It also generated a 300-foot-high burst of flame, so the airspace above the engine test had to be cleared for 3,000 feet every time they ran it.

The 4084 had been in existence in some form for nearly three years now. Individual components had been laboratory tested, and redesigned if necessary. The whole assembly of components had

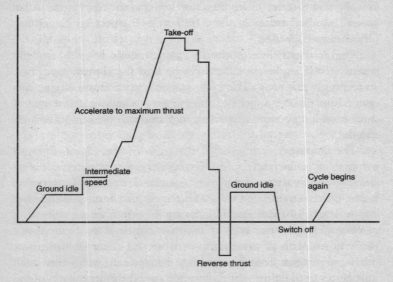

4084 engine test cycle - duration 17 minutes 34 seconds

undergone more lab testing to see that the engine delivered the performance that Pratt had promised Boeing. Tests like the strobo-scopic illumination of the vibrating engine had identified those pieces that might develop a harmonic interaction with the engine's vibration cycle and shake off or fracture. All of these tests had led to a successive elimination of potential problems. But physics and materials science still have a way of surprising engineers, as new and strange modes of fatigue or temperature deterioration suddenly occur in the hostile environment.

What the engineers needed to know was that the engine could endure regular cycles of different levels of thrust – from a maximum at take-off, through a lower level for cruising, and then reverse thrust to brake the plane after landing – over and over again for the equivalent of several months' scheduled flying.

The 3,000-cycle engine tests had begun at the Pratt plant in Florida in October. Boeing had asked for permission to start the 1,000-cycle ETOPS flights as soon as the engine had undergone 1,500 cycles successfully, although they were prepared to stop the ETOPS flights if a problem then developed in the test engine. After several hundred cycles of the 3,000-cycle engine tests something unfortunate happened.

The Pratt engineers noticed a change in engine note, and the sensors in the engine sent messages back to the control room that something was wrong. The cycle was aborted and the engine was opened up. Inside, a piece of the engine – a vane actuator arm, a three-inch-long component – had fractured and broken off at high speed.

The continual cycling of all the parts of the engine through extremes of temperature, pressure and stress would be expected to show up any weakness in design or manufacture. There was an extra factor which accentuated this. The engine had been put together with a degree of imbalance, to simulate the effects of the worst sort of wear and tear. Over years of use, particularly if an engine is not properly maintained, unevenness of wear and dents in blades and other components from foreign-body damage can lead to very small imbalances in the distribution of weight round the central pin of the engine. At the sort of rotation speeds the engine experiences at full thrust, just a tiny fluctuation in the distribution of weight can lead to a major vibration in the engine. This in turn can shake pieces off the outside, such as brackets and pipes, or even lead to fracturing of components inside. So, when a brand-new engine was prepared for its 3,000-cycle test, it was made with a deliberate imbalance, to produce conditions similar to the worst case, or worse than the worst case, just to make sure that the engine could still operate safely for the required number of regular flights.

When the component broke, there was a swift redesigning process in order to start the 3,000 cycles again, as soon as possible. But it was no small task. Although only one actuator arm had fractured, every one of them had to be replaced, and there were seventy-eight of them shared among four different stages of the turbine. Furthermore, of course, all five planes flying had engines with the faulty design, and their components had to be replaced as well.

Now, on 9 December, the much awaited 1,500th cycle was reached at last. In the early Florida evening, as the mosquitoes hovered around the maintenance engineers, the engine was powered through its 1,500th cycle, with a final roar as its thrust-reverser operated, and Bob Mazurkivich and his colleagues faxed a hastily improvised certificate back to Seattle to mark the occasion.

The role of clouds in the psychology of everyday life is often underrated. So important is the presence or absence of sun, blue skies and daylight that there is a psychological condition called Seasonal Affective Disorder – SAD – whose depressive aspects are entirely due to the gloom of short days, low cloud and absence of sunshine. And yet pilots and frequent fliers know how evanescent such feelings are, since they are continually crossing, almost in an instant, the border between gloom and glory, leaden clouds and brilliant sunshine. When a fully laden 747 takes off from Heathrow on a rainy Friday morning, the 400 or so irritable people who have struggled against the rush-hour traffic, past roadworks and through drizzly rain, shuffled forward in a queue with heavy cases, undergone interrogation and suspicion from surly security guards, and finally sunk into cramped seats and stared out of raindrop-spattered windows, can then experience a transformation scene worthy of any pantomime when the gauze of the cloud layer falls away and the plane bursts into a world of peace, calm and light that had been secretly coexisting all the time with the gloom and the wet and the unpleasantness of urban life on a rainy day.

The pilot of an aircraft plays the part of a traveller between two worlds, crossing and recrossing the border on one side of which is the mundane and unpredictable journey through life below and on the other the clean, crisp passage of an aircraft along predetermined paths at easy-to-calculate speeds with predictable arrival times in a space about which, barring storms and turbulence, almost everything is transparent and predictable.

Jim Metcalfe had a reminder of the sharpness of this border – in fact several reminders in quick succession – when he tried to land WA 004 at Glasgow, Montana, on Thursday 12 January 1995. The plane had already gone through eighty-nine flight cycles since the go-ahead was given after the successful 1,500 cycles of the engine, and it was now scheduled to start the cold weather portion of the 1,000-cycle ETOPS test. They had set off from Boeing Field at about 9.30 a.m. for a routine ninety-minute flight to Glasgow. The Glasgow airfield is a desolate 13,500-feet runway, thirty miles from the Canadian border, surrounded by buildings in various states of homely disrepair. It used to be a Strategic Air Command base, and the disused control tower still possesses a red telephone, receiver swinging idly in an unheated room with broken window panes. Boeing took over the establishment some years ago, and it is now used for any test flights that require guaranteed cold weather and a lot of unobstructed airspace to fly around in.

When WA 004 left Seattle there was no hint that the weather might be a problem. But about half an hour away from Glasgow the meteorologists reported poor visibility at the airfield due to a layer of cloud from the ground up to about 500 feet. Fog, in other words.

The plan had been that the plane would arrive at about noon with the intention of completing five cycles that afternoon. Now the fog posed a threat to that schedule. Great Falls, Montana, was clear but no one wanted to land there and hang around, perhaps until Friday, with all the associated bother of finding hotel rooms and rental cars for eighty people (and cancelling the same in Glasgow.) In normal operations, not surprisingly, the 777 was designed to land in the worst possible conditions, down to zero visibility, provided the airfield was equipped with the necessary sophisticated electronics to link up with the plane's own autoland system. But Glasgow did not have the necessary equipment, and so the procedure for landing was more primitive.

The thickness of the cloud seemed to vary from moment to moment. The only way to land was to descend along the glide path until a point about fifty feet above the ground where the runway would be visible. If it wasn't, the plane would have to 'go around', accelerating rapidly upwards until it was clear of the fog and then making a circuit to line it up with the runway to try again. Like all standard manœuvres, the procedure was formalized. On the approach, the copilot, an FAA pilot who was there to observe the 1,000-cycle ETOPS process, would watch the altimeter until the plane reached what was called the decision height. He would then call out 'Decision!' and the pilot would have to make up his mind on the basis of what he could see out of the cockpit windscreen. Because the cloud layer was so thin and so low, for most of the descent the plane was flying in clear skies. All around stretched the flat north-eastern Montana landscape with its layer of white cotton wool.

On the first attempt, at about 500 feet the sunlight disappeared and the plane sliced smoothly into the cloud layer. A few seconds later, as Metcalfe peered through the windscreen, hand on the throttles, the copilot shouted 'Decision!' and, barely before the word had left his mouth, Metcalfe replied 'Going around' at the same time as pulling back the joystick and increasing the throttles.

In the back of the plane, the eighty or so flight engineers, test crew and maintenance staff felt the smooth surge of the powerful plane as it rose out of the clouds and into the sun. The change in the engine noise was undramatic, even though the manœuvre was quite sudden – with such a lightly laden plane there had been no need to exert a huge increase in thrust to lift the plane above the clouds. Metcalfe came on the cabin speakers and said that they were going to try three or four times to get down at Glasgow before considering the option of seeking a clear airfield and sitting it out.

Metcalfe made four more attempts, and each time he wasn't satisfied by what he saw at decision height. Although there was no real danger, the cloud layer was so narrow that everything happened very quickly. For the people on the ground, waiting to see the plane in, it was a frustrating experience. On several of Metcalfe's attempts they could actually see the dark-blue belly of the plane dip beneath the thickest part of the fog and skim along above the runway before shooting up out of sight for another try.

On the sixth attempt, just when everyone in the plane thought they really were destined to spend the night in Great Falls, the copilot shouted 'Decision!' and Metcalfe said, already suiting the action to his words, 'Going in' as he eased the plane into its flare, held the throttles steady, and brought the plane on to the runway with barely a bump. Through the mist the snow-covered surface of the runway and airfield stretched away with only the occasional black streak where the snowploughs had been at work. Putting the engine into reverse thrust, Metcalfe slowed to a crawl and steered the plane into the taxiway. There was little of interest visible through the windows, apart from the distant shapes of the control tower and several two-storey buildings. There was an escort truck to lead the plane, but no other planes on the airfield.

When the plane drew to a halt and the steps were pushed up to the plane, the door opened and Mary Armstrong, the Glasgow station manager, appeared, pink-cheeked and pregnant. She was originally from Tacoma, near Seattle, and had been sent by Boeing to manage the Glasgow facility four years before. She was queen of the airfield, and used her authority lightly but firmly. She had sole responsibility for dealing with all the accommodation, food and administrative needs of up to 100 Boeing staff who might descend on Glasgow for several weeks at a time and then disappear as quickly, leaving the facility deserted, apart from snow hares and deer. Hers was also the voice the pilots heard on the radio as they went through the routine communications procedures to obtain take-off and landing clearance.

Armstrong gave a short welcoming address to the team, telling them where to find their rental cars, how to get to their hotels, and where they could drive on the base. Jim Otey, the test director for the first group of cycles due to be carried out that afternoon, then made an announcement that there would be a pre-flight briefing at 2.30.

As the engineers and administrative staff straggled down the steps and across the snow to their cars, Otey, a short, red-headed man, expressed concern that, if the weather stayed as bad as it was, they might well never take off that afternoon. They had already lost more than an hour in abortive attempts to land, and the start time for the first five cycles had been pushed back. If the weather delayed them further they might have to cancel today's activities and try to start the ETOPS tests tomorrow.

The programme of cycles had been worked out very carefully to simulate as wide a range as possible of the sorts of conditions the plane would have to fly when it entered into service. Some of these conditions were weather-related. Some of the 1,000 cycles had to be conducted in ground temperatures below 0°F – hence Glasgow – others in temperatures above 100°F – usually somewhere like Phoenix, Arizona. Other conditions related to engine thrust on take-off, position of the centre of gravity, whether or not the APU was running, the weight of the plane, and so on.

Gary Vassallo, who ran the team that devised the schedule, explained how it was done:

We started with five specific flight profiles, covering the normal range of United routes. Then we took the five profiles and came away with fifty-one different variations. Those variations provide something in the neighbourhood of 5,000 different requirements, little bits and pieces here and there – there's always something happening in one of these cycles. In a nutshell, we're presenting a mission mix of everything – altitude from 2,500 feet all the way up to 43,000 feet, with a lot of extensive cruise duration at 18,000 and 35,000 feet. We're looking at a full range of temperatures from anywhere from –20 degrees to greater than 100 degrees.

We're operating all the systems in a full-up configuration as well as selected degraded modes of operation. So, as an example, we're going to do eight full 180-minute engine diversions where we shut one engine down and cruise on the other for 180 minutes. When we do some of those diversions we're going to be demonstrating maximum continuous thrust capability. On others we're going to demonstrate the airplane's drift-down capability in a single-engine scenario. On one of them we're going to put a second failure on top and simulate a rapid decompression down at 10,000 feet. The APU is going to be started 1,900 times or so.

We've got other things in there, such as one of the engines being made unbalanced, in order to induce vibratory wear. The other engine is actually a used engine, on the right-hand side, that's been properly used in ground-based endurance testing at the engine manufacturer in order to wear it in, and we use that engine to demonstrate to the FAA that there is no appreciable flight effect.

Other things include maintaining the airplane, demonstrating that tooling, our training and our procedures in manuals as well as the human factors – the people involved – all can work together to maintain a 777 in a cold environment.

At 2.30 the team for the afternoon's test assembled in an overheated conference room in a building underneath the disused control tower. The decor was 1950s fake-wood laminate on the walls and shag-pile carpet on the floor, all in sombre browns and dull yellows. There was a warm fug throughout the building, and people shed layers of cold-weather clothing as the meeting got under way. In addition to the flight-test team, Mary Armstrong was there, sitting in a corner, along with representatives of the Glasgow airfield fire service. The whole focus of the meeting was Jim Metcalfe, the man in the driving-seat. Although Otey was the test director, everyone deferred to Metcalfe when issues of routing, procedure, weather and safety came up. It was typical of Boeing's whole philosophy that the last word was with the pilot, however skilled the other members of the team and however autonomous the systems and equipment that engineering ingenuity could devise.

That afternoon, the main question was the weather. There was a list of five conditions that had to be ticked off in the temperature range 20–40°F, the current temperature levels at Glasgow. But there was still plenty of fog outside: thinner perhaps than earlier in the day – even a glimmer of sun to be seen – but no one could guarantee that it wouldn't close in again. And the tests really would receive a setback if the plane had to be diverted to another Montana airport, or even further afield.

After sifting through the weather reports from around the state and chewing over the options, Metcalfe and Otey decided that they would try to stay on schedule and start the next five cycles. As a precaution, those people going on board were told to take overnight bags.

By now the light was fading outside and a much smaller group headed for the plane. Most of the eighty people who had flown to Glasgow were members of other shifts or of the maintenance staff. For the cycles themselves only five people needed to be on board – two pilots, a test director and two other engineers to monitor the data-gathering. In the cockpit there was a final flurry of communications over the radio, and then Otey came out to break the news that they had decided the risk was too great. Even in the few minutes since the pre-flight briefing the weather had closed in, and it now looked as if it was entirely possible that once the plane had taken off for its first cycle it would be unable to land again in Glasgow.

Overnight bags in hand, the small group trudged off the plane and back to the overheated meeting-room. There was more discussion of the weather, this time in an attempt to decide what to do about the scheduled tests for the following day. Using the heavy beige telephone in the middle of the table, Metcalfe enlisted the aid of one of the Boeing weather staff back in Seattle. Contingency plans had to be made. Perhaps, if the bad weather continued, the whole team would have to decamp to another part of the United States where the weather was cold enough and clearer than at Glasgow.

Although cost must clearly be a factor in decisions like these, there was a refreshing absence of concern about the financial implications of the decisions that were being made. Fuel costs, landing fees, extra hotel and car-hire costs – all of these would be a consequence of a change in location for the tests, even for a few days. But the main focus was on 'How can we get them done?' not 'How can we avoid extra expenditure?', even though the amounts at risk ran into tens of thousands of dollars.

In the end, nobody felt confident enough to make any plan for the following morning other than to turn up at 6.30 a.m. for an updated weather briefing from the Boeing man in Seattle, who was asked to get up in time to be in his office at 5.30 Seattle time, and accepted with cheery resignation.

Glasgow, Montana, is, in the words of Dennis Floyd, 'a town

with a woman behind every tree'. This is intentionally ironic, since there are no trees worth speaking of on the flat, open streets of the town. You know it's farming country from the 'For Sale' advertisements in the local paper, offering bales of alfalfa, 'Black and White W.F. Bangs Vaccinated Bred Heifers', and '35 Coming 2 Year Old Hereford Bulls' ('They are Big and Rugged High Performing Rascals'). The town is about eighteen miles from the airfield, and reached by a straight, featureless road with one slight rise and fall a few miles outside Glasgow. On Thursday night it was still foggy, and as some of the 777 team drifted into town, they had to peer through the windscreen to see familiar landmarks like the Cottonwood Inn and Sam's Supper Club off Route 2 through the centre of town.

The ceiling of Sam's Supper Club is festooned with graffiti, encouraged by the management, who will issue you with a permanent marker pen if you can find a space. Many of them relate to Boeing test programmes, since teams of engineers have been coming to Glasgow for seven or eight years and have made Sam's their home. Recently the ceiling has acquired evidence of the 777 programme, such as 'WA 2 comes first' and 'WA 4 ETOPS comes again and again and again.' There's even a cocktail called a 777.

On Thursday evening many of the newly arrived team from Seattle sought out Sam's for a drink or a meal. There isn't a Sam, although there was once a Samantha. On duty that night was Diane, one of the three managers of the restaurant, a plumply smiling woman who gives the impression that she sees life as one big party. In a town like Glasgow – pop. 5,000 or so – the influx of 100 or so healthy, mostly young, mostly male engineers and technicians is an opportunity not to be missed, and, although there are other restaurants in town, Sam's seems to have cornered the Boeing market with a combination of good food, relaxed fun and the clean, innocuous charms of Diane and her partners.

In spite of her suggestive slogans on the ceiling and the presence, in fact if not on a printed menu, of a cocktail called a 'Cowboy Cocksucker', there is a surprising wholesomeness about Boeing people enjoying themselves off duty. They're a polite crowd who rarely swear, even when they've had a bit to drink, and are not prone to the kind of boisterous behaviour that can come from hardworking people in stressful occupations when they let their hair down.

They're more likely to say 'shoot' than 'shit' and 'gosh' than 'God', and, in spite of the usual badinage with waitresses that goes on in any bar, you get the sense that there's little danger of predation when the Boeing crowd have a night out at Sam's.

For some years Sam's has helped out with some of the catering that the Glasgow base requires when the numbers are more than Mary Armstrong's small kitchens can cope with. During this Thursday evening Sam's kitchen is in the throes of preparing fifty or so chicken noodle dinners to be driven eighteen miles to the Boeing people who have stayed on base to prepare the plane during the night for the hoped-for tests on Friday morning. But, while noodles boil, Diane is out front, keeping the party atmosphere alive by challenging all-comers to perform a 'Waterfall'. This is a manœuvre where two small glasses are filled with different drinks – Bailey's and vodka, say. The glasses are then held in the gaps between the first, second and third fingers and tilted so that one is above the other. The drinker is supposed to drink from the bottom glass while making the liquor in the top glass pour into the bottom one, to be drunk in one continuous process. Unlike many of these tricks, like whipping the tablecloth off a laden table, the art is not to do it very quickly. One Boeing engineer tried it that way and ended up bathing his face and neck with both drinks simultaneously. But a female test engineer called Jeri Haggard, who perhaps had done it before, performed a faultless Waterfall by a slow, disciplined twist of the hand, accompanied by a steady gulping of two liquids as they poured into her mouth.

Diane watched all this with motherly interest, and then brought out a transparent folder of memorabilia connected with previous Boeing test teams. Among her favourite flight-test engineers is Dennis Floyd, the good-natured test director of some of the Edwards Air Force Base tests carried out last September and October. Floyd earned Diane's undying affection for the way he reacted when one of the supper-club waitresses accidentally poured a drink down his back while she was serving customers. Such an event might make some people vow never to return to the restaurant, but Floyd took it all in good part. He returned to Sam's the following day, but he did take the precaution of wearing a giant plastic binliner, and Diane kept the photograph of this in a folder behind the bar. She also had a photo, taken on board one of the 777 test flights, of a sandwich she had prepared for Floyd. Part of the catering service provided by the club consisted of supplying the box lunches that Boeing provided for the crews. Normally, these were supplied in the necessary numbers and people just helped themselves once they were on the plane, but on one flight Dennis Floyd found a box with his name on it. Thinking this was an especially delicious lunch prepared for him personally by Sam's, he opened it and took out a particularly luscious-looking sandwich with layers of meat and salad and . . . something else. Trustingly he bit into the sandwich and found himself chewing on a neatly folded pair of panty-hose. A glutton for punishment, Floyd took all this in good humour too, and sent Diane the photograph of the event to add to her collection.

At about 10 p.m. Diane and a colleague loaded up several steaming tureens of chicken and set off in her van to drive to the airfield, leaving behind her a tavern full of Boeing engineers drinking Cocksuckers, 777s and Waterfalls.

At 6.30 the following morning a small group gathered in the conference room at the airfield. On the other end of the telephone, relayed by loudspeaker, was the weatherman from Seattle with the results of a quick survey of weather prospects for the next few days around the northern United States. He gave a cautiously optimistic account of the likely weather conditions in Glasgow, but also suggested Yellowknife in Canada if the temperature didn't drop as much as they needed for the tests. But for today, in spite of the murky darkness outside the window, it seemed as if they would be able to carry out five cycles of tests and land back in Glasgow as planned.

The small group trudged out to the plane again. It had been prepared for flight during the even earlier hours of the morning, and had now been released into the hands of Metcalfe and his copilot. At least one of the engineers on board had been at Sam's the night before, enjoying a birthday celebration. On the plane, she opened the obligatory freezer box of canned drinks, picked one out, and complained that no ice had been supplied, as she gazed out at the sub-zero landscape.

Outside the plane, de-icer was sprayed on the wings. A strong smell of the de-icing chemical filled the cabin, and the pilot called for the engineers in the back of the plane to see if they could find the source of the smell. One of them thought he could see a thin spray of chemical inside the plane, and the odour lingered long after the spraying had stopped. Metcalfe 'squawked' the incident (reported it as a problem), although it later turned out that there hadn't been long enough between switching off the ventilation system using outside air and beginning de-icing, and the plane then took off for cycle number 90. There were only another 910 to go.

TWENTY-THREE

Finishing Touches

For those who appreciate coincidences, there was something sadly symbolic about the accident that happened to Alan Mulally's wife, Nicki, in January 1995. The night before the static test plane was due to have its wings stressed to breaking-point, she fell and broke her hip. So Mulally was nowhere to be seen during the early phases of the test, as he stayed with his wife in the hospital while she underwent surgery. But, on the second floor of Building 40-26 at Everett, most of the other senior figures were there to observe the final rites on one of the two 777s that would never fly.

During the course of a year, a plane with wings, fuselage and empennage, but without engines or fly-by-wire systems, had been stretched and twisted in various ways to ensure that the design would cope with the worst battering that wind and poor piloting could subject it to. In particular, the wings had been subjected to loads that were 100 per cent above the worst to be expected in normal or in abnormal but natural flight. This was an FAA requirement, and, although the loads tugging up on each wing had already pulled them fifteen feet or so higher than their rest position, everything had held. But Boeing wanted to go further. They decided to see how far the wings could be bent until they snapped. To do this, they arranged powerful pistons and jacks that could generate the weight of another 777 on each wing of the static plane. This was not some end-of-term prank to destroy a plane that had achieved its purpose: it would supply some very useful commercial knowledge to be used in the future development of the 777 family. If the wings, as built for the first 777s, could be taken up to a maximum load that would still be legal for larger and heavier versions of the plane, that would save considerable redesign work.

Airplane wings sometimes find themselves in situations where they need every ounce of strength that has been designed into them, and occasionally more. Boeing's history is littered with examples of wings that have behaved above and beyond the call of duty.

A PanAm 707 was once flying from Paris to New York when it experienced a lot of buffeting and build-up of speed. The aircraft had a system, called 'trim', for maintaining level flight in the face of such conditions, but it had not been switched on by the crew after the plane reached cruise height. Because of this, the plane began to roll and started diving towards the ocean at almost the speed of sound. The *g* forces immobilized the crew, producing two black eyes in the captain, who managed to roll the wings level under a force of 4.5 times the force of gravity, when the plane had been designed to survive only up to 3.75g. The plane managed to land successfully and had a permanent two-inch bend in the wings. (Some pilots said it flew better because of this.)

In 1965 the outboard engine on a 707 taking off from San Francisco caught fire and exploded, destroying twenty-five feet of the plane's wing. The plane managed to stay in the air until it landed safely. Six months later a 707 collided with a Constellation at 11,000 feet and lost thirty-five feet of wing. Nineteen minutes later, this plane too landed safely. After these two incidents someone sent a message over TWA's teletype system: 'EFFECTIVE IMMEDI-ATELY ALL BOEING 707S MAY BE DISPATCHED WITH RIGHT OR LEFT WING MISSING.'

When the 767 static test plane was subjected to high loads, the aircraft was so robust that the fuselage broke before the wings.

On the day the 777 was to be subjected to the test, there was a pre-event briefing at which one of the speakers showed on the projection screen a quote from Theodore Roosevelt:

It is not the critic who counts, not the man who points out how the strong man stumbled or where the doer of deeds could have done them better.

The credit belongs to the man who is actually in the arena; whose face is marred by dust and sweat and blood; who strives valiantly, who errs and comes up short again and again; who knows the great enthusiasms, the great devotions, and spends himself in a worthy cause; who at the best knows in the end the triumphs of high achievement; and who at the worst, if he fails, at least fails by daring greatly; so that his place shall never be with those cold and timid souls who know neither defeat nor victory.

It was a gesture that was entirely without pretension – a contribution to morale-boosting and a celebration of achievement that was entirely in keeping with the tone Alan Mulally had set for the team. Everyone then trooped out of the meeting-room, some to witness the event from a specially protected area level with the left side of the plane, a few to the control room from where the test would be run.

Just visible from the viewing-gallery, when it was pointed out, was a small plastic duck, someone's bath toy, taped to the very tip of the left wing. It took good eyesight or a pair of binoculars to see, and it had been put there by one of the test engineers. 'It's OK – it's weight won't distort the measurements,' he said – 'unless it flaps its wings, of course.'

The event was pure choreographed tension. A graph of the likely progress of the test showed a series of staged loads, starting at 10 per cent above the upward pressure that would support the whole plane. The engineers in charge of the test predicted that the wings would snap at 157 per cent of the normal load. For the first phase, when the load was taken up steadily above 100 per cent, there was a party atmosphere on the viewing-gallery. Phil Condit was here, and Ron Ostrowski and Dale Hougardy and other senior engineers, as well as representatives of customer airlines.

After about 130 per cent, the hubbub died down as people spoke more quietly or just stared at the wing. The loudspeaker from the control room gave each new step, and the red digital meters showed the extension in feet. The prediction was that the wing would snap when it was bent up about twenty-four feet. As it went over eighteen feet, Alan Mulally slipped into the crowd unannounced and Ron Ostrowski went to offer whispered commiseration about his wife's accident. Mulally looked a little pale, but still responded to Ostrowski and his other colleagues with handshakes and bearhugs.

At 150 per cent the whole area fell silent, apart from the test engineer who announced each percentage over the loudspeaker.

Someone pointed out that the fuselage had developed ripples across the green shiny metal as the wing root twisted upwards. '151 per cent,' the speaker announced. The group watched the wing – and the little yellow duck – move up a few more inches. '152 per cent . . . 153 per cent . . . 154 per cent.'

Then there was an almighty cracking, rending sound – like several claps of thunder superimposed one on another. Mulally flinched, almost as if he feared an attack. Others jumped, startled by the loudness of the noise, as the upward loads finally rent and buckled the layers of steel, aluminium and carbon-fibre composite in a fraction of a second. There was a moment's pause and then cheers and applause from the VIPs, followed by a distant echo from a much larger crowd on the factory floor. Shreds of cables that had transmitted the loads swung wildly above the wing; metal panels hung free or poked above the previously smooth wing surface. And on the observation floor the breaking of the wing to release the tension was matched by a loud and excited ripple of laughter, exuberance and conversation as people pointed out to each other over and over again the carnage that had been wrought on the wing. One or two people noticed what had happened to the duck. Remarkably, the force and speed at the wing tip, which might have propelled the duck to the roof beams, had actually sent it on a modest journey to a position on the floor just beneath the wing, where it sat, upright and unnoticed by most of the excited engineers.

Astonishingly the other wing – the one with the folding wing tip – had snapped at the identical moment, a tribute to the exacting standards of design that were built into the 777.

Thursday 2 February was not a good day for Boeing. The company was in the newspaper headlines for two reasons. After the year-end results for 1994 showed a drop in earnings due to the effects of the continuing recession on the airlines, Boeing announced the planned lay-off of seven thousand workers. They were going to cut back production of 737s and 767s due to lower than expected new orders and cancellation of existing ones. Coming a month after a clever PR announcement from Airbus that, yet again, they had overtaken Boeing in quarterly orders for similar-size planes, the lay-offs painted a picture of a company under threat. In fact the lay-offs didn't affect the 777 programme, but what did cast a chill over the team's customary ebullience and optimism was an event that also occurred on Thursday and made front-page headlines in the Seattle papers on Friday.

'777 Loses Pressure in Flight,' the newspaper headlines said, '7 Hurt.'

A rapid decompression had occurred while WA 002, United's first airplane, was flying at 43,000 feet thirty miles north of Seattle, and the pilot had had to make a fast dive to get to an altitude where the pressures inside and outside the aircraft would equalize. The crew members who were hurt had not managed to put their oxygen masks on in time. One of the people who was affected had been standing by the flight-deck door when the decompression occurred, away from his oxygen mask. On his way to find the mask he passed out, and a colleague who came to help him also fainted.

What made the whole thing doubly unfortunate was the fact that there was a big media gathering at Boeing Field to see the first landing of British Airways' first airplane, WA 076. This was an important event because delays in GE's engines had made everyone impatient to get the plane flying. Within an hour of receiving its test certificate, the plane was up on its first flight, piloted by Frank Santoni. As Santoni headed back to the Boeing Field after a successful flight he was held up for fifteen minutes while the assembled journalists watched a plane they didn't expect land to a reception committee of fire engines and ambulances.

The cause was a double failure: of a clamp around a duct and of a check-valve, an eleven-inch-diameter aluminium flap in the low-pressure ducting that should have stayed closed to maintain cabin pressure. The valve was supplied by a company with whom Boeing had had no problems before, although in the early days of assembling the plane there had been problems with how the ducting was installed.

The word went out to beef up the valve on all the planes, a process that was expected to take about a week. In spite of the media excitement, there was no major hiccup in the test programme, merely an FAA order to keep the planes below 25,000 feet until the new valves were fitted. In fact, perhaps to reinforce the point that

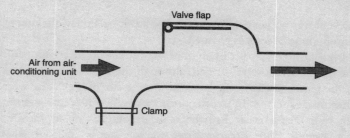

Valve flap

Air from air-conditioning unit

Clamp

Normal operations

Pressurized air flows towards interior – valve flap open

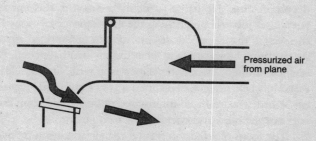

Pressurized air from plane

Single failure – clamp

Clamp fails – pressure drops – valve flap shuts to prevent depressurization

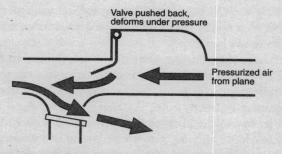

Valve pushed back, deforms under pressure

Pressurized air from plane

Double failure – clamp and valve

Clamp fails – valve flap breaks – pressurized air escapes from interior

this event was no big deal, WA 002 flew again on Friday, sticking to its programme of tests as planned.

Initially, no one was certain quite why either of the components – the clamp or the valve – failed, although there was some concern that the temperatures in the bay that was the site of the failure were higher than expected. In fact the previous day WA 003, carrying out flight tests near Hawaii, had the same decompression problem at lower altitude. But, because there weren't hordes of journalists waiting at the airport when it returned, there wasn't the same attention.

Neal McClusky was driving home with his car-pool colleagues when he heard on the news that WA 002 had experienced a sudden decompression. He had a particular interest in this news item since part of his job was supervising the installation of various elements in the system that supplied air-conditioned pressurized air to the 777. At the time, he wasn't sure what exactly had happened, but by nine o'clock at night, when his supervisor rang, it was clear that the relaxing weekend he had planned was not going to be possible. Early on Saturday morning an improvised design–build team assembled to sort out the mess and decide what to do next.

The focus of attention was on the air-conditioning packs, two of them, on either side of the underbelly of the plane just forward of the main landing-gear. When the plane had landed and after the injured flight-test engineers had been taken to hospital, a group of engineers had opened up the panels that gave access to the air-conditioning unit. It was immediately apparent that all was not well. Everything was OK on the left, but on the right side of the plane, where an eleven-inch duct carried cooled pressurized air into the plane, there was havoc.

The large duct leading from the air-conditioner to the plane interior had come apart and got pushed up against the roof of the bay. There was a wide gap in between two pieces of ducting that were meant to be tightly sealed. A clamp had failed, allowing air that was on its way to the plane to be diverted into the bay. When the clamp came loose, the air pressure from the air-conditioner couldn't be maintained since the air could now escape into the belly of the plane and thence to the outside. Such a drop in pressure would normally allow the higher-pressure air in the plane to flow back towards the air-conditioner. Since clamps do occasionally fail, or ducts get punctured, there was a valve at this point that was meant to slam shut if the pressure in the duct dropped. The valve did, in fact, operate, pushed into place by the back pressure from the plane's interior. But the force of the air trying to escape slammed the valve flap against the duct opening and bent or broke it. So there was still a hole through which the air could escape, and as it did so, with some force, the airflow generally bashed the ducting about a bit in the bay, pushing the main pipe up against the roof of the bay and creating the havoc that met the eyes of the engineers when they opened the bay after the plane landed.

A few days after the event, while the engineers were still trying to work out how it all happened, McClusky explained their current theories:

> We were under battery power and we'd been running for approximately three minutes. We were not only at the outside envelope of our flight ceiling, we were also at the maximum temperature output for the pack. And at about the three-minute mark, during this battery test, one of the couplings in the pack outlet system actually separated. Once that joint separated, we no longer had flow going into the airplane from the pack. And when you have a loss of airflow the flapper inside the check-valve wants to close very rapidly. And, as we understand it, the flapper, shaped like a disc, went to close and it actually deformed and extruded out of the other end of the check-valve, The hinge broke, and it just headed right on out into the pack bay and into the unpressurized area. From that point on you now have an eleven-inch-diameter hole for the pressurized air to flow through and we had decompression.

It was one of those 'unk-unks', a double unknown – two parts failing one after the other – that can bedevil flight testing at any time.

McCluskey and his colleagues now embarked on the task of finding out how to make sure it didn't happen again:

> When we came in the day after, we knew that we needed to provide a more robust design for our flapper and check-valve. We

got back with our supplier and we spent two or three days just talking back and forth with our system stress people to not only come up with the design but also come up with an agreed-upon method to test this part, because we wanted to make sure that not only did we understand the failure analytically, we needed to understand it physically as well, by going out and actually testing it to show that we did understand the failure, and then at the same time take our new, more robust, design, which we came up with over the weekend, and test it.

And that's actually what we ended up needing to do for the FAA. The FAA was in the picture probably the Monday following the incident, and that was when we really sat down with them and said, 'This is what we feel happened. We understand analytically that our new design will be good, and here's how we propose to test it.' The FAA agreed with that, and we went and tested the parts on the following Tuesday. So five days after the incident we had the new parts, the new analysis, and we went into a lab and tested them successfully.

A useful test of the redesigned valve occurred on a later test flight when, yet again, the same duct clamp failed. This time the drop in pressure on the air-conditioner side of the valve led, as intended, to a rapid closure of the beefed-up valve, which held firmly in position and averted the decompression it was designed to prevent.

While the flight tests continued at a hectic pace, there was a crucial ground test that the plane had to pass that had been delayed for several weeks but couldn't be left much longer if the plane was to stay on target. Way back in the earliest stages of door design, the Passenger Doors DBT had put a lot of effort into designing what's called the 'bustle' of the door, the bulge in the lower half that it's very tempting to sit on as you stand in a queue for the lavatory. Under the bustle is a miracle of compaction: a huge deflated escape slide compressed into a few cubic feet. There are eight passenger doors on the 777, each with a slide for use if the plane stops on the ground and passengers have to be evacuated quickly.

There is a mandatory test, supervised by the FAA, that the plane has to pass before it can be certified for regular revenue flying. The plane-makers had to show that the 777 was designed in such a way that a full complement of passengers could escape from the plane in ninety seconds or less. The test is made even more stringent by restricting the number of doors through which the passengers can escape to four, on the assumption that it is quite possible that some of the doors will be jammed or inaccessible because of fire or some other hazard.

On Saturday 11 February 1995 about 500 Boeing employees, chosen from staff volunteers who knew nothing about the emergency evacuation procedure, filed into a darkened hangar in Everett and walked up a covered stairway into the plane. The stairway was covered to conceal the layout of the plane in the hangar, which would have revealed the side through which the evacuation would take place. The criterion that all the passengers should be able to get out through half the doors was being met by making the doors on the right side of the plane unopenable.

Neither the cabin staff nor the flight crew of this non-flying flight knew which side of the plane would be the active one. They would have to find that out for themselves, just as they would have to do in a real emergency. There was room for 420 passengers, but Boeing had arranged for a few extra in case of drop-outs – the double-booking habit dies hard in the airplane business. They were each to be paid for the test, at each person's normal overtime rate for a Saturday morning. Although there were no very young children, there had to be a specific age/sex mix, including older people who might be more susceptible to injury. There were always a few injuries in this sort of test, and down on the hangar floor an expert medical team waited for the inevitable casualties.

The passengers settled into their seats until every one was filled. They were not allowed to bring any baggage on the flight, but after everyone was seated test staff went through the cabin scattering 125 bags and briefcases, to simulate the likely obstructions to a quick getaway.

No one on the plane knew when the test was going to happen. The signal to the flight attendants would be when the normal lights went out and emergency lighting went on. This would be triggered

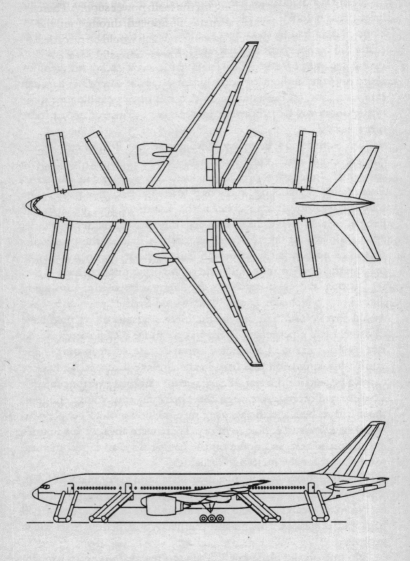

The 777 evacuation slides deployed

from outside the plane by switching off the main power supply: There were fourteen low-light video cameras positioned throughout the cabin to provide pictures of every passenger which would be recorded and analysed to determine whether the test was successful or not.

As the minutes ticked away the passengers could be seen chatting to their neighbours, yawning or looking bored, undiverted by inflight movies or airline meals. After about half an hour of this, one of the test team in the hangar went up to the plane and switched off the power from the outside. The lights went down, and on the monitors people could be seen to leap up out of their seats in response to the orders of the flight attendants, who had unfastened their own seat belts and begun to check doors to find which ones were operative. On the flight deck, the crew had been told to stay in their seats for thirty seconds – time that might have been taken up in a real emergency with shutting down the engines and switching off any active equipment. In fact it is likely that they would be able to leave the cockpit sooner and help the cabin staff with the evacuation. Once a flight attendant had discovered a door could be opened, he or she turned the large handle and the huge slide unfurled and inflated in about eight seconds.

From outside the plane everything looked as if it was going smoothly. As the four slides inflated, the plane resembled an insect emerging from its chrysalis and unfurling its wings. Dozens of passengers, each with a numbered vest, tumbled out of the four doors and slid down the slides, some of them whooping as if they were on a ride in Disneyland. But inside there were a couple of 'anomalies' as the test engineers called them.

Bob Satterfield, supervisor of the Emergency Escape Systems Group, described what happened:

Number one, there was a passenger who was injured even inside the airplane, when she attempted to get out of her seat belt. It appears that some of the aisle debris, the carry-on luggage that had been scattered in the aisles, caused her to twist her ankle and fall. And for a short period of time she effectively blocked the left-hand aisle of the airplane, just after the door 2 position. The flight attendants did an admirable job of assisting that person, and she was able to go on and leave the airplane via one of the slides at door 2. But in the meantime a good bit of confusion had been created and the cabin attendants had redirected some of the people that were in the immediate vicinity of this unfortunate passenger who had tripped and fallen down in the aisle. To make a long story short, we had one person who appeared very apprehensive, disoriented and confused, who made her way all the way back to door 4, which is the rearmost door of the airplane, from a seated position in the forward centre portion of the airplane, and we had 419 people on the ground four or five seconds before she even got to the door.

The test engineer's account of what happened next was carefully worded: 'There were vocal and reasonable commands to attract her to the rear of the airplane, and then there was physical assistance, once she got to the door-4 area, to get her down the slide.' In other words, she was shouted at, and then thrown down the slide, as any good flight attendant would be expected to do in an emergency.

The rest of the passengers had all left the plane within eighty-seven seconds, but the final passenger led to the evacuation exceeding the target of ninety seconds:

By the time she and the two flight attendants who had stayed behind to assist her got on the ground, we were up somewhere in the 93½-second time frame. So we experienced what we've assessed as approximately a six-second delay, because of the circumstance of that last passenger getting off.

It could have been worse. On a 747 evacuation test one passenger hid in the lavatory until everyone else had left and it was assumed that the test was over. When the count on the ground revealed one missing passenger, his head was then seen peeping out of the doorway.

There was some anxiety among the 777 test team as to whether the FAA would consider that they had passed the test or not. But a few days later, after studying the videotapes, which established that the delay was due neither to the plane design nor to some fault in the evacuation drill, the FAA granted the 777 one more certificate to add to its growing collection, bringing the plane ever nearer to the day when it would be allowed to fly paying passengers in revenue service.

TWENTY-FOUR

An 'All-Girl' Flight

By late April 1995, WA 004, which had started its 1,000-cycle ETOPS flight at the end of 1994, had flown about 960 cycles, simulating the amount of wear and tear on the plane and its engines that it would have experienced in nearly two years of scheduled flying. The tests had done two things: they had confirmed that the plane was so well designed and tested that there were no major surprises lurking in the interstices of the systems or the structures or the engines, but they had also shown that there was a steady drip of faults, or less than optimum design decisions, that Boeing needed to tackle before the plane went into service. Some of these involved actual faulty designs, like clips or brackets that didn't hold under the stresses of constant use. Others were more to do with inadequate maintenance instructions in the manual, or rather in the many thick volumes of manuals that lay around in the plane in large boxes.

For example, one problem that arose halfway through the 1,000 cycles was the result of an over-enthusiastic (or ignorant) ground engineer spinning one of the engines dry of oil after the plane had landed. A little mild spinning was required before fresh oil was put in the engine, but in this case the engine was spun far beyond the specifications of the manual, and the engine seized up and had to be sent back to Pratt. It was an event that tested to the full the ability of the Boeing engineers to adhere to the principle of 'no blame' in considering problems – or challenges, as they called them.

At flight number 910 the rules changed. Up till then, Boeing engineers and staff had been flying the plane, observed by FAA pilots. But, with ninety cycles to go, United now got into the act, and the complexity of the tests increased. Instead of making a series of short cruises between take-off and landing, the plane now entered a schedule that was more like regular airline flying, with a series of flights that went from one airport to another on United's regular routes. The purpose of this final phase was to show that United were competent to operate the 777 in regular service, and so these flights took on much more of the appearance of passenger flights, with uniformed flight attendants, meals cooked in the galleys, proper safety announcements and demonstrations, and realistic maintenance procedures at each stopover. Underlying this last aspect was the complicated logistics of making sure that there were United maintenance engineers at each airport, trained specifically on the 777. Each flight would have both Boeing pilots and United pilots on board, to share the flying, as well as one or two FAA pilots observing that United flew the plane according to the airline's own set of procedures. There was one oddity about the whole set-up that was nevertheless essential if this was to be a successful test of United's competence: if anything went wrong, it was United staff who had to solve the problem for themselves, even if a Boeing pilot on board felt he could lean forward and give the answer himself. Only in an extreme situation would United be allowed to use the knowledge and experience of the Boeing people they carried along with them.

On a warm sunny Wednesday evening in Honolulu towards the end of April, Captain Wally Tweden and his crew checked in to United's operations room at Honolulu Airport to file a flight plan for a flight to Washington DC, one of the longest legs of the ninety cycles. They had been in Hawaii for three days, having flown in on WA 004 early the previous Monday morning. On that flight, in addition to the normal operations of flying the plane, they had decided to try cold-soaking the APU and then switching it on in flight. This was the process the auxiliary engine had been put through many times in Alaska during the winter of 1993–4, when it had been randomly started by computer. There was an APU engineer on board to monitor the process and he, like everyone else, was disappointed when it took five tries before the thing would start. To make the APU work as hard as possible, the engineers switched some of the power systems in the cabin to battery, instead of being powered by the main engines. One unforeseen consequence of this was that the snack served shortly before landing – a meat-filled bun – was warmed on top but icy cold underneath: the switch to batteries made the oven in the galley conserve power by generating a lower temperature.

While WA 004 flew on with another crew, the United crew and flight attendants had spent their enforced stay in Hawaii at the Honolulu Seaside Hotel, two blocks back from the seafront, a hotel that United appeared to monopolize with their cabin crews and pilots, although it was surprisingly unluxurious compared with the harbourside Ilikai where Boeing put up its staff. The weather had been rather mixed over the last few days – always mild, but cloudy and showery as well. Tweden, like most long-haul pilots a veteran of overnight stays in exotic but boring places, had spent some of Tuesday hiking up and around Diamond Head, the extinct volcano that forms a backdrop to Honolulu.

Tweden was another pilot, like John Cashman, who could have come from Central Casting. Tall, moustached, with a drawly laid-back voice, he could nevertheless make quick, firm decisions when necessary. He was an ideal expositor of what United called Cockpit Resource Management, a system designed to encourage a shared approach among the flight crew to flying the plane and dealing with emergencies. By studying the causes of aircraft accidents, United had found in the past that some could have been avoided if a less senior member of the flight crew had had the courage – or felt he had the right – to point out mistakes made by his superior, the captain of the plane. Even when lives were at risk, there had been situations where a pilot was clearly missing or ignoring a crucial piece of data or a cockpit alarm or warning and his colleagues had been inhibited about drawing it to his attention for fear of annoying the person who was in some sense their boss. Cockpit Resource Management was a system of training that encouraged everyone to share in the task of flying – not to the extent of flying by committee, but certainly to be on the alert for important data and to share the decision-making about what to do in tricky situations. Tweden was one example of a captain who, by his relaxed lack of egotism on the flight-deck, tried his hardest to give permission to those he flew with to say what they liked without fear of retribution.

The first thing that was apparent when Tweden and his crew arrived at the airport was that the incoming flight would be about an hour and a half late. If they were to operate like a normal flight schedule, it would therefore be important to catch up some time on the turn-around. As Tweden chewed on a platter of sashimi thoughtfully provided by one of the United ground staff, he discussed the situation with his colleagues. The turn-around might be complicated as a result of a further piece of news – there was a fault with one of the high-frequency radios which would be necessary for communications over the Pacific on the way back. In addition to normal maintenance procedures, someone would have to take a look at that.

At about eight o'clock a knot of people waited by Stand 5 out on the ramp at the airport. There would be about twenty people on the flight back, at liberty to spread themselves around the three hundred seats of the plane. In addition to the flight and cabin crews, and the FAA pilots, there were Boeing flight-test engineers, a United operations manager, Bob Ireland, who worked with Gordon McKinzie, and a sprinkling of maintenance and technical people. There would also be some of the people who were on the incoming aircraft and would remain on it flying two back-to-back flights totalling about 10,000 miles in a day or so.

One of the ground staff pointed to lights in the south-western sky. It was WA 004, currently named Flight 9431, the number given to the Washington–Honolulu leg of an itinerary that had criss-crossed the United States making several stops since the plane had visited Hawaii on Monday. The plane approached from the east, making a long, low trajectory parallel with the southern coast of Oahu, the most populous Hawaiian island, and then turned 180 degrees to land on one of the two main runways. A few minutes later, after taxiing in the warm night air against the background of the lights of Honolulu, the plane drew up at Stand 5. Because of the lateness of the plane, the pace of activity was more hectic than the usual mêlée that surrounds a large airliner when it lands. Refuelling began almost immediately, while the incoming crew met Tweden and his colleagues to brief them on the plane's state of health. One of the crew came down the steps in search of Bob Ireland, and of some crucial computer discs.

It was Thursday 27 April, and the plane's navigation computers were due for a change of data that took place every thirty days. Airport details, routes and flight levels around the world, special notices about restrictions over certain areas: all of these were stored in the computer and brought into service as part of the normal automated flight-planning system on the plane that was initiated when the pilot fed in the details of the flight plan he would be given an hour or so before the flight. The new data for the computer update had to be installed by midnight on the thirtieth day. The crew had intended to do the update a day or so ago on the mainland, but Bob Ireland had inadvertently carried the discs off to Honolulu. Now they were relieved to get their hands on them, and one of the engineers took them up to the cockpit to begin the installation.

The high-frequency radio system also had to be fixed before take-off. It was one of many duplicated systems on the plane, and was used for voice communication, particularly on flights over long stretches of water, away from the regular radio communications networks that operated over the more crowded airways of the mainland. By nine o'clock two United engineers from the Honolulu maintenance team were thirty feet up in the air on a cherry-picker platform, removing screws from the bright blue tail fin of the plane. There seemed to be several dozen screws holding the panel that gave access to the HF aerial, the suspected cause of the problem, and – in a familiar replay of the problem that often taxes DIY specialists – the final few screws were impossible to turn.

By now the plane had been on the ground for more than an hour, and it looked as if the radio problem was going to prevent the speedy turn-around everyone had hoped for. On the plane, those people not involved in the radio problem or in loading the navigation data were spread about the cabin in various states of relaxation from horizontal sleep to vertical perambulation. Naomi and Yang, the two flight attendants, supplied coffee and soft drinks to all, and began to prepare the meal trays that had been loaded earlier, sliding them into the food-warmers in the shining new galley. Like all Boeing planes – indeed all Boeing establishments – the 777 was 'dry'. On board tonight was Jeri Haggard, who had demonstrated such prowess at drinking Waterfalls in Sam's Supper Club when WA 004 was based in Glasgow, Montana, in the early days of the 1,000 cycles. Asked how she was coping without any alcoholic drink on the plane, she said, rather mysteriously, 'Oh, you just have to improvise.'

Along with the non-alcoholic drinks, the two flight stewardesses prepared to serve small plastic ramekins of the finest mixed nuts, delicately warmed in the galley ovens. Unfortunately – well, it *was* a new plane and they were bound to face teething troubles – the oven temperature was too high and Yang's face fell as she pulled out a tray of a dozen containers, all of which had assumed drooping and Dali-esque shapes due to the plastic having melted under the fierce heat. Hurriedly improvising, the women poured the nuts into coffee-cups and carried them round to the passengers as if nothing had happened.

Two hours after the plane had landed, the ground engineers had managed to find a powerful enough screwdriver to remove the remaining screws on the tail panel. They replaced the faulty antenna and screwed the panel back in place. In the plane, Wally Tweden sat in the first-class section, in seat 3D, eating a dinner of lamb cutlets. There was no room for him and the other pilots in the cockpit, as the engineers were still working on the navigation computers. Bob Ireland hovered around, anxious to get the plane off the ground and worried by the suspiciously long time it was taking to transfer the contents of two floppy discs into the computers. It turned out that the loading process was not working. They would think they had put the data in correctly and then, when they tried to test the system, it displayed various glitches. However many times they reloaded the data, they still got the same faults. At about eleven o'clock, Tweden and the other pilots gathered in a huddle to discuss whether there was any way they could go without the data for the flight back to Washington. Tweden believed that there were no changes in the navigational information they needed for the particular route they planned to follow, but the fact was they were not permitted to travel with old navigational data in their computers, however harmless they might believe it to be.

The most astonishing thing about the whole business was that in the back of the plane, among the assorted personnel travelling back to Washington, was one of Boeing's most experienced computer engineers, and there was every possibility that he knew how to solve the problem. But, because the whole purpose of these flights was for United to show that they could operate the plane on their own, the United maintenance engineers in the cockpit were not allowed to seek the help of Boeing people in the back of the plane. To take this charade to its admirably rigorous conclusion, when it became apparent that the United people could not fix the problem, they did what they would do if the plane was in service: a United engineer went to a communications van on the ground by the plane and rang the maintenance headquarters in San Francisco to report the problem. The United HQ said, 'This sounds like a problem for Boeing', and rang the Boeing computer people in Seattle for advice. The Boeing people said. 'You need to speak to one of our computer experts, and it so happens that we have one on the ground in Honolulu.' Thus the quest came full circle and the United people were put in touch with the Boeing engineer. Or they were about to be, when Wally Tweden decided to call a halt to the whole business. It was now two o'clock in the morning, and Tweden decided that, even if the problem was solved now, the crew had been on duty for too long to allow them to set off on an eight-hour flight to Washington.

As if by magic, two minibuses appeared at the foot of the steps, ready to take everyone off to a couple of dozen rooms that had just been booked at the Honolulu Airport Holiday Inn. The new plan was to ask United in San Francisco to fly in a new computer that would arrive by eleven o'clock the following morning. Meanwhile the ground maintenance team would work away at the computers during the rest of the night and see if they could fix them. In this way, they hoped to show that United were capable of dealing with the problem on their own rather than admitting defeat and calling Boeing to their aid.

Wearily, the crew and the handful of passengers assembled on the tarmac and then got into the two buses. In the hotel lobby, they all meekly lined up at the counter while a clerk laboriously went through the checking-in routine. The pilots and Dick Clark and Jim Otey, the flight-test directors, gathered in a huddle to discuss options for the following morning. Everyone was told to be ready to depart at 11.15, when it was expected that the new computer would have arrived and been installed. Then they all trudged off, along interminable dull corridors, to find their identical Holiday Inn rooms, many with a view of a wide, desolate construction site. In comparison with this, memories of the Honolulu Seaside Hotel were rapidly acquiring a patina of affectionate nostalgia.

The following morning was bright and sunny. Flight crew had received a call to say that they should go to the plane half an hour earlier than expected, while the rest of the test team could still go at 11.15. It turned out that the navigation data had been successfully loaded during the night, while the new computer was still halfway between San Francisco and Honolulu. In a brilliant stroke of improvisation, the United ground crew had swopped the plane's two computers around and managed to load the data without any further trouble. So United had narrowly escaped having to ask Boeing for help, and were quietly proud that they had shown that they could handle the problem themselves – which was one of the purposes of the ninety cycles they were now flying.

Loaded with the new navigation data – which, on the route they were flying, was probably indistinguishable from the old – the plane took off to the west, over Diamond Head, and then curved round back to the east towards the US mainland and Washington DC. It was eighteen hours late. If it had been a scheduled flight the passengers would have been put on to other flights the night before, but there was no real spirit of depression or frustration over the problem the plane had faced. It was one of Alan Mulally's 'gifts', that had provided a small proof to the FAA that the airline was capable of operating the plane on its own.

Significant events came thick and fast in May 1995, as United Airlines continued preparations to take delivery of their first 777. On Thursday 11 May a United team led by Bob Ireland took WA 006, the first plane they would purchase, up in the skies over Washington and systematically went through every single aspect of the plane to check that it worked. Each seat was reclined, each footrest extended, each earphone socket checked. They even activated the release mechanism for the oxygen masks in the ceiling above each passenger seat. But, because it would have been a day's work to put back the masks on their long twisted air lines – almost like pushing toothpaste back into the tube – they had secured the masks to prevent them falling out when the quick-release hatches fell open. The need for this precaution became apparent when one mask did unfurl entirely and an engineer had an infuriatingly fiddly task to get it back.

But on the whole United were satisfied. The plane worked, and, as they landed back in Seattle, Bob Ireland was ready to give his seal of approval to set in motion the events that would lead to the exchange of rather a lot of money.

What nobody knew while they were flying was that there was something wrong with one of the engines. After landing, a routine inspection of the fan blades showed that one engine had been hit by something, possibly a bird, that had damaged one of the blades. FOD had struck.

Nobody knew when it had happened – it hadn't been noticed during that flight, and could have happened any time in the previous few days. There was only one course to take, with pressure building up to the following Monday when United wanted to buy the plane: the plane had to have a new engine. In a space of hours, the whole engine was taken off the plane and another engine was removed from one of the other 777s to replace the faulty one.

Very early on the morning of 15 May WA 006 took its last flight as a Boeing plane, so that the United team could reassure themselves about the hurriedly replaced engine before the plane changed hands. When Ireland and his colleagues gave it the thumbs up, a complex series of phone calls was set in motion that was to be repeated on eleven occasions before the end of 1995, as one by one United's first eleven planes were sold to them by Boeing.

The financial events that took place when United bought their first 777 from Boeing were every bit as complex and carefully considered as the design of the aerodynamically efficient surface of a wing. Both accountants and engineers tried to do things in the most cost-effective way possible. In the case of the purchase of WA 006, United wanted to get the best possible value for $100 million or so, making use of US tax loopholes, lease-back arrangements, even the proximity of Canada. The idea of simply giving Boeing the money and then owning the plane was laughable – or at least that was only the beginning of the process. Whatever amount United and Boeing agreed as a sale price was a result of the hard bargain driven nearly five years ago late at night in Chicago. Along with the fine print (or small handwriting) of that agreement went discussion of payment schedules, deposits, guarantees, penalties and even who paid for what in the rather murky area of the interior fit-out of the plane. But, on top of that, there was a further way open to United to get the most for their money. Within hours of buying the plane from Boeing, United were planning to sell it to someone else – a leasing company that would rent the plane straight back to United. Depending on what taxation laws applied at the time, there could be tax advantages to United in renting the plane rather than disposing of their capital.

There was a further potential advantage. The purchaser of the plane, representing a group of banks, might buy it from United at a higher price than United paid Boeing, allowing United to make a profit on the deal. There was nothing underhand about this. In a free market, United presumably said, 'We have a brand-new 777 – what will you buy it for and how much will you charge to lease it back to us?' The fact that they might have paid Boeing less than they received for it was neither here nor there: if the leasing company felt that the return from regular leasing payments was a justifiable return on their investment of a certain lump sum, then everyone was happy. In fact, in a process called 'double dipping', the leasing company could even pass the plane on to another company or consortium, perhaps one in a foreign country, so that further tax advantages could accrue in the interstices of international tax law.

All of this was decided beforehand. Now at 6 a.m. in Seattle the United team, led by Gordon McKinzie and Bob Ireland, sat around in a conference room with several phones at Boeing's Customer Service Centre, along with a bevy of lawyers and accountants and a lot of paperwork. Everyone looked very smart. At the same time, at the FAA offices in Oklahoma City, where it was 7 a.m., two lawyers acting for United sat by their phones, waiting for the moment when they would be told by Bob Ireland to walk down the corridor and buy a five-dollar registration certificate for the plane. In Chicago, where it was 8 a.m., there was a group of lawyers and accountants listening in at United's corporate headquarters, where the airline's relationship with the 777 was first sealed. And in New Castle, Delaware, where it was 9 a.m., a solitary Citibank employee, Brian Todd, sat by his computer waiting for the phone to ring.

In Seattle, people were waiting for the paperwork that was being prepared as a result of United's early-morning acceptance of WA 006. In the background to the hubbub of conversation in Seattle could be heard the speakerphone relaying sounds from the FAA offices in Oklahoma City. The two law-firm representatives were discussing a topic far away from the expenditure of $100 million – one of them was describing a beautiful and fragrant pot-pourri she had been given by a relative, unaware, perhaps, that senior airline executives were in on the conversation a thousand miles away. Just before 6.30, Bob Ireland was handed the papers he needed and leaned forward to interrupt the pot-pourri conversation and set the ball rolling.

There was a formal written script for the purchase, covering various points that had been confirmed by Boeing and United to the FAA before the lawyers could register the plane. One by one a lawyer in Oklahoma City asked the series of questions and got formal answers from Ireland, checking carefully on the paperwork he had in front of him. These included a unique Boeing registration number for the plane. When the long list of questions was answered, Ireland had a second thought and looked back over the paperwork. Suddenly he said to Oklahoma City, 'I think I've given you the wrong number.' It turned out that the number was mistyped on his paperwork, and he had passed on to the FAA a number that was 3,000 larger than the correct one – a number that would be borne by a 777 made some time in the middle of the next century, if Boeing were still making them then.

After the certification application had been corrected, the two FAA women walked out of their office and down the corridor and stopped at a counter. They handed over the application and a cheque for five dollars, and the woman behind the counter took them and then just waited. 'I'm waiting for the next minute,' she said. She had to time-stamp the paperwork, and wanted to stamp every piece of paper with exactly the same time. If she had started straight away, the time might have changed between documents. Who knows what legal shenanigans might have ensued if the application had been stamped at 8.43 and the certificate at 8.44?

The timer-stamp clicked to 8.44, the documents were stamped, and the first 777 was registered to United Airlines as its owner.

In Seattle, once they received this news, the next step could be taken. Now United were the registered owners, they had to pay Boeing.

Ireland dialled the number of Citibank in Delaware and was answered by Brian Todd, who had been waiting for the call for the last half-hour. 'Could you transfer the agreed amount now?' said Ireland. Todd rang a colleague in the Citibank treasury department, checked some figures, tapped a few keys on his computer, and then told United in Chicago and Seattle that the money had gone from United's account to Boeing.

In the half-hour that Brian Todd sat twiddling his thumbs, United's $100 million earned about $400 that would have been Boeing's if the transaction had happened on time.

There were now three weeks to go before United's first scheduled flight. In anticipation of this delivery date, set about four years ago, United had arranged a huge party for two days after the purchase, and they brought to Seattle selected United employees from Chicago, who each stayed with a Boeing employee and then had a flight on the plane down to San Francisco and back. Behind the scenes, flight crew and flight attendants had been training in simulators and mock-ups and with CD-ROM-based teaching material, and maintenance engineers at United's maintenance headquarters in San Francisco had been learning how to deal with routine maintenance tasks and rarer malfunctions. Thousands of people who would fly and maintain the plane and look after the passengers were preparing themselves for 7 June and, more important, for the regular daily flights across the Atlantic and the United States that would follow every day *after* 7 June.

There was one outstanding event that Boeing desperately hoped would occur before the first passenger flight. This event more than any other would mark out the 777 as a different plane from all the rest. The FAA had still not pronounced on ETOPS when United took over the plane. United didn't in fact need 180-minute ETOPS for their first routes, although they would as soon as they planned to go to Hawaii, but the idea of a new twin-engine plane that *before it entered service* was allowed to fly up to three hours away from a suitable airport was so captivating that to have approval come only a day after entry into service might have knocked the gilt off the gingerbread. As it was, Boeing were told that the FAA would deliver their verdict on 30 May, and they had organized yet another ceremony to celebrate what they anticipated would be a favourable announcement.

But the suspense was kept up till the last moment by the FAA. Anthony Broderick, the FAA administrator who oversees all aircraft certification, was interviewed in the *Wall Street Journal* published on 30 May, and said that approval was 'likely to be granted'. If *he* didn't know for certain, who did? But Broderick also said, 'It's really quite a remarkably designed and engineered airplane.'

In fact, because Boeing 'worked together' with the FAA, during the last year or so of tests they had been kept in close touch with any concerns that the FAA might have had about the plane's reliability, and these concerns would have been attended to by putting in extra tests, carrying out design modifications, and providing yet more data – which did, in the end, set them free, from the fear of falling short of the most publicly promoted of all their targets.

On 30 May what Broderick thought 'likely' became certain, and the years of effort of all those involved in the ETOPS planning paid off. 777 customers under the jurisdiction of the FAA – so far only United and Continental – were allowed to fly 777s over almost any part of the world apart from a small pocket of the south Pacific, which three hundred people were unlikely to want to visit all at the same time anyway.

United had taken delivery of three 777s by early June and slotted them straight into their schedules, starting on 7 June. Two of them were on internal routes, out of Chicago and Denver, but the first to fly would be the transatlantic trip from London to Washington DC. For some of the people on the inaugural flight the 777 was just another plane: they had needed to travel from London to Washington on that day and they or their secretaries had just booked a seat on the most convenient flight, which happened to be UA 921, leaving Heathrow at 11.40. The fact that flight UA 921 was the first scheduled revenue-generating flight of the 777 became apparent to some of them only as they turned up at Terminal 3 and encountered a degree of hullabaloo that started modestly with check-in staff wearing 777 baseball caps, increased in intensity when passengers discovered a party going on at the departure gate, and culminated in a flight where, among other marvels, they found themselves being consulted in person by the presidents of two major

American corporations – Boeing and United – who walked up and
down the aisle for all the world as if they were selling duty-free
merchandise.

US Navy Lieutenant Commander Rowland Huss had booked
himself on to the flight the day before because he wanted to get
home from Oman. When he checked in at Heathrow he was
pleasantly surprised to be told by the English-accented check-in
attendant that he had got himself on to an 'all-girl' flight. Further
questioning produced the disappointing news that she was talking
about an 'inaugural' flight. 'Well,' Huss said, 'you can't help it after
being in the Gulf for an extended period.'

While Huss and the other passengers were checking in, the flight
crew were inspecting the flight plan, and Captain Wally Tweden,
allocated as one of the crew members on today's flight, was walking
around the plane kicking tyres in the time-honoured way pilots do
before a flight – a relic of the days when tyres were not half the
height of the pilot with rubber several inches thick. Tweden had
learned only last Friday that he would be allocated to this flight, and
he was very pleased – particularly since he had recently heard that he
was to be promoted to fly a desk in San Francisco and so his regular
piloting would diminish. For the first month or so United were
taking no chances. Although on a seven-hour flight like this only two
crew were strictly necessary, there were going to be extra pilots
around for a while, including more experienced pilots like Tweden,
who had taken part in the ETOPS flights.

As the plane taxied, some of the radio messages monitored by
Tweden and his colleagues had an informality that seemed to
contravene the legally imposed brevity designed to ensure clear, safe
communication. Other pilots waiting on the runway noticed the
unusually large twin-engine plane as it meekly stood in line for the
always crowded take-off line-up at Heathrow. 'Nice pair of engines,
United!' said the pilot of one waiting plane, and it got a laugh in the
777 cabin, where air-traffic-control talkback was fed through to
audio channel 9 on the passenger entertainment system.

There were seventeen cabin staff to look after the passengers:
because of the newness of the plane, United had added two flight
attendants who had had detailed training on the plane to the normal
complement of fifteen. Helen Buss, a trim young Englishwoman,

was one of these, and she was there to help convey some of the nuances of the 777 to flight attendants who were not too familiar with the plane. Some, like today's purser, Antonia Wysong, had never flown in the plane before, and she and her colleagues valued Buss's help with opening out the Connoisseur-class footrests or answering passengers' questions about the armrest televisions.

It is a little-known fact about flight attendants – little known to many passengers, anyway – that by far the most important part of their job is connected with safety. The care taken with the plane's first full evacuation test showed how crucial it was in an emergency for the flight attendants to know exactly how to act fast in opening the doors, marshalling the passengers, checking for stragglers, shouting instructions, and so on; and they had to learn a similarly choreographed routine for every possible hazard on the plane, even though most of them would never have to carry out these routines in earnest during their entire working career. It is with good grace, therefore, that flight attendants do spend so much of their time being nice and polite to passengers in matters of food and drink, not to mention cleaning up after them and their children. One flight attendant mentions a typical example of what they face. On a recent flight, she asked a five-year-old-child what he would like to drink. 'Coke!' was the abrupt answer. 'Isn't there another little word we say?' said the flight attendant, charmingly. Rather hesitantly the child said, 'Please . . .' 'You don't *have* to say "please",' the mother butted in – 'she's *paid* to serve you.' 'I am *paid* to look after your safety,' said the attendant, and walked away.

There was a round of applause as the plane took off, and people settled into their seats, tried to work out the new fixtures and fittings, and turned to the passenger sitting next to them to find out whether they were travelling on a paid ticket or a freebie. Everybody had a story about why he was on the flight. Jim Sibbald and his wife, Carolyn, had won a competition in *Director* magazine. They had only been told last Friday that they had won, and had run around arranging for their children to be looked after. As the plane reached cruise height, Carolyn tried to work the plane telephone to call and see how her eighteen-month-old daughter was getting on without her.

There were other passengers who were first-flight groupies,

making a point to be first to fly on any new airplane. One of these was a businessman from Salt Lake City whose previous claim to fame was an entry in the *Guinness Book of Records* because he once played eighteen holes of golf at the North Pole. Today he hoped to set up a new record by flying on all three United 777s on this inaugural day. If all the planes were on time, after he got to Washington he would board a 777 flight to Chicago and then take another 777 from Chicago to Denver. From Denver he'd have to travel to Salt Lake City on a boring old 737, after being in the air or in airports for twenty-four hours.

One of the passengers opened a newspaper he'd bought at London Airport and read a story about the 777s engines, which worried him somewhat until he realized it was about the GE engines, not Pratt's. The *Financial Times* reported an announcement by General Electric the day before which said that its engines had suffered problems when bird-strike tests had led to an imbalance after damage to the fan blades. Any serious trouble there could delay British Airways' first 777s going into service – an eventuality that would cause no heartache to United, who had spent the last three months upstaging the British airline with a publicity blitz and promotional flights.

It wasn't entirely a flawless flight. In a repetition of the 'molten nut-containers' incident on the delayed Honolulu–Washington ETOPS flight, the first-class ovens burned the rolls. 'Fortunately,' said Helen Buss, 'it wasn't a disaster, because we had some more rolls.' She also discovered that the plates in the plate cupboard had been stacked too high by the people who loaded the plane, and she had made a note for a report that would be discussed in a conference call the following morning with flight attendants who had been on other 777 flights.

There was general confusion among the non-Americans on the flight about the inflight telephones placed at several points in the cabin. There were no instructions by the phones, and, like a trial-and-error task for a rat in a cage, people would be seen undergoing the slow process of working out that there was a slit for a credit card, which way up you had to put the card, what you had to dial to reach the country of your choice, and so on. Even at ten dollars a minute there was a queue for these phones, as people made souvenir phone calls to home or journalists filed their copy. Four hours into the trip, Ron Woodard, President of Boeing Commercial Aircraft Group, decided to call Dale Hougardy and tell him how great the plane was, but Dale was out of town and Woodard spoke to Lyle Eveland instead, conveying the general sense of excitement and partying that prevailed in the plane.

Of course it was precisely the electronics that was the plane's Achilles' heel. There should have been no queues for the few active phones, because every seat was meant to have one. United were disappointed with Boeing, and Boeing were disappointed with GE/Marconi, and everybody was throwing man-hours at the most complex electronics in any airliner, and the accountants were wrangling about who should pay for what. But in United's favour on this inaugural flight was that if you don't expect every seat to have a telephone and computer games then you don't miss them, and it was likely that most of the passengers were pleased enough with six channels of video and nineteen channels of CD-quality sound.

One of the passengers today knew all about the electronics. Vin Prothro, from Dallas, Texas, was chairman of the board of the Dallas Semiconductor Corporation, which manufactured a key component in the 777 fly-by-wire system. For him, being on the inaugural flight was a must, and he had asked his travel associates to monitor the United computer closely to book seats for him and his wife as soon as reservations became available. Prothro's component was described as 'a serial interface module, or SIM, which converts digital data from the terminal controller into analogue voltage waveforms and transmits these to the coupler over a cable called the stub cable', and there were 300 or so of them in each 777. With so much data flowing back and forth along the plane, such devices and many others helped to separate out one set of messages from another when they had very cleverly all been sent down the same pair of twisted wires. As Prothro settled into his seat he felt a quiet confidence that *his* part of the plane, at any rate, would perform with 100 per cent efficiency and accuracy during the flight.

For every component there was a Prothro, although few of them were on the plane. If Roger de Rudder had been there he would have been pleased at the success of the APU at keeping the plane

cool and supplied with power on the ground. Tom Gaffney, long
ago promoted to a job in China, would have swelled with pride as
the ground staff swung his passenger door into position on its
simplified common hinges, and turned the handle that forced the
redesigned door seal into every tiny crevice of the door-frame. Old
Jim Flanagan would have looked out of the window as the Pratt &
Whitney 4084 engines revved up and would have imagined the
fierce build-up of heat that was bathing his carefully crafted turbine
case. Tom Davenport, recently moved to a new job that had to do
with small engines rather than large ones, might have listened for the
boom-crack sound of an engine surge, not in any expectation that it
would happen but as a wry memory of one of the most stressful
periods of his relationship with the 777. Al Tyler would have been
glad that there was no need to test the restraining power of the
rudder to keep the plane on course during take-off after engine
failure.

Sharon Macdonald-Shramm, who was to leave Boeing towards
the end of the month, would have appreciated, on behalf of her
colleagues, the occasional overheard remark about the mellow
comfort of the air-conditioning and the way the cabin pressure
didn't seem to make your ears pop as the plane descended. Mike
Nichols's bins also generated approving comment, although one
passenger, as short as a Pacific Rim inhabitant, had a bit of a struggle
to push it closed after he deposited his heavy bag. The ultimate
tribute to the 777 bins came in a United commercial shown on one
of the six video channels. Bigfoot, the Pacific North-West equivalent
of the Abominable Snowman, was shown enjoying the 'bigness' of
the plane, including the fact that he (or the actor playing him) could
fit most of his body into the overhead bin.

Bob Cullen would have been pleased that there was no sagging
in the floor, which used to happen with previous layouts of the floor
beams and gave some passengers cause for a moment of concern. As
the plane burned up fuel heading for its cruise altitude, there were
no leaks through Glenda Barnes's excellent sealing work on the wing
interiors. During the few bouts of turbulence of the flight, Ed
Kacalek would have looked out of the window and seen how well
the wing-to-body join worked at keeping the wings on the plane.

And it goes without saying that, had he been on the flight, Alan

Mulally would have lifted and dropped the lavatory seat several times for the sheer pleasure of seeing it sink silently into contact with the bowl, with no hint of a 'big-bang' sound.

Of course, whatever pride each person had in any one component would be shared by dozens or hundreds of other 777 team members in the DBT that led to the existence of that component in that particular form, and by their managers' managers up to Condit, Mulally, Hougardy, Ostrowski, Howard, Standal and Eveland. And the trust that the components would fly once they were all assembled came out of the work of Cashman and the Higgins brothers, and the Dennises – Floyd and Mahan – and the rest of the flight-test team.

None of these people was on board, because most of them were hard at work designing and assembling and testing the dozens of 777s that would roll out over the next two or three years – dozens that Boeing hoped would turn into many hundreds during the next two or three decades.

In the end, though, what really made this first flight a significant event was the fact that ordinary fare-paying passengers were on board. Boeing and United were entering a period when they would see whether their gamble had paid off. If word got around that the 777, particularly when it got its electronics sorted out, was truly a better ride in every way, passengers might begin to do what they hadn't done since the early days of the 747 and ask to travel on a specific plane. For the next few months that could only mean a United plane, and if the inaugural press and publicity campaign stuck in people's minds the airline might keep its head start.

One businessman in economy class, whose seat had been booked as a matter of routine by his secretary, sat through most of the flight untempted by videos and music, working away with documents and figures. The eight-hour party swirled around him, made worse for him by his being in the front row of a section just by the galleys, so he couldn't escape the drinking and socializing. But he worked on, buried in his figures and oblivious to the fun.

This passenger was what the previous five years' work had really been about – to make this executive pay good money to sit in a comfortable armchair at a height of 37,000 feet and travel at four-fifths the speed of sound to his destination. It was for this one aim that Boeing had spent millions of personhours and billions of dollars on advanced aerodynamics, increased thrust and engines, lightness of materials, sophistication of electronics and multiple redundancy of systems, and over the next few years this man, and others like him, would tell them whether they had made the right judgements.

Epilogue

The second airline to fly 777s was British Airways. Sir Colin Marshall, who had flown to Seattle in late September 1995 as a guest speaker at an aviation industry lunch, clearly hoped to fly back on the first BA 777, due to be delivered the day of his visit. But the GE90 engine was still having problems completing its certification tests and when Marshall was asked at the lunch what the delivery date was he looked pointedly at Frank Shrontz, sitting at the head table, and said, 'You'll have to ask Boeing about that.'

Barry Gosnold, BA's representative in Seattle, played down any suggestion of this being a major problem. 'We just keep the old planes flying a bit longer,' he said. Later, when Gosnold looked back over the first six months of service, he could find only good words to say about the plane: 'The first plane came back from a trip to the Gulf with no faults and everybody thought, "Hey that's a bit of luck." But it went back and forth with very few problems, and we supplemented it with a second plane on 28 September, and a third a little bit later and they're all fine. Flight crew, cabin crew and passengers all think it's a damn fine airplane.'

It might still seem surprising that a problem-free plane would attract comment, but Gosnold has some experience of the delivery flights of other new planes. 'I've been out of here on a new 737 when you get a generator failure, you run short of oil, you get a VHF problem, you have a snag with the air-conditioning, the brakes pull – all sorts of problems. Most of the 777s and a lot of the 747s go out of here in pretty good shape.'

Another significant event for Boeing in October, in addition to the delivery of BA's first plane, was the start of a strike of machinists. It was a company-wide strike of 32,000 workers and affected the

777 by putting a stop to factory work. Those planes that were at an advanced enough stage were taken out of the factory on to the flight line outside, and the final finishing work – completing the interiors, incorporating customer changes and certain pre-flight testing – was done by management while the strike lasted. Lyle Eveland, in charge of manufacturing and also, as it happens, responsible for coordinating Boeing management's response to the strike, was sanguine about the strike and its effects. 'It was emotional rather than rational. There was an issue over "outsourcing" – getting some work done in countries like China – and the international labour unions want to stop this.' The strike lasted sixty-nine days, and although Eveland denies that the final management work on the 777s involved any loss in quality, Gordon McKinzie, who was overseeing the United deliveries, wasn't so sure.

'After the strike, we were seeing more than the usual number of pre-service problems so we elected to take no chances on compromising our ETOPS operation and kept them closer to repair opportunities here in the States by flying them on domestic routes before we headed into international destinations. We jokingly referred to those airplanes as "management built" just to get Boeing's attention.' (Whether or not management planes were finished off worse than the rest, United certainly suffered from late deliveries of four of their planes, and had to postpone using the 777 on some routes.)

Weirder still was a letter that appeared out of the blue at Boeing in February 1996 from United's Executive Vice-President of Fleet Operations, Joe O'Gorman.

Another instance of 'getting Boeing's attention' surfaced in mid-February, when Joe O'Gorman, United's Executive Vice President of Fleet Operations, sent a letter to Boeing expressing United's concern with mechanical reliability. 'We had such high expectations,' said McKinzie, 'based on our extensive readiness programmes and thorough familiarity with the airplane and its systems, that the slightest hiccup in our operation became an issue of great distress.' O'Gorman's letter pointed out a series of twelve recurring problems that had led to delayed or cancelled flights over the eight months that the plane had now been in service. The airline owned ten planes which were flying on routes across the States and between North America and Europe.

It wasn't the fact that United had some complaints that puzzled people in Boeing. Indeed, Boeing was already working on most of them, having been informed in a routine way as the problems were discovered during early delivery inspections or early maintenance checks, or – occasionally – on the ground as a plane prepared to take off. One of the most troublesome problems, which caused a number of flight delays in the severe Chicago winter, was a problem with the passenger doors. The doors that Tom Gaffney and his team had taken such trouble and expense to get right, even to the extent of testing to see whether they would open in −20 degrees, sometimes *wouldn't* open in subfreezing temperatures. The lever that the flight attendants had to turn to arm or disarm the door on the ground was connected to a cable which in certain cold weather conditions would freeze up. And the problem wasn't confined to one aircraft – it happened on most of United's early 777s. Over Christmas 1995 there were some Boeing engineers who didn't see as much of their families as they would have liked, as they wrestled with this problem. and the delays to flights were sometimes made worse by the maintenance engineers on the ground trying to fix the door, using instructions which, in the words of one Boeing senior engineer, were 'not as user-friendly as maybe they should have been'.

As flight attendants struggled to turn the handle and a plane-full of increasingly irritated passengers looked on, the reputation of the 777 as the most service-ready plane ever delivered suffered a little more with each incident. What was happening was that water or water vapour was getting into the duct surrounding the cable and freezing. Although the door-freeze test had sprayed the exterior liberally with water all through the night of 16 June 1992, the other side of the door mock-up, representing the interior of the plane, was dry and, in fact, the mechanism was open to the air, so the problem didn't arise. Presumably the water that was causing the problem now was condensed humidity from the interior of the plane, something which the team hadn't tested for.

That was problem number one, and there were eleven more on O'Gorman's list. They included electrical malfunctions, computer software bugs, a faulty landing-gear door, a damaged circuit breaker, and fluid leaking into the APU. But there were two things that stuck in Boeing's craw more than the actual problems. One was the use of words like 'intolerable', which astonished and puzzled the 777 engineers when they received the letter. Not the sort of language to be expected from a member of a 'Working Together' partnership. The other was that three weeks after Boeing received the letter it was on the front page of the *Wall Street Journal*, with headlines like '777 "A MAJOR DISAPPOINTMENT"'. *That* was not good news at all. The down side of promoting a product you have just made as very reliable is that reports of its *un*reliability attract disproportionate attention.

Looking back in June 1996 over a year of scheduled flying, McKinzie felt that it was ironic that the publication of O'Gorman's letter caused so much fuss. 'By the time the letter appeared,' he said, 'Boeing had corrective action identified and already on its way to United.'

There wasn't as much surprise about the problems within the industry as there was out of it. 'We've got dozens of letters like that from United,' said a Pratt source. 'It's just that they don't get into the *Wall Street Journal*.'

There are suggestions in the industry that O'Gorman was under intense pressure from his boss, Gerry Greenwald, a comparative newcomer to the aviation world. Greenwald had previously run a major automobile manufacturer and was unused to the situation where a little defect can cause a big problem.

As a succession of flights were delayed and passengers – often influential people – who had paid a lot of money for their tickets made highly vocal protests, United reacted. The situation wasn't helped by the fact that some of the classy new seats in the 777's highly attractive new Connoisseur interior broke. The recline button disappeared – sometimes irretrievably – inside the seat arm, and occasionally Connoisseur passengers had to be reseated back in economy, 'where the passengers sit' in Lord King's memorable words.

The twelve problems were eventually fixed, and there were fewer delays in service. But United's 777 passenger entertainment system, operating in a rudimentary mode on the inaugural flight, never improved during the following year of regular flying, no matter what pressure was exerted or threats made.

'Even before the first airplane was delivered,' McKinzie said, 'we were beginning to realize that the complexity of the Interactive Video System was going to be a troublesome nut to crack.' As an alternative, United activated the system without the interactive elements of games or catalogue shopping or telephones, but with six channels of video and nineteen of digital audio to each seat.

'While we continued to ask GEC-Marconi (the UK developer of the system) to continue working towards full interactivity, its schedule slippage eventually brought the programme to a standstill and both sides resorted to litigation to resolve the issues.'

The planes were still being delivered with the full system, including the phones which didn't work. McKinzie described what happened next: 'We rip all 300 phones out of each plane, so I've got 3,000 telephones in a bunch of boxes.'

But inside Boeing there was a general air of confidence created by what was actually an overwhelmingly favourable reaction to the 777. Even Joe O'Gorman, after his fit of anger over the plane, was heard to praise it lavishly at a ceremony a few weeks after his letter, to give the 777 team one of the aviation industry's most coveted accolades, the Collier Award. But perhaps it was inevitable that among four million parts there were some which hadn't quite turned out right. 'There are little disappointments rather than big ones,' said Ron Ostrowski, who had been made 777 Manager when Dale Hougardy retired in 1996. 'Nothing where we've said "Oh my goodness, we've really screwed this one up."' One of these 'little disappointments' was a seal, called the kiss seal, in a duct that led heated air from the nacelle around the engine into the air cooler for cabin air. In the early weeks of regular flying, maintenance inspections showed up cracks in the kiss seal that surrounded the GE engine. Two airlines in particular suffered from the effects of the discovery. Although this was not a safety issue, the seal had to be replaced each time cracks were discovered, and British Airways and China Southern found themselves with planes on the ground, waiting for replacement seals. It was less of a problem for BA, where the parts were speedily replaced, than for the Chinese airlines, where a combination of distance, flight schedules and customs led to long delays while new parts were flown in.

Back in Seattle a 'Tiger Team' was working on the problem, but it wasn't easy to solve. Something in the conditions the seal had been exposed to in service caused the seal, as currently installed, to crack. 'We still don't understand the dynamic conditions that exist there,' said Ostrowski in mid-1996. 'We think it's to do with how much you clamp the thing down when it's installed. The team has gone through one part refinement already and it's still happening.'

In such a situation one question Boeing asked itself was, of course: 'How did all the flight testing we did fail to show up the defect in the part.' Interestingly, the answer seems to be that some of the flight testing was done with a different part. While the testing was being carried out with one design, a small change was made in the part to simplify the manufacturing process, and it seems that this change might have made the part more liable to cracking under one particular set of cowl movements at high thrust.

Another issue that rumbled on during the year after the 777 went into service had its origins in an incident that occurred on a Cathay Pacific 747 in November 1993. One of the 747's four engines lost a fanblade, and the shaking of the unbalanced engine as the airflow caused it to 'windmill' led to extremely worrying levels of vibration in the cockpit, making it difficult for the crew to handle the plane. As part of its routine testing of the 777 engines, Pratt and the other engine manufacturers carried out vibration tests to see what levels of vibration would occur in such a situation. In fact, any *major* vibration of a damaged engine would lead to the engine dropping off the wing, to make the plane safer to fly. But there was a lower level of vibration that wasn't forceful enough to shear the bolts that held the engine to the wing but might still affect the structure of the plane.

And in the case of the 777, with larger engines than the 747, as John Cashman put it: 'The first impression you have is "big engines, big fanblades – big problem."' Boeing dutifully investigated the possible consequences of a blade out on a 777 engine and satisfied themselves that this would not lead to damage to the structure of the plane that would endanger the flight. As Cashman put it, they wanted to see if 'the structure and the engine stayed put and was the electronics going to stay in the rack?' But the FAA had other concerns. They wanted to be sure that any vibration that occurred after such an event wouldn't threaten the crew's ability to fly the plane. During 1995, right up to the certification of the United configuration in May, correspondence between Boeing and the FAA centred on this issue, and eventually, by putting a hundred engineers on the data analysis, Boeing convinced the FAA that the plane was safe in a blade-out situation.

But obviously somebody in the FAA still wasn't happy because the story then reared its head in public in an article in *Business Week* in January 1996.

Like many so-called 'scoops' *Business Week* had not discovered anything that wasn't known to Boeing, the FAA and the airlines. What they had discovered, or been sent, was an internal FAA memorandum about the series of tests Boeing were carrying out to solve a new aspect of the problem. The tests that had originally satisfied the FAA had related to the Pratt and GE engines, but the Rolls-Royce engine, the third to be completed and tested, had shown that if it lost a blade its vibrations would be right at the limits of what was covered by the tests Boeing had already submitted. This meant that new data were necessary and, according to the article, Boeing were not supplying enough details, at least as far as some of the FAA people were concerned. DID THE FAA GO EASY ON BOEING? was the headline on the article, raising all the old accusations of cosiness between Boeing and the FAA that came up from time to time. In fact, at the time the article was published, Boeing were still planning some of the tests that would eventually settle the issue, and the answer they wanted wasn't really obtained till the spring.

Boeing had misinterpreted the FAA's requirements and concentrated on structural issues rather than crew ability to perform. Now, in February and March 1996, they set up a vibrating platform and equipped it with crew seats, control column and instruments and shook it about at various frequencies to see the effect on pilots. John Cashman was the first to try it out and he found no problems, even at the most vigorous vibration frequencies. They were uncomfortable but he didn't think they would actually prevent a pilot doing his job in a situation where one engine had been switched off because of a blade out: 'Between adrenaline and self-preservation you can put up with a lot in order to survive. You do what you've got to do. It may not be what you want to do on a Sunday afternoon, but you would definitely survive and be able to get the airplane there.'

All along, Boeing had been convinced that the data showed that this was not a serious problem. The extra tests they carried out to their own – and the FAA's satisfaction – suggested that their view had been correct.

In mid-1996 Alan Mulally was still at Boeing, in the job to which he had been promoted nearly two years before, Vice-President of New Engineering Development. His ability to persuade people to behave in extraordinary ways was undimmed. On one of his trips back to Everett to address the 777 team at a Project Review Meeting, the entire complement of engineers greeted him wearing ties which bent up in the mid-air pose of a cartoon character called Dilbert, the archetypal nerd. Carefully engineered wire frames had been distributed to the meeting beforehand to achieve this frozen instant of time – and a big laugh.

Mulally's new job didn't seem to provide the same heady excitement of building a new plane, and there were rumours that he had been offered a higher salary and a multimillion dollar bonus to head another major plane manufacturer. But he didn't leave Boeing. Perhaps his closeness to Phil Condit, who was made Frank Shrontz's successor as Chief Executive Officer in early 1996, led him to swallow any dissatisfactions he might have had and stay on in the company he had worked in for the past twenty-seven years.

And in spite of the fact that the first 777s were well established and doing what was expected of them, there was still a big team of engineers at Everett, working away on the next planes in the family Mulally had always envisaged. The basic model was the 777–200 and there had always been the intention to make what was called a B-market plane, and a stretch. These terms had changed during 1996, so that the B-market became the IGW – increased gross weight – and the stretch became the 777–300. British Airways had ordered the IGW to fly some of its longer routes, since it had a range that was 3,000 miles further than the basic 777, and it would take delivery of its first plane in December 1996.

The factory, now the strike was over, was producing one airplane every six days. Because of a continuing boom in orders this was planned to step up to one every four days in October 1996, and to an astonishing one every *three* days on 10 March 1997.

Lars Andersen, formerly in charge of the 777s ETOPS testing and certification, had been made Chief Engineer for 777 Design, and he had at his fingertips all the data that came in every day from the airlines flying the plane. He was intimately acquainted with the details of every single problem that the plane had thrown up as the airlines took Boeing at its word and threw the planes straight into service within days – sometimes hours – of taking them 'out of the box'. But in mid-1996, he was still smiling. His long fingers turned over the pages of carefully collated statistics that measured the plane's performance.

As far as the engines were concerned, in a year of scheduled flying the engines that had flown most, the PW4080s, had not experienced a single in-flight shutdown in 73,000 hours of flying and 22,000 take-offs and landings. In fact, if it had – if even one engine had had to be shut down once in flight – it would have been a disaster for Boeing and Pratt, since their promise was that the engines would fly for more than 250,000 hours and still not suffer a problem that would require the captain to shut one down.

Andersen also had figures for what was called 'Schedule Reliability', an index of the plane's success, defined as the proportion of flights that were delayed for more than fifteen minutes because of a technical problem with the plane. Boeing's target was to achieve

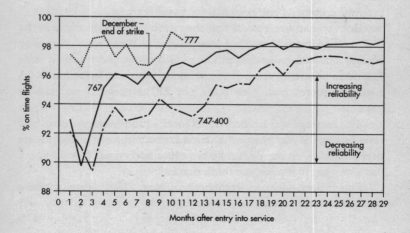

98 per cent reliability – that's no more than two delayed flights per hundred – within two years of entry into service.

In a perfect airline system, one plane in every fifty taking off late might not seem a very ambitious target. But as frequent fliers know, the fifteen-minute target is frequently missed for reasons that are nothing to do with malfunctions of the plane, but are the result of congestion or weather or even oversleeping flight crew, with technical problems being a small signal buried in the noise of more major factors. Even so, one glance at Andersen's statistics shows that, ambitious or not, such an achievement within two years would be the best that any Boeing plane – or any other new large airliner, for that matter – had ever done. And as the data came in, the graph for the 777 was staying consistently above the data for two previous comparable planes, the 767 and the 747-400. There was a dip in reliability during the period of the strike, although the 777 team disagreed with Gordon McKinzie that there was any connection, but as the planes flew through the early part of 1996 and the weather improved, optimistic observers sensed a trend towards achieving a consistent 98 per cent much earlier than the 24-month mark.

For Boeing, this was the evidence they were looking for, the proof that their new way of building a plane had paid off as everyone had hoped. It had been a long haul but for them these data gave the lie to the critical newspaper headlines, and the snide reporters, and even the frustrated voices of delayed passengers.

But there was one voice that they were happy to listen to as the 777 built up its flying hours during 1995 and 1996. It was that of an anonymous maintenance engineer at Heathrow, and was relayed to Seattle in an e-mail from Andy D'Agata who had helped as a BA customer representative to make the 777 as easy to maintain as possible:

The message was headed '777 Quote of the Month'. It read:

'Terminal 4 Supervisor: "Do you know, some of the blokes 'ere prefer to work on the 777s than the other fleets now."

D'Agata: "Why do you think that is?"

Supervisor: "It's an engineer's aircraft. They seem to have thought about us when they designed it." '

Index